Against the Wall

THE CITY IN THE 21ST CENTURY
Eugenie L. Birch and Susan M. Wachter, Series Editors

A complete list of books in the series is available from the publisher.

Against the Wall

Poor, Young, Black, and Male

EDITED BY ELIJAH ANDERSON

PENN

University of Pennsylvania Press

Philadelphia

Published by
University of Pennsylvania Press
Philadelphia, Pennsylvania 19104-4112

Printed in the United States of America on acid-free paper

10 9 8 7 6 5 4 3 2 1

A Library of Congress Cataloging-in-Publication record is available from the Library of Congress
ISBN-13: 978-0-8122-4097-9

Contents

Foreword: Strong Men Keep A-Comin On

CORNEL WEST

In 1932 Sterling Brown, one of the great black men of the twentieth century, published a monumental work of poetry, *Southern Road*. In Part I, called "Road So Rocky"—a phrase that still describes what young brothers encounter in so many chocolate cities—is a poem called "Strong Men." In this catastrophic moment for so many black brothers growing up in impoverished communities, we must recall and invoke the tradition of strong men, men of courage, wisdom, and dignity, as did Sterling Brown in his time.

I grew up in the 1950s and '60s, and when I think of black men I think of my grandfather, Rev. Clifton West, Sr., and my late father, Clifton West, Jr. I always associated black men with tremendous style, elegance, resiliency, and agency. I associated black men with being able to overcome, to look darkness in the face unflinchingly and still smile like Louis Armstrong, or "keep on pushing" like Curtis Mayfield. That's my conception of black men, but that is not a hegemonic or predominant perception these days. Why so?

The current view of black men has something to do with the fact that we have been living for forty years in an ice age where it is fashionable to be indifferent to poor people suffering, the most vulnerable citizens suffering. Young black men are a significant slice of the most vulnerable, so they are rendered invisible. In the great metaphor of Ralph Ellison, they become so invisible that the dilapidated housing, the disgraceful school systems, the lack of access to jobs that pay a living wage, the underemployment and unemployment that afflict young men in the inner city—all these have now become part of the norm. When we hear stories documenting racial discrimination in hiring today, we almost have to laugh to keep from crying as we see how that legacy of white supremacy still operates. We say to ourselves, my God, is the culture still that sick, is society still that pathological, is the U.S. still that indifferent to the full-fledged humanity of black men? The philosopher William James used to say that indifference is the one trait that makes the very angels weep, and I say that heaven must be overflowing with a flood when we look at the ways in which the wounds, bruises, and scars of black people in general and black men in particular are still overlooked, ignored, and downplayed. No doubt. As we call for national action to address the desperate situation of young men in America's chocolate cities today, we are also issuing an indictment of national inaction; the two go hand in hand.

In late 2004, the grand freedom fighter, my dear brother Tavis Smiley, conceived of a covenant with black America. We wanted it to become so popular that people had to talk about it, that young folk felt as if they had to get in on it, or they were missing out on it. This historic book, *The Covenant with Black America* (2006), was number one on the *New York Times* bestseller list, owing to Smiley's visionary leadership and inexhaustible energy. On national tours (with Professor Eddie Glaude and myself) speaking about *The Covenant with Black America* and the sequel, *The Covenant in Action*, we visited churches and communities where we interacted with young folk. We're trying to get the young folk to see that there are ways in which we can reproduce the strength, courage, and wisdom of past generations of black men.

My question is this: What are the conditions under which we reproduce strong black men, self-respecting black men, self-regarding black men, self-loving black men, who recognize they're in a kind of war? It's a war not against whiteness, but against injustice, white supremacy, male supremacy, homophobia, wealth inequality, and imperial arrogance. That's the best of the history of black people, the best of the history of black men. As we reflect on the miserable statistics documenting the deplorable conditions in which so many young black men exist today, let us not downplay the crucial roles in our history played by the strong black men in every generation.

We remember their names: David Walker, heroic author of the 1829 *Appeal* to "colored citizens" to make common cause with their enslaved brothers and sisters and rise up against slavery and discrimination, dead in a Boston hotel room in 1831 after his incendiary pamphlet was circulated clandestinely in the South; Frederick Douglass, the most eloquent ex-slave in history and author of three powerful autobiographies recounting his self-emancipation; A. Philip Randolph, socialist journalist and organizer of the Brotherhood of Sleeping Car Porters, the largest autonomous black labor union in the country, which was a leading force in civil rights struggle in many communities; Marcus Garvey, Jamaican-born leader of the Universal Negro Improvement Association, which mobilized black working people in cities across America to treasure their African heritage and seek collective self-determination; and Martin

Luther King, Jr., whose radical critique of war and poverty resonates anew today. How do we make their example, their courage, and their vision more palpable, more intelligible, and more attractive to a younger generation so that when they talk to their children and grandchildren they can say what I can say: I knew black men who were strong, who had courage, who were willing to think for themselves, who were willing to bear witness for love and justice, who were willing to hold up a banner not of cheap optimism but of hope born of determined struggle.

When I think of our great scholars in previous generations—W. E. B. Du Bois, St. Clair Drake, and Horace Cayton, sociologists who studied and interviewed the black folk then congregating in urban ghettos—and our twentieth-century literary artists—Richard Wright and James Baldwin, who called for social change in forms that captivated the imagination— I ask: where's their memory, where's their fire, where's their commitment and conviction in relation to who we are and what we are doing? Where are our R&B, rap, and hip-hop artists like Kenneth Gamble, Curtis Mayfield, Chuck D, and KRS-One? We've got to make sure when we talk about the history of black men who grow up poor, we recognize men like Louis Armstrong. He was once a poor black young man who rose to become the great revolutionary of jazz music; he defined the greatest art form of American civilization, working though a culture of black folk that produced the best of the human spirit.

What I love about the history of strong black men is they understood the complex dialectical interplay between roots and routes, so you use your roots as a springboard but you become global, international, universal. You're willing actually to speak your mind with a soul, with a level of insight, in such a way that the whole world has to take notice precisely because you reject the parochial and the conventional, the chauvinistic and the sectarian, in the name of live and justice. This is a grand tradition.

For an exemplary approach, I turn to Du Bois's great text of 1924, *The Gift of Black Folk*. This book deserves more attention; too many people read only the 1903 classic, *The Souls of Black Folk*. In *The Gift of Black Folk* Du Bois talks about the emancipation of democracy and the reconstruction of freedom. The gift of black folk and in particular of black men (which in no way excludes black women) to this nation and the world is, first, a Socratic gift, the gift of asking questions that cannot be evaded forever, that when confronted and answered make this a better, more equal, more human place. It was the determination of black slaves that turned the U.S. Constitution from a proslavery document into a freedom document. It was the determination of the slaves and freedpeople that created the possibility for the Fourteenth Amendment, which gave due process to every citizen in this fragile democratic experiment. It was A. Philip Randolph who connected the exploitation of labor to the denial of equal citizenship rights. Don't ever think you can talk about the vicious legacy of white supremacy and say nothing about the asymmetric relation between bosses and workers, between capital and labor, between the profit-driven, market-obsessed society in which we live and the globalization of that capital. Corporate globalization has affected not just urban ghettos in Philadelphia and Los Angeles but also New Delhi and South Africa. We've got to think globally. There's a democratic awakening taking place, and the Socratic gift of black folk is to ask questions. Socrates says in his final speech, as reported in Plato's *Apology*, line 38A: "the unexamined life is not worth living."

Malcolm X, the great twentieth-century prophet who grew up in poverty, said that the examined life is painful. What did he mean by that? He meant that it is black folk, and especially black men, who have forced America to wrestle with the most frightening question: what does it really mean to be human? The Greek original actually says, the unexamined life is not a life of the human. Our English word human comes from the Latin *humando*, bury; the very fact that you can't talk about humility or humanity unless you're talking burial, soil, earth keeps it real. Black folk in general, and black men in particular, have been the truth tellers when it comes to America's death-dodging, death-denying, and death-ducking orientation, its melodramatic narrative of self-celebration and self-congratulation. Any society that denies death easily inflicts death on others: Amerindians, black folk, Filipinos, or Iraqis, as long as they remain invisible. Here come the truth tellers. There's a night side, a dark side, death in myriad forms: the social death signified by slavery, the civic death imposed by Jim and Jane Crow; the spiritual death of teaching black people that they ought to hate themselves; the psychic death of telling black people they ought to doubt themselves, you're less beautiful, less moral, less intelligent. Yet some strong men rejected these lies and helped keep afloat a fragile and precious democratic experiment. What a tradition.

We must engage in what Socrates called *parrhesia* in line 24A of Plato's *Apology*. In explaining why he had been sentenced to die, Socrates said that *parrhesia*, bold speech, frank and plain speech, "was the cause of my unpopularity." Telling it like it is means paying a price, knowing there's gonna be a consequence. Let's be very honest. Our talk about the crisis of leadership is connected to the crisis of organizational capacity, the world-weariness of black people feeling as if we don't want to organize and mobilize anymore. We feel so jaded, we think that somehow we can just muddle through. That weariness has everything to do with the lingering effects of institutionalized contempt against black folk and especially black men. You cannot downplay that, although it's not the only factor. There's no way to tell the history of every generation of these precious, young human beings, these babies of mothers of African descent who happen to be male, and see the level of their suffering and act as if nobody loves them, or black folks somehow don't care enough for their own babies to raise them up to be strong and tell the truth about what's going on. That's the tradition we're talking about. It's a bold speech, and you make it knowing that you're very likely to be crushed, marginalized, demeaned, and defaced. Why? Because the powers that be understand that black men and black people are a sleeping giant and when they wake up they wake up in such a way that the *demos*, the people, becomes galvanized and mobilized. That's the great gift of black people, the Socratic gift that says we're gonna raise questions, we're going to interrogate you, America, in such a way that we will out-democratize your truncated democratic practices. We will teach you a lesson about democracy even though you treat us undemocratically. Never forget Malcolm X's scientific definition of a nigger as a victim of American democracy. Our neoconservative brothers and sisters are absolutely wrong, we've never been solely victims, we've been victimized but we've always been agents. We still want to raise questions, to organize and mobilize, to bear witness. We want to bequeath a legacy to our children so they can feel that we didn't fall for the hype of success, we didn't confuse prosperity with magnanimity, we didn't confuse status with service to others. That's the tradition we're talking about. If we cannot recover and revive that tradition, then we will lose the tradition of struggle that was given to us by those who came before. That's why the focus on young people is so important: so many of them have reached the conclusion that America is not merely a lie, but it doesn't even have the structural capacity to treat poor black people decently, humanly, and equally. And they've got good evidence for their despair.

Now our leadership is so decrepit, our leadership has caved in so easily and sold out so quickly, that the young folk had to create their own connection, their own black structures of meaning and feeling. That's what hip hop is, an indictment of black leadership and the black middle class that says for so long now you have been so preoccupied with your own careers, your own hedonism and narcissism, that we feel we have to raise ourselves. We don't feel loved enough, we don't feel cared for enough, you haven't given us enough attention, we're rootless, we're deracinated, we're floating on our own, we're gonna raise each other. That's what hip hop is, at least in part. How do you do this? How do you do that? We used to ask the fathers and the uncles and the mothers; now they ask themselves. What do you get when children are raising children? Resiliency and tremendous limitation. The market forces kick in with tremendous ferocity, and young folk believe that freedom, material prosperity, and personal security have very little to do with self-respect and self-determination. I call this the peacock effect. Freedom is all about becoming a peacock and letting everybody see what your foliage is, showing off your level of achievement and accomplishment, I'm so successful, I'm so rich, I'm so smart, I'm so professional. There is a difference between peacocks and eagles. Peacocks strut because they can't fly. We need to be producing eagles. We've got a peacock generation that just wants to strut; they can't get off the ground no more.

We must talk about the problem of national inaction in relation to corporate elites in the private sector and the political elites in the White House and Congress who are so often beholden to corporate interests. But let us not overlook the national inaction among the black bourgeoisie. Where is the moral outrage? Where is the truth telling? Cosby engages, Cosby has a point about irresponsibility, yes, but if you don't inform your language of correction with a language of compassion it will fall on deaf ears. We should start our indictment of irresponsibility with Enron and WorldCom and corporate elites, and then confront our middle-class friends and the black upper class. Where is the political courage of an entrepreneurial genius like my sister Oprah Winfrey? Where's the political courage of a spiritual genius like my dear brother T. D. Jakes? Where is the political courage of so many of the hip hop artists walking around with $350 million acting so big and bad? They're not courageous enough to speaking truth to power in relation to the social misery of black folk, the very folk who support them.

How do you talk about these issues in a way that is loving? I love Cosby; I just think he's wrong in his approach sometimes. I love Oprah; I think she's wrong in her timid orientation sometimes. I spent time with Bishop T. D. Jakes; I think he's wrong at times even as he matures politically. Why is this important? There is not going to be any national action forthcoming from us if we can't respect one another enough to come together in a democratic dialogue to generate vision and courage, to disagree with respect and civility, but also recognize that we're dealing with suffering so much greater than ourselves.

I think that we could very well be seeing the very early moments of a new wave of social momentum. Not a social movement; that takes a confluence of conditions here and around the world and a whole generation of leaders who are willing to live and die for the movement. That's a very rare thing. When I ask young people today what leaders would die for you, they can hardly name one. I knew who would die for me: Martin and Malcolm, Fanny Lou Hamer and Ella Baker, and so many more. They had that irreducible combination of service and love and being willing to pay a price. Social movements arise when you have a whole group of those people acting at a particularly pregnant historical moment. I do not think we're near a social movement now, but social momentum, yes.

In the ice age, even motion is progression. Some awakening is taking place. People are becoming more alert. The sleepwalkers are beginning to wake just a little bit. Any such awakening is like falling in love: you care so much that you can't help yourself. We need leaders—namely, each one of us—to fall awake in this way.

Mustering the courage to engage critical reflection is what we're trying to do. By itself, though, critical reflection is not enough. We are told that Socrates never shed a tear. Something is wrong with Socrates if he never wept. He loved wisdom but he didn't love concrete individual folk—as Plato's *Symposium* put it, he couldn't stay with the fleshified, imperfect, incomplete creatures. That's the difference between Plato and the genius of the Hebrew scriptures: the oppressed people, hated people, despised people had tears in their eyes when Amos and Micah spoke. And a Palestinian Jew named Jesus wept for Jerusalem.

This second gift of black folk—prophetic witness of love and justice—is crucial. We're engaging in Socratic reflection, but we know the case for national action must be informed by tears 'cause some folk catching hell out here. It's those tears, that love and compassion, what the great John Coltrane called Love Supreme, the link between the spirituality of Socratic questioning and the spirituality of genuine compassion, to be willing to sacrifice for others, to find joy in service to others. That's a great part of the tradition of strong black men.

The third gift of black people is the blues. You can't overlook the blues. Black folk should never confuse their situation with the Hebrews of the Old Testament, for black folk are on both sides of the bloody Red Seas. We're between a rock and a hard place. We've got the indifference of the white majority, we've got the complacency of too many of the black middle class, we've got the rage and despair of the black working poor and very poor—so what we gone do? How you gonna keep moving? How will you not sell out to the majority? How will you not become part of the complacency of the black middle class? How will you not give in to your despair of the very folk you love and are concerned about? Look at the prison industrial complex and all of the various other forms of losing sight of the humanity of people, especially young black men. The blues—as tragicomic hope—is a great gift. Listen to Muddy Waters, Robert Johnson, and B. B. King, guitarists and singers of the Mississippi Delta. Blues became the dominant idiom of the most barbaric century of all recorded time, the twentieth century, the century of the European holocaust and imperial atrocities. Blues has become the way in which people conceive of making music, from the genius of Jewish brother Stephen Sondheim to classical music's tilt from the major toward the minor keys. Trying to stay in contact with the underside is a major gift of black folk. We made dissonance a way of life, as Duke Ellington said in his autobiography, *Music is My Mistress*. We made the blue note the very thing you hang on for dear life because the chances seem so narrow.

Yet strong black men keep a-coming, strong black men get stronger. This tradition means raising Socratic questions, bearing witness and issuing a call for national action, but knowing that you got a blues sensibility and therefore you better learn to make disappointment your constant companion without allowing the disappointment to trump your agency or foreclose your willingness to act. That sorrow that is always already with you is the blues sensibility. You just gotta learn how to fortify yourself. Young folk are becoming more sentimental and melodramatic as they chase after success. They're losing the ability to fortify themselves and be strong and straighten up their backs and deal with the inescapable realities that confront them. In the end I would argue that in an ironic kind of way, the nation now has the blues after 9/11, which was the first time in the history of this country that all Americans felt unsafe, unprotected, subject to random violence, and hated for who they are. To be a nigger in America for 400 years is to be unsafe, unprotected, subject to random violence, and hated for who you are. So in that sense this is the first time the whole nation has the blues. If you don't learn something from a blues people then maybe you end up losing the best of your democracy. Just be honest about yourself, America; you're still plutocratic and pigmentocratic, you're imperially arrogant. Don't tell the lie about democracy. We folk who have lived the underside of democracy love democracy too much to see that word on the lips of the very folk who would demean it. We strong black men pledge to keep alive the gifts of black folk in America: their heroic Socratic questioning, courageous prophetic vision, and stylish blues resiliency as the ice age begins to melt.

Part I
Facing the Situation of Young Black Men in Inner Cities

Chapter 1

Against the Wall: Poor, Young, Black, and Male

Elijah Anderson

Living in areas of concentrated ghetto poverty, still shadowed by the legacy of slavery and second-class citizenship, too many young black men are trapped in a horrific cycle that includes active discrimination, unemployment, poverty, crime, prison, and early death. When they act out violently, or are involved in dramatic crimes that make the news, the repercussions for the general image of the young black male can be far-reaching. Strongly identified with violent criminality by skin color alone, the anonymous young black male in public is often viewed first and foremost with fear and suspicion, his counter-claims to propriety, decency, and law-abidingness notwithstanding. Others typically don't want to know him, and in public seek distance from him and those who resemble him. Aware of his place as an outsider, he may try to turn the tables when he can, expressing himself on his own terms, behavior that is viewed, especially in public, as threatening, "oppositional," and justifiable given their initial reactions.

The young ghetto male's self-presentation is often consciously off-putting or "thuggish," a "master status" that overpowers positive qualities (Hughes 1944; Becker 1963; Anderson 1990). In a bid for respect, many value this image as part of a hip style that deters insults and attacks in the local 'hood. But the image may have unintended consequences, giving potential employers reason to discriminate in favor of less threatening workers—often from the pool of recent immigrants, who appear clean-cut, hard-working, and willing to work for less and without the benefits and protections expected by the ghetto male. According to a Center for Immigration Studies survey cited in Preston (2007), 37.9 million immigrants, live in the United States today: one in eight people, the most since the 1920s. At least in the short run (see Jaynes, this volume), this steady stream of immigrants, many of them impoverished, along with mothers leaving welfare, high school dropouts, and retirees, make the low-wage job market more competitive, further diminishing the black ghetto male's already dismal job prospects. Beset with preexisting fears, negative assessments, or prejudice (Kirschenman and Neckerman 1991), the employer may consciously exclude the stereotypical "black ghetto male," contributing to his persistent joblessness and desperation.

As these circumstances become more widespread, the negative stereotype is perpetuated and strengthened, leading to more suspicion, discrimination, and marginalization—the wholesale diminution of social capital that energizes and intensifies the country's racial divide.

To understand the origin and nature of the problems and prospects of the black inner-city male, we must situate him in postindustrial urban America, as distinct from industrial America before the civil rights movement. In that past, the stereotypical hardworking factory man or construction worker and his female partner most often accepted the social conventions of their time. Their perspectives and orientations might be characterized as accommodating compared to those of their present-day counterparts. In many respects, society was more homogeneous, and the binary system of race relations gave quiet support to an oppressive racial order of white domination in virtually all areas of life.

In the 1950s more militant black people emerged to challenge the system collectively via the civil rights movement. Young people marched and led sit-ins, and political assassinations followed. Formerly moderate Americans, both black and white, lost their innocence. Yet in those last days of the industrial era, black men continued to work hard in factories and on construction while their wives worked as domestics, dishwashers, nurse's aides, and janitors. Though menial, these jobs gave a certain stability to the poor inner-city community, even as dissatisfaction with the socioeconomic position of black people was rising.

In time, this situation gave way to the postindustrial era with its recurrent recessions, major economic shifts from manufacturing to service and high technology, and the departure from the inner city of relatively high-paying and low-skilled jobs through deindustrialization and globalization (Harrison and Bluestone 1982; Perrucci et al. 1988; Wilson 1987, 1996; Wacquant and Wilson 1989; Anderson 1990). Persistent waves of immigrants, legal and illegal, gravitated to the urban centers to compete with African Americans for what was left of the manufacturing jobs (see Borjas 1999). Meanwhile, large portions of the safety net, including social programs such as child welfare, a mainstay since the New Deal, were chipped away. In this climate of political reaction, the union movement atrophied, becoming increasingly ineffective. A major result was that working people, black and white, slowly came to realize that they were on their own and had to fight for jobs and services. Among blacks, a nascent urban militancy became closely associated with the fight for civil rights, culminating in riots in which city after city burned. This militancy gave way to cultural nationalism in the urban ghetto.

In these circumstances, the image and stereotype of the black inner-city male ceased to be one of docility. Rather, it was rapidly transformed into a portrait of militancy mixed with anger directed toward the system of white domination in general, and white people in particular. In the minds of many whites, the figure of the black male became more and more mysterious, dangerous, and fearsome. Occasionally, he would act out this image, talking back to whites and challenging white authority. The common view among whites was of the young black man with an Afro asserting himself and disputing racial apartheid (Massey and Denton 1993), with expressions of militancy ranging from the peaceful civil disobedience of Martin Luther King, Jr., to the calls for revolution of Malcolm X and H. Rap Brown (Kerner Commission 1968).

Incessant urban turmoil, underscored and spread by the ubiquitous television coverage, encouraged and supported young blacks in questioning white authority. Among black middle-class people it became legitimate to fight for "your full rights" and first-class citizenship. Militant, and to a large degree oppositional, attitudes spread through the urban ghetto, settling in some of the most entrenched and disfranchised working-class and poor communities, where alienated young people were quick to act them out.

This unrest and activism did have the positive effect of encouraging whites in authority to open up the system somewhat and make accommodations to the aspirations of black people (Anderson 2001). The combination of affirmative action, set-asides, and fair housing facilitated the exodus of better-off blacks from the ghetto. The emerging black middle class increasingly gravitated to white neighborhoods, and many inner-city neighborhoods gradually underwent a process of transformation from all-white middle- and working-class to racially mixed but still economically stable to all-black working-class, poor, and destitute (Wilson 1987; Anderson 1990; Massey and Denton 1993).

In these circumstances, the black middle class was temporarily able to make a halting peace with the wider white society, while many of those residing in the increasingly isolated ghettos could not. Although only a small segment of middle-class people actively participated in the "race" riots, many whites were unable or unwilling to distinguish one class of black persons from another, and stereotypes spread. The distinctions blacks made among themselves often went unnoticed or were confused, and almost any white person living in close proximity to blacks was inclined to place as much distance as possible between him- or herself and *them*.

Amid the economic collapse wrought in the inner city by suburban decentralization, urban deindustrialization, and globalization, great numbers of the young blacks who remained in the ghetto found themselves subject to poor schooling, employment discrimination, and powerful negative stereotypes, all of which seriously diminished their human and social capital. As a result of these factors, they were unable to make an effective adjustment to the new economic realities, and the inner-city black community sank into entrenched structural poverty. In order to survive, residents created a thriving irregular, underground, and often illegal economy. The crack cocaine trade offered a way to make money, but entailed grave risks to individual and social health (Williams 1992). The violent crimes perpetrated by desperate addicts and greedy dealers reinforced deeply negative public images of the black urban ghetto.

All this set the stage for the situation we face today. The social costs of impoverishment fell particularly hard on the heads of the young black men who were feared by the rest of society and left to fend for themselves by white authorities. In his alienation and use of violence, the contemporary poor young black male is a new social type peculiar to postindustrial urban America (Anderson 1999). This young man is in profound crisis. His social trajectory leads from the community to prison or cemetery, or at least to a life of trouble characterized by unemployment, discrimination, and participation in what many are inclined to view as an oppositional culture—which is how he goes about dealing with his alienation from society. The wider social system is deeply complicit in this scenario, but, as indicated above, it relates to the impoverished black male by stigmatizing and further marginalizing him, informing him that he has no place in respectable society (Becker 1973; Goffman 1963; Anderson 1978, 1990, 1999).

His plight has vast social and racial ramifications in the city: on the bus, trolley, and subway; on sidewalks and street corners; in newspapers; in corporate offices and boardrooms; in grocery stores and shops; in restaurants and taxis. In many places of public accommodation, the anonymous black male is too often feared and considered guilty until proven innocent, and even that proof, when demonstrated, is not fully accepted. People—black as well as white—necessarily avoid him, and through their avoidance behavior teach him that he is an outsider in his own society. His image as bad and potentially dangerous is so powerful that it spreads to anyone who resembles him. This stereotype has implications for black males more generally, even those who are upper- or middle-class in education, achievement, and social standing. All males of color are then referenced by the stereotype of the "bad boy."

When the black male appears in public, common codes of civility are severely tested. Systematic observations on trains show that the anonymous black male is often the last person others will sit next to. Black men generally agree that they spend entire journeys seated alone, unless the train is crowded and seating is scarce. Black men of all social classes understand that most whites and some other blacks avoid them on public transportation. The black male may "put white people off" just by being black, and the younger he is and the more "ghetto" he looks, the more distrust he engenders. Many adopt the working conception that white people, their protestations to the contrary notwithstanding, generally dislike or fear black people, but especially black males.

As young black men talk among themselves, each man has a story of police harassment or public discrimination in which strangers go to great lengths to avoid him. Regardless of the degree to which this is true objectively, this belief leads the black male to develop his own sense of position vis-à-vis the wider society, especially whites. Black men compare notes and develop elaborate strategies for managing or avoiding such arbitrary treatment and salvaging their self-respect.

At times, young men attempt to turn the tables. Deciding they would rather ride with a seat to themselves—which may well be in part a "sour grapes" rationalization—they sometimes puff themselves up and adopt an off-putting appearance, displaying looks geared to make others uptight and determined to avoid them, to reject the "other" first. Strikingly, other blacks will also avoid anonymous young black males they are uncertain about, though blacks are usually more savvy about distinguishing those who pose an authentic threat from those who do not. Familiar with black life, they are generally capable of making finer distinctions than are their white counterparts.

Upwardly mobile males of color generally try to avoid the stereotype by using every means available to distance themselves from the "bad" black male, including his dress and demeanor. Parents teach their sons that to look, talk, or walk like him is to be associated with him and to suffer his stigma. At the same time, it may be assumed that the black male can wield the stereotype strategically in negotiations with whites and the dominant society, striking fear in their hearts. Many others embrace the image simply to look tough and hip and to be cool, often in the name of "street credibility." The image has been perversely glorified, but it carries heavy costs for the status and situation of those people who cannot switch this identity on and off. It can serve, nonetheless, as an important defensive strategy for the black male who operates with a provisional status in white-dominated settings (Goffman 1963; Anderson 2001).

The poor inner-city male is subject to even more overwhelming challenges. To understand why, we must shift back from interactions and negotiations in public places to the fundamental structural factors that shape the increasingly isolated and impoverished urban black ghetto. The inner-city economy at "ground zero" rests on three prongs: (1) low-wage, casualized jobs that offer little continuity of employment and few if any benefits; (2) welfare payments, including Aid to Families with Dependent Children and its successors, food stamps, and other government transfer programs; and (3) the informal economy, which encompasses (a) legal activities carried on outside the marketplace such as bartering labor and goods among friends and relatives, (b) semi-legal activities such as small businesses operated out of the home under the radar of regulation, and (c) illegal activities such as drug dealing, prostitution, and street crime. Members of families, households, and neighborhoods engage in non-market exchanges, borrowing and lending and, in the process, transferring and transforming these resources. While individuals obtain financial resources from one or more of these sources, resources also circulate between and among them.

Until recently, poor black people relied on all three ways of gaining income simultaneously. For example, welfare checks and earnings from employment not only supplemented one another but provided capital and consumers for small business, such as braiding hair, washing cars, or watching children. If any one of these elements is unproductive or fails to deliver financial resources, people are pushed to engage in the remaining two.

With the recent drastic reductions in welfare payments and the latest contractions in job opportunities for less educated workers, many inner-city residents have increasingly relied on the informal economy. The more desperate people become, the more the underground economy becomes characterized by criminality and violence. The marginalization of black inner-city men by economic forces is profoundly exacerbated by the legacy of racism in America.

The reality of daily life for too many young black men in areas of concentrated poverty revolves around simply meeting the challenge of "staying alive." To avoid being killed as they navigate their way in public within the disfranchised community, they acquire personas with a street-toughened edge. This image becomes generalized, supporting the negative stereotype that has become a dominant image of the black man throughout white society. Employers often reject young black male applicants on this basis, undermining their prospects for legitimate employment (Kirschenman and Neckerman 1991). Joblessness has deeper ramifications that feed on themselves, leading many young men to rationalize their involvement in the illegal, and often violent, underground economy.

At the same time that our elected leaders have made major cuts in the safety net, including welfare and other social supports, poor people must compete more fiercely for low-paying jobs and scarce resources with new immigrants to the U.S. as well as with poor working people around the globe. Globalization has completed what suburbanization and deindustrialization began. When corporations send their manufacturing operations to other places that offer plentiful supplies of low-wage labor, now including China and India as well as the U.S. South and West, Mexico, and the Asian Pacific region, even more jobs leave Philadelphia and other industrial centers, creating an employment vacuum. And inner-city black men have many competitors for the few jobs that do exist. Black women may have an advantage in customer service positions; immigrants may get a foothold in key employment niches. For the truly disadvantaged, especially high school dropouts or men with criminal records, jobs are very difficult to obtain (Pager 2003, 2007).

The "end of welfare as we know it" coincided with a brief period of unusual expansion in the labor market, fueling the illusion that most people would be able to move from welfare to work, but the recessions that followed have exacerbated the effects of these structural shifts, and joblessness and distress are now widespread. Under these conditions, the informal, underground economy expands to pick up the slack. For the poorest residents of the inner city, this third prong of the economy has become increasingly salient. More and more people engage in irregular exchanges, hustling, and at times, outright street crime in order to survive.

The jobs held by people living in the inner city qualify them as the working poor. They toil as night watchmen, janitors and office cleaners, street sweepers, dishwashers, construction laborers, car washers, landscapers, fast food workers, nurse's aides, office assistants, and domestic workers. Most of the available jobs pay little, and provide few if any benefits. They are also insecure, to some degree a function of a favorable economy. In an economic downturn, these people are among the first casualties, thus encouraging their participation in the informal economy. Moreover, even the steady jobs do not generate enough income to get people out of poverty. Despite the rise in the official employment rate in the community, conditions in many inner-city black neighborhoods have not improved, with the impact felt most acutely by uneducated young black men (see Mincy 2006). And a great many people who do find employment remain impoverished while working. In these circumstances, the "neighborhood effects" of concentrated poverty described by Wilson (1987) become ever more salient, exacerbating local problems.

The inner city is frequently the scene of many irregular business ventures that fall close to the blurry line between legality and criminality. For example, a party host might sell dinner platters for six or seven dollars. People routinely gamble on card games; a minimum stake of twenty or thirty dollars a person is required, and the game goes on all evening, with people joining in and dropping out. People organize other forms of gambling in their homes, in the back rooms of barbershops and bars, or on the street. Illegal forms include playing the numbers, dog fights, cock fights, and dice games. Legal gambling, in the form of the state lottery, is also highly popular.

All these exchanges turn on cash or credit. The barter system works through the exchange of goods and services instead. For example, a person repairs a neighbor's car on the weekend, helps paint someone's steps, performs a plumbing job, or styles someone's hair, but takes no money for it; rather, the individual waits to be paid back with a favor in the future. Mothers routinely trade child care in the same manner.

In the inner-city community, money earned is quickly spent. One common scenario begins with a paycheck from a legitimate employer. Many inner-city residents don't have bank accounts, so they cash their paychecks at the "cash exchange," which charges exorbitant fees. Often, the man then goes to the corner tavern for "a taste," a drink of liquor with friends. Typically, the man has accumulated debts to associates on the corner which he must pay back when he sees them or answer to the lender. Debts accumulate in part because the man's earnings are insufficient to cover all his expenses between paychecks; he must often borrow money from friends "to make ends meet." Through the week before payday, men can be heard soliciting others to "let me hold ten [borrow ten dollars] until Friday." When payday comes, if the debt is not paid, the lender's sense of self-respect may be on the line; arguments and altercations leading to outright violence may ensue over the money owed. When a debtor is observed using the money for something else, the lender can feel disrespected, or "dissed." So he may need to set the debtor straight. And if the debt is not paid promptly enough, the lender is not likely to extend credit again. This informal economic system has built-in sanctions.

Since the tavern is often one of the first places the man visits after receiving his pay, his wife, if he is married, may try to intercept him there, demanding the check or the money before he has a chance to "mess it up." Some men will give their women a large portion of the check to hold for them. In other cases, a bartender or proprietor of the tavern will hold the man's money for him, with predictable results (Anderson 1978). The money is passed on, in this case to the proprietor and his bank account. Much money leaves the community in just this manner.

The third element of the ghetto economy, the irregular component, overlaps with and influences the local circulation of money from wages. On the legal side are various interpersonal accommodations, such as bartering or trading favors with friends and relatives, and outright begging. Illegal activities include gambling, robbery, burglary, fencing, dealing drugs, and "loan sharking." Marginal forms of work merge into the informal economy: freelancers may work on their own, doing odd jobs or engaging in petty entrepreneurship as street vendors, or for someone else, most notably at the car wash for tips only. In this sector of the economy, relations are informal, characterized by age-related peer groups, family relationships, and personal connections, reminiscent of the marginal urban economies in developing or underdeveloped nations.

Crime, in various low-level forms, has taken up some of the slack left by the termination of government transfer payments and the contraction of wage-earning from legitimate jobs. Illegal activities supply some income to the neighborhood. More men can now be heard in barbershops and bars saying such things as "I'm gon' get mine somehow" and "Somebody's gon' pay me." These allusions to street crime made by men who appear peaceful do at times get acted out. It's hard to quantify such impressionistic evidence, but an observer gains a clear sense of the high frustration levels in the community. While many people are managing to adjust, many others develop short fuses, and anger is easily aroused. The Korean grocers who have opened stores in otherwise all-black neighborhoods appear to be bearing the brunt of this frustration. Not only are they of a different ethnic group and national origin, but they appear to be making money off the black community. To be sure, many proprietors are solicitous of local people and employ them in visible positions, but enmity can build, and occasionally this tension mounts to the point that a Korean is killed in a robbery of the family's grocery store. There is an observable connection between frustration levels and the number of robberies and assaults occurring on the streets. When frustration levels are high, the potential for violence rises.

In these circumstances, informal social transactions become an increasingly common way to deal with life. Strikingly, these exchanges are made essentially without the benefit of civil law. In the local community, the civil law and its agents have limited credibility, and over time confidence in the law has been seriously eroded. "Street justice" fills the void, becoming an important principle of local social relations. And matters of reputation or street credibility become all the more important, serving as a form of social coin. But "street cred" cannot be attained once and for all; it is high maintenance and must be husbanded, nurtured, and replenished from time to time. Strikingly, it is replenished most effectively not by talk and recriminations, but through actual deeds, which must be performed repeatedly to earn the desired effect: respect. Ironically, certain inner-city residents constantly look for opportunities to develop and have others validate their street credibility. In these circumstances, shows of disrespect must always be addressed, creating a stimulus for interpersonal violence.

The peculiar forms of social capital and regulation that develop in the isolated inner-city community, street justice and street credibility, not only sustain the drug trade but exacerbate its violence and extend its reach. Residing in areas of concentrated poverty in which hustling and crime flourish, poor inner-city males see possibilities for making money just outside their door. Drugs are everywhere, as the illegal enterprise moves in where the wider economy has failed local residents. Young men, who cannot avoid confronting the drug network, often seize the economic opportunities made available by the drug trade and the remunerative street crime that accompanies it.

Although the dominant society fears the violence of alienated young people, the inner-city neighborhood itself suffers the greatest harm at their hands. In response to persistent structural poverty, failures of public policy, and intensifying joblessness, the irregular economy expands, but its fallout is violent crime perpetrated primarily by desperate young males (Jones 2004; Ness 2004).

Many alienated and otherwise idle youths enter the drug trade voluntarily, motivated by a street culture that emphasizes material objects, such as new sneakers, gold chains, and leather jackets, which function as signs of status and may help a man win the attentions of young women and prestige among his peers. For many of these young people, participating in the drug trade is a strong bid for financial success. Aspirations for well-being exist alongside a desperate desire for "street cred."

In Philadelphia, the drug trade is organized hierarchically, in terms of "top dogs," "middle dogs," and "low dogs" (Anderson 1990), similar to a pyramid scheme. The top dogs are believed to make the most money, operating essentially as drug "king pins," but to local residents they are mostly invisible, known largely in the abstract or as urban legends. As aging babydaddys, homeboys, brothers, cousins, nephews, and sons, the middle dogs are more visible and often have an everyday presence in the community. Ranging in age from twenty-five to thirty-five, they visit the local street corner carryouts, clubs, barbershops, and car washes and drive around the neighborhood in a Lexus, Mercedes, or BMW, their flashy "rides" attesting to their financial success and drawing the attention of youthful wannabes. On their rounds, they "do their business," but also are on the lookout, or even an outright hunt, for young recruits to the trade. Their most likely prospects are financially strapped young boys in need of self-esteem. Typically, these boys lack a "decent" and strong father figure or other male presence in their lives, but the draw of the street is so powerful that boys from even the most intact families can be taken in.

Upon spotting vulnerable boys, sometimes as young as thirteen or fourteen, the middle dogs seek to cultivate them and turn them into "low dogs." By showing them attention, the middle dogs overtly or subtly court them, perhaps letting them "hold" (borrow) a few dollars or doing other small financial favors for them. The task, or the challenge, may be as simple as serving as a lookout. With each completed task, a bond is struck between the young boy and the middle dog, and mutual confidence grows. As their relationship develops, the middle dogs "let" them do incrementally larger favors, with completed tasks earning them more trust. Eager to please the middle dogs, the boys return their favors so as to gain the middle dog's approval. The young boy wants to "step up to the plate" and to prove that any degree of faith, which may well be confused with respect, shown by the middle dog was justified and not misplaced—to show that he is "ready." In time, these little favors turn into "odd jobs" and other tasks for which the boys may be paid, encouraging dependence and bonding the boy to the middle dog. At times, benefiting from the occasional largesse of the middle dog, the young boy may use his credit and build up a debt that becomes ever harder to repay. As the young boy becomes increasingly dependent on this relationship, his street credibility is ever more strongly tied to his job performance as evaluated by the middle dog.

This hierarchical relationship has elements of coercion as well as seduction, given the differences in age and power between the middle dog and the low dog. When directly approached by an older man to work for him, a young boy may take the offer as a threat, and after discovering that the man is a real dealer, he may feel intimidated, believing it is too risky not to work for the man, and that if he refuses, his life may be in danger. But with the promise of "living large" with ready money and enhanced street credibility, why not? To seal the deal and initiate him into the drug trade, the middle dog may offer the young boy a "package" to hold, or even a corner to stand on and sell drugs. Deeply flattered, but also anxious, he detects a certain dilemma, but the young boy may find it easier to comply with the wishes of the middle dog than to refuse.

The stage is now set for the boy to become a full-fledged low dog in the local drug trade. Consummating his new status, he stands on the corner "holding" or selling drugs to passersby. The young boy stands on the corner day and night, typically making drug transactions and handling large sums of cash. In the neighborhood and on the streets, the boy is now "clocking," which means that the middle dog has "fronted" him drugs to sell, often on consignment. But it also means that the young boy has taken on the burden of a drug bill, a promissory note that must be paid, either in money or by the return of the unsold product.

If the youth is unable to meet his account, his very life may be on the line. These debts can easily grow to unwieldy proportions, since "interest" rates of fifty cents on the dollar are not uncommon. If the boy borrows money from a dealer and fails to repay in the allotted time, a middle dog may allow him to repay by working in the trade. Failure to pay his debt is to place the middle dog's street credibility in jeopardy, leading the middle dog to exact payment in some form, through physical harm or even assassination.

Making matters worse, conditions of endemic poverty have encouraged the emergence of "stick-up" boys, who roam the ghetto streets robbing the low dogs who stand on the corner selling drugs; money or drugs is what they are after. If a boy is robbed and is unable to account for his drugs by producing the right amount of cash, he may be told by his middle dog that, "If you don't pay up, you have twenty-four hours to live." Under pressure to come up with the money on short notice, the boy may well resort to robbery and other forms of street crime. Before scores can be settled, several people may die. Violence and counter violence have a place in many transactions. Through the erosion of civil law, street justice becomes the only way of mediating disputes, and in these circumstances, street credibility becomes the coin, for both expressive and instrumental reasons.

In these circumstances, for his own sense of security, the young boy becomes highly motivated to "get himself a gun." Acquiring a weapon begins largely as a matter of personal defense. Typically, the gun is seen as standing between the young dealer and his own death. He must be prepared to defend what is his, be it money, drugs, or street credibility. From his experience of the streets, he knows that his very life depends on it.

Possession of a gun provides instant street credibility, which is why weapons are so sought after. Guns are readily available and quite easy to acquire; young boys beg, borrow, rent, and steal them. Once he has a weapon, the boy often carries it, but also likes to present himself as "strapped," adopting elaborate ruses including a hunched or labored style of walking that, for those who are streetwise, sends the unmistakable message, "I'm packing." Through the multifarious drug transactions that "go down" on the corner, the young boy becomes involved in a web of social and financial relations that are regulated not by civil law but a "code of the street" (Anderson 1999) that makes street credibility all the more critical to the young man's survival. Beefs can arise from most anywhere at any time, and the youth must be prepared to deal with them. For protection, the youth carries his "piece" to the Multiplex, to Mickey D's, to his girlfriend's house, sometimes even to school, to any "staging area" where trouble might arise and beefs might be settled.

This almost insatiable need for street credibility, reinforced by a "code of silence" that prohibits and penalizes "snitching," contributes powerfully to the high murder rate that Philadelphia and other cities are presently experiencing. A primary root cause is persistent urban poverty, which leaves no clear way to acquire money other than engaging in this criminal, violent dimension of the underground economy.

Young black men face extreme disadvantages just by living in areas of concentrated urban poverty. Most families in inner-city communities—even those who are most impoverished—hold "decent" or mainstream values, but they are under extreme pressure in the neighborhood. They try to socialize their children into decent values, but the open display of these values is dangerous, calling the youths' street credibility into question. Young boys from decent families must learn to code-switch, developing an exquisite ability to tell "what time it is" and to behave accordingly.

Even in childhood, these boys are often criminalized. Police officers guard the entrances and hallways of their schools. If a youth is involved in an altercation, disruption, or disorder, he often does not go to the principal's office but is handcuffed on the spot. His name is entered into a computer database as someone who has violated the law, so he gets an instant record. Meanwhile, his neighborhood peer group smokes marijuana cigarettes or blunts, experimenting with mind-dulling drugs. By the time a black male gets out of school and approaches the job market, he can't pass the background check or the drug test. The employer then has a ready excuse not to hire dark-skinned young males, typically discriminating in favor of immigrants or young people from the suburbs.

The life course of the young black male in the inner city is shaped by the concentration of poverty in an isolated, segregated community. Almost everyone around him is beset by problems, and he is subject to these concentration effects as he grows up. Instead of seeing adult males who are successful in family life and at work, he is exposed to alternate role models who engage in drug dealing and other underground activities. In the segregated environment, he has no contacts with the wider society and real people not in his situation. The black youth sees others similarly situated and naturally identifies with them. This limited experience and perspective forms his orientation and outlook on life, its possibilities and limitations. He thrives in the company of his peers. A large part of his formation comes from watching TV, with its messages that are like cartoon cutouts of the real world. Typically his home life is female-centric; he lives with his mother, perhaps along with his grandmother or an aunt, but not with a father. The men in his life are his brothers and cousins, occasionally an uncle or a grandfather. Seldom does he have the direct influence of a father who lives nearby and stays in touch. When a father figure is present, he is rarely an effective role model. This man may be compromised by poverty to the point where he is involved in crime and hustling. He might take or sell drugs. He is unlikely to be a strong, upstanding man with a job and a sense of connection with mainstream society and the wider culture.

Everyday life pushes boys in other directions. Young boys and men twelve to twenty years old hang out on the corner, on their way to and from school if they still attend school and for the greater part of the day if they do not. Here they sell drugs, shoot craps, and discuss their situation. The big issue for them is having enough money. The whole community is in the pit of poverty, and it seems like there is never enough. Everything is about getting money so that they can acquire the trinkets that are so important to social identity: the gold bracelet or neck chain, the iPod, the jacket, the sneakers. The oversized white T-shirt worn over pants that hang well below the waist is the urban uniform. It makes one suddenly presentable, and at three, four, or five dollars, it is cheap and allows everyone to be part of the crowd. Given the competitiveness that pervades youth culture, the youth needs to show others that he is better than they are, and expensive accessories do that. Dress becomes a visible sign of belonging and status.

Many young men get spending money from their mothers or uncles. They borrow from one another; a few have part-time jobs. But if respectable money is not forthcoming, a certain urgency comes over a boy, and he becomes vulnerable to the street ethic. Before he knows it, he is out there doing what he feels he must do: sticking someone up, snatching a pocketbook, or picking up a package. Hustling is a way of life, but there are consequences when things go awry—as they almost always do eventually. Violence terminating in jail or death is the common result. Young black people at ground zero know full well the fatal consequences of resorting to these expedients, but they seldom see any alternative. Like soldiers in a war zone, they focus simply on staying alive and adopt the postures that survival on the streets demands.

It is with this orientation that the maturing inner-city male approaches the world outside the ghetto as well as institutions inside the ghetto that interface with the wider society: schools, churches, stores, the police, the criminal justice system, and TV shows that blend the fictive with their own slant on reality. Here the young black male encounters efforts to bridle and control him that are sometimes quite negative, as well as messages that are filled with blame toward him. From these he learns early on that he is a problem. As this stigma mixes with other messages from his peers, he learns how to prevail in spite of being a problem. The code of the street orients him toward a survival mentality. He learns to present himself as tough and able to engage in a peculiar form of exchange that is primarily defensive. He is encouraged to give as good as he gets and often presents himself aggressively in order to deter attacks from others.

Being black and male in this society is to hold second-class citizenship as a legacy of the past that profoundly limits the present and blights the future. Even as a child, the black male is subject to the remnants of suspicion that go along with that racial and gender position. His identity is shaped by the repeated expressions of these attitudes, and he inevitably becomes alienated. He is caught in the tension between "decent" and "street." Generally, at home and at school, he is encouraged to be "decent" and to accept and manage his situation, but his peers encourage him to be "street." Most kids make their peace with these two poles and learn code-switching in order to function in both settings. To an extent, all youths face this situation, but for black males the pressure is more insistent. It is especially important for them to be hip and cool and show themselves to be at odds with the wider culture. They must not sell out to the dominant culture but embrace their distinctiveness. They may even confound street behavior with their black identity.

The civil rights and Black Power movements stimulated cultural nationalism, which emphasized racial particularism in contrast to mainstream social conventions. Young people were in the vanguard of this development, wearing Afros and dashikis, being politically active, questioning the system, and talking black. By doing these things, they were celebrating blackness in a white-dominated world. This dynamic still shapes the forms of expression for black youths' alienation. Extremely isolated black youths have a rationale, even a script, for acting like outlaws or hoodlums. In some ways, their alienation is legitimated by the exclusion that confines them, so that the persona they have scripted for themselves turns their alienation into a positive value. Their life circumstances are deeply intertwined with the ways the economy of the ghetto has developed, both in the effects of poverty on the young men themselves and in the effects of their behavior on the economy. So what began as a protest strategy has now become an oppositional stance whose primary victims are black people themselves, especially young males.

With every crime, especially those that involve a gun, the wider society finds more reasons to distrust inner-city men with dark skin. Poverty becomes ever more racialized, and young black men are increasingly marginalized. These involuntary outsiders invest in their own alienation, attempting to invert their outcast status into something positive, if only for themselves. Within their peer group, they are encouraged to present themselves with an oppositional style. Many who adopt this dress and demeanor may be decent kids underneath, with a sour grapes attitude but no criminal intentions or violent tendencies. Yet members of the dominant society, motivated by an anxious desire to protect themselves, identify the stereotype and make no distinctions among individuals. In time, for black youth, any fruits associated with the mainstream culture pale against the psychic rewards of the oppositional culture. This process feeds on itself, gaining increasing numbers of models, wannabes, and adherents.

The trademark clothing styles of so many of these young men become attractive even to black men who are law-abiding and decent. Part of the attraction has to do with the "edge" that clothing and other "presentation rituals" (Goffman 1959) suggest. They connote the toughest aspect of the inner-city ghetto community, and are emulated for that reason. A measure of prestige can be attained simply by mimicking this style. When this is done well, people are then able to look the part of "tough guy" and never have to "throw down," to make a stand, to risk a "fight to the death." This demeanor is protective, which explains part of its attraction. But aesthetic considerations are also in play. Over time, as this particular look has become closely associated with the tough inner-city male, it has become absorbed in the mental life of youth as signifying cool and hip. The "thug look" has both practical and aesthetic uses. But, as the look becomes commonplace, many young people become inured to its significance, unaware of where it came from and the initial reasons for its emergence. In effect, the look becomes institutionalized, and its present-day adherents have no sense of why they wear what they wear or look the way they do. But the wider society keeps careful notes on these displays, taking them as the latest manifestation of the alienation born of a ghetto existence. What has become relatively obscured and is taken for granted among its young black male adherents becomes central to white society's limited understanding of black male existence.

Much, perhaps even most, of the violent crime that is a key aspect of the growing oppositional culture is directed within the inner-city community. These men are much more concerned about one another than they are about those outside the community, but at the same time they understand that violence against any one of them means less to the authorities than violence against white people. If anyone—even a peer—insults another man (although young women are increasingly acting out violently as well), his mother, his sister, or his friend, he takes it personally, and the offense must be avenged lest others try to get away with such acts. If someone steps on another person's foot or shows the slightest disrespect in a myriad of other ways, it may feel good to the injured party to put the offender back in his place physically, by hitting or subduing him. Small matters can easily escalate and get out of hand, resulting in increasing amounts of intraracial violence and crime. Inner-city residents are firm in their belief that the public authorities do not care about what happens in their community.

Sometimes simply being broke is reason enough to steal or commit burglary. These young people have very few legitimate ways of obtaining money. When a young man wants some cash, he cannot always go to his mother or his father; they have little to spare. If he is broke, he may resort to the ample opportunities offered by the streets of his community. When he runs out of prospects or prey, his attention turns toward the nearby middle-class communities, and crime rates there rise. In these neighborhoods, the goods that signify prosperity and privilege are plentiful. When white people are robbed or assaulted and their homes are burglarized, and the assailant is known to be or identified as black, every dark-skinned man becomes suspect. Every black male is approached as though he has a deficit; he has a hole to climb out of before he can be trusted as an ordinary law-abiding person. Every newspaper or television story that associates a young black man with a violent crime sends a message to everyone that reinforces the stereotype of class: the dark-skinned inner-city male who is to be closely watched, feared, not trusted, and employed only as a last resort. Decent, law-abiding black males suffer as they are drawn into this aura of distrust (Anderson 1990). Black males become ever more marginalized and alienated. Race becomes more inextricably intertwined with crime and violence, and the public racial divide becomes ever more intractable.

Shawn's experience is instructive. A law student in Washington, D.C., Shawn grew up in Philadelphia. He comes from the inner city but was able to attend private schools, where he did very well, and went on to college and a prestigious law school. He and the handful of other black law students were the only nonwhite residents of the affluent neighborhood near the law school. One evening after classes, Shawn was waiting for a bus to go home. His apartment was only a ten-minute walk away, but he had just stopped by the local grocery store, so he had groceries and books to carry, and he decided to take the bus that stopped just across the street from the law school. Shawn was talking to his girlfriend on the phone as he waited for the bus when he noticed a police car drive slowly by. Then it drove by again, and circled a third time. On the fourth pass, the officer pulled up behind him and sat for approximately three minutes, with the car floodlight shining on the bus stall in which Shawn sat. Then Shawn was startled to hear a blowhorn order for him to put his hands out where they could be seen and to turn slowly toward the light. Shawn did so, with his phone still in his hand. As he turned toward the officer, who had stepped out of the cruiser, he saw that the officer was reaching for his holster and drawing his gun. Another law student, a white female whom Shawn did not know but who had also been waiting for the bus, yelled out to the officer that what he had in his hand was only a cell phone. The officer yelled for Shawn to drop it, which he did. The officer then told Shawn to place his hands against the wall and not move. The officer immediately handcuffed and frisked him.

Shawn asked what was happening and explained that he was a student at the law school just across the street and was waiting for the bus to go home. The officer ignored his explanation and continued frisking him. By this point, approximately seven other police cars had arrived and had blocked off the street to traffic. At the same time, students and professors from Shawn's law school began to form a crowd across the street, but no one made a move to assist him. He was humiliated. The police cursed at him and yelled at him to cooperate. He did so, confused by what was going on. They repeatedly kicked at his legs and ankles, forcing his legs further and further apart until he was spread-eagled. They kept pushing his face against the wall or down toward his chest, telling him to keep his head down and stop resisting. He was frisked two more times, and his wallet taken. His school books and laptop were dumped out on the sidewalk; his grocery bags were emptied as well. He was restrained by three officers who held his handcuffed hands together with the slack from the back of his shirt and pants to prevent him from running away. They questioned him roughly, showing no respect for him as a law-abiding citizen.

When Shawn again asked what was going on, he was told he fit the description of someone involved in a shooting a few blocks away. Just then, one of the officers' radios crackled, "Black male, 5'8", blue button-down shirt, khaki tan dress pants, brown dress shoes." The description fit Shawn exactly. Having heard himself being described over the radio, he was convinced he was going to jail. After ten minutes of being forced to stand straddled, physically restrained, and handcuffed in front of his peers and professors, another radio announcement let the officers know that the suspect had been apprehended. Shawn was uncuffed and told to have a seat. The officers who were standing around returned to their vehicles and drove off. The officer who made the initial stop remained and took down Shawn's information for the police report. As the officer filled out the form, he attempted to make small talk with Shawn, who felt humiliated and still afraid, but mostly angry at the lack of respect he had received and the clear racial profiling that had just taken place.

During the commotion, a group of neighbors had congregated on an adjacent corner behind the police car barricade. As the officer took down Shawn's information, a neighbor came up to the officer and, in front of Shawn, asked if Shawn was "the guy." The officer replied that no, it turned out to be someone else. The neighbor, whispering within Shawn's hearing, offered to follow Shawn home to make sure. The officer said that would not be necessary. Shawn later learned from local news that the actual suspect was the victim's college roommate, who was just playing around and accidentally discharged the gun. He was a white male. Shawn realized that it was the neighbors who had called the cops and provided his description. They had heard that there was a shooting in the neighborhood and when they saw Shawn, who had been living in the neighborhood for three years, standing on the corner at night, they called the police, having concluded that this black male must be the suspect. These were the neighbors who had stared at him every day and avoided eye contact as he walked by them on the sidewalk on his way to and from law school.

Because the young black male is essentially disfranchised and considered a troublemaker or at best a person of no account, his is a provisional status. Every black male is eligible for skeptical scrutiny, which renders him vulnerable to harassment for any infraction, real or imagined. His credibility is always shaky. The constant confusion between the street-oriented and the law-abiding black male means that all are subject to suspicion in white eyes, and such a public reception then encourages many blacks not to trust whites. Thus both blacks and whites assign provisional status to the other, deepening the racial divide.

Outsiders see the "tough" stance adopted by the black male as hostile, an indication that he has a chip on his shoulder against the outside world, but this is a strategy he has learned to deal with adversity. Through the myriad negative encounters he has—with peers, teachers, police, parents, and other adults in the community and the outside environment—the maturing inner-city male does toughen up, and he develops a negative view of the outside world. This is the persona with which he meets a prospective employer, who already has a certain mistrust of young black men. Until he proves otherwise—if he is even given the chance to do so—he is assumed to be guilty of attitudes and behavior that the employer sees as antithetical to work. Everything that is needed is absent from his repertoire, including the required physical appearance.

When the young male applies for a job, he does not change from his oppositional uniform to something more acceptable to the white establishment, nor does he think it appropriate to do so if it is suggested to him. As a result, the prospective employer readily dismisses him out of hand. If he is hired, it is only as a last resort. And when this negative message is communicated to him and he begins to make mistakes, the employer thinks he has acted true to form. This dynamic often culminates in the young man being fired, which then colors the employer's assumptions about the next young black male who comes along. The youth is thrown back to the ghetto to make it any way he can. The easiest way is to sell drugs, which sets him on a path toward the cemetery or jail. The system generates and reinforces this all-too-common trajectory for the young black inner-city male.

An important element that limits and destroys the lives of young black men growing up in concentrated poverty, especially the violence and social disconnection ghetto youths experience, is that adult men are basically absent. Fathers are rarely present, and many of those who are around are ineffectual. There is a fundamental disconnect between fathers and their sons and daughters. Many poor black fathers lose touch with their children within a few years after they are born, especially if both parents have moved on to other relationships. They are not raising boys to be men, a situation that has significant consequences for how they turn out. The boys' mothers may be engaged in their lives, but they can only do so much. The culture is quite prepared to place a woman in a weak position, even as a supplicant. So young boys turn to peer groups to raise them. This dynamic generates profoundly ineffective parenting for young men and, in turn, makes those young men unable to parent their own children.

Poor inner-city men continue to father high numbers of children outside marriage. Their limited employment prospects render many black men "unmarriageable" in Wilson's sense (1987), and they are increasingly unable to provide for the babies they sire. Yet, many are emotionally needy with a strong drive to procreate, or at least to be credited with impregnating women. For their part, the women often hold a persistent dream of a middle-class life of comfort and respectability while understanding their limited ability to achieve it by themselves. Typically, the woman searches for a "dream" man, but instead encounters a man running a confidence game. Designed to "get over" her sexual defenses, his game involves a "rap"—smooth and flattering words.

When the young man's game meshes with the young woman's dream, sexual intercourse often results in pregnancy, sometimes planned, but often simply not prevented and left up to fate. The young man's courtship game, which may involve window shopping and talking about the home they will make someday, encourages the young woman to accept the prospect of motherhood, even if the young man is unable to "play daddy." As this phrase suggests, the role of father is often not taken very seriously. Yet the strength of her own desire for a baby and marriage to an upstanding young man often inclines the woman to be taken in by her suitor's game, especially if he is older than she. Men of twenty-one or so are more convincing in their raps than younger men; young women are more gullible and likely to believe that they are ready to settle down. The young man's need to control the woman surfaces time and again during "lovers' quarrels." In these spats, he may constantly put her down, contributing to her low self-esteem—which is already shaky given her life circumstances. This treatment may well make the young woman even more vulnerable to his entreaties. For her part, getting pregnant can be a strong play for authority, independence, and respect. She embraces maternity as a way of getting out on her own, of showing that she is grown up.

When pregnancy occurs, a social crisis ensues, setting the stage for the young man's retreat. Because of his typically weak financial situation, his peer group's unflattering view of women, and, often but not always, his close relationship with his own mother, the young man expresses little or no interest in committing himself to marriage. The situation becomes clarified as the couple experience the social trauma of pregnancy. The young woman and her peer group strongly embrace motherhood and babies, with new babies often representing a form of social capital and bonding.

Most young men are intensely ambivalent about the prospect of fatherhood. Many play the "father" role symbolically and part-time at most, rejecting the responsibility, social constraints, and demands marriage would make on them. The men want to be free to "come as I want and to go as I please," a strong value articulated and enforced by the male peer group. The young man does not want to be "tied to one woman" in a way that allows her any say in how he conducts his life. To some degree, this preference may be a rationalization of his limited financial power to form a household in the manner of the "Mr. Johnson" of the past. For so many of these young men, "playing house" means being in control of a household and heading a family, being a "family man" consistent with the norms of American working-class culture. In this scenario, first and foremost, the man must be an effective breadwinner and provider. Given the long-standing social and political marginalization of black men in America, for many, it has become extremely important to play this role well—or not at all. But playing the role even minimally requires a decent job with a steady income. Without financial resources, it is difficult from the standpoint of being not just an adequate provider but regarded as the titular "head" of the household, a position whose value increases among those who are often unable to attain it (see Anderson, 1990, 1999).

In order to gain and retain the respect of his mate and his community, the man must bring home a paycheck, an accomplishment that is crucial to his identity as a married adult. Without this, his self-esteem suffers. Without steady employment, he is unable to control his household—a feat his community keeps track of. The black inner-city man's social and economic situation prevents him from fulfilling the demanding roles of husband and father; those who make the attempt can do so incompletely at best. This assessment, which overwhelming numbers of such men readily make, discourages them from even trying life as married men, and most often they do not. In these circumstances, they do what they can—have sex, and babies, with as many willing females as possible. But most fail to follow through with marriage. Those who do set up a household take a profound social risk, the management of which often leads to domestic strife and ultimately to physical abuse of their spouse or live-in mate.

When experiences with available men dash their dreams, women often get on with their lives, having the baby, rearing the child, and adapting to single motherhood, but with an eye to attracting other men who might better serve as a mate. Many women raise their children while being supported socially by their extended families, including their own fathers, brothers, and uncles. The baby is viewed as a "heavenly gift," and the grandmother and other kin often take a supportive role that allows the young woman to recover socially from her pregnancy and get back into the mating game as soon as possible. "Baby clubs," informal groups of young women who affirm and nurture one another, provide significant emotional support. These women's peer groups are often competitive as well, encouraging the young women to spend their limited resources on "looking good" and distancing themselves from being "messed up."

Strongly related to this life course is the young woman's limited sense of future and her strong desire for a baby as a means of affirmation, or even compensation. This pattern is strongly related to the community's impoverished circumstances. The structural poverty in which the inner city is mired severely circumscribes the outlook of both men and women. In this context, a woman can readily infer—even when this is not true— that she has no possible future that differs significantly from her current circumstances. Often the men she encounters support this view of the situation. So she drops down her buckets where she is, so to speak, settling for what she often views as the consolation prize of her life—a baby.

A volatile mix of these factors contributes to the young woman's decision to have a child out of wedlock. Of course, in many cases it is no decision at all. Rather, faith and fate play important roles, especially as the mother-to-be tries to rationalize her situation: everything "happens for a reason," and who is she to intervene? Abortion is rarely a consideration. The baby is hers to love and nurture, and her child "loves her back" unconditionally. The "new woman," especially if she has already had disappointing experiences and has grown accustomed to adult independence, is unimpressed by the young men who seek her favors. She demands much of any male suitor. The man must work and deliver on his promise, or else.

Many young men end up unemployable, without a stable life partner, and with one or more children they may see sporadically. Men in this situation quite naturally seek to get whatever they can in any way they can without regard to the rules. They readily buy into the code of the street, settling for what is feasible even if it is not optimal or even viable over the long term. As the young man engages in oppositional behavior, as he celebrates his alienation, he contributes to the stereotype of the angry, aggressive young black male. This stereotype enables employers, police, schoolteachers, and others to respond with suspicion or even outright rejection to the dark-skinned youth they encounter on the streets and in other public settings. The image becomes a reference point against which every black man is understood in the public mind's eye, as he either approaches it or distances himself from it. All public interactions are negotiated, and many are perilous. In these encounters, the young black man tends to lose. He is downgraded and devalued, regardless of how he approximates or differs from the stereotype. Consequently, he enters the encounter with a deficit no matter what he is about. In an environment filled with white women and immigrants competing with black men for the few decent jobs available, the black male is put at a profound disadvantage. Whites feel justified in distancing themselves from him. In this context, he becomes not only alienated but even more aggrieved. The young black male becomes invested in his outsider status and buys into it as an end in itself. This dynamic makes his situation utterly intractable.

Young black males increasingly make up an urban underclass. Neighborhoods of concentrated poverty in Philadelphia and other economically distressed cities are pervaded by high levels of crime, mayhem, and murder. These indices of decay are found not only in rust-belt cities such as Pittsburgh, Youngstown, Cleveland, Flint, and Detroit, but also in so-called sunbelt cities such as Los Angeles, Dallas, Houston, and New Orleans. The urban environment continues to decline, economically, socially, and physically. Jobs and economic opportunities are sorely needed, along with improvements in the infrastructure and housing. Policy makers must reverse the prevailing trend to cut the social safety net. In these circumstances, a Marshall Plan for the cities would be a significant beginning. Without a massive program of reconstruction, inner-city residents, especially young black men, will remain mired in hopeless circumstances, and the stereotype of the dangerous dark-skinned male will become increasingly entrenched. This stigma will afflict all young men of color, leading to an erosion of social capital even among the middle class and putting at risk the hard-won gains of the civil rights movement.

References

Anderson, Elijah. 2004. The cosmopolitan canopy. In *Being Here and Being There: Fieldwork Encounters and Ethnographic Discoveries*, ed. Elijah Anderson, Scott N. Brooks, Raymond Gunn, and Nikki Jones. *Annals of the American Academy of Political and Social Science* 595 (September): 14–21.

———. 2001. The social situation of the black executive. In *The Problem of the Century: Racial Stratification in the United States*, ed. Elijah Anderson and Douglas S. Massey, 405–36. New York: Russell Sage.

———. 2000. The emerging African American class structure. In *The Study of African American Problems: W. E. B. Du Bois's Agenda, Then and Now*, ed. Elijah Anderson and Tukufu Zuberi. *Annals of the American Academy of Political and Social Science* 568 (March): 54–77.

———. 1999. *The Code of the Street: Decency, Violence, and the Moral life of the Inner City*. New York: W.W. Norton.

———. 1998. The social ecology of youth violence. In *Youth Violence*, ed. Michael Tonry and Mark H. Moore. *Crime and Justice* 24: 65–104.

———. 1994. Sex codes among inner-city youth. In *Sexuality, Poverty, and the Inner City*. Sexuality and American Social Policy. Menlo Park, Calif.: Henry J. Kaiser Family Foundation.

———. 1990. *Streetwise: Race, Class, and Change in an Urban Community*. Chicago: University of Chicago Press.

———. 1978. *A Place on the Corner: A Study of Black Street Corner Men*. Chicago: University of Chicago Press.

Becker, Howard S. 1973. *Outsiders: Studies in the Sociology of Deviance*. New York: Free Press.

Borjas, George J. 1999. *Heaven's Door: Immigration Policy and the American Economy*. Princeton, N.J.: Princeton University Press.

Goffman, Erving. 1963. *Stigma: Notes on the Management of Spoiled Identity*. Englewood Cliffs, N.J.: Prentice-Hall.

———. 1959. *The Presentation of Self in Everyday Life*. New York: Anchor Books.

Harrison, Barry, and Bennett Bluestone. 1982. *The Deindustrialization of America: Plant Closings, Community Abandonment, and the Dismantling of Basic Industry*. New York: Basic Books.

Hughes, Everett C. 1944. Contradictions and dilemmas of status. *American Journal of Sociology* 50: 353–59.

Jones, Nikki. 2004. It's not where you live, it's how you live: How young women negotiate conflict and violence in the inner city. In *Being Here and Being There: Fieldwork Encounters and Ethnographic Discoveries*, ed. Elijah Anderson, Scott N. Brooks, Raymond Gunn, and Nikki Jones. *Annals of the American Academy of Political and Social Science* 595 (September): 49–62.

Kerner Commission. 1968. *Report of the National Advisory Commission on Civil Disorders*. Washington, D.C.: U.S. Government Printing Office.

Kirschenman, Joleen, and Kathryn Neckerman. 1991. "We'd love to hire them, but . . . ": The meaning of race for employers. In *The Urban Underclass*, ed. Christopher Jencks and Paul E. Peterson, 203–34. Washington, D.C.: Brookings Institution Press.

Massey, Douglas S., and Nancy A. Denton. 1993. *American Apartheid: Segregation and the Making of the Underclass*. Cambridge, Mass.: Harvard University Press.

Mincy, Ronald, ed. 2006. *Black Males Left Behind*. Washington, D.C.: Urban Institute Press.

Ness, Cindy. 2004. Why girls fight: Female youth violence in the inner city. In *Being Here and Being There: Fieldwork Encounters and Ethnographic Discoveries,* ed. Elijah Anderson, Scott N. Brooks, Raymond Gunn, and Nikki Jones. *Annals of the American Academy of Political and Social Science* 595 (September): 32–48.

Pager, Devah. 2007. *Race, Crime, and Finding Work in an Era of Mass Incarceration.* Chicago: University of Chicago Press.

———. 2003. The mark of a criminal record. *American Journal of Sociology* 108 (5): 937—75.

Perrucci, Carolyn Cummings, Robert Perrucci, Dena B. Targ, and Harry R. Targ. 1988. *Plant Closings: International Context and Social Costs.* New York: Aldine de Gruyter.

Preston, Julia. 2007. Immigration at record level, analysis finds. *New York Times,* November 29.

Wacquant, Loïc J. D., and William Julius Wilson. 1989. The cost of racial and class exclusion in the inner city. In *The Ghetto Underclass,* ed. William Julius Wilson. *Annals of the American Academy of Social and Political Science* 501 (January): 8–25.

Williams, Terry. 1992. *Crackhouse: Notes from the End of the Line.* Reading, Mass.: Addison-Wesley.

Wilson, William Julius. 1996. *When Work Disappears: The World of the New Urban Poor.* New York: Knopf.

———. 1987. *The Truly Disadvantaged: The Inner City, the Underclass, and Public Policy.* Chicago: University of Chicago Press.

Chapter 2
David's Story: From Promise to Despair

Raymond Gunn

When I approached the school where I had been conducting field research for the past three years on an unseasonably warm morning in late October, I was startled by two Philadelphia police cars with flashing lights. Police cars outside a public high school in Philadelphia are hardly newsworthy; law enforcement officers are routinely summoned to these imposing gray structures with steel doors and grated windows. Parents often have little choice but to entrust their children to these unwelcoming institutions. Crowded, bored, and frustrated, students act out from time to time, although less often than might be expected given the conditions they endure every day. Students deemed the most disruptive or violent are taken by police off school grounds and transferred to one of several alternative schools. Sadly, it is all too common to spot students—most often, black male students—being escorted off school premises. But this sight is uncommon at what I call Multicultural High School, a small, academically elite public school in the School District of Philadelphia. It is even more startling when the student being led out of the building in handcuffs by uniformed police officers is someone I have come to know. As I approached Multicultural High that morning, I could not help but think that David had never looked smaller and his baggy school uniform of white shirt and khaki slacks more ill-fitting than when I saw him shoved into the back of a squad car.

I had met David only two weeks prior to the incident. He was a sophomore whom the guidance counselor thought I should meet. Janis Nussbaum often introduced me to the black male students at Multicultural High whom she thought "academically promising." Were not all students at a college preparatory school like Multicultural High supposed to be academically promising? David's grades from the year before were not stellar, but of the twenty or so black males in his class, he was the highest ranked.

Several teachers who watched the incident shook their head. "He was always such a good boy." "I never thought him capable of anything like this." "It's the quiet ones you got to look out for." We all stood and watched helplessly as the squad car pulled away, and the back of David's head disappeared from view.

Over the next several days, I managed to piece together the events that led to David's expulsion from Multicultural High. Admittedly, the only part of the story that I am entirely certain of is that David was taken out of the school by police for being in possession of a pocket knife. The rest of what I know about it relies heavily on what David has told me.

The incident whose disastrous ending I witnessed began with another boy in David's neighborhood making sexually suggestive comments to David's thirteen-year-old sister. David feels an obligation to look after his younger sister, especially since their father moved to another part of the city to start a new family. His mother, who works long hours as a certified nursing assistant, is forced to leave David in charge while she is away. David is well aware of his responsibilities to his sister. When David confronted the neighborhood kid, an altercation ensued, and the other kid warned David to "watch his back" because he was going to get his boys to "jump" David. Frightened for his personal safety, David felt he needed some protection in his West Philadelphia neighborhood, especially for the three-block walk between his house and the elevated train he takes to and from school. He grabbed the pocket knife that is kept in the utility drawer at home before he left for school that morning. Once on the El, he forgot all about the weapon in his pocket, programmed the iPod his mother had given him for his birthday two months earlier, settled into his seat, and prepared for the long ride to school on the north side of town. By the time he walked the six or so blocks from the station to Multicultural High, he had entirely forgotten about the object in his pocket—until the metal detector went off as he sauntered through it. He simply did not think about the metal detectors the Philadelphia school district had mandated to be placed at the front entrance of all high schools when he shoved the knife deep in his pant pocket.

After the incident, David was sent to spend between 120 to 180 days in one of two privately managed alternative education programs. Called "soft jails" by critics, these sex-segregated programs are highly regimented (Fuentes 2005). During the past few years, these discipline-oriented programs have been established in several cities around the country with large African American and/or Latino populations, even though independent evaluations have found that they fail to promote student achievement (Fuentes 2005). Upon completion of the program, David will not be allowed to return to Multicultural High. Instead, he must go to his neighborhood high school, where as of 2006, according to standardized test scores, only 7 percent of eleventh-grade students are proficient or advanced in math and only 18.1 percent are proficient or advanced in reading (School District of Philadelphia 2007).

David's story illustrates how easy it is for young black males in poor inner-city communities to go from being full of promise to hypervulnerable. Boys like David, whose academic skills are strong enough to qualify them for a competitive high school, are a rare find. Too often, boys from neighborhoods like David's are not looked upon as having such potential. In fact, as Ferguson (2000) shows in her insightful book *Bad Boys*, adults often predict that a jail cell is in these boys' not too distant future. As social services continue to be cut, job opportunities vanish, and family structures are redefined, this prophecy is far too readily fulfilled.

The streets become a refuge for young people who are alienated from school and see no future ahead of them. Here hegemonic masculinity— an expression of gender identity that males attempt to use to establish dominance over females and other males (Connell 1996)—is on full display. Yet in impoverished urban ghettos these boys' hypermasculine posturing makes them hypervulnerable (Cassidy and Stevenson 2005; Stevenson 2004). Homicide rates are at record highs, and run-ins with law enforcement are commonplace. Indeed, to navigate these streets safely, youth must have masterful social skills. Anderson (1990, 1999) points out that it is imperative that everyone on the streets remain vigilant at all times, lest they fall victim to anything from petty thievery to homicide. Youth learn and adapt to a "code of the street," Anderson (1999) posits, which is largely the result of the severely weakened ties between these urban communities and the rules of civil law.

In this environment, it becomes imperative for young black males to prove their masculinity at a very early age. Masculinity can be demonstrated in a number of ways, through basketball, rap music, hustling, and sexual prowess. Like all the boys in his neighborhood, David is all too familiar with the code, and because of this knowledge he was quick to jump to his sister's defense. Had he not, his sister would be seen as an easy target, and he would have been regarded as a "punk" and targeted also. While the vast majority of the parents and guardians in these communities—most of whom are mothers and grandmothers— want educational success for their children, the boys are keenly aware that academic success carries very little currency when they or someone they love is threatened with interpersonal violence. With fathers and other adult males so often missing from children's homes and lives in these poor communities, the pressure on young boys to be able to protect themselves and their families occurs at a much younger age than for boys growing up in other environments. The urgency is quite high for these boys to display a convincing performance of toughness and street smarts. While the boys in my study have managed to perform well enough academically to be admitted to a selective, college preparatory high school, I find that they must devote enormous energy to their performance of hegemonic masculinity, which in turn subtracts from their academic performance.

In inner-city communities, residents tend to have very definite ideas about what masculinity looks like. Mothers, fathers, and other relatives of small boys who would rather push a baby carriage than bounce a basketball seek to "correct" the boys' behavior in no uncertain terms. A little boy who cries during roughhousing is rebuked for being a "little girl" or "faggot." Mothers and fathers often refer to their sons as "my little man" and show them off to friends, neighbors, and relatives in adult-like outfits tailored to fit their little bodies (Anderson 1989, 1999). Young boys are encouraged not be "soft" or a "little bitch." Feminized attributions such as "girl" or "bitch" are highly derogatory, and boys learn about masculinity, as Kimmel (2003) says, as a kind of negation to femininity. Boys are told "not to be a bitch," "not to be a girl," "not to be soft" far more than they are told in the affirmative what masculinity is supposed to be.

Similarly, boys coming of age in the inner city are constantly shown displays of masculinity and, even more often, they are shown the penalty for lacking masculinity as it is understood in these communities. I do not mean to suggest that residents of inner-city communities understand masculinity any differently from the way other Americans do; hegemonic masculinity rules the day throughout American society. In mainstream America, boys—through family relations, homosocial interactions such as peer groupings and sports, school structures, and media representations of gender performances—are socialized to be emotionally detached, competitive, and active participants in the objectification of women (Bird 1996). Although mainstream culture eschews violence unless it is in acceptable forms such as in sports or war, middle-class parents strive to have their sons demonstrate mastery in an area that signifies leadership, a decidedly masculine trait. Middle-class American parents often encourage their sons to excel in sports and/or academics, with the hope that these boys will grow into adults who can use their mastery to garner a leadership position of some kind, which they can then use over others.[1] Middle-class parents who are particularly anxious about their effeminate sons are likely to seek professional advice usually in an attempt to root out any feminine traits the parents perceive the boy as having (Langer and Martin 2004), or much less often to learn how to adapt the family's lifestyle to the boy's effeminate behavior.

Although the following illustration is an admittedly extreme example, it clearly shows the role socioeconomic class plays in how parents rcspond to sons who do not display conventionally masculine traits. A December 2, 2006, *New York Times* article about families with young children who do not conform to their assigned gender roles profiles a northern California couple whose five-year-old son has insisted he is a girl since the age of three. The mother, an attorney, and father, a public school administrator, have decided to support their child's decision to dress as a girl after consulting with a psychologist and observing their son's "newfound comfort with his choice." The article explains that the parents have "carefully choreographed his life, monitoring new playmates, selecting a compatible school, finding sympathetic parents in a babysitting co-op," because they fear that their child might encounter individuals who are less understanding of his preference. Meanwhile, the schoolmates of a little boy in the Bronx who had been deemed effeminate by his peers dumped him in a trash bin for failing to live up to their standards of masculinity. The principal of the school in the Bronx chided the boy's mother for not teaching him how to defend himself properly against bullying (Brown 2006).

While bullying is a problem for everyone, wealthier parents of less masculine boys can call on far more resources to protect their sons than can parents with less means. Affluent parents can physically remove their son from the environment where the bullying takes place, changing schools or even moving to a new neighborhood if they deem the bullying severe enough and cannot stop it any other way, for example, by complaining to the school or to the other boys' parents. They can insulate their children's social world to lessen the likelihood that they will encounter overt hostility. Inner-city parents rarely have the means to do likewise and are expected to use different strategies to protect their children. The most important is teaching boys to protect themselves from physical violence.

Despite the class differences in strategies for eliminating effeminate behavior in boys, families of all class backgrounds agree that the stakes are high. In societies like the United States, masculinity is equated with power and dominance, and femininity is defined as the lack of both, as powerlessness and subordination. While maleness is regarded as a birthright in a patriarchal society, *masculinity* is always contested terrain. For most of American history, only able-bodied straight white males could assume the privileges of hegemonic masculinity. In spite of the advances in our thinking about masculinity that came in the wake of the civil rights, women's, and gay rights movements, as well as the advent of information technology that makes physical prowess inessential for mastery,[2] the definition of masculinity that has dominated much of American history continues to be the touchstone by which everyone else is measured, often unsuccessfully. The dominant society, then, views a boy who exhibits effeminate behavior as effectively giving up any chance of possessing power. Unlike the northern California family profiled in the newspaper article, most American families do not allow young children to make such important decisions about their life. In the same way that parents decide where and how their children will be educated and what and when their children will eat for dinner, parents monitor their children's gender-identity behavior. American parents, regardless of background, may want similar things for their children, but how they go about ensuring them is often determined by family circumstances. In poor, urban communities, parents are well aware of the dangers that await their sons on the streets, but they can rarely consult psychologists and other professionals who may help by suggesting strategies to avoid such dangers. They must, instead, rely on their wits.

If boys in inner-city communities have not learned sufficiently from their family to perform in a hyper-masculine fashion by the time they are ready to be in the world apart from their family, then their peers and neighbors will want to know why and challenge the boy's masculinity in very direct ways. Boys who do not act sufficiently masculine will often become the target of interpersonal violence. Their peers in the neighborhood and in school will challenge them physically, using these boys as a way to establish their own masculine credibility. More aggressive boys will usually take advantage of them by physically dominating them and by taking away or destroying their possessions. In some cases, less aggressive boys will even be taken advantage of sexually by more aggressive boys as a way to feminize and thereby disempower them. In short, less aggressive boys are made into objects to be acted on in a zero-sum game that emasculates them as it builds up the masculine credibility of the perpetrators. Sometimes, parents or older siblings will intervene on the less aggressive boys' behalf, but in many cases that is impossible, and the young boys must learn to survive this hostile environment on their own. The boys can use any number of strategies, but the most common is to simply toughen up, to perform masculinity in ways that are recognized by other residents of that community.

By the time the boys reach high school age, they are well versed in the acceptable performances of masculinity for their community; and it is at this juncture in their development that their performances intersect in significant ways with the myriad stereotypes teachers and school administrators very likely hold about urban poor, young, black males. Even at academically selective institutions such as Multicultural High, it matters little that the boys had to pass a rigorous admissions process to gain entry to the school. It is the boys' performance of masculinity that is most salient for many school officials. Consequently, a close watch is kept on these students, and the slightest infraction of school rules is treated as confirmation of what teachers and administrators already "knew" about these boys.

While the adults in the school train their gaze on the African American boys, the boys are far more preoccupied with their peers than they are with the adults. It is the peers who matter, and the boys are often willing to sacrifice a healthy relationship with the adults in the school in order to win the respect of their peers. The attention the boys give to their peers is hierarchical, with the order of attention varying according to the demographics of the particular school. At Multicultural High School, with a majority African American population, the boys first focus on the other African American boys, because it is necessary to size them up. They then focus on the African American girls because the kind of attention they receive in return from these girls will add or detract from their performance of masculinity. Other students are often of far less importance.

As these boys travel from inner-city Philadelphia neighborhoods to an elite high school, they struggle to figure out how to assert their masculinity enough to deter interpersonal violence from their peers outside school, to gain the respect of their peers in school, and to win the favor of their teachers and other school personnel—or at least not to provoke their disapprobation. It is extremely tricky social terrain, and few of the boys navigate it successfully.

Because a college degree has never been so important in determining one's access to employment that offers economic stability and prospects for upward social mobility, a school like Multicultural High is vitally important for poor black students' future. With a population that is comprised mostly of students of color from low-income and poor families, Multicultural High maintains high academic standards, sending about 70 percent of its graduates to selective four-year colleges, with the remaining students going off to community college, trade schools, and the military. Many of the parents of the African American boys at the high school think of the school as a "godsend." One mother commented that if her son could not attend Multicultural High, "he'd have to go to [the neighborhood school], and those kids go wild in there." She is, understandably, happy that Multicultural High helps to keep her son out of harm's way. But, what about her son's academic performance there? His math teacher shrugs his shoulders and sums up the general impression of this student: "He's not serious. All he wants to do is fool around with the girls in class."

African American males make up about one-fourth of a typical freshman class at Multicultural High, but they comprise only about one-tenth of a typical senior class. Of those who manage to stay through graduation, in most years only one black male student ranks in the top 10 percent of the class. At first blush, it appears that the math teacher is right: the boys may not be serious about academics. Upon closer inspection, we see that their energies are being diverted elsewhere. All these boys have high aspirations for themselves, and a "good" college figures prominently in their goals. Nevertheless, they are unclear about what steps they need to take to gain admission to a good college and to be successful there. Many of them believe, rightly or wrongly, that the guidance counseling staff is not forthcoming with information to help them attain this goal.

There is ample evidence that a college education increases the quality of life for poor blacks appreciably; and the more selective the college, the better a person's quality of life is likely to be. In *The Shape of the River* (1998), Bowen and Bok (former presidents of Princeton and Harvard respectively) show quite convincingly the myriad advantages that poor black youth gain from attending elite undergraduate institutions. These students are much more likely to graduate from college, go on for advanced professional degrees, increase their economic prospects dramatically, participate in civic activities, and have a higher level of satisfaction with their work and personal lives than their peers who attended less selective colleges. Major universities such as Harvard, MIT, Brown, Princeton, Penn, and Stanford have reconfigured their student financial aid packages to allow qualified low-income students to matriculate at little or no cost to their families. This is indeed exciting news. But it will be meaningless to young black males from poverty-stricken, troubled neighborhoods unless we ensure that they are no longer left behind, unprepared for and excluded from higher education by the myriad failures of their public secondary schools.

The disciplinary policies and practices of Multicultural High are designed to treat all students the same, regardless of the differences the students may bring to school. On the surface, this sounds fair. The Philadelphia school district, which enrolls over 210,000 students in its public and charter schools, mandates that each school adhere to a "code of student conduct"[3] when making official decisions in response to students' infractions of rules and policies. Uniform rules for student conduct can be useful as a guide for maintaining a safe environment for a large urban school district.

At the same time, blind adherence to these rules and their blanket application in all situations effectively targets certain members of the student body who must abide by a different "code" to protect themselves from interpersonal violence on the streets. Many young black males like David are forced to meet the exigencies of everyday life in their impoverished, dangerous neighborhoods in ways that often militate against academic success or result in disciplinary actions that expel them from college preparatory programs. Schools must understand these circumstances and provide viable ways for these boys to maintain a delicate balance between their lives in school and their lives outside school that enables them to survive and succeed in both worlds. Certainly, schools should not tolerate students bringing weapons onto school premises or engaging in any behavior that is disruptive or violent. But the blind application of zero-tolerance policies only serves to exacerbate the difficulties faced by students like David. Sending David to a "soft jail" for the rest of the school year where he will fall far behind academically, or shrugging our shoulders to the mediocre academic performance of very capable students, serves to curtail the life chances of poor young black males—often irreparably.

Schools like Multicultural High are vitally important because they are one of the few pipelines that poor black students have to getting the preparation necessary to gain admittance to selective colleges and universities. But the mismatch between the demands of the school and those of the neighborhood make it particularly difficult for African American male teens who reside in inner-city neighborhoods to navigate this transition. They are susceptible to the pitfalls of street life as they travel to and from school. Hyper-masculine stereotypes about young black males leave them hyper-vulnerable to challenges to their personhood in ways that most other young people do not have to contend with. Consequently, many young African American males from poor communities attempt to present themselves in ways that deter interpersonal violence against them on the street, but in doing so they also invite unwanted attention to themselves from school personnel. The result is social terrain filled with land mines that may end a promising student's academic career as abruptly and unjustly as David's ended that warm October morning. We must facilitate and support black male students' success by designing school- and community-based programs that realistically address their day-to-day circumstances and enable them to handle the myriad and often contradictory demands of their neighborhoods and the dominant society.

References

Anderson, Elijah. 1999. *Code of the Street: Decency, Violence, and the Moral Life of the Inner City.* New York: W.W. Norton.

———. 1990. *Streetwise: Race, Class, and Change in an Urban Community.* Chicago: University of Chicago Press.

———. 1989. Sex codes and family life among poor inner-city youths. In *The Ghetto Underclass*, ed. William Julius Wilson. *Annals of the American Academy of Political and Social Science* 501: 59–78.

Bird, Sharon R. 1996. Welcome to the men's club: Homosociality and the maintenance of hegemonic masculinity. *Gender & Society* 10 (2): 120–32.

Bowen, William G., and Derek C. Bok. 1998. *The Shape of the River: Long-Term Consequences of Considering Race in College and University Admissions.* Princeton, N.J.: Princeton University Press.

Brown, Patricia Leigh. 2006. Supporting boys or girls when the line isn't clear. *New York Times,* December 2.

Cassidy, Elaine F., and Howard C. Stevenson. 2005. They wear the mask: Hypermasculinity and hypervulnerability among African American males in an urban remedial disciplinary school context. *Journal of Aggression, Maltreatment and Trauma* 11 (4): 53–74.

Chafetz, Janet S., and Joseph A. Kotarba. 1995. Son worshippers: The role of Little League mothers in recreating gender. *Studies in Symbolic Interaction* 18: 217–41.

Coakley, Jay. 2006. The good father: Parental expectations and youth sports. *Leisure Studies* 25 (2): 153–63.

Connell, R. W. 1996. Teaching the boys: New research on masculinity, and gender strategies for schools. *Teachers College Record* 98 (2): 206–36.

Cooper, Marianne. 2000. Being the "go-to-guy": Fatherhood, masculinity, and the organization of work in Silicon Valley. *Qualitative Sociology* 23 (4): 379–405.

Ferguson, Ann Arnett. 2000. *Bad Boys: Public Schools in the Making of Black Masculinity.* Ann Arbor: University of Michigan Press.

Fuentes, Annette. 2005. Failing students, rising profits. *The Nation,* September 1. www.thenation.com/doc/20050919/fuentes/2, accessed May 18, 2007.

Kimmel, Michael S. 2003. Masculinity as homophobia: Fear, shame, and silence in the construction of gender identity. In *Privilege: A Reader,* ed. Michael S. Kimmel and Abby L. Ferber. Boulder, Colo.: Westview Press.

Langer, Susan J. and James Martin. 2004. How dresses can make you mentally ill: Examining gender identity disorder in children. *Child and Adolescent Social Work Journal* 21 (1) (February): 5–23.

School District of Philadelphia. 2007. Regional offices and school information. sdp-webprod.phila.k12.pa.us/OnlineDirectory/Directory, accessed May 18, 2007.

Stevenson, Howard C. 2004. Boys in men's clothing: Racial socialization and neighborhood safety as buffers to hypervulnerability in African American adolescent males. In *Adolescent Boys in Context,* ed. Niobe Way and Judy Chu, 59–77. New York: New York University Press.

Chapter 3

Young, Black, and Male: The Life History of an American Drug Dealer Facing Death Row

Waverly Duck

In *Code of the Street* and *Streetwise*, Elijah Anderson illustrates the complex effects on the urban poor of unemployment, spatial concentration and isolation, ineffective schools, the drug trade, and rampant violence. He describes how a street culture, the "code of the street" governing behavior, appearance, and moral values, often arises in the inner city in response to the weakening or absence of economic resources, education, and civil law. The code represents some young men's desperate quest for self-respect in the midst of urban decay. Because violence arises from the competition that is central to street culture, and what policing exists is counterproductive, communities of concentrated poverty are left to fend for themselves. Furthermore, Anderson argues, the criminal justice system contributes to the spiral of violence as young men fight and even kill one another to avoid being locked away for what seems like forever because of mandatory sentencing. Under these conditions, young men use informal means of negotiating their way through a community plagued by violence, while they struggle to maintain some sense of decency and self-respect. Even young men who aspire to escape poverty through education and employment must learn the code to navigate tough streets that test manhood through violence and sexuality.

The life story of Jonathan Wilson illustrates the code Anderson describes. Jonathan has been in the criminal justice system since the age of thirteen. He was incarcerated at twenty-two and only narrowly escaped the death penalty at twenty-six. Legal experts often argue that there are many young people who grew up in circumstances similar to Jonathan's who never committed a crime such as using or selling, and certainly never became involved with murder. While this may be true in a number of cases, it is undeniable that the desperate conditions Anderson describes will produce countless men like Jonathan. This life history aims to answer this question. What options do young men have when unemployment is chronically high; when schools are unable to provide a safe environment for learning and teachers are incapable of teaching basic reading, writing, and math; when neighborhoods are overrun by crime; when law enforcement does not respond consistently or constructively and the community is filled with drug users and dealers, gangs, sex workers, and violence? What are the rational choices for children growing up in these circumstances, especially when they and their parents are unable to change their environment?

Meeting Jonathan Wilson

In September 2004, I was asked to give a presentation to a group of defense attorneys in federal capital murder cases. My talk was based on the social situation of economically depressed urban areas, and much of the presentation was based on Anderson's *Code of the Street*. In the course of preparation, I met Jonathan Wilson, who at the time was a federal prison inmate awaiting trial. After my talk, I was asked to work on two cases against him. Jonathan was charged first with conspiracy to murder a federal witness, and second with the murder of a rival drug dealer. In the latter case, the federal prosecutor's office was seeking the death penalty.

Initially I was hesitant to accept the assignment. As an aspiring ethnomethodologist, I had done research on gender, health, and class and racial inequality. But I soon realized that I had not been asked solely based on my academic background. The lead defense attorney, John, stated that he wanted my help because I was young and black and had grown up in Detroit in an environment that resembled Jonathan's. For this reason, he believed that I could provide valuable insights into the defendant's social situation. Knowing that my personal and academic background would appeal to the jury, I decided to volunteer as an expert witness in the capacity of a sociologist, working alongside Elijah Anderson.

In this essay, I present a life history of a young, poor, black man facing a capital murder charge, written in the method originally outlined by John Dollard in his classic *Criteria for the Life History* (1935) and in the tradition of Clifford Shaw and Howard Becker's *The Jack-Roller* and Fox Butterfield's *All God's Children*.

I interviewed Jonathan Wilson at the federal prison where he was incarcerated. Over a period of eight months, I visited the prison on twelve different occasions for a minimum of two hours per visit. I also interviewed his parents and siblings and spent a lot of time in the community collecting field notes. For legal reasons, I was not allowed to tape-record my conversations with Jonathan or members of his family, and my note-taking was closely monitored by the defense attorney. Because this biography is based on interviews in which Jonathan presented his own version of events and justified his behavior, I initially had some concerns about the factual accuracy of the information he gave me. My account was submitted to the prosecution before I testified in federal court as an expert witness, so accuracy was essential. I did not have access to school or arrest records, but later, during the trial, I learned that most accounts he gave me matched up precisely with the facts.

The approach I brought to the case of Jonathan Wilson was shaped by my personal history and academic training. Ethnomethodology examines the methods by which people construct their assumptions about the world, so I am interested primarily in "how" rather than "why." Working on this case, I was consumed by this question: How do a hard-working married couple with two incomes, who own their own home and are committed to what Anderson calls "decency" or "middle-class values," end up with two drug-dealing sons on trial for murder and facing the death penalty? I believe that the answers may be found by examining the social context in which these children grew up.

As a sociologist, I have had little interest in crime, criminology, or criminal justice. My apprehensions about studying crime may stem from a desire to distance myself from the environment of my youth. I grew up in poverty in the inner city on the east side of Detroit, which provided me with enough information about crime and violence to last a lifetime. I witnessed the beginning of the crack epidemic, its subsequent decline, and the entire cycle of the "War on Drugs." I attended Osborn High School in Detroit, the second most populous high school in the city, with approximately 4,000 students. My freshman class in 1991 had over 1,200 students; at graduation in 1995, approximately 230 of us walked across the stage. Most of my classmates were murdered, in prison, or had dropped out of school, largely because of situations related to the crack cocaine drug trade.

My academic understanding of crime as a sociological subject was in sharp contrast to many of my life experiences. While I was growing up, murders were rarely solved and many people committed crimes as nothing more than a means to an end. Crime had a functional utility for many of my peers: simply put, it helped to ensure their social, mental, and economic survival. In college, I was fascinated by the theories of Marx, Weber, and Durkheim and studied ethnomethodology with well-known social theorist Anne Rawls (daughter of John Rawls, who wrote *A Theory of Justice*, and protégé of Harold Garfinkel, founder of ethnomethodology). I went on to do graduate work with Elijah Anderson at the University of

Pennsylvania. I was most interested in the study of social inequality based on gender, age, race, and/or class and its effects on families. Initially, I intended to have only one brief meeting with Jonathan Wilson.

Before that meeting, I read his federal indictment on line. The hundred-page document described an archetypical model of how inner-city children are systematically socialized into the drug trade at a very young age. The progression goes something like this: look-out kid (ages 7–11), drug holder (12–13), seller (14 and up). Jonathan had begun dealing at age nine. Before going to trial, the prosecution gave him the option to plead guilty to conspiracy to murder a federal witness, in addition to two other murders, in exchange for a lighter sentence. The plea agreement required Jonathan to confess to a litany of crimes, some of which he claimed he did not commit. He was, however, willing to serve time for the crimes he acknowledged committing. Against the advice of his attorney, Jonathan declined the plea bargain, causing his case to proceed to trial.

When I met Jonathan Wilson, he had spent four years in federal prison awaiting trial. He was an imposing 6'1", 210 lbs. Initially he did not look at me and refused to make eye contact. He was cagey and kept his answers to my questions very brief. When I asked him where he grew up, he said, "Bristol." I asked about life in Bristol, and he said, "Life was okay." A breakthrough occurred about an hour into our meeting when I asked Jonathan about his wife, with whom he was not on speaking terms at that time. When I asked why they were not communicating, he told me that she kept accusing him of cheating with a former sex partner with whom he had fathered a child. When I asked him if he received conjugal visits he said no, and I replied, "What's your secret? Because unless you're a magician how is it possible for you to cheat with another woman in a maximum security federal prison?" He burst out laughing and said, "Thank you!"

Jonathan's conflicts with his wife are representative of the disorganization, confusion, and suspicion surrounding his entire life. The more we talked, the more he opened up and told me about his life in and beyond Bristol. In court, I testified about my findings as an expert witness, placing Jonathan's life in the context of an ethnographic account of the community. The interviews produced helpful information for the defense that ultimately led to Jonathan's receiving a life sentence instead of the death penalty.

Family History

Jonathan's family of origin consisted of Lynn Wilson, his mother, an African American in her early fifties; Winston Wilson, his father, a

Jamaican immigrant in his early sixties; Nicole, his older sister, twenty-nine; and Antonio, his older brother and partner in drug dealing, twenty-eight. Jonathan grew up in Bristol, a small city near a major metropolitan area in the Northeast. Typical of many cities with a manufacturing base, Bristol's economy has been experiencing a long period of decline. The local unemployment rate is around 20 percent, and about a quarter of the city's population live below the poverty line ($4,000 per person, $16,000 for a family of four). Bristol's population is around 36,000, predominately African American (75 percent) and Hispanic (18 percent).

Jonathan knows that his mother is originally from Georgia and grew up in Bristol, and that his father is from Jamaica. He had no contact with any of his grandparents because they died when he was very young. Lynn and Winston Wilson married when they were in their late twenties, began having children, and purchased a house together in Bristol. When Jonathan was ten or eleven years old, Lynn learned that Winston had had a long-term extramarital affair with a babysitter who was also Lynn's friend. The relationship produced two children who were near in age to her children. Lynn left the family for a year and a half, returned when Jonathan was fourteen or fifteen, and left permanently two years later. Lynn's reasons for leaving the home included her husband's infidelity, her sons' drug selling and dropping out of high school, and her own inability to control Nicole, who dropped out of private school so she could attend the neighborhood public school with her friends. Lynn had what she described as a "stressful situation" that required her to leave the home.

Jonathan's parents have remained married, but live separately. Lynn refuses to divorce Winston for financial reasons associated with ownership of the house they jointly purchased, the cost of a divorce, and perhaps because of feelings they have for each other. Winston refuses to move because of the investment in the house. Both are employed in Bristol, Lynn as a nurse's aide and Winston at the shipping yard unloading boats. Winston had worked at a factory until its closure in 1999.

Jonathan reports having witnessed his father smoking marijuana often, a habit Jonathan himself picked up at fifteen. He quit at eighteen when medication he ingested to "clean" his urine for a drug screen made him so sick he required hospitalization. Winston states that he smokes marijuana in order to sleep and have an appetite. He talks about working for a pharmaceutical factory as a janitor for seventeen years, which, he says, led to his marijuana smoking. During his fifteenth year at the factory (around the same time Lynn left), new management took over. The previous year Winston had been honored as "employee of the year," but now he felt he was under scrutiny. He felt that his new manager was racist and anti-immigrant (Winston has a very distinct Jamaican accent). His consistent 9 to 5 schedule was replaced by sudden weekly shift changes. Managers and other employees made racial slurs toward him, and once he was tripped by a fellow employee.

Initially Winston was reluctant to report his supervisor and coworkers to the union representative for fear he might lose his job, but after a year he filed a grievance. Two months after the grievance was filed, Winston was laid off indefinitely. Two years later the factory relocated from Bristol. Winston collected unemployment compensation, and when it ran out he applied for food stamps and did odd jobs for a wealthy suburban woman. Winston, who was raising the kids alone during this time, stated that he never took government money, only food stamps to feed his family. It was during this time that he took money from his children.

According to Jonathan, his parents had a very laissez-faire attitude toward discipline, which was based on their belief that their own children were far more "decent" than the other children in the neighborhood. Both parents worked long hours. Lynn had one job and served as primary caregiver while Winston held two jobs to support two families, his family with Lynn and his second family with the former babysitter.

The Street Boys and the Young Boys

Jonathan was first exposed to the "Street Boys" (later renamed the "Old Heads") when he was about ten years old. According to Jonathan, the Street Boys were fixtures in the neighborhood, young men who sold drugs on the corner and ranged in age from mid-teens to early twenties. They would go by slang names to evade law enforcement officers, whom Jonathan saw constantly harassing them with drug raids, arrests, and sometimes beatings. Jonathan experienced similar treatment himself on occasion. One altercation with the authorities influenced his entry into drug selling, moving him from a cocaine holder to an actual dealer.

For Jonathan, the Street Boys were more than just drug dealers; they were an organic part of the neighborhood. On various occasions, in public spaces such as parks, basketball courts, and street corners, the Street Boys would play basketball or move around between different houses and invite some of the "Young Boys" in the neighborhood to play video games. In public places, the Street Boys would have the younger kids compete to run errands to the store, the prize being the change left from whatever they purchased.

Jonathan describes organized fights between the Young Boys that were orchestrated by the Street Boys. These wrestling and boxing matches involved what he describes as "body blows," such as punches to the chest and body slams to the concrete, to see which boy in the neighborhood was the toughest. Sometimes there would be matches where teams of Young Boys would double- or triple-team a single Street Boy, skirmishes that Jonathan understood to be "playful." However, the Young Boys' interactions with the Street Boys were not only recreational. It was common practice for the Street Boys to make the Young Boys hold drugs whenever law enforcement officers appeared. If a Young Boy were asked to hold a package, it was nearly impossible for him to refuse. The consequences of saying no could keep a young boy from going outdoors; he was subjected to the constant threat of being beaten by an older Street Boy, and the Young Boys might retaliate by beating him up, ostracizing him, or calling him a punk or a coward.

Jonathan's First Drug Deal (Age 11)

The incident that sparked Jonathan's transformation from errand boy to drug holder and dealer began with the forced holding of powder cocaine. When Jonathan was eleven years old, a Street Boy told him to hold a package. Jonathan knew it was wrong but took the package anyway, mindful of the consequences of defying a Street Boy. As law enforcement officers began to question and arrest people in his neighborhood for drug activity, Jonathan walked away from the police toward a neighbor's porch. The neighbor demanded that he get away from the porch, and when the police witnessed the confrontation Jonathan was searched and arrested. His pleas to the police that the drugs were not his were disregarded, and Jonathan was questioned at the police station without his parents. During questioning, Jonathan continued to deny that the drugs were his and asserted that he did not remember which Street Boy had given him the drugs. When his mother came to the police station to pick up Jonathan, he told her the truth: that he had been forced to hold the package and that he did not remember the Street Boy who gave it to him. Jonathan's mother believed her son and, seeing the terror in his eyes, cursed out the arresting officer and took him home. Jonathan was later sentenced to probation in Juvenile Court. When he returned to his neighborhood, he was accorded respect and status for not snitching, and the Street Boy he took the rap for gave Jonathan forty dollars' worth of powder cocaine, which Jonathan then sold for a profit—his first drug sale. At age 11 Jonathan had unwittingly learned the lessons that would open the door to his life as a cocaine dealer.

From Seventh Grade to Tenth Grade (Age 14–17)

By the time Jonathan was in the seventh grade he had his own drug operation, making money by selling powder cocaine. Middle school was merely a place of recreation where he could display his latest fashions and use his free time to hang out with his sweetheart Susanna, whom he described as his "dream girl." Susanna lived a few blocks away from Jonathan. She was extremely attractive, smart, went to private schools, and was a virgin. Jonathan was her first sexual experience and, to his knowledge, the only one. He later married Susanna and had two children with her. Jonathan admired her family as "decent" middle-class people who did not associate with the negative elements in the neighborhood. Oddly, this view remained unchallenged even though Jonathan knew that members of her family sold drugs and had, in fact, at one point provided him with money to purchase drugs for his own operation.

Between the ages of fourteen and seventeen, Jonathan smoked marijuana heavily and was arrested several times. In school, he made it to the tenth grade in spite of the fact that he was diagnosed with a learning disability that interfered with reading comprehension. According to Jonathan, he dropped out of high school because Bristol High was too dangerous to attend and he faced pressure because he "represented" the Gray Gardens area. Newspaper articles and anecdotal evidence substantiate his claims about the dangerous conditions at the school. The city school district, which had ranked at the bottom of the entire state, was taken over by state authorities in the early 1990s. In 2001, a private educational firm was contracted to run the schools in Bristol. In 2005, the educational firm withdrew from Bristol High School at a $30 million loss, citing uncontainable violence as one of the causes.

Three Attempts at Decent Adulthood

In the years following his departure from high school, circumstances in Jonathan's life changed significantly. He tells of three instances in which he tried to turn his life around.

ONE: THE PROBATION OFFICER WHO CARED

Jonathan dropped out of high school and was arrested again later for drug possession. This time his mother turned him in. He was sentenced to probation, which stipulated that he be subject to random drug screening. In an attempt to mask his urine with an over-the-counter medication, Jonathan fell ill from drug poisoning and was placed in a hospital. He was assigned to a young white female probation officer who seemed to him sincere and caring. She arranged for him to take his GED (which he never finished), stopped by his home for visits, went to court dates, and kept up with him. During this time, at seventeen, he believed he was on the right track. However, Jonathan was caught again with drugs and received probation, this time as an adult. The juvenile court officer, who had been so sympathetic, lost track of Jonathan when he was rearrested, moved, and was reassigned to another district.

TWO: THE ID PROBLEM

When he was eighteen, Jonathan decided to find a legitimate job working for a plumbing company. Until that point in his life he had never worked for hourly pay in a regular occupation. After struggling through the application and interview process, Jonathan was hired. He had to present a valid government-issued ID to begin working. The job was held for him for a month. He asked his mother for his birth certificate, but she never produced it. Jonathan blamed his parents and his run-ins with law enforcement for his lack of preparedness for the social expectations of finding a job: "They never told me about how to fill out a job application, or even that I needed an ID." In the meantime, Jonathan and his brother continued to sell drugs. Drug money, which his parents accepted without question while openly condemning it, helped pay the family's expenses. Jonathan's father was laid off during this time. None of the three children finished high school, all were involved in drugs, and the daughter dated a neighborhood drug dealer.

THREE: STARTING A FAMILY

At eighteen, Jonathan left home with the help of Susanna, who rented an apartment for him in her name. Jonathan managed to save $30,000, decided once again that he was tired of the drug-dealing lifestyle, and considered signing up for Job Corps. He concluded that the only way he would ever be able to leave the "drug game" would be to leave Bristol; Job Corps requires you to move for six months. But Susanna became pregnant with their first child and told him it would be unfair of him to leave her and the baby. Susanna arranged for GED materials to be sent to Jonathan's home, but he never applied for any of the programs.

When he was eighteen Jonathan and Susanna had their first child, a daughter named Joanna. A year later, he had a daughter named Violet with Sharon, with whom he had sex occasionally. Two years later Jonathan and Susanna had their second child together, Jonathan Wilson, Jr. Jonathan still considers Susanna the love of his life and sincerely believes she feels similarly toward him even though he had a child with another woman while they were together. Jonathan describes Sharon as someone he used "to kick it with. She just my baby's mama." Sharon has a history of mental health problems, and her children were once wards of the court. Violet's stepfather, Omar Moore, is one of the people Jonathan was accused of killing. By the age of twenty, Jonathan was supporting two different families, as his father had, and giving occasional support to his mother and father.

Street Boys to Old Heads

When he was younger, Jonathan had looked up to the Street Boys because they had the money, the clothes, the jewelry, and the cars. Although at one time Jonathan said he wanted to be a lawyer, night-to-night life in Bristol with the Street Boys made their lifestyle a more attainable and realistic possibility. As he grew older, the Street Boys began to be referred to as the "Old Heads" because of their age and their experience. When Jonathan became a successful dealer—he claimed that he and one other young man were the best street hustlers in the neighborhood—he became a target of stick-ups as the Old Heads became envious of him.

It was the stick-ups that Jonathan feared the most. The Old Heads were known to take drugs and money by brute force. At times they would stick someone up and torture their victim until he revealed where his stash was located. Jonathan tells a story of how a prominent Old Head, who worked as a bus driver by night and sold cocaine on the side, showed him the ropes. The Old Head picked Jonathan up and took him to a house in an expensive neighborhood, which he pretended was his. Standing at the door of the house without going in, the Old Head explained the rules of the drug game and how to turn a major profit, assuring Jonathan that he too could have a house like that. While this Old Head was winning Jonathan's trust, Jonathan volunteered information such as how much "weight" he was moving, where he kept his stash, and how much money he made a month. Jonathan later found out that this particular Old Head, whom he had known for most of his life, was setting him up to get robbed.

The Criminal Charges

Janet Dallas, Jonathan's cousin through marriage, was murdered on October 11, 2001. Janet had grown up with Jonathan and his brother Antonio; she had known them since they were nine and ten respectively. At the time of her murder, Janet was under arrest by federal agents for purchasing and distributing guns, including rifles, pistols, and automatic weapons, to neighborhood drug dealers; two men were arrested with guns she had purchased. One of the two men arrested was Jonathan's brother Antonio. In return for her testimony, Janet was to receive three years in probation and the men she testified against were to receive three years of prison each. Janet told both Antonio and Jonathan that she was going to testify only against Antonio, who was under house arrest because of these charges. She wanted Antonio and Jonathan to help her get her guns back so that she would not have to testify against all of the parties involved.

One of the men to whom Janet sold guns was Byron Church. According to Jonathan, Byron killed Janet Dallas because he was fearful she would testify against him. Jonathan described Byron's history of mental illness; he was the son of drug-addicted parents and was raised entirely in group homes. A week passed without an arrest in the murder, and Byron was one of the fifty or so drug dealers on Lyford Street who appeared to get away with the crime.

Another Lyford Street drug dealer, Blake Night, became convinced that the police had become so complacent that they would not investigate any murders in the neighborhood. A week after Janet Dallas's murder, Blake killed a very popular, well-respected, and honest neighborhood policeman named Officer Tate. Officer Tate's murder on October 16 caused state, federal, and local law enforcement agencies to question and subpoena the entire block of Lyford Street.

The murder of Janet Dallas, a federal witness, was still being investigated. She had agreed to testify against at least five men, all of whom sold drugs on Lyford Street. Federal authorities arrested Officer Tate's murderer, Blake Night, who in return for a lesser sentence told authorities that Byron Church had murdered Dallas. A year after Church confessed to the murder and was given a life sentence without parole, Jonathan Wilson was charged with conspiracy; until then, he had been charged only with selling and possession of cocaine. Similar charges were made against Antoine Grey, Jonathan's friend since age 10; Howard Church, Byron Church's cousin and fellow drug dealer on Lyford Street, whom Jonathan had known since age fifteen; Deshawn Wright, a Lyford Street drug dealer, whom Jonathan had known since age fifteen; and Hakim Lincoln and Eddie Richardson, two Young Boys who had known Jonathan for three years prior to the arrest. Byron Church told law enforcement officers that the order for Janet Dallas's murder had come from Antonio and Jonathan Wilson.

Two years later, based on confessions from Wright, Lincoln, and Richardson, as well as Church, Jonathan Wilson was charged with the murders of Darnell Harris, a middle school acquaintance who was supposedly murdered over a dice game that went wrong, and Omar Moore, stepfather of his daughter Violet, supposedly murdered over "turf."

According to Jonathan, Wright, Lincoln, Church, and Richardson all testified against him to save themselves. Jonathan pointed out that he has never gotten along with any of these guys. He believes that Deshawn

Wright turned him into law enforcement three years earlier, which caused his parents' home to be raided for drugs. Jonathan stated that at one point Howard Church pulled a gun on Antonio to settle a wrestling match "gone wrong"; Jonathan said that he resolved that situation peacefully so that no one was injured. Jonathan believes that a majority of the testimonies against him stem from jealousy, because he was the top-selling drug dealer in the neighborhood, with a steady girlfriend. He pointed out that Deshawn in particular refused to buy drugs from him, purchasing drugs from his competition across town instead. Jonathan says that he has never owned or been caught with a gun.

Jonathan contends that, after Officer Tate's death, law enforcement and the media created the term "Lyford Street Gang." In the newspaper they were called the Lyford Street Boys, the Gray Gardens Gang, Lyford Street Gang, and the like. According to Jonathan, Lyford Street was just a place of convenience to sell drugs because it is located right off of the Interstate. Between thirty and fifty guys sold drugs on Lyford Street at any given time. Jonathan says that he, Antoine Grey, Byron Church, and Deshawn Wright share a tattoo on their arms that reads LOYALTY, which he has covered up. A well-known neighborhood rapper tattooed them while they were drinking and smoking marijuana. Jonathan stated that only four of the eight guys charged have the tattoo and that it does not symbolize anything in his eyes.

Jonathan refused to plead to any of the charges made against him because he says he is not guilty of all the things he is accused of doing in Bristol. He pointed out that the sequence of crimes with which he was charged was based on confessions by people who are facing possible jail time. First came his arrest on drug charges; a year later, he was charged with conspiracy to murder Janet Dallas; and two years later, again while he was incarcerated, he was indicted for accessory to the murders of Omar Moore and Darnell Harris. Jonathan feels that life in prison without parole is the equivalent of a death sentence. He pointed out that Janet Dallas's murderer received only life.

Because Janet Dallas was a federal witness, the U.S. attorney, rather than the state or local district attorney's office, handled the case. The group of seven drug dealers was charged under RICO, a federal law enacted to control organized crime. The prosecutor alleged that the pattern of their actions demonstrated that they belong to an "ongoing criminal organization."

Jonathan Wilson was found guilty of conspiracy to commit murder of a federal witness and accessory to two other murders and sentenced to life in prison without the possibility of parole. He is currently housed in a federal prison in a northeastern state.

Placing Jonathan's Case in Context

In order to understand Jonathan's life history, we must consider the situation in which he grew up. His family was disorganized, especially with regard to the supervision and education of the children. Neither the children nor the parents completed high school. Constant arguments between Jonathan's parents and extramarital affairs that produced other children affected Jonathan's life. According to Jonathan, there were virtually no decent role models, no moral grounding, and no adult mentoring to speak of.

The neighborhood offered little or no economic opportunity and lacked resources such as job training. It had very few, if any, strong institutions—not even churches. It was vacant of parks, recreational centers, Little League, music programs, and museums. Safe public spaces for children and families were almost nonexistent. Like many inner-city neighborhoods with concentrated poverty, it was drug infested and violent, with easy access to firearms. The police were not held accountable for their actions and people lacked faith in law enforcement, creating a perceived need for what Elijah Anderson calls "street justice" to take the place of civil law.

The schools were unable to provide a safe and adequate learning environment. Jonathan never received special education services after his learning disabilities were discovered. He may even be functionally illiterate. Bristol Upland School District is among the worst-performing school districts in the state.

Lacking parental guidance, an adequate education, and marketable skills, Jonathan was ill-prepared for adult life. Racial stigma and immersion in street culture, with its drug trafficking and violence, entail profound alienation. Jonathan tried several times to abandon the drug lifestyle, but failed. The systematic failure of schools, the criminal justice system, and parental guidance left Jonathan trapped in a cycle that ultimately led him to prison. Yet, even faced with the possibility of receiving the death penalty, Jonathan maintained a sense of hope for the future.

My involvement with the Jonathan Wilson cases grew once I became convinced that he did not deserve to die. Before working on this case I had never thought seriously about the death penalty, but I found the prospect of this young man's execution deeply unsettling. First, although I am not a lawyer, I was troubled by the decision to pursue the death penalty for Jonathan's crime, which seemed to be the byproduct of circumstances and legal wrangling. Jonathan's brother Antonio, the initial primary target for the prosecution, was deemed mentally retarded, which disqualified him as a candidate for the death penalty. Most of the information being used against Jonathan was based on testimony from individuals who had made plea deals with the prosecution, and the individuals who actually committed the murders were not given the death penalty. There were few character witnesses, often a mitigating factor in death penalty cases, because most of the young men Jonathan grew up with were either dead or in prison. Even the victim's family did not want Jonathan put to death. Ultimately, though, what motivated me the most was concern for Jonathan's three children; his execution would have additional damaging effects on them.

The Limitations of Rational Choice Theory

Upon concluding my talk to defense attorneys in state and federal death penalty cases, I was initially met by silence. Then, one after another, they alluded to the oft-heard argument that individuals have choices, a theory known formally as Rational Choice Theory. The Rational Choice theorist argues that individuals are rational beings who act in their own best interests by constantly analyzing costs and benefits. According to criminologists Cornish and Clarke, offenders seek to benefit themselves by their criminal behavior, which involves making decisions limited only by the constraints of time, ability, and the availability of relevant information (Cornish and Clarke 1986, 1). While I do not disagree with Rational Choice Theory in the abstract, I want to draw attention to the context within which these choices are being made. What choices are being weighed when there is nothing sacred in these communities, when schools fail to teach basic reading, writing, and math, when law enforcement fails to provide consistent protection? What are the choices when parents do not guide and protect their children, and neighborhoods are filled with chaotic families and overrun by drug use, drug sellers, and violence? What are the choices when even churches do not help? Ultimately, what choices would anyone have within the bureaucracy of poverty in which the state controls the quality and availability of schools, neighborhood policing, and welfare, and where a majority of the social institutions such as families, schools, and churches do not perform in the "taken-for-granted" ways many think they should? The individual in such an environment ends up in a situation in which all of his choices, born of neglect and despair, are bad choices regardless of potential personal benefit.

Tragically, Jonathan's life history is symptomatic of the continued decline of American inner cities, and he can be counted among the innumerable men and women who have little hope because of the imminent possibility of an early death or incarceration and because of the absence of even one functional, supportive institution. The consequences are especially dire for poor black men, who aspire to be self-sufficient but no longer have the tools to achieve this goal adequately without proper guidance. Deindustrialization and the shift to a lower-paying, service-oriented economy have left very few economic choices for the urban poor and the ill-educated, especially for young men who want to succeed but lack the necessary resources. In this environment, within the predominant street culture, masculinity is often performed in destructive acts of sexuality and violence. Jonathan's behavior reflects the code of the street in both regards. Interestingly, both Jonathan and his father made good choices in their selection of spouses who stuck by them through difficult marital situations. Their wives remained loyal despite their infidelity, perhaps because they realized that infidelity was not the primary cause of their problems. Under the circumstances, the Wilson men were lucky to have married particularly strong women; other men were less fortunate.

In the end, the best that can be hoped for Jonathan Wilson is that he spends the rest of his life in prison without the possibility of parole. But the real tragedy is outside the prison walls, in the world into which Jonathan's children were born. In his old neighborhood, poor schools, a dangerous environment, and the criminalization of children continue to destroy young people's prospects even when their parents have the best of intentions and aspirations for upward mobility into the middle class. Children who grow up in these circumstances are presented with an interconnected array of countless bad choices.

References

Anderson, Elijah. 1999. *Code of the Street: Decency, Violence, and the Moral Life of the Inner City*. New York: W.W. Norton.

———. 1990. *Streetwise: Race, Class, and Change in an Urban Community*. Chicago: University of Chicago Press.

Butterfield, Fox. 1996. *All God's Children: The Bosket Family and the American Tradition of Violence*. New York: Avon Books.

Cornish, Derek B., and Ronald V. Clarke. 1986. *The Reasoning Criminal: Rational Choice Perspectives on Offending*. New York: Springer-Verlag.

Dollard, John. 1935. *Criteria for the Life History, with Analyses of Six Notable Documents*. New Haven, Conn.: Yale University Press.

Garfinkel, Harold. 1967. *Studies in Ethnomethodology*. Englewood Cliffs, N.J.: Prentice-Hall.

Garfinkel, Harold, and Anne Rawls. 2002. *Ethnomethodology's Program: Working Out Durkheim's Aphorism*. Lanham, Md.: Rowman and Littlefield.

Rawls, John. 1971. *A Theory of Justice*. Cambridge, Mass.: Belknap Press of Harvard University Press.

Shaw, Clifford, and Howard Becker. 1966. *The Jack-Roller: A Delinquent Boy's Own Story*. Chicago: University of Chicago Press.

Part II
Structural Analyses of Joblessness Among Black Youth

Chapter 4

The Economic Plight
of Inner-City Black Males

WILLIAM JULIUS WILSON

The economic predicament of black men in the inner city today resembles the situation documented by Elliot Liebow in his classic book *Tally's Corner: A Study of Negro Street Corner Men.* Liebow wrote *Tally's Corner* in the mid-1960s, yet his arguments concerning the work experiences and family lives of black men in a Washington D.C. ghetto are still applicable to contemporary urban communities. In analyzing the data collected by our research team on poverty and joblessness among black males in inner-city Chicago neighborhoods, I was repeatedly reminded of Liebow's analysis. Liebow was perhaps the first scholar to call attention to the fact that ongoing lack of success in the labor market lowers a man's self-confidence and gives rise to feelings of resignation that frequently result in a temporary, or even permanent, abandonment of the job search. "The most important fact is that a man who is able and willing to work cannot earn enough to support himself, his wife, and one or more children," declared Liebow. "A man's chances for working regularly are good only if he is willing to work for less than he can live on, sometimes not even then" (Liebow 1967, 50–51).

The jobs filled by the low-status black men in Liebow's study were poorly paying, dirty, physically demanding, and uninteresting. They offered neither respect nor opportunity for advancement. Like others in this society, the street corner man viewed such jobs with disdain. "He cannot do otherwise," stated Liebow; "he cannot draw from a job those values which other people do not put into it" (51). Understandably, the work histories of the street corner men were erratic. Menial employment was readily available, and workers drifted from one undesirable job to the next.

The New Urban Poverty

Although the job prospects for low-skilled black men were bleak when Liebow conducted his field research in the early 1960s, they are even worse today. Indeed, the employment woes of low-skilled black men represent part of what I have called "the new urban poverty." By the new urban poverty, I mean poor, segregated neighborhoods in which substantial proportions of adults are unemployed, have dropped out of the labor force, or never participated in it at all. This jobless poverty today stands in sharp contrast to previous periods when the working poor predominated in urban ghettos. In 1950, for example, a substantial portion of the inner-city adult population was poor, but they held jobs (Wilson 1996). Now many adults are disconnected from the labor market.

When I speak of "joblessness" I am not referring solely to official unemployment. The unemployment rate includes only those workers in the official labor force, that is, those who are actively looking for work. I use the term "jobless" to refer not only to those who are looking for work but also to those who are outside of or have dropped out of the labor market, including millions of adult males who appear in the census statistics but are not recorded in the labor market statistics.

These uncounted males are disproportionately represented in inner-city neighborhoods. For example, take the three neighborhoods that form the historic core of Chicago's Black Belt: Douglas, Grand Boulevard, and Washington Park. In 1950, 69 percent of out-of-school males age fourteen and over who lived in these three neighborhoods worked for pay during a typical week, and in 1960 64 percent of this group were employed. However, by 1990 only 37 percent of out-of-school males age sixteen or over in these neighborhoods held jobs during a typical week. Over the last three decades, low-skilled African American males have encountered increasing difficulty gaining access to jobs—even menial jobs that pay no more than minimum wage. The ranks of idle inner-city men have swelled since 1970, and include a growing proportion of adult males who routinely work in and tolerate low-wage jobs when they are available (Wilson 1996).

The impact of this joblessness is reflected in real earnings, that is, earnings adjusted for inflation. For example, between 2000 and 2004 the average real annual earnings of twenty-four-year-old black males in the bottom quarter of the earnings distribution (the 25th percentile) were only $1,078, compared with $9,623 and $9,843 respectively for their Latino and white male counterparts.[1] For purposes of comparison, in the 75th percentile of the earnings distribution, average annual earnings for twenty-four-year-old black males were $22,000, compared with $22,800 and $30,000 for Latino and white males respectively. The really significant discrepancy is for those in the 25th percentile.

The extremely low annual average earnings for black males at the 25th percentile of the earnings distribution results from the fact that many of them were jobless during this period, including those who had completely given up looking for work and had virtually no reported income. These men are heavily concentrated in poor inner-city neighborhoods.

Many of these jobless men are high school dropouts. The situation for black male high school dropouts is especially bleak. A recent report by Andrew Sum and his colleagues at Northeastern University's Center for Labor Market Studies reveals that "only 1 of every 3 young black male high school dropouts was able to obtain any type of employment during an average month in 2005" and only 23 percent of these males were able to find full-time employment during an average week. The report appropriately points out that "many of these young men will end up being involved in criminal activity during their late teens and early twenties and then bear the severe economic consequences for convictions and incarceration over the remainder of their working lives" (Sum et al. 2007, 2–3).

Given the severity of unemployment and underemployment, the relatively low proportion of young African American men with higher education has significant social ramifications. There has been a growing gender gap in college degree attainment in recent years, with women exceeding men in the rate of college completion. This discrepancy is particularly acute among African Americans. Black women have significantly higher college completion rates than black men, and the gap has widened steadily over the past 25 years. In 1979, for every 100 bachelor's degrees awarded to black men, 144 were received by black women. In 2003–2004, for every 100 bachelor's degrees granted to black men, 200 were conferred on black women. By contrast, for every 100 bachelor's degrees earned by white and Hispanic men respectively, 131 were earned by white women and 155 by Hispanic women (Sum et al. 2007).

The significant and growing discrepancy in the college attainment rate of black men and black women has important social and economic consequences for the black community as well as the larger society because the economic returns to college investment are very high for black males. Figure 4.1, which provides data on the employment/population ratio—the percentage of young men who were not in school and who were employed in 2005—reveals that there is very little difference in employment rates of black and white college graduates: 88.3 percent for whites and 86.2 percent for blacks. The employment gap widens with lower levels of education. The gap between white and black young males ages sixteen to twenty-four who were not in school in 2005 declined from 20 percentage points for high school dropouts to 16 percent among high school graduates, 8 percent for those completing 1 to 3 years of college, and only 2 percent for four-year college graduates. Education plays a key role in enabling black men to secure employment.

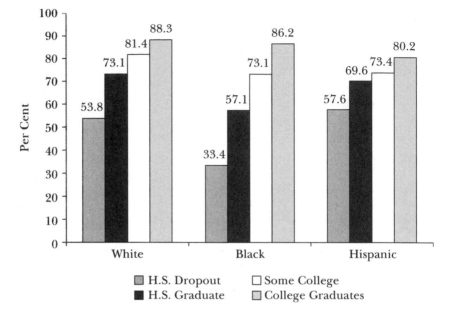

Figure 4.1. Employment/population ratios of non-enrolled sixteen- to-twenty-four-year-old males by educational attainment and race/ethnic group, 2005. Adapted from Andrew Sum, Ishwar Khatiwada, Joseph McLaughlin, and Paulo Tobar, "The Educational Attainment of the Nation's Young Black Men and Their Recent Labor Market Experiences: What Can Be Done to Improve Their Future Labor Market and Educational Prospects?" Center for Labor Market Studies, Northeastern University, Boston, February 2007.

Similarly, the relative size of the gap in annual earnings between black men and all men ages twenty to twenty-nine decreases as the educational attainment of black men rises. The median annual earnings of black male dropouts in 2004–2005 were only equivalent to 15 percent of those of male dropouts in all racial-ethnic groups. However, that figure increased to 64 percent for high school graduates and 96 percent for those with bachelor's degrees. The disparity in the earnings of black and non-black men is much less among high school graduates than among dropouts and almost vanishes among college graduates (Figure 4.2).

Explanations of the Economic Plight of Low-Skilled Black Men

What has caused the deterioration in the employment prospects of low-skilled black males and hence their remarkably lower earnings? I highlight several major factors, both structural and cultural, in explaining

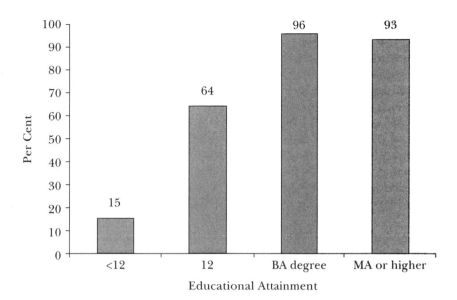

Figure 4.2. Ratio of median annual earnings of twenty- to-twenty-nine-year-old black men to all men by educational attainment, 2004–2005. Adapted from Andrew Sum, Ishwar Khatiwada, Joseph McLaughlin, and Paulo Tobar, "The Educational Attainment of the Nation's Young Black Men and Their Recent Labor Market Experiences: What Can Be Done to Improve Their Future Labor Market and Educational Prospects?" Center for Labor Market Studies, Northeastern University, Boston, February 2007.

this situation. The structural factors include those that are nonracial and are shared more or less by all low-income males, and those that are racial and pertain specifically to black males.

STRUCTURAL FACTORS

Although African American men continue to confront racial barriers in the labor market, many inner-city black males have also been victimized by the declining relative demand for low-skilled labor. The propagation of new technologies is displacing untrained workers and rewarding those with specialized, technical training, while the globalization of the economy is increasingly pitting low-skilled workers in the United States against their counterparts around the world, including laborers in Third World countries such as China, India, and Bangladesh. Because of the decreasing relative demand for low-skilled labor, workers face the growing threat of wage declines and job displacement (Katz 1996; Schwartzman 1997).

Over the past several decades, black males have experienced sharp job losses in the manufacturing sector. While Hispanics have suffered the largest loss in manufacturing jobs over the long term, more recent losses have been worse among African Americans. According to John Schmitt and Ben Zipperer of the Center for Economic and Policy Research, the proportion of black workers who are employed in manufacturing decreased from 23.9 percent in 1979 to 10.1 percent in 2006. Whites experienced slightly smaller drops (from 23.5 to 11.9 percent), while Hispanics experienced a larger decline (from 30.2 percent to 11.9 percent). However, since 1996 black declines in manufacturing (from 16.0 to 10.1 percent) slightly exceeded those of whites (from 16.5 to 11.5 percent) and Hispanics (from 18.1 to 12.6 percent). The dwindling proportion of African American workers in manufacturing is important because manufacturing jobs, especially those in the auto industry, have been a significant source of better-paid employment for black Americans since World War II (Schmitt and Zipperer 2007).

The declining proportion of black workers in manufacturing parallels their decreasing involvement in unions. From 1983 to 2006 the proportion of all African American workers who were either in unions or represented by a union at their employment site dropped considerably from 31.7 percent to 16.0 percent (Schmitt and Zipperer 2007). This reduction (down 15.7 percentage points) was greater than that for whites (down 8.9 percentage points) and Hispanics (down 13.5 percentage points). The lack of union representation renders workers more vulnerable in the workplace, especially to cuts in wages and benefits.

Labor markets today are mainly regional, and long commutes in automobiles are common. Most ghetto residents cannot afford an automobile and have to rely on public transit systems that make the connection between inner-city neighborhoods and suburban job locations difficult and time-consuming, or even impossible. For example, research conducted in the Chicago ghetto areas revealed that only 19 percent of residents have access to an automobile. To make matters worse, many inner-city residents lack information or knowledge about suburban job opportunities. In isolated inner-city neighborhoods, the breakdown of the informal job information network aggravates the problem of the spatial mismatch between workplace and residence (Wilson 1996).

The heavy child support payments now required of noncustodial parents under federal law present a daunting problem, as Harry Holzer and his colleagues remind us. Such payments represent an employment tax of 36 percent of a worker's wages, and if the noncustodial father is in arrears, the federal law allows states to deduct as much as 65 percent of his wages. Many of those who face this higher tax are ex-offenders whose delinquent child support payments accumulated while they were in prison. High child support payments function as a disincentive to remain in the formal labor market and an incentive to move into the casual or informal labor market (Holzer, Offner, and Sorensen 2003).

For inner-city black male workers, the problems created by these nonracial factors have been aggravated by employers' negative attitudes. This racial factor affects black males especially seriously. Interviews of a representative sample of Chicago-area employers conducted by my research team in the late 1980s revealed that a substantial majority of employers considered inner-city black males to be uneducated, uncooperative, unstable, or dishonest (Wilson 1996).[2] For example, a suburban drug store manager commented:

It's unfortunate but, in my business I think overall [black men] tend to be known to be dishonest. I think that's too bad but that's the image they have.
Interviewer: So you think it's an image problem?
Respondent: An image problem of being dishonest men and lazy. They're known to be lazy. They are [laughs]. I hate to tell you, but. . . . It's all an image though. Whether they are or not, I don't know, but, it's an image that is perceived.
Interviewer: I see. How do you think that image was developed?
Respondent: Go look in the jails [laughs].

The president of an inner-city manufacturing firm expressed a different reservation about employing black males from certain ghetto neighborhoods:

If somebody gave me their address, uh, Cabrini Green I might unavoidably have some concerns.
Interviewer: What would your concerns be?
Respondent: That the poor guy probably would be frequently unable to get to work and . . . I probably would watch him more carefully even if it wasn't fair, than I would with somebody else. I know what I should do though is recognize that here's a guy that is trying to get out of his situation and probably will work harder than somebody else who's already out of there and he might be the best one around here. But I think I would have to struggle accepting that premise at the beginning.

Because of the prevalence of such attitudes, the lack of access to informal job networks is a notable problem for black males. The importance of knowing someone who knows the boss is suggested by another employer's comments to our interviewer:

All of a sudden, they take a look at a guy, and unless he's got an in, the reason why I hired this black kid the last time is cause my neighbor said to me, yeah I used him for a few [days], he's good, and I said, you know what, I'm going to take a chance. But it was a recommendation. But other than that, I've got a walk-in, and, who knows? And I think that for the most part, a guy sees a black man, he's a bit hesitant.

These attitudes are classic examples of what social scientists call statistical discrimination: employers make generalizations about inner-city black male workers and reach decisions based on those assumptions without reviewing the qualifications of an individual applicant. The net effect is that many inner-city black male applicants are never given the opportunity to prove their qualifications. Although some of these men eschew entry-level jobs because of the poor working conditions and low wages, many others would readily accept such employment. Statistical discrimination, although involving elements of class bias against poor urban workers, is clearly a racially biased practice. Far more inner-city black males are effectively screened out of employment than Hispanic or white males applying for the same jobs.

Unfortunately, the restructuring of the economy has compounded the negative effects of employers' attitudes toward inner-city black males. Today, most of the new jobs for workers with limited education and experience are in the service sector, which includes jobs that tend to be held by women, such as waitstaff, sales clerks, and nurse's aides. Indeed, "employment rates of young black women now exceed those of young black men, even though many of these women must also care for children" (Holzer, Offner, and Sorensen 2003). The shift to service jobs has resulted in a greater demand for workers who can effectively serve and relate to the consumer. Many employers in our study felt that, unlike women and immigrants (who have recently expanded the labor pool for service-sector jobs), inner-city black males lack these qualities. Instead, low-skilled black males are perceived as dangerous or threatening. In the past, all that men had to demonstrate was a strong back and muscles for heavy lifting and physical labor in a factory, at a construction site, or on an assembly line. They did not have to interact with customers. Today, they have to search for work in the service sector, and employers are less likely to hire them because they have to come into contact with the public. Consequently, black male job-seekers face rising rates of rejection.

The difficulties experienced by low-skilled black males in the labor market are even greater for those who have prison records. The ranks of ex-offenders have increased significantly over the past several decades. Indeed, rates of incarceration have soared even during periods when the crime rate has declined. Finding employment has become exceedingly difficult for poor black males for many reasons, but the problem is even worse for those with prison records. According to one estimate, as many as 30 percent of all civilian young adult black males ages sixteen to thirty-four are ex-offenders; a significant proportion of them are high-school dropouts with prison records. Becky Pettit and Bruce Western estimate that "among [black] male high school dropouts the risk of imprisonment had increased to 60 percent, establishing incarceration as a normal stopping point on the route to midlife" (2004). <u>Their high incarceration rates are closely connected to their high jobless rates.</u> It is a vicious cycle. Initial joblessness prompts illegal money-making activities that result in incarceration, which then leads to even more intractable joblessness.

The Role of Culture

Forced to turn to the low-wage service sector for employment, inner-city black males, a significant proportion of whom are ex-offenders, have to compete with the growing number of female and immigrant workers. Often they are unsuccessful. The more these men complain or manifest their job dissatisfaction, the less attractive they seem to employers. They therefore encounter greater discrimination when they search for employment. Since the feelings many inner-city black males express about their jobs and job prospects reflect their plummeting position in a changing economy, it is important to link attitudinal and other cultural traits with the opportunity structure (Wilson 1996).

According to my colleague Orlando Patterson, not enough attention is given to the cultural dimension of urban black men's employment problems. Patterson argues that "a deep seated dogma . . . has prevailed in the social science and policy circles since the mid-1960s: the rejection of any explanation that invokes a group's cultural attributes—its distinctive attitudes, values and predispositions, and the resulting behavior of its members—and the relentless preference for relying on structural factors like low incomes, joblessness, poor schools and bad housing." He asks, "Why do so many young unemployed black men have children—several of them—which they have no resources or intention to support? And why . . . do they murder each other at nine times the rate of white youths?" Why do young black males turn their backs on low-wage jobs that immigrants are happy to fill? (Patterson 2006). Referring to research conducted by Roger Waldinger (1996), Patterson states that these jobs enabled the chronically unemployed to enter the labor market and to acquire basic work skills that they later used to secure better jobs, but that the takers were mostly immigrants.

Patterson also refers to anecdotal evidence collected several years ago by one of his students, who visited her former high school to discover why "almost all the black girls graduated and went to college whereas nearly all the black boys either failed to graduate or did not go on to college." Her distressing finding was that all the black boys were fully aware of the consequences of failing to graduate from high school and go on to college; they told her indignantly, "we're not stupid!" So, Patterson asks, "why were they flunking out?" The candid answer that these young men gave to his former student was their preference for what Patterson called the "cool-pose culture" of young black men, which they found too fulfilling to give up.[3] "For these young men, it was almost like a drug, hanging out on the street after school, shopping and dressing sharply, sexual conquests, party drugs, hip-hop music and culture" (Patterson 2006).

Patterson maintains that this culture blatantly promotes the most anomalous and counterproductive models of behavior in urban lower-class neighborhoods, featuring "gangsta-rap," predatory sexuality, and irresponsible paternity. "It is reasonable to conclude," he states, "that among a large number of urban, Afro-American lower-class young men, these models are now fully normative and that men act in accordance with them whenever they can" (2000, 217). For example, Patterson argues that male pride has increasingly become defined in terms of the impregnation of women. This orientation is not unique to the current generation of young black males, he notes. Several decades ago the sociologist Lee Rainwater (1969) uncovered a similar pattern. A majority of the inner-city young black male respondents he interviewed stated that they were indifferent to the fact that their girlfriends were pregnant; some even expressed pride because getting a girl pregnant proves that you are a man! The fact that Elijah Anderson and others discovered identical patterns (Anderson 1990; Majors and Billson 1992; Nightingale 1993) decades later suggests a process of cultural transmission within black communities (Patterson 2000).

Patterson maintains that social scientists have shied away from cultural explanations because of the widespread belief that such explanations inherently blame the victim, that a focus on internal behavioral factors leads to the conclusion that the poor are responsible for their own poverty and social problems, rather than assigning causality to the nefarious and deleterious aspects of the environment. He contends that this view, which has often been put forth by conservatives, is "utterly bogus." To hold an individual responsible for his behavior is not to rule out any consideration of the environmental factors that may have evoked the questionable behavior to begin with. "Many victims of child abuse end up behaving in self-destructive ways," he argues, so "to point out the link between their behavior and the destructive acts is in no way to deny the causal role of their earlier victimization and the need to address it" (2006). Likewise, he contends, a cultural explanation of black male self-destructiveness not only speaks to the immediate relationship between their attitudes and behavior and the undesirable outcomes, but it also examines their brutalized past, perhaps over generations, to investigate the origins and changing nature of these attitudes. Patterson maintains that we cannot understand "the high rates of homicide, predatory sexuality and irresponsible fathering" of young black males without a deep examination of African Americans' collective historical experience.

Although I believe that Patterson tends to downplay the importance of immediate socioeconomic factors that are currently affecting black males' life chances, I fully concur with his view that cultural explanations should be part of any attempt to account for such behavior and outcomes. When we speak of cultural attributes we are referring to distinctive values, norms, attitudes, and predispositions held by a group, and the behavior of a group's members that stem from such attributes.

Not only is it exceedingly difficult to determine the relative importance of cultural and structural factors in explaining the situation and actions of young black males, but I firmly believe that to attempt to analyze them separately, rather than examining how they interact, is a serious mistake. If we are going to consider social and economic factors that over time contributed to the development of certain cultural traits and behavior patterns, we also have to give serious attention to the immediate effects of structural conditions. Social structures and cultures combine and interact to shape attitudes and behavior in a myriad of complex ways. A few examples illustrate this process.

Patterson contends that low-skilled black males do not pursue menial jobs that immigrants readily accept. However, he fails to discuss developments that were uncovered in our ethnographic research in Chicago: that many young black males, who now have to compete with women and immigrants in the low-wage service sector, have experienced repeated failures in their job search, have given up hope, and no longer even bother to look for work.[4] This defeatism was due in no small measure to employers' negative attitudes and actions toward low-skilled black males. Repeated failure results in resignation and the development of cultural attitudes that discourage the pursuit of steady employment in the formal labor market.

Furthermore, it is difficult to account for the higher dropout rate and lower academic achievement of black males in comparison with black females without taking into account the negative experiences of young black males in the labor market, even those who have graduated from high school. Black males are far less likely than black females to see a strong relationship between their schooling and post-school employment. I believe that the evolution of "cool-pose culture" is partly a response to that feeling of discouragement and sense of futility.

The relative lack of commitment to fatherhood among many inner-city men is a cultural problem that may have its origins in past experiences over the generations, but it is also related to more immediate restrictions on opportunities. Many inner-city fathers today, even those who are not typically street corner men, have low self-efficacy when it comes to fatherhood, whether they are willing to admit it or not. Included among the norms of fatherhood is the obligation to provide adequate and consistent material support. Continuing lack of success in the labor market reduces the ability of many inner-city men to support their children adequately, which in turn lowers their self-confidence as providers and creates antagonistic relations with the mothers of their children. Convenient rationalizations emerge, shared and reinforced by the men in these constricted economic situations, which reject the institution of marriage in ways that enhance, rather than diminish, their self-esteem. The outcome is a failure to meet the societal norms of fatherhood that is even more widespread than reported by Liebow in 1967.

I strongly concur with Orlando Patterson that an adequate cultural explanation of young black male self-destructiveness must explore the origins and changing nature of attitudes that go back for generations, even centuries. Such analyses are complex and difficult. For example, Kathryn Neckerman provides a historical perspective to explain why so many black youngsters and their parents lose faith in the public schools. She shows in her book, *Schools Betrayed* (2007), that a century ago, when African American children in most northern cities attended schools alongside white children, the problems commonly associated with inner-city schools were not nearly as pervasive as they are today. She carefully documents how and why these schools came to serve black children so much more poorly than their white counterparts. Focusing on Chicago public schools between 1900 and 1960, Neckerman compares the circumstances of blacks and white immigrants—groups that had similarly little wealth and status yet received vastly different benefits from their educations. Their divergent educational outcomes, she contends, were the result of decisions made systematically by Chicago officials to deal with the increasing African American migration to the city by segregating schools and denying equal resources to African American students. Those decisions reinforced inequality in the schools over time. Ultimately, these policies and practices eroded the schools' legitimacy in the lower-class black community and dampened aspirations for education. "The roots of classroom alienation, antagonism, and disorder can be found in school policy decisions made long before the problems of inner-city schools attracted public attention," Neckerman concludes. "These policies struck at the foundations of authority and engagement, making it much more difficult for inner-city teachers to gain student cooperation in learning. The district's history of segregation and inequality undermined school legitimacy in the eyes of its black students; as a result, inner-city teachers struggled to gain cooperation from children and parents, who had little reason to trust the school" (2007, 74). We need more studies like this to fully understand the current cultural dynamics in inner-city neighborhoods.

Finally, Patterson argues that while culture "partly determines behavior, it also enables people to change behavior" (2006). He states that culture provides a frame for individuals to understand their world. By ignoring culture or only investigating it at a superficial level, as a set of styles or performances, social scientists miss an opportunity to reframe attitudes in a way that promotes desirable behavior and outcomes. I concur. However, reframing attitudes is often difficult without accompanying programs to address structural inequities. For example, I argue that programs focusing on the cultural problems pertaining to fatherhood, including attitudes concerning paternity, without confronting the broader and more fundamental issues of restricted economic opportunities have limited prospects of success. In my view, the most effective fatherhood programs in the inner city will be those that address attitudes, norms, and behaviors in combination with local and national attempts to improve job opportunities. Only then will fathers have a realistic chance to care for their children adequately and envision a better life for themselves.

Social Policies and Programs

What social policies and programs are most likely to improve the employment prospects of young low-skilled black males, including those with prison records, and could be instituted alongside activities intended to change self-destructive attitudes?

First, programs such as the Job Corps and Youth Build should be expanded to help young people who are unemployed and in need of training and assistance in locating and securing jobs. Skilled training programs, similar to STRIVE and Project Quest, which include instruction in both soft (or "people") skills and hard (or technical) skills and job placement, should also be expanded. Restoring funding for job training under the Workforce Investment Act would be helpful in this regard, as would providing more funds to increase job placement and transportation programs, such as America Works, in inner-city neighborhoods (Giloth 2003).

We should review ways to relieve the work disincentives associated with mandatory child support payments. I agree with Harry Holzer and his colleagues that various forms of "arrearage forgiveness" ought to be considered, especially for men who fell far behind in child support payments while spending time in prison (Holzer, Offner, and Sorensen 2003).

Transition programs should be created to facilitate the successful reentry of incarcerated men into society. These programs might include a period of soft and hard skills training and job counseling prior to the prisoner's release and job placement assistance upon release.

Since joblessness is closely associated with incarceration, ideally we want programs to improve the employment prospects of young men before they commit crimes. According to the U.S. Bureau of Labor Statistics, only 42 percent of black youths who had not enrolled in college had jobs in October after graduating from high school in June, compared with 69 percent of their white counterparts. The figures for black youngsters in inner-city neighborhoods, especially black males, are even lower.

Accordingly, I think that it is vitally important to promote school-to-work transitions in inner-city neighborhoods through internships and apprenticeships, especially for high school seniors. Successful school-to-work programs will depend on the cooperation of employers, who should be encouraged by political leaders to create internship and apprenticeship opportunities for secondary-level students. The Career Academies programs, which increased the post-school earnings of the young men who participated, should be widely publicized in efforts to generate support for such initiatives.

Nearly 2,500 high schools have career academies, which have three distinguishing features: an organizational structure featuring a school-within-a-school; curricula that combine academic and occupational courses organized around a career theme; and partnerships with employers. The Manpower Demonstration Research Corporation (MDRC) recently evaluated this program using a random assignment design and found that school academies had substantial long-term effects on the earnings of young men, especially minority men. These programs included summer and after-school jobs provided by employers, which enabled these young men to gain work experience. Such programs should be widely publicized and expanded, especially in poor communities of color.

Finally, the City University of New York (CUNY) recently instituted a program called the Black Male Initiative to increase enrollment in college. This program could become a model for other universities and colleges around the country. In 2004, campuses in the CUNY system were funded to establish demonstration projects designed to improve both enrollment and college graduation rates of disadvantaged students, particularly black males; to increase opportunities for individuals without a high school diploma to enroll in GED courses oriented toward college preparation; and to provide support for formerly incarcerated individuals to enroll in college. The importance of increasing the educational attainment of black men cannot be overstated; that is why the CUNY Black Male Initiative is so timely and important.

All these programs are modest and realistic and ought to receive the support of policymakers who are concerned about the worsening plight of young black men growing up poor in the inner city. If these structural programs are combined with those dedicated to addressing self-destructive attitudes and norms, programs focused on patterns of behavior will be more effective.

References

Anderson, Elijah. 1990. *Streetwise: Race, Class, and Change in an Urban Community.* Chicago: University of Chicago Press.

Center on Budget and Policy Priorities. 1996. The Administration's $3 Billion Jobs Proposal. Washington, D.C.

Giloth, Robert, ed. 2003. *Workforce Intermediaries for the 21st Century.* New York: American Assembly.

Holzer, Harry J. 1995. *What Employers Want: Job Prospects for Less-Educated Workers.* New York: Russell Sage.

Holzer, Harry J., Paul Offner, and Elaine Sorensen. 2003. What explains the continuing decline in labor force activity among young black men? Paper presented for Color Lines Conference, Harvard University, August 30, 2003.

Katz, Lawrence. 1996. Wage Subsidies for the Disadvantaged. Working Paper 5679. Cambridge, Mass.: National Bureau of Economic Research.

Lerman, Robert I., and Martin Rein. Forthcoming. *Social Service Employment: An International Perspective.* New York: Russell Sage.

Liebow, Elliot. 1967. *Tally's Corner: A Study of Negro Street Corner Men.* Boston: Little, Brown. Reprint with new introduction by William Julius Wilson. Lanham, Md.: Rowman and Littlefield, 2003.

Neckerman, Kathryn M. 2007. *Schools Betrayed: Roots of Failure in Inner City Education.* Chicago: University of Chicago Press.

Nightingale, Carl Husemoller. 2003. *On the Edge: A History of Poor Black Children and Their American Dreams.* New York: Basic Books.

Majors, Richard, and Janet Billson. 1992. *Cool Pose.* Lexington, Mass.: Heath.

Patterson, Orlando. 2006. A poverty of the mind. *New York Times,* March 26, Section 4, 13.

———. 2000. Taking culture seriously: A framework and an Afro-American illustration. In *Culture Matters: How Values Shape Human Progress,* ed. Lawrence E. Harrison and Samuel P. Huntington, 202–18. New York: Basic Books.

Pettit, Becky, and Bruce Western. 2004. Mass Imprisonment and the life course: Race and class inequality in U.S. incarceration. *American Sociological Review* 69: 151–69.

Rainwater, Lee. 1969. The problem of lower-class culture and poverty-war strategy. In *On Understanding Poverty,* ed. Daniel P. Moynihan, 229–59. New York: Basic Books.

Schmitt, John, and Ben Zipperer. 2007. The Decline in African American Representation in Unions and Manufacturing, 1979–2006. Center for Economic and Policy Research Report. March 20.

Schwartzman, David. 1997. *Black Unemployment: Part of Unskilled Unemployment.* Westport, Conn.: Greenwood Press.

Sum, Andrew, Ishwar Khatiwada, Joseph McLaughlin, and Paulo Tobar. 2007. The educational attainment of the nation's young black men and their recent labor market experiences: What can be done to improve their future labor market and educational prospects. Prepared for America's Graduates, Alexandria, Virginia, February.

Tobin, James. 1965. On improving the economic status of the Negro. *Daedalus* 94: 878–98.

Waldinger, Roger, 1996. *Still the Promised City? African Americans and the New Immigrants in Postindustrial New York*. Cambridge, Mass.: Harvard University Press.

Waldinger, Roger, and Michael I. Lichter. 2003. *How the Other Half Works: Immigration and the Social Organization of Labor*. Berkeley: University of California Press.

Wilson, William Julius. 1996. *When Work Disappears: The World of the New Urban Poor*. New York: Knopf.

Young, Alford A. 2004. *The Minds of Marginalized Black Men: Making Sense of Mobility, Opportunity, and Future Life Chances*. Princeton, N.J.: Princeton University Press.

Chapter 5

Blacklisted: Hiring Discrimination in an Era of Mass Incarceration

DEVAH PAGER

Jerome arrived at a branch of a national restaurant chain in a suburb twenty miles from Milwaukee. He immediately sensed that he was the only black person in the place. An employee hurried over to him, "Can I help you with something?" "I'm here about the job you advertised," he replied. The employee nodded reluctantly and went off to produce an application form. Jerome filled out the form, including information about his criminal background. He was given a math test and a personality test. He was then instructed to wait for the manager to speak with him. The manager came out after about ten minutes, looked over Jerome's application, and frowned when he noticed the criminal history information. Without asking any questions about the context of the conviction, the manager started to lecture: "You can't be screwing up like this at your age. A kid like you can ruin his whole life like this." Jerome began to explain that he had made a mistake and had learned his lesson, but the manager cut him off: "I'll look over your application and call if we have a position for you."

Jerome could have been any one of the hundreds of thousands of young black men released from prison each year who face bleak employment prospects as a result of their race and criminal record. In this case, Jerome happened to be working for me. He was one of four college students I had hired as "testers" for a study of employment discrimination. An articulate, attractive, hard-working young man, Jerome was assigned to apply for entry-level job openings throughout the Milwaukee metropolitan area, presenting a fictitious profile designed to represent a realistic ex-offender. Comparing the outcomes of Jerome's job search to those of three other black and white testers presenting identical qualifications with and without criminal records gives us a direct measure of the effects of race and a criminal record, and of possible interactions between the two, in shaping employment opportunities. In this essay I consider the ways in which high rates of incarceration among African Americans may fuel contemporary stereotypes about the criminal tendencies of young black men. The evidence reviewed here suggests that the disproportionate growth of criminal justice intervention in the lives of young black men and the corresponding media coverage of this phenomenon, which presents an even more skewed representation, has likely played an important role in reinforcing deep-seated associations between race and crime, with implications for employment discrimination and broader forms of social disfranchisement.

Racial Stereotypes in an Era of Mass Incarceration

Over the past three decades, we have seen an unprecedented expansion of the criminal justice system, with rates of incarceration increasing more than fivefold from 1970 to 2000. Today the United States boasts the highest rate of incarceration in the world, with over two million individuals currently behind bars. The expansive reach of the criminal justice system has not affected all groups equally: African Americans have been more acutely affected by the boom in incarceration than any other group. Blacks comprise over 40 percent of the current prison population, although they are just 12 percent of the U.S. population. At any given time, roughly 12 percent of all young black men between the ages of twenty-five and twenty-nine are behind bars, compared to less than 2 percent of whites in the same age group. Roughly a third of young black men are under criminal justice supervision (Bureau of Justice Statistics 2006, 2000, Table 1.29).[1] Over the course of a lifetime, nearly one in three young black men—and well over half of young black high school dropouts—will spend some time in prison. According to these estimates, young black men are more likely to go to prison than to attend college, serve in the military, or, in the case of high school dropouts, to be in the labor market (Bureau of Justice Statistics 1997; Pettit and Western 2004). Imprisonment is no longer a rare or extreme event among our nation's most marginalized groups. Rather, it has now become a normal and anticipated marker in the transition to adulthood.

In addition to the unprecedented reach of incarceration in the lives of young black men today, these trends have troubling consequences that may extend well beyond the prison walls. There is good reason to believe that the mass incarceration of black men contributes to continuing discrimination against the group as a whole, not only those with criminal records, by reinforcing the association of criminality with African Americans that has long been a feature of racial prejudice in the U.S. African American men have long been regarded with suspicion and fear. In contrast to progressive trends in other racial attitudes that have occurred in recent decades, associations between race and crime have changed little. Survey respondents consistently rate blacks as more prone to violence than any other American racial or ethnic group, endorsing stereotypes of aggressiveness and violence most frequently in their ratings of African Americans (Sneiderman and Piazza 1993; Smith 1991). The stereotype of blacks as criminals is deeply embedded in the collective consciousness of whites, irrespective of their level of prejudice or personal beliefs (Devine and Elliot 1995; Eberhardt et al. 2004, 7; Graham and Lowery 2004).

Although the current prevalence of racial stereotypes cannot be traced to any single source, the disproportionate growth of criminal justice intervention in the lives of young black men, compounded by skewed media coverage of this phenomenon, has likely played an important role. Experimental research shows that exposure to news coverage of a violent incident committed by a black perpetrator not only increases punitive attitudes about crime but further increases negative attitudes about blacks generally (Gilliam and Iyengar 2000; Gilliam, Iyengar, Simon, and Wright 1996; Entman 1990). The more exposure whites have to images of blacks in custody or behind bars, the stronger their expectations become regarding the race of assailants and the criminal tendencies of black strangers.

The consequences of mass incarceration may well extend far beyond the costs to the individuals behind bars, the families that are disrupted, and the communities whose residents cycle in and out.[2] The criminal justice system may itself legitimate and reinforce deeply embedded racial stereotypes, contributing to the persistent chasm in this society between black and white.

The Credentialing of Stigma

For each individual processed through the criminal justice system, police records, court documents, and corrections databases detail arrests, charges, convictions, and terms of incarceration. Most states make these records publicly available, often through online repositories, accessible to employers, landlords, creditors, and other interested parties.[3] As increasing numbers of occupations, public services, and other social goods become off limits to ex-offenders, these records can be used as the official basis for determining eligibility or exclusion. The state serves as a credentialing institution, providing official and public certification of those among us who have been convicted of wrongdoing. The "credential" of a criminal record, like educational or professional credentials, constitutes a formal and enduring classification of social status, which can be used to regulate access and opportunity across numerous social, economic, and political domains.

In the labor market, the criminal credential has become a salient marker for employers, with increasing numbers making use of background checks to screen out undesirable applicants. The majority of employers claim that they would not knowingly hire an applicant with a criminal background. These employers show little concern about the specific information conveyed by a criminal conviction and its bearing on a particular job, but rather view this credential as an indicator of "general employability" or trustworthiness (Holzer 1996, 60).[4] Well beyond the single incident at its origin, the credential comes to stand for a broader internal disposition.

The power of the credential lies in its recognition as an official and legitimate means of evaluating and classifying individuals.[5] The negative credential of a criminal record offers formal certification of the offenders among us, and official notice of those demographic groups most commonly implicated. But credentials have effects that reach beyond their formalized domain. Particularly in cases where the certification of a particular status is largely overlapping with other status markers, such as race, gender, and age, public assumptions about who is and is not a "credential holder" may become generalized or exaggerated. Because blacks are so strongly associated with the population under correctional supervision, it becomes easy to assume that any given young black man is likely to have, or to be on his way to acquiring, a criminal record. According to legal scholar David Cole, "when the results of the criminal justice system are as racially disproportionate as they are today, the criminal stigma extends beyond the particular behaviors and individuals involved to reach all young black men, and to a lesser extent all black people. The criminal justice system contributes to a stereotyped and stigmatic view of African Americans as potential criminals" (1995, 2561). Invoking this formal category may legitimate forms of social exclusion that, based on ascriptive characteristics alone, would be more difficult to justify.[6] In this way, negative credentials make possible a new rationale for exclusion that reinforces and legitimates existing social cleavages.

To understand the workings and effects of this negative credential, we must rely on more than speculation as to when and how these official labels are invoked as the basis for enabling or denying opportunity. Because credentials are often highly correlated with other indicators of social status or stigma, especially race, gender, class, we must examine their direct and independent impact. In addition, credentials may affect certain groups differently from others, with the official marker of criminality carrying more or less stigma depending on the race of its bearer. As increasing numbers of young black men are marked by their contact with the criminal justice system, it becomes a critical priority to understand the costs and consequences of this now prevalent form of negative credential.

Applying for Jobs in White and Black, With and Without a Criminal Record

This study uses an experimental audit methodology to measure the extent to which race and criminal backgrounds represent barriers to employment. The basic design of an employment audit involves sending matched pairs of individuals, called testers, to apply for real job openings in order to see whether employers respond differently to applicants on the basis of specific characteristics. The current study included four male testers, two black and two white, matched into two teams; the two black testers formed one team, and the two white testers formed a second. The testers were college students from Milwaukee who were matched on the basis of age, race, physical appearance, and general style of self-presentation. They were assigned fictitious resumes that reflected equivalent levels of education (high school degree) and work experience (steady employment across a range of entry-level jobs). Within each team, one tester was randomly assigned a "criminal record" for the first week; the pair then rotated which member presented himself as the ex-offender for each successive week of employment searches, so that each tester served in the criminal record condition for an equal number of cases.[7] By varying which member of the pair presented himself as having a criminal record, unobserved differences within the pairs of applicants were effectively controlled.

The testers participated in a common training program to become familiar with the details of their assumed profile and to ensure uniform behavior in job interviews. The training period lasted for one week, during which testers participated in mock interviews with one another and practice interviews with cooperating employers. The testers were trained to respond to common interview questions in standardized ways, and were well rehearsed for a wide range of scenarios that emerge in employment situations. Frequent communication between myself and the testers throughout each day of fieldwork allowed for regular supervision and troubleshooting in the event of unexpected occurrences.

A random sample of entry-level positions requiring no previous experience and no education beyond high school was drawn each week from the Sunday classified advertisement section of the *Milwaukee Journal Sentinel*. In addition, I drew a supplemental sample from Jobnet, a state-sponsored website for employment listings that was developed in connection with Wisconsin's W-2 Welfare-to-Work initiatives.[8] I excluded from the sample those occupations with legal restrictions on ex-offenders, such as jobs in the health care industry, work with children and the elderly, jobs requiring handling firearms (e.g., security guards), and jobs in the public sector.

Each of the audit pairs was randomly assigned fifteen job openings each week. The white pair and the black pair were assigned separate sets of jobs, with the same-race testers applying to the same jobs.[9] One member of the pair applied first, with the second applying one day later; whether the ex-offender came first or second was determined randomly. A total of 350 employers were audited during the course of this study, 150 by the white pair and 200 by the black pair. The black team performed additional tests because black testers received fewer callbacks on average than whites did; in this situation, a larger sample size enables the calculation of more precise estimates of the effects under investigation.

Immediately after submitting a job application, testers filled out a six-page response form that coded relevant information. Important variables included type of occupation, metropolitan status (city/suburb), wage, size of establishment, and race and sex of employer. Additionally, testers wrote detailed narratives describing the overall interaction and recording any statements on application forms or comments made by employers specifically related to race or criminal records.

The study focused only on the first stage of the employment process. Testers visited employers, filled out applications, and proceeded as far as they could during the course of one visit. If testers were asked to interview on the spot, they did so, but they did not return to the employer for a second visit. I therefore compare the results on the basis of the proportion of applications that elicited callbacks from employers. Individual voice mail boxes were set up for each tester to record employer responses. I focus on this initial stage of the employment process because it is the stage likely to be most affected by the barriers of race and a criminal record. Early on, employers have the least individualizing information about the applicant and are more likely to generalize on the basis of group-level, stereotyped characteristics. In a parallel case, a recent audit study of age discrimination found that 76 percent of the measured differential treatment occurred at this first stage of the employment process (Bendick, Jackson, and Reinoso 1994). Given that both race and a criminal record, like age, are highly salient characteristics, it is likely that as much, if not more, of the overall effects of racial criminal stigma will be detected at this stage.

A second advantage of the callback rather than a job offer as the key outcome variable is that it does not require employers to narrow their selection down to a single applicant. At the job offer stage, if presented with an ex-offender and an equally qualified non-offender, even employers with little concern over hiring ex-offenders would likely select the applicant with no criminal record, an arguably safer choice. Equating the two applicants could magnify the impact of the criminal record,

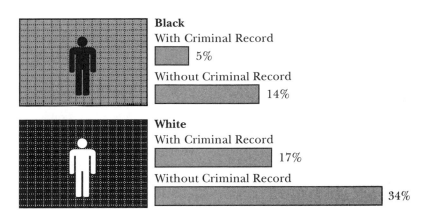

Black

With Criminal Record

5%

Without Criminal Record

14%

White

With Criminal Record

17%

Without Criminal Record

34%

Figure 5.1. Effects of race and criminal background on employment. Bars represent percentage of callbacks received by each group. The effects of race and criminal record are large and statistically significant ($p < .01$). The interaction between the two is not significant in the full sample.

as it becomes the only remaining basis for selection between the two (Heckman 1998). The callback does not present such complications. Typically employers interview multiple candidates for entry-level positions before selecting a hire. In a telephone survey following the audit, employers in this study reported interviewing an average of eight applicants for the last entry-level position filled. At the callback stage, employers need not yet choose between the ex-offender and non-offender. If the applicants appear well qualified and the employer does not view the criminal record as an automatic disqualifier, he or she can interview them both.[10]

Racial Disparities in Hiring Outcomes

Results are based on the proportion of applications submitted by each tester which elicited callbacks from employers. Three main findings appear in the audit results, presented in Figure 5.1. First, there is a large and significant effect of a criminal record for white job seekers, with 34 percent of whites without criminal records receiving callbacks relative to only 17 percent of otherwise equally qualified whites with criminal records. A criminal record thus reduces the likelihood of a callback for whites by 50 percent. Second, there is some indication that the magnitude of the criminal record effect may be even larger for blacks than whites. While the interaction between race and criminal record is not statistically significant, the substantive difference is worth noting. While the ratio of callbacks for non-offenders relative to offenders for whites was two to one (34 versus 17 percent), this same ratio for blacks was close to three to one (14 versus 5 percent).[11] Finally, looking at the callback rates for black and white tester pairs side by side, the fundamental importance of race becomes vividly clear. Among those without criminal records, black applicants were less than half as likely to receive a callback compared to equally qualified whites (14 versus 34 percent). This disparity implies that young black men needed to work more than twice as hard, applying to twice as many jobs, to secure the same opportunities as whites with identical qualifications. Even more striking, the powerful effects of race rival the strong stigma conveyed by a criminal record. In this study, a white applicant *with a criminal record* was just as likely to receive a callback as a black applicant without any criminal history (17 versus 14 percent).[12] Despite the fact that the white applicant revealed evidence of a felony drug conviction and reported having recently returned from a year and a half in prison, employers seemed to view this applicant as no more risky than a young black man with no history of criminal involvement. Racial disparities have been documented in many contexts, but here, comparing the two effects side by side, we are confronted with a troubling reality: in terms of one's chances of finding a job, being black in America today confers just about the same disadvantage as having a felony conviction.

In presentations of this research, I have often heard an audible gasp from the audience when I display these results. Could the effect of race really be so large? The magnitude of these effects stands in striking opposition to the prevailing wisdom that such blatant forms of discrimination have become vanishingly rare. It is tempting to think that there is something peculiar about this study, or about the time and place in which it was conducted, which offers an exaggerated view. When this study was conducted, Milwaukee was the second most segregated city in the country, implying great social distance between blacks and whites.[13] If race relations were more strained in Milwaukee than in other parts of the country, then the effects of race found there might be larger than what would be found in other urban areas. In fact, however, the magnitude of the race effect found in this study falls squarely within the range found in previous audit studies (Pager 2007a). An audit study in Washington, D.C., found that blacks were 24 percentage points less likely to receive a job offer than their white counterparts, a finding strikingly similar to the 20 percent difference between white and black non-offenders found here.[14]

Likewise, a recent field experiment by Marianne Bertrand and Sendhil Mullainathan (2003) found large effects of race among employers in Boston and Chicago. In this study, the researchers mailed resumes with racially identifiable names to employers in the two cities. Their sample was restricted to listings for sales, administrative support, clerical, and customer service positions. Despite the narrower range of occupations and the higher level of qualifications presented in this study, these authors find clear evidence of racial bias. White male names triggered a callback rate of 9.19 percent, compared to 6.16 percent among black male names. The ratio of callbacks for whites to blacks (1.5), while smaller than the ratio of callbacks to white and black non-offenders from this study (2.4), strengthens our confidence that Milwaukee is not the only city in which race continues to matter.[15] A replication of our study in New York City obtained very similar results, with whites receiving callbacks at twice the rate of similarly qualified blacks (31 percent versus 15 percent), and white felons receiving callbacks at rates similar to those of blacks with no criminal history (17 percent versus 13 percent) (Pager, Western, and Bonikowski 2007).

Each of these studies reinforces the conclusion that race represents an extremely powerful barrier to job entry. The matched designs allow us to separate speculation about applicants' qualifications (supply-side influences) from the racial attributions or biases of employers (demand-side influences). While these studies remain silent on the many supply-side factors that may also contribute to the employment difficulties of young black men, they speak loud and clear about the significance of employers' racial biases or attributions in shaping the opportunities available to young black and white job seekers. Before applicants have an opportunity to demonstrate their capabilities in person, a large proportion are weeded out on the basis of a single categorical distinction.

Driving While Black: Associations Between Race and Crime

I received a call from Andre at about two o'clock one afternoon. He was calling me from his cell phone while sitting in the back of a police car. The police had stopped him at a freeway entrance on the way to one of his assignments. Though Andre had not committed any traffic violation, the police explained they were looking for someone who matched his description: "a black man, between the ages of 21 and 25." Andre was instructed to step out of his car and asked to take a seat in the back of the police vehicle. Passersby craned their necks to catch a glimpse of the latest criminal suspect who had been apprehended. The police asked him a long series of questions and called in his information to the station to have his background thoroughly checked. In the end, the police were satisfied that Andre was not the guy they were looking for and let him go. Andre had spent over an hour in the back of that police car.

We often hear popular accounts of the problems of "driving while black," the phenomenon that blacks are pulled over arbitrarily for police checks, with the implication that in some places any black man is automatically suspect (Harris 1994).[16] Over the course of the fieldwork for this study, I witnessed some of these episodes first hand. The young men serving as testers in my field experiment were bright college kids, models of discipline and hard work; yet in the course of their daily lives, they were at times mistaken for the troublemaker types featured on the nightly news. Particularly in casual encounters, while driving or when entering a place of business, there seemed little they could do to signal their distance from the dominant stereotype of the black male.[17]

On several occasions, black testers were asked in person, before submitting their applications, whether they had a prior criminal history. For these employers, a young black man immediately aroused concern about criminal involvement, and this issue took center stage before getting to matters of education, work experience, or qualifications. None of the white testers, by contrast, was asked about his criminal history up front.[18] These experiences are consistent with Elijah Anderson's account of the suspicion with which young black men are often viewed. According to Anderson, "the anonymous black male is usually an ambiguous figure who arouses the utmost caution and is generally considered dangerous until he proves he is not" (1990, 190).[19] Overcoming this initial stereotype is one of the first challenges facing the young black male job applicant, particularly in low-wage labor markets where fewer objective indicators, such as a college degree or related work history, are available for, or relevant to, the evaluation.

The effect of race demonstrated here is especially striking by virtue of its contrast with the effect of a criminal record. Seeing the two categories side by side drives home just how much race matters in employment contexts; being black is viewed as tantamount to being a convicted felon. These effects, however, should not be seen as independent. In an era of mass incarceration, when one in three young black men will wind up in prison, black men are readily associated with criminal activity in the minds of whites. High levels of incarceration cast a shadow of criminality over the black population as whole, implicating the majority of black men who have remained crime-free.

Race and Crime on TV

Racial stereotypes of black criminality are fueled by media coverage of crime, which tends to depict criminal episodes in a heavily racialized context. A study of local television news in Chicago found that the largest share of news stories featuring blacks (on any topic) portrayed blacks as perpetrators of violent crimes (Entman 1990),[20] more often than news about Oprah, Michael Jordan, or Barack Obama (all Chicago residents), and more often than news about the thousands of black corporate leaders and community organizers in the city.

The frequency of coverage focusing on black criminals does have some basis in reality; higher arrest rates for blacks logically translate into greater news coverage of black accused criminals. But direct comparisons of local crime reports with corresponding arrest rates do not support a straightforward explanation. When Travis Dixon and Daniel Linz (2000) compared news reports about crime in the Los Angeles metro area with arrest rates from the California Department of Corrections, they found that blacks were 75 percent more likely to be represented as perpetrators in crime reports than their actual arrest rate would have predicted. White offenders, by contrast, were shown on television about 25 percent less often than their arrest rate would have predicted.[21] Existing racial disparities in criminal justice involvement tend to be exaggerated in the news, with blacks more often, and whites less often, shown in custody than actual crime statistics reveal to be true.

Other studies of race and crime in the news have found media coverage of black criminals to be skewed not only in frequency, but also in kind. A study by Richard Entman and Andrew Rojecki (2000) found that news coverage of blacks in custody was more likely to present mug shots (as opposed to a live image or an image taken prior to arrest), or images of blacks in handcuffs and under the physical restraints of a white police officer, than was coverage of whites in custody. Moreover, in coverage of individuals accused of violent crimes, local news broadcasts were nearly twice as likely to provide an on-screen name for whites (47 percent) as for blacks (26 percent). According to Entman and Rojecki, "The presence of the accused's name provides a sense of his or her individual identity. Its absence may suggest that individual identity does not matter, that the accused is part of a single undifferentiated group of violent offenders: just another Black criminal" (82). The more menacing and less individualized images of black suspects provide vivid "evidence" in support of racial stereotypes depicting blacks as dangerous, violent, and criminal.

With roughly 70 percent of Americans identifying television as the source of "most of your news about what's going on in the world today," media distortions of the frequency and severity of offending among blacks can have important consequences for how Americans think about race and how they think about crime (Mayer 1993; Sheley and Ashkins 1981). To begin with, the vast over-representation of black criminals in the news is linked to distorted images of the race-crime connection. A 1991 survey, for example, asked, "Of all the people arrested for violent crimes in the United States last year, what percent do you think were black?" The modal response to this question was "60 percent," an exaggeration by roughly 35 percent of the actual proportion at that time.[22] Similarly, an experiment in which individuals were shown a short news clip describing a murder—in which the race of the alleged perpetrator was not identified—found that over 40 percent of subjects falsely recalled having seen a black perpetrator.[23] When the most common image of blacks on TV shows blacks as criminal offenders, the associations between race and crime become virtually automatic.[24]

Indeed, racial stereotypes of blacks as violent or crime-prone are among the most salient dimensions of contemporary stereotypes about African Americans. The associations remain deeply embedded in the unconscious, and can affect the cognitive processing and behavior of even those individuals who consciously repudiate racial stereotypes or discrimination (Eberhardt et al. 2004; Devine 1989; Payne 2001). Social psychological experiments have found that subjects are more likely to interpret ambiguous actions as threatening when the actor is portrayed as African American (Duncan 1976; Sagar and Schofield 1980).[25] Subjects instructed to "shoot" potentially armed targets (presented in a videogame) are more quick to do so when the target is African American (Correll, Wittenbrink, and Judd 2002). Through some combination of higher crime rates, media distortions, and cultural biases, race has become a powerful heuristic with which to assess danger.[26] Particularly in interactions that contain some ambiguity, or in decisions made under pressure, evaluations are easily colored by these pervasive (and largely unconscious) stereotypes about black aggressiveness or threat.

Findings such as these suggest that the characteristic of criminality is readily ascribed to blacks. Consequently, even blacks with no history of criminal involvement are likely to suffer some of the same penalties as do ex-offenders of any race. Despite the lack of official conviction record, their job candidacy is nevertheless suspect by virtue of membership in a group with high incarceration rates and pervasive images of criminality.[27] This is not to say that employers are indifferent to a criminal record among blacks; blacks suffer a larger penalty for a criminal record compared to whites. But this research suggests that even without an official marker of criminality, blacks are viewed as high-risk employees. Once again, then, we return to one possible far-reaching consequence of our crime policies: steeply rising incarceration rates among blacks cast a shadow of criminality across the black population. The effects of race shown in this study should not be thought of as unrelated to employers' concerns about crime. Rather, it seems to be the case that blacks with or without criminal records are likely to be viewed by employers with suspicion.[28]

By focusing on discrimination at the point of hire, this study uncovers an important and under-investigated source of racial disadvantage in the low wage labor market. Blacks are less than half as likely to receive consideration by employers as equally qualified whites, and black non-offenders fare no better than even whites with prior felony convictions. The sheer magnitude of these findings underlines the continuing significance of race in employment decisions.

This research cannot identify the precise source of employers' reluctance to hire blacks. Indeed, it is difficult if not impossible to "get inside employers' heads" to determine what combination of conscious or unconscious considerations may lead to the racial preferences we observe. High incarceration rates among blacks and their amplification in the media are one possible source of racial bias. Indeed, the available evidence points to the pervasiveness of images associating blacks with crime and the power of these images to strengthen negative feelings about blacks as a group. It may be the case, then, that increasing rates of incarceration among blacks, and their disproportionate coverage in the media, heighten negative reactions toward African Americans generally, irrespective of their personal involvement in crime.

While the true concerns underlying employers' decisions are difficult to discern, the prima facie evidence shows that race carries important meaning to employers, and can often represent the sole basis for dismissing a candidate. According to the results presented here, black men must work at least twice as hard as equally qualified whites simply to overcome the stigma of their skin color. Rather than being merely a problem of the past, direct racial bias continues to shape employment outcomes in ways that contribute to persisting racial inequality.

References

Anderson, Elijah. 1990. *Streetwise: Race, Class, and Change in an Urban Community.* Chicago: University of Chicago Press.

Becker, Howard. 1963. *Outsiders: Studies in the Sociology of Deviance.* New York: Free Press.

Bendick, Marc, Jr., Charles Jackson, and Victor Reinoso. 1994. Measuring employment discrimination through controlled experiments. *Review of Black Political Economy* 23: 25–48.

Bertrand, Marianne, and Sendhil Mullainathan. 2003. Are Emily and Brendan More Employable Than Lakisha and Jamal? A Field Experiment on Labor Market Discrimination. National Bureau of Economic Research Working Paper 9873. Cambridge, Mass.: NBER.

Blumstein, Alfred. 1982. On the racial disproportionality of United States prison populations. *Journal of Criminal Law and Criminology* 73: 1259–81.

———. 1993. Racial disproportionality revisited. *University of Colorado Law Review* 64: 743–60.

Bodenhausen, Galen V., and Meryl Lichtenstein. 1987. Social stereotypes and information processing strategies: The impact of task complexity. *Journal of Personality and Social Psychology* 52: 871–80.

Bureau of Justice Statistics. 2006a. Survey of State Criminal History Systems. NCJ 210297. Washington, D.C.: U.S. Department of Justice.

———. 2006b. Prison and Jail Inmates at Midyear 2005. Washington, D.C.: U.S. Department of Justice.

———. 2003. Characteristics of Drivers Stopped by Police, 2002. Washington, D.C.: U.S. Department of Justice.

———. 2000. Correctional Populations in the United States, 1997. NCJ 177613. Washington, D.C.: U.S. Department of Justice.

———. 1997. Lifetime Likelihood of Going to State or Federal Prison. Washington, D.C.: U.S. Department of Justice.

Bushway, Shawn. 2004. Labor market effects of permitting employer access to criminal history records. *Journal of Contemporary Criminal Justice* 20: 276–91.

Bussey, Jenny, and John Trasvina. 2003. Racial Preferences: The Treatment of White and African American Job Applicants by Temporary Employment Agencies in California. Berkeley, Calif.: Discrimination Research Center of the Impact Fund.

Cole, David. 1995. The paradox of race and crime: A comment on Randall Kennedy's "Politics of Distinction." *Georgetown Law Journal* 83: 2547–71.

Correll, Joshua, Bernd Wittenbrink, and Charles M. Judd. 2002. The police officer's dilemma: Using ethnicity to disambiguate potentially threatening individuals. *Journal of Personality and Social Psychology* 83 (6): 1314–29.

Crocker, Jennifer, Brenda Major, and Claude Steele. 1998. Social stigma. In *Handbook of Social Psychology*, ed. Daniel Gilbert, Susan Fiske, and Gardiner Lindzey, 504–53. Boston: McGraw-Hill.

Devine, Patricia. 1989. Stereotypes and prejudice: Their automatic and controlled components. *Journal of Personality and Social Psychology* 56: 5–18.

Devine, Patricia, and Scott Elliot. 1995. Are racial stereotypes really fading? The Princeton trilogy revisited. *Personality and Social Psychology Bulletin* 21 (11): 1139–50.

Dixon, Travis L., and Daniel Linz. 2000. Overrepresentation and underrepresentation of African Americans and Latinos as lawbreakers on television news. *Journal of Communication* 50 (2): 131–54.

Dovidio, John F. 2001. On the nature of contemporary prejudice: The third wave. *Journal of Social Issues* 57 (4): 829–49.

Duncan, Birt L. 1976. Differential social perception and attribution of intergroup violence: Testing the lower limits of stereotyping of Blacks. *Journal of Personality and Social Psychology* 34 (4): 590–98.

Eberhardt, Jennifer L., Phillip Atiba Goff, Valerie J. Purdie, and Paul G. Davies. 2004. Seeing black: Race, crime, and visual processing. *Journal of Personality and Social Psychology* 87: 876–93.

Entman, Robert M. 1990. Modern racism and the images of Blacks in local television news. *Critical Studies in Mass Communication* 7: 332–45.

Entman, Robert M., and Andrew Rojecki. 2000. *The Black Image in the White Mind: Media and Race in America*. Chicago: University of Chicago Press.

Farmer, Amy, and Dek Terrell. 2001. Crime versus justice: Is there a trade-off? *Journal of Law and Economics* 44 (October): 345–66.

Feagin, Joe R., and Melvin P. Sikes. 1994. *Living with Racism: The Black Middle-Class Experience*. Boston: Beacon Press.

Fiske, Susan. 1998. Stereotyping, prejudice, and discrimination. In *The Handbook of Social Psychology*, 4th ed., ed. Daniel Gilbert, Susan Fiske, and Gardner Lindzey, 357–411. Boston: McGraw-Hill.

Garfinkel, Harold. 1956. Conditions of successful degradation ceremonies. *American Journal of Sociology* 61: 420–24.

Gilliam, Franklin D., and Shanto Iyengar. 2000. Prime suspects: The influence of local television news on the viewing public. *American Journal of Political Science* 44 (3): 560–73.

Gilliam, Franklin D., Shanto Iyengar, Adam Simon, and Oliver Wright. 1996. Crime in Black and White: The violent, scary world of local news. *Harvard International Journal of Press/Politics* 1 (6): 6–23.

Goffman, Erving. 1963. *Stigma: Notes on the Management of a Spoiled Identity*. New York: Prentice-Hall.

Gooden, Susan T. 1999. The hidden third party: Welfare recipients' experiences with employers. *Journal of Public Management & Social Policy* 5: 69–83.

Graham, Sandra, and Brian S. Lowery. 2004. Priming unconscious racial stereotypes about adolescent offenders. *Law and Human Behavior* 28: 483–504.

Harris, David. 1994. Factors for reasonable suspicion: When black and poor means stopped and frisked. *Indiana Law Journal* 69: 659–93.

Heckman, James J. 1998. Characterizing Selection Bias Using Experimental Data. NBER Working Paper 6699. Cambridge, Mass.: National Bureau of Economic Research.

Holzer, Harry J. 1996. *What Employers Want: Job Prospects for Less-Educated Workers*. New York: Russell Sage.

Holzer, Harry J., Steven Raphael, and Michael Stoll. 2006. Perceived criminality, criminal background checks and the racial hiring practices of employers. *Journal of Law and Economics* 49 (2): 451–80.

Klite, Paul, Robert A. Bardwell, and Jason Salzman. 1997. Local TV news: Getting away with murder. *Harvard International Journal of Press/Politics* 2: 102–12.

Lacy, Karyn R. 2004. Black spaces, Black places: Strategic assimilation and identity construction in middle-class suburbia. *Ethnic and Racial Studies* 27 (6): 908–30.

Legal Action Center. 2004. *After Prison: Roadblocks to Reentry. A Report on State Legal Barriers Facing People with Criminal Records*, ed. Paul Samuels and Debbie Mukamal. New York: Legal Action Center.

Lodder, LeAnn, Scott McFarland, and Diana White. 2003. *Racial Preferences and Suburban Employment Opportunities*. Chicago: Legal Assistance Foundation of Metropolitan Chicago.

Mayer, William G. 1993. Poll trends: Trends in media usage. *Public Opinion Quarterly* 57 (4): 593–611.

Nunes, Ana, and Brad Seligman. 2000. *A Study of the Treatment of Female and Male Applicants by San Francisco Bay Area Auto Service Shops*. Berkeley, Calif.: Discrimination Research Center of the Impact Fund.

Oliver, Mary Beth. 1994. Portrayals of crime, race and aggression in "reality-based" police shows: A content analysis. *Journal of Broadcasting and Electronic Media* 38 (2): 179–92.

Pager, Devah. 2007a. *Marked: Race, Crime, and Finding Work in an Era of Mass Incarceration*. Chicago: University of Chicago Press.

———. 2007b. The use of field experiments for studies of employment discrimination: Contributions, critiques, and directions for the future. *Annals of the American Academy of Political and Social Sciences* 609: 104–33.

Pager, Devah. 2003. The mark of a criminal record. *American Journal of Sociology* 108 (5): 937–75.

Pager, Devah, and Bruce Western. 2005. Discrimination in low trust labor markets. Paper presented at the Annual Meetings of the American Sociological Association, Philadelphia, August.

Pager, Devah, Bruce Western, and Bart Bonikowski. 2007. Discrimination in low-wage labor markets. Working paper, Princeton University.

Payne, B. Keith. 2001. Prejudice and perception: The role of automatic and controlled processes in misperceiving a weapon. *Journal of Personality and Social Psychology* 81 (2): 181–92.

Pettit, Becky, and Bruce Western. 2004. Mass imprisonment and the life course: Race and class inequality in U.S. incarceration. *American Sociological Review* 69: 151–69.

Quillian, Lincoln, and Devah Pager. 2001. Black neighbors, higher crime? The role of racial stereotypes in evaluations of neighborhood crime. *American Journal of Sociology* 107 (3): 717–67.

Romer, Daniel, Kathleen H. Jamieson, and Nicole J. deCouteau. 1998. The treatment of persons of color in local television news: Ethnic blame discourse or realistic group conflict? *Communication Research* 25 (3): 286–305.

Sagar, H. A., and Janet Ward Schofield. 1980. Racial and behavioral cues in black and white children's perceptions of ambiguously aggressive acts. *Journal of Personality and Social Psychology* 39: 590–98.

Sampson, Robert J., and Janet L. Lauritsen. 1997. Racial and ethnic disparities in crime and criminal justice in the United States. *Crime and Justice: Ethnicity, Crime and Immigration: Comparative and Cross-National Perspectives* 21: 311–74.

Sheley, Joseph F., and Cindy D. Ashkins. 1981. Crime, crime news and crime views. *Public Opinion Quarterly* 45 (4): 492–506.

Smith, Tom W. 1991. *What Americans Say About Jews.* New York: American Jewish Committee.

Sneiderman, Paul M., and Thomas Piazza. 1993. *The Scar of Race.* Cambridge, Mass.: Belknap Press of Harvard University Press.

Tonry, Michael. 1995. *Malign Neglect: Race, Crime, and Punishment in America.* New York: Oxford University Press.

Turner, Margery, Michael Fix, and Raymond Struyk. 1991. *Opportunities Denied, Opportunities Diminished: Racial Discrimination in Hiring.* Washington, D.C.: Urban Institute Press.

Wacquant, Loïc. 2000. Deadly symbiosis: When ghetto and prison meet the mesh. *Punishment and Society* 3 (1): 95–134.

Word, Carl O., Mark P. Zanna, and Joel Cooper. 1974. The nonverbal mediation of self-fulfilling prophecies in interracial interactions. *Journal of Experimental Social Psychology* 10: 109–20.

Chapter 6

The Effects of Immigration on the Economic Position of Young Black Males

Gerald D. Jaynes

The charge that immigrants, especially the undocumented, put downward pressure on wages and take jobs from native-born Americans has become one of the most contentious issues in the debate over immigration and "control of the U.S. border." Support for these charges appears readily available, and disturbing evidence is disseminated widely. Recently, the Center for Immigration Studies, a Washington, D.C., think tank that advocates and lobbies for tighter restrictions on immigration to the U.S., issued an alarming report discussing the effects of undocumented immigration on the employment of native-born workers. One of the report's starkest findings concerned job growth between March 2000 and March 2005, a period that the White House boasts about as characterized by high rates of job growth during the economy's recovery from the 2001 recession. During this five-year period, native-born workers, who accounted for 6 of 10 people making up the net increase in the population aged eighteen to sixty-four, accounted for slightly less than 1 of 10 of the net increase in jobs received by adults (Camarota 2006). The numbers were confirmed by the U.S. Department of Labor (DOL), although an economist at DOL felt obligated to point out that as job growth strengthened during 2005 the proportion of native-born job seekers finding jobs rose to 4 of 10, an increase unlikely to calm their anxieties (Scherer 2006).

Facts as stupefying as these job gain numbers explain in dramatic fashion why the labor market effects of immigration on the native born have emerged as a tempestuous public policy issue. In addition to an abundance of anecdotal evidence showing immigrant "takeover" of specific jobs (Jaynes 2000, 23), both common sense and straightforward economic reasoning explain why in a continuing stream of public opinion surveys many Americans say they believe that immigrants tend to decrease wages and displace native-born workers from jobs. The common sense behind these fears emerges from the most basic principles of supply and demand; mass immigration of millions of migrants looking for work in a new country should exert a large and negative effect on the wage rates and employment opportunities of workers already in the country. This effect is supposed to be particularly severe for low-skilled native-born men, especially young black men in the inner city.

Despite the highly organized and publicly visible forces touting evidence of immigrants' devastating effects on native-born workers, how immigrant workers affect labor markets remains a topic of uneasy debate among ordinary citizens and economists. Some people argue that current levels of immigration are literally destroying communities because undocumented workers are driving blue-collar wages so low that a middle-class standard of living is becoming unattainable for many working Americans. These arguments often claim that foreign workers are particularly detrimental to the job prospects of young African American men lacking high school diplomas. Yet, according to opinion polls, at least until very recently, a majority of American citizens believe otherwise. Many Americans are more likely to believe that immigrants fill jobs that would otherwise remain vacant and that their labor is actually accelerating economic growth and expanding overall employment.

Because they fear providing fuel to some of their nastier opponents in this highly charged debate, many supporters of immigration and immigrant rights are reluctant to acknowledge immigration's deleterious effects on native-born workers' labor market prospects. However, we can acknowledge that immigration probably hurts the employment and wages of some less educated citizens and still favor immigration. Apparently, large numbers of African Americans hold just such ambivalent views. Many African Americans who insist that immigrants lessen blacks' employment opportunities also say they favor immigration. These findings from surveys of Americans' attitudes toward immigration are especially significant since less educated African Americans and Latinos are the native-born citizens and permanent residents whose wages and employment opportunities are most affected and would appear to have the most to lose from immigration.

How can we make sense of these apparently inconsistent views? In this essay, I first summarize recent trends in the employment position of young black males, showing how the simultaneous occurrence of their deteriorating employment position and rapidly rising immigration lends prima facie credence to the argument that immigration has negative effects on them. However, a review of rigorous analyses of the effects of immigration on less educated blacks and other native-born workers suggests that these effects are relatively small and in any event secondary to other causes of less educated blacks' dismal employment experience. A brief summary of black and white Americans' views toward immigration reveals that only a minority of Americans think immigrants take jobs from citizens. Surveys also reveal significant differences in blacks' and whites' attitudes toward immigration: blacks are less likely to support draconian measures to stop immigration. I argue that this viewpoint is due to African Americans' continuing adherence to principles of equal justice and their realization that the long-term effects of immigration favor greater population diversity and equality for all Americans.

Recent Labor Market Experience of Young Males

One significant difficulty encountered in any attempt to estimate the effects of immigration on native-born workers' employment status is determining the number of undocumented workers in the United States. The Census Bureau, basing its analyses on numbers from the 2000 census, estimates there are about 9 million undocumented immigrants in the nation. However, most analysts agree the 2000 census seriously undercounted undocumented immigrants. Alternative estimates range from about 11 million to more than 20 million; a minimum figure of 12 million has been widely used in public debates. All analysts agree that the number of undocumented immigrants entering the country has increased significantly during the past few years. Less educated Mexicans and Central Americans have entered the labor market in substantial numbers, and they appear to be near-perfect substitutes for native-born high school dropouts and less skilled high school graduates of all races and ethnicities. Steven Camarota of the Center for Immigration Studies estimates that between 2000 and 2005 the number of immigrants entering with no more than a high school degree increased about 1.5 million. He also estimates that the number of employed native-born workers with a similarly low level of education dropped by about 3 million (Camarota 2006). Moreover, the average wages of native-born high school dropouts are very similar to the average wages of Mexican immigrants into the United States. Their similar wage structures suggest strongly that less skilled Latino immigrants and similarly educated native-born workers do compete with one another for jobs.

Straightforward supply and demand analysis implies that competition from immigrants should decrease less educated native-born workers' job opportunities. The theory is supported by the fact that the surge in immigration during the past thirty-five years occurred simultaneously with a large drop in the inflation-adjusted wages of less educated American workers. The adverse trend in the wages of less educated men was both absolute and relative to the wages of college educated men (Jaynes 2006). As the average education levels of arriving immigrants declined significantly after 1980, the compensation of less educated U.S. workers fell dramatically relative to the earnings of the highly educated. One way to understand the increases in earnings inequality is to compare the earnings of high school and college graduates who work full time. The earnings of male high school graduates fell significantly compared to the earnings of male college graduates of the same age. Underlying the disadvantageous change in male high school graduates' relative wages were two basic trends: while the earnings of college graduates increased significantly after the mid-1970s, the earnings of high school graduates at best stagnated and at times declined.

The largest reductions in earnings occurred among less educated men and women in all racial-ethnic groups. During the decade and a half from the early 1970s through the late 1980s, the earnings of the poorest 10 percent of working men fell more than 30 percent while the earnings of the most affluent 40 percent held steady. To illustrate the point, between 1969 and 1984 (measuring in 1984 constant dollars) the mean weekly wages of white male high school graduates fell from $481 to $393, a reduction of 18 percent. The fall in mean weekly earnings among white male high school dropouts was much sharper; 37 percent. Even steeper declines occurred in the already lower wages of comparably educated African American men, and employment conditions for young black males deteriorated especially dramatically. During this fifteen-year period, black male high school graduates' mean weekly wages fell by 22 percent, from $357 to $278, while black male dropouts' mean weekly wages were in a free fall, dropping 32 percent from $312 to $213.

Falling inflation-adjusted wages and rising inequality in earnings were accompanied by increasing male joblessness. Throughout the recent socioeconomic history of the United States, joblessness and low earnings have been especially severe among young black males. Declining opportunities had already precipitated severe reductions in young black men's employment during the 1970s, but their labor market position deteriorated even further during the 1980s; rates of joblessness in inner-city neighborhoods became shockingly high. Overall, the official unemployment rate of black men exceeded 20 percent during the early 1980s. At the midpoint of that decade, the average black male aged twenty to twenty-four who had dropped out of high school earned only $146 per week when employed; even more unfortunately, these young black male dropouts had an unemployment rate of 45 percent. Their high school graduate counterparts fared little better, averaging earnings of $165 per week. White dropouts that age earned a third more and faced half the risk of unemployment, a situation still burdensome for their families and communities but less disastrous than that among black males. The response to these catastrophically low wages was the marked detachment of many young black men from the formal labor market. In 1970, black high school graduates and college graduates aged twenty-five to thirty-four had similar employment rates (90 percent versus 90.4 percent), but by 1985 the employment rate of black high school graduates was 13 percentage points lower than for college graduates (66.3 versus 79.6 percent). In 1970, black high school dropouts aged twenty-five to thirty-four enjoyed an employment rate of 85 percent; by 1985, the employment rate of black high school dropouts aged twenty-five to thirty-four was only 57.2 percent, 9 percentage points lower than high school graduates and 22 points lower than college graduates. The proportion of black high school dropouts in this age group reporting no earnings more than tripled, from 7 percent in 1970 to 23 percent in 1985.

The more recent labor market experience of young men has continued to bolster the claims of critics of immigration who say immigrants worsen the employment prospects of African American males. The ten-year period beginning in 1995 and ending with 2005 began with a healthy upsurge in employment and wages. After 2000, some of the earlier wage gains were lost, but wages remained higher than during the early 1990s. A brief look at the labor market experience of young black men during this ten-year period helps explain why criticism of immigration may be increasing from within the African American population. At any given time, the economic fortunes of the contemporaneous cohort of young black high school graduates who work full time are important indicators to younger blacks of the possibilities available to them in the work world. This cohort provides disadvantaged black youth their most salient examples of the economic payoff of accomplishing two objectives highly touted by society, graduating from high school and securing full-time employment. Unfortunately, the deteriorating situation of African American men aged eighteen to twenty-four who are high school graduates and full-time workers has probably diminished the labor market expectations of young black males from disadvantaged socioeconomic backgrounds.

While the wages of full-time employed white and Latino male high school graduates rose sharply during the economic boom between 1995 and 2000, the wages of similar black men were flat, leading many African Americans to speculate that heavy Latino immigration during this period was linked to the declining employment and wage opportunities for black men. Figure 6.1 illustrates the general deterioration in the wages of young American men of each racial-ethnic group since 2000. The fact that the wages of young Latino men overtook the wages of young black men during this period merely fans the flames of discontent over immigration.

These trends lend credence to some Americans' demands that Congress construct a wall along this country's southern border to stem the

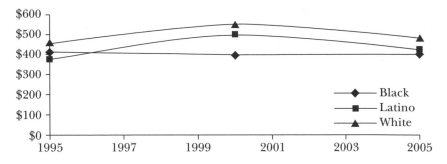

Figure 6.1. Weekly wages of male high school graduates age eighteen to twenty-four by ethnicity. Data calculated from CPS Annual Social and Economic Supplement, 2006, Table PINC-04; 2001 March Supplement, Table PINC-04; 1996, Table PINC-06A. Weekly wages of full-time workers calculated as annual earnings divided by 52. All three groups include both native-born and immigrants.

tide of undocumented migrants. Some critics of immigration go further, calling for the government to seize all illegal immigrants and deport them. In addition, they say, legal immigration should be severely limited, and only highly educated and skilled applicants should be allowed entry.

Assessing the Evidence of Immigration Labor Market Effects

Critics of current U.S. immigration policies need not search hard to find disturbing and apparently unimpeachable evidence that recent immigrants are exerting far-reaching effects on the American labor market. But how convincing is the evidence? Social scientists require stronger proof than mere correlation between rising numbers of immigrants and deteriorating job market conditions for native-born Americans, and public policy should be constructed on firmer foundations than general impressions. The host of socioeconomic changes that have occurred in the U.S. over the past four decades requires us to consider a wide range of alternative explanations for the deteriorating economic circumstances of low-skilled workers. Structural shifts in the economy have borne down upon young black males with particular force. No remotely credible argument blames immigration for the large and nearly steady reduction in blue-collar jobs in the U.S. that began during the 1950s. Nor did immigration cause the weakening of labor unions, spread of automation, growth of the computerized information economy, or the deteriorating U.S. import-export balances that continue to suck up good jobs—full-time positions that offer stable employment, decent wages, and benefits.

Indeed, social scientists' rigorous statistical analyses initially stood upon its head the common-sense logic of supply and demand. Until well into the 1990s, the great preponderance of rigorously designed and executed studies of immigration's effects on the economic position of U.S. citizens concluded either that the effects were ambiguous or negligible or that immigrants actually had a positive effect on the employment and wages of native-born workers. These results held for both skilled and unskilled workers, for both women and men, and for members of racial-ethnic minority groups and whites. The one exception was recent immigrants, whose employment prospects were damaged by those who arrived after them.

The counterintuitive results of this research were explained in the following terms. The job skills brought into the country by less educated immigrants were complementary to the skills of more educated and better trained native-born workers; therefore immigrants did not compete with the native born for the same jobs. On the contrary, the rising supply of immigrant workers ready and able to work hard for low wages is said to spur the expansion of existing firms and the growth of new firms that were able to profit from paying low wages. The expanding firms based on low-wage immigrant labor also hired more skilled native-born workers as their revenues grew. Janitorial services, car washes, and poultry processing plants with growing numbers of employees require more supervisors, clerical workers, accountants, and other white-collar employees. Using this scholarship, proponents of less stringent immigration policies argued that immigrants in fact improved the position of native-born workers. Subsequent researchers, however, have contended that the previous findings that immigrants raise the wages of native-born workers may be a statistical artifact of the cross-sectional data used in such studies. If, as seems very likely, immigrants are more likely to migrate to geographic areas where jobs and capital are flowing, then statistical analyses will find a positive correlation between the number of immigrant workers and higher wages and job growth for all workers. However, the immigrants need not be responsible for the higher wages; their arrival may in fact be slowing the rate of increase even in these areas. In this case the quantity of immigrant labor in a geographic area is treated as an explanatory variable, but it should be treated as both an explanatory variable and a dependent variable in a simultaneous equation system. The original estimations are based on a mis-specified statistical procedure and are likely to be biased; a more complete model should take account of the complex, dynamic interactions of labor supply and economic growth.

Dissatisfaction with the statistical methods used in studies of the effects of immigration on the employment opportunities of native-born workers led to the development of different models. Using more sophisticated statistical methods than previous scholars, Borjas, Freeman, and Katz (1992) estimated that during the 1980s both increased imports of goods produced abroad with lower-skilled labor and rising immigration of lower-skilled labor into the U.S. were important contributors to the adverse turn in the weekly wages of American high school dropouts as compared to the weekly wages of American college graduates. These authors estimated the "implicit" increase in the supply of lower-skilled labor within the U.S. that is consistent with the increased volume of U.S. imports and immigrant labor supply. They then estimated that between 30 percent and 50 percent of the decline in the relative weekly earnings of high school dropouts between 1980 and 1988 should be attributed to increased immigration and trade. Wilson and Jaynes (2000, 22–23) decomposed the effects of immigration on geographic labor markets into separate effects of flows and stocks of immigrant workers. Our analysis also estimated separate effects for various native-born racial-ethnic groups and different skill and education levels. We found that immigration flows across geographic areas were a negligible factor in the declining wages and employment of less educated African Americans. That finding is consistent with earlier findings. However, we also found that the increasing size of the immigrant population within a given area did have a modest negative effect on the employment of less educated African Americans. A simple way of interpreting this result is to recognize that immigrant populations may have a threshold effect on employment opportunities within local labor markets. When immigrants are a small proportion of the local labor market, they have negligible effects on the terms of employment. When the stock of immigrants reaches a certain threshold size, however, employers are able to institute hiring and wage pricing procedures that utilize the strong social networks within a given ethnic group which feature the exchange of information and referrals about jobs. These practices allow an immigrant group that has reached a critical mass to become a dominant factor in employment conditions (Waldinger 1996).

More recently, Borjas and Katz have refined statistical methods even further and extended the analysis of the effects of Mexican immigration on low-skilled workers through the 1990s. They conclude that the large growth in immigration during the 1980s and 1990s, particularly of low-skilled Mexican laborers, lowered the wages of native-born high school dropouts by about 8 percent and exerted a modest influence in widening wage inequality within the U.S. (2005, 37–38, 63, table 11).

Despite the relatively small overall effects of recent rises in immigration on native-born workers' employment rates and average earnings in the U.S., there are obviously some job markets where immigrants exert significant influences on native-born workers' job prospects. The argument that immigration improves the position of native-born workers is related to a major myth concerning immigration and jobs: that immigrants take jobs native-born workers do not want. If this statement were true in the simple and straightforward manner in which it is usually stated, there would be no native-born workers in the same kinds of jobs held by large numbers of immigrants. However (with the possible exception of migrant agricultural labor in harvesting crops), native-born workers, either now or in the recent past, composed large proportions of the laborers in jobs currently associated with immigrant workers. A more correct statement of the assertion "immigrants take jobs that Americans won't take" is that in some types of jobs the availability of immigrant workers—especially undocumented workers—causes enough deterioration in the wages and working conditions of low-skill jobs that native-born workers exit, abandoning jobs they feel are not worth having. Once immigrants enter a labor force previously composed of native-born workers, the fact that immigrants can be hired for lower wages to toil under poorer conditions allows employers to earn larger profits than they could with native-born workers. Employers benefiting from this boon say that American citizens are not willing to accept these difficult, low-paying jobs. Generally, this statement is correct on its face. Native-born workers who have alternatives generally do not want these jobs once the pay and conditions of work become defined by an immigrant work force with no options but to accept exploitative conditions.

Meatpacking is a salient example of an industry where case studies provide strong evidence that low-wage immigrant workers have displaced native-born workers. Meatpacking jobs have always been dirty, physically demanding, and dangerous, and historically the occupation has attracted only the least educated members of the workforce. In the past, the industry employed large numbers of African Americans. Today immigrants predominate in meatpacking jobs, and the undocumented are a significant part of the labor force. During the late 1990s, the Immigration and Naturalization Service estimated that undocumented workers composed 25 percent of the labor in meatpacking plants in Iowa and Nebraska. Over the past two decades, immigrant labor has come to dominate the poultry industry in the southern states. In these earliest years of the twenty-first century, Latino immigrants comprise about three-fourths of the workers in the poultry plants located in northwest Arkansas; the vast majority of the remaining workers are from Southeast Asia and the Marshall Islands. Native-born workers are now rare (Human Rights Watch 2005).

Through the 1970s and into the 1980s, nearly half (46 percent) of the industry's workers were represented by labor unions, and larger meat packing firms were heavily unionized. The large, unionized plants paid a wage premium; in 1982 their base wage rate was $10.69 per hour ($22.33 per hour when adjusted for inflation to 2006). A rapid influx of workers from Southeast Asia, Mexico, and Central America during the 1980s coincided with firms' demands that workers accept wage cuts. Extremely turbulent employer-union relations, with bitter strikes and corporate attacks on unions, characterized the 1980s. During the period 1983–1986 there were 158 work stoppages involving some 40,000 workers in cattle and hog plants. By 1987, the proportion of the work force that was unionized had been cut to 21 percent and wages were down to the $8 to $9 range in both union and non-union plants. A sharp decrease in workers' health and safety accompanied the unions' collapse. Although the meatpacking industry already had the highest rates of occupational injuries and illness of all U.S. industries, on-the-job illness and injury rates rose still further, peaking in 1991 at 45.5 per 100 workers. Jobs in the industry deteriorated so badly that only the steady influx of cheap immigrant labor compensated for the extraordinarily high turnover rates, reaching 100 percent annually at some plants during the 1990s. Under these conditions, it is true—and not surprising—that meatpacking plants have difficulties attracting native-born workers (Macdonald et al. 1999, 15–16). Many employers of less educated labor say they prefer immigrants over African American men or native-born workers of any racial-ethnic group. The immigrants, employers say, "show up on time" and "get along with the boss"—a euphemism for doing what they are told without complaining no matter how distasteful it may be.

What are the policy implications of findings that the availability of low-skill immigrants negatively affects the employment opportunities of less educated black males? If the United States allocated substantially more resources to border security and managed to reduce the number of undocumented workers significantly while also tightening channels for legal immigration, would the reduction in the number of immigrant workers result in more and higher paying jobs for American citizens? The easy answer is that a reduction in the labor supply would force an increase in wages and enable more native-born workers to find employment. However, as with any question of economic effects, the demand side of the equation must also be considered. Although we have rejected the simple assertion that immigrants are willing to take jobs the native born refuse, we have noted that immigrants take jobs for lower pay and do them under more undesirable working conditions. Hiring immigrant workers lowers employers' labor costs. Take away the immigrants, and the result would be rising wages and less pliable work forces, which would lower business profits. Where possible, a greater proportion of jobs would be outsourced—sent to lower-cost labor markets abroad. Some of the more marginal businesses that had to pay higher wages to workers who are not as productive would not survive, and the demand for less educated workers would likely decrease. The net effect would be that wages and employment of native-born workers would likely rise, but not nearly as much as a simple comparison of raw numbers suggests.

A reasonable assessment of the effects of immigration on the employment prospects of young black males is that the overall effect is negative but small, except for specific industries and some geographic locations where the effects are significant. In addition to meatpacking jobs in many areas of the south, less-skilled work in construction across the country has seen a major shift to immigrant labor. However, the evidence also supports the conclusion that, economy-wide, the negative effects of immigration on the opportunities for and terms of employment of young black males are not nearly as large as the worst-case scenarios suggest.

Views of Immigration

Interestingly, the conclusion supported by the social scientific evidence that immigration has had negative but modest effects on less-skilled workers nationwide is consistent with what Americans seem to be saying when they are surveyed about immigration-related issues. The first thing to note from such surveys is that only a minority of American citizens believe that immigrants exert a negative effect on the labor market prospects of the native born. Both black and white citizens express moderate views. Majorities of blacks and whites (53 and 65 percent) believe "immigrants take jobs Americans don't want," while clear minorities of blacks and whites (34 and 25 percent) say that "immigrants take jobs away from U.S. citizens."

One of the most interesting results from surveys of U.S. citizens on attitudes toward immigration is that, despite the fact that the news media devote nearly all coverage of African Americans' views on this topic to competition between blacks and Latinos and dwell on the negative views held by a minority of black citizens, black Americans hold more favorable views of immigrants and immigration than do white Americans.

Summarizing its April 2006 survey of Americans' attitudes toward immigration, the Pew Research Center concluded: "The issue of immigration leaves many Americans deeply conflicted. But the social and economic cross-pressures may be greatest on African Americans, who express relatively positive opinions of immigrants even as they view them as competitors for scarce job opportunities" (Doherty 2006). The data leading to this conclusion may be summarized succinctly. Compared to whites, blacks are more likely to believe they have lost a job to an immigrant (22 to 14 percent) and more likely to believe immigrants take jobs from U.S. citizens (34 to 25 percent).[1] Even so, while whites favor sending illegal immigrants back to their country of origin by a preponderance of nearly 2 to 1 (59 to 33 percent), blacks are evenly divided on this question (47 to 47 percent). Blacks are slightly more likely to believe that legal immigration into the U.S. should be either increased or remain at present levels than are whites (56 versus 52 percent). Many more blacks than whites (78 versus 52 percent) say "jobs are difficult to find" in their communities. Logically, this experience should interact with blacks' beliefs that immigrants take jobs to create opposition to immigration, but it does not.

These 2006 findings that blacks view immigration more favorably than do whites are based on a snapshot of American citizens' attitudes toward immigration, but they are consistent with long-standing racial differences in Americans' views on immigration. Blacks' attitudes toward immigration and immigrants have been more favorable than the attitudes of whites for some time. Polls conducted in the early 1990s showed that African Americans were more likely than other Americans to associate immigration with negative labor market outcomes for themselves. Nevertheless, although Americans generally favored lower immigration levels by 2 to 1, black Americans were evenly divided between those who supported a reduction in immigration and those who welcomed immigrants at current or even higher rates (Jaynes 2000, 3).

Blacks were also more likely than whites to express the view that once immigrants arrive they should be given fair and equal treatment. For example, African Americans are far more likely than white Americans to say that even immigrants who have arrived in the U.S. illegally should be eligible to receive a host of government services, particularly social services and public schooling for their children. In 2006, blacks were more than twice as likely as whites (43 percent to 20 percent) to agree that illegal immigrants should be eligible for social services. Although both groups are quite liberal on the issue, 4 of 5 blacks (79 percent) compared to 2 of 3 whites (67 percent) agreed that children of undocumented immigrants should be allowed to attend public schools (Doherty 2006).

These differences in the views held by black and white Americans toward immigration and immigrants seem counterintuitive, since blacks are more directly affected than whites by the presence of immigrants as potential competitors in the labor market. How are these seemingly surprising group sentiments to be explained? We believe that African Americans, who have long espoused strong beliefs in principles of equality of opportunity, the rights of the downtrodden, and respect for humanity viewed in its broadest terms, are especially cognizant of the hypocrisy embedded within ethnocentric demands for an end to immigration. Given African Americans' historical commitment to these values, black citizens have the most to lose both psychologically and politically by engaging in such hypocrisy.

In a 2006 press release discussing the ethnic and racial composition of the U.S. population, Census Bureau director Louis Kincannon emphasized that the "mid-decade numbers provide further evidence of the increasing diversity of our nation's population" (U.S. Census Bureau 2006). In 2005, the U.S. minority population reached 98 million, making it 33 percent of a national population totaling 296.4 million. With one in three Americans counted as nonwhite or Latino and their numbers growing rapidly, the culture is undergoing a deep and far-reaching transition. Like white Americans, black Americans voice concerns that the growing number of new immigrants coming into the U.S. may threaten American values. However, what African Americans regard as foundational American values are not necessarily the same as those many white conservatives regard as traditionally American. Black citizens welcome socioeconomic and public policy changes that some whites regard negatively, especially those that undermine whites' customary positions of privilege and ethnic superiority. Significant alteration of society's basic institutions threatens many whites with the possibility of significant psychological and material loss. White conservatives may find that threat especially salient; ethnicity and party affiliation are strong correlates of dissatisfaction with both immigration policies and immigrants.

Immigration on the scale this country has sustained during the past three decades will surely bring significant change in some of our most important social, political, and cultural institutions, as well as those we might classify as primarily economic. Beyond short-term, localized effects on low-wage labor markets, immigration carries with it more general effects throughout society that in the medium and long term are likely to benefit African Americans in profound ways. Increases in the proportion of American citizens who belong to minority racial-ethnic groups are likely to put more pressure on political institutions to improve the allocation of educational resources to students in low- and moderate-income communities, for example. Growing numbers of Americans who identify themselves as members of minority groups are likely to have a strong interest in changing the ways in which such public institutions as the criminal justice system and the health care system are organized and managed. Over the long term, the resulting changes will be good for African Americans. Recognizing these possibilities in no way underestimates the likelihood that blacks will sometimes find themselves in competition with new groups for resources. However, the competition will likely be over relative shares in an expanding pool of private and especially public goods and services.

In conclusion, although immigration has probably had modest negative effects on the overall employment position of less educated young black males, it is just as likely that the relative importance of young black men's job losses that are due to the competition of immigrant workers is swamped by a constellation of other factors diminishing their economic status. A sizable minority of black men persists in low educational achievement, dropping out of high school, and engaging in negative behaviors such as criminal activity and interpersonal violence. These behaviors interact powerfully with preexisting societal views, reinforcing negative stereotypes that in turn foster fear of and distaste for associating with young African American men. Suppose immigration's depressing effects on young black men's wages were as high as 10 percent. Without denying that any increase in the average earnings of black males would bring some benefit, we must note that a 10 percent increase in the wages earned by black high school dropouts would still leave them in a pathological condition. Substantial improvement in the economic status of young black males will require considerable change in their social status on many other dimensions. Immigration's wider effects on American society offer far greater prospects for positive change than support for myopic policies designed to choke off the flow of immigrants into the U.S.

References

Borjas, George J., Richard B. Freeman, and Lawrence F. Katz. 1992. On the labor market effects of immigration and trade. In *Immigration and the Work Force: Economic Consequences for the United States and Source Areas*, ed. George J. Borjas and Richard B. Freeman, 213–44. Chicago: University of Chicago Press.

Borjas, George J., and Lawrence F. Katz. 2005. The Evolution of the Mexican-Born Workforce in the United States. Working Paper 11281. National Bureau of Economic Research, Cambridge, Mass. April.

Camarota, Steven A. 2006. Dropping Out: Immigrant entry and Native Exit from the Labor Market, 2000–2005. Center for Immigration Studies, Washington, D.C. March.

Doherty, Carroll. 2006a. Attitudes Toward Immigration in Black and White. Pew Research Center for the People and the Press. April 26.

———. 2006b. Attitudes Toward Immigration in Red and Blue. Pew Research Center for the People and the Press. May 9.

Human Rights Watch. 2005. Blood, Sweat, and Fear: Workers' Rights in U.S. Meat and Poultry Plants, 2004. http://hrw.org/reports/2005/usa0105/index.htm.

Jaynes, Gerald D. 2006. Two Evolutions: Black affluence, Black poverty—The economics of African American citizenship since Emancipation. Manuscript, Yale University.

————. 2000. *Race and Immigration: New Dilemmas for American Democracy.* New Haven, Conn.: Yale University Press.

MacDonald, James, Michael Ollinger, Kenneth Nelson, and Charles Handy. 1999. Consolidation in U.S. Meatpacking. Agricultural Economic Report 785. Washington, D.C.: Economic Research Service, United States Department of Agriculture.

Scherer, Ron. 2006. Immigration debate crux: Jobs impact. *Christian Science Monitor,* March 30, 1.

U.S. Census Bureau. 2006. Nation's population one-third minority. Press Release CB06-72. May 10.

Waldinger, Roger. 1996. *Still the Promised City? African Americans and New Immigrants in Postindustrial New York.* Cambridge, Mass.: Harvard University Press.

Wilson, Franklin D., and Gerald D. Jaynes. 2000. Migration and the employment and wages of native and immigrant workers. *Work and Occupations* 27 (2) (May): 135–67.

Chapter 7
Immigration and Equal Opportunity

DOUGLAS S. MASSEY

African Americans have long watched successive waves of immigrants enter the United States at the bottom of the economic ladder only to bypass them in a generation or two. Prior to the civil rights era, African Americans faced systematic exclusion from and discrimination within most U.S. labor markets, while immigrants were generally able to gain access and advance within these same markets, though not entirely without resistance (Alba and Nee 2003). Over time, immigrants moved steadily up the socioeconomic ladder while African Americans did not.

It is not at all clear that today's immigrants will repeat this historical experience. Contemporary immigrants from Asia, Latin America, and the Caribbean are racially more distinct from the dominant group of Americans than were European immigrants in the past. Although some southern and eastern European groups were also widely perceived as nonwhite when they first arrived (Jacobson 1998; Roediger 2005), most immigrants today are darker skinned and more phenotypically distinct from white Euro-Americans. Immigrants from the Caribbean, in particular, are often of mixed African and European origins, and a large fraction are very African in appearance. Immigrants from the rest of Latin America are generally a mixture of European and Amerindian origins, a blend that people in the region generally label mestizo.

The arrival of growing numbers of dark-skinned immigrants over the past several decades has triggered a new round of racial formation in the United States. Latinos, in particular, have increasingly been framed as a racialized "other" whose presence threatens the culture, values, living standards—indeed, the very existence—of the United States. In keeping with this framing of social reality, discrimination against Latinos has risen to equal or exceed that directed against African Americans (Charles 2003), with discriminatory treatment being triggered by foreign accent, appearance, and skin color rather than class (Massey 2007, 113–57). At the same time, increasingly harsh immigration and border policies have combined to raise the number of people living in the United States without social, political, or economic rights, a trend that has worked to the disadvantage of all low-wage workers, including African Americans (Massey and Bartley 2005).

As a result, in the contemporary political economy Latino immigrants and their children are not bypassing African Americans in the socioeconomic race but are joining them in marginalized positions at the bottom of the U.S. class structure. Because Latinos and African Americans increasingly share the same structural position, they have much to gain by joining together to demand civil rights and equal opportunity. In this sense, immigration reform—legalizing current undocumented migrants and granting them and future arrivals from abroad full labor rights in the United States—is very much in the interest of African Americans and, in fact, represents an essential part of a broader movement toward egalitarian reform in the United States.

Framing Latinos as a Threat

The upsurge in immigration from Latin America over the past several decades has been accompanied by a new portrayal of Latinos as a threat to the nation's culture, economy, and security. In order to assess shifts in the public portrayal of immigrants over time, Chavez (2001) analyzed U.S. magazine covers devoted to immigration between 1965 and 2000 and classified them as affirmative, alarmist, or neutral in their portrayal of foreigners. Covers coded as "affirmative" used text and images to celebrate immigration; "alarmist" covers used text and images to convey problems, fears, or dangers associated with immigration; and "neutral" covers were accompanied by articles that offered balanced and factual coverage of the issue.

Chavez found that alarmist themes overwhelmingly dominated in coverage of immigration after 1965, characterizing two-thirds of all covers devoted to the topic, compared with just 9 percent classified as neutral and 19 percent as affirmative. Moreover, the frequency of alarmist covers increased over time. Only 18 percent of the alarmist covers appeared in the 1970s, 38 percent were published in the 1980s, and 45 percent appeared in the 1990s. Upsurges in alarmism coincided with periods of economic recession in the United States (Chavez 2001, 21–24).

Immigration-related magazine covers were selective with respect to their portrayal of race, ethnicity, and gender. For example, Massey (2007) took Chavez's classifications of the characteristics of people shown on magazine covers and compared them to data from the U.S. Census and U.S. Office of Immigration Statistics to show that males and nonwhites were overrepresented compared to their actual frequency among immigrants who arrived in the same period. Whereas females now comprise a slight majority of immigrants, three-quarters of those depicted on magazine covers were male. Although immigrants from Europe made up around 15 percent of the total who arrived in the 1990s, none of the cover illustrations showed whites and just 10 percent of the cover photographs did so. In contrast, whereas immigrants from Africa and the Caribbean comprised only 15 percent of all immigrants during the 1990s, 23 percent of the cover photos and 46 percent of the cover illustrations depicted people who were black or visibly of African descent; Latin Americans comprised 37 percent of immigrants, but they made up 45 percent of cover illustrations (Massey 2007, 133–35).

At the same time, African Americans and Latinos were underrepresented in depictions of native-born U.S. citizens on magazine covers. While in 2000 around 13 percent of all Americans identified themselves as black, only 2 percent of the non-immigrants shown on magazine covers had black faces. Likewise, Hispanics comprised just 1 percent of photographs of non-immigrants compared with 13 percent in the U.S. population. In short, magazine covers were manipulated to overstate the nonwhite origins of immigrants while understating the nonwhite origins of natives (Massey 2007, 134).

The texts that accompanied these images reinforced the sense of alarm and urgency communicated by the pictures (Chavez 2001). In time-honored fashion, editors made heavy use of marine metaphors, depicting immigration as a "tidal wave" that was "flooding" the United States and threatening to "inundate" the dominant culture. During the 1980s, a new metaphor appeared with growing frequency as immigrants and immigration were framed increasingly in martial terms. Coinciding with the escalation of the Cold War in Central America and elsewhere, the Mexico-U.S. border was portrayed as a "battleground" that was "under attack" from "alien invaders" who constituted a "time bomb" waiting to explode and destroy American culture and values. In this militarized portrayal, Border Patrol Officers became "defenders" who were "outgunned" as they tried to "hold the line" against attacking "hordes" (Dunn 1996; Andreas 2000). Whether the metaphorical language was martial or marine, it always portrayed immigration as a "crisis."

During the 1980s, Ronald Reagan brought the anti-immigrant hysteria to a head by framing immigrants as a threat to "national security" in the Cold War. He predicted, as a result of communist insurgencies in Central America, "a tidal wave of refugees—and this time they'll be 'feet people' and not boat people—swarming into our country seeking safe haven from communist repression to the south" (*Washington Post*, June 21, 1983). In a 1986 speech the president reminded Americans that "terrorists and subversives are just two days driving time from [the border crossing at] Harlingen, Texas" (quoted in Kamen 1990), and his 1987 Task Force on Terrorism reported that immigrants constituted a potential "fifth column" in the United States because extremists would "feed on the anger and frustration of recent Central and South American immigrants who will not realize their own version of the American dream" (quoted in Dunn 1996).

The year 1986 was pivotal in the institutionalization of animus against immigrants. Late that year Congress passed the Immigration Reform and Control Act (IRCA), which contained two far-reaching provisions that drastically reshaped the political economy of migration and transformed the position of Latinos in the United States (Durand, Massey, and Parrado 1999). First, IRCA sharply increased funding for border enforcement, initiating an unprecedented expansion in the Border Patrol that has continued unabated for two decades. Second, it criminalized the hiring of undocumented workers and applied sanctions against employers who knowingly did so. Unfortunately, these measures backfired by increasing the number of undocumented migrants living in the United States while simultaneously undercutting their bargaining position within U.S. labor markets, thereby undermining wages and working conditions for all Americans competing for low-wage employment.

After 1986, the size and budget of the Border Patrol were expanded rapidly and in increasing disproportion to the underlying volume of migration (Massey, Durand, and Malone 2002). In 1986 the agency had 3,700 officers and an annual budget of $151 million, but by 2002 it had 6,200 officers with a budget of $1.6 billion and had become the largest arms-bearing branch of government save the military itself (Nevins 2001, Andreas 2000). The budget of the Immigration and Naturalization Service ballooned from $474 million to $6.2 billion as it came to operate a growing network of prisons where inhumane treatment and abuse became routine, establishing a new "American gulag" that paralleled the boom in the incarceration of African Americans (Dow 2004).

Despite vast expenditures on border enforcement, the rate of illegal entry remained virtually constant after IRCA's passage (Massey, Donato, and Liang 1990; Donato, Durand, and Massey 1992a). According to data from the Mexican Migration Project, the overall probability of taking a first undocumented trip has fluctuated narrowly around 1 percent for the past 25 years and the probability of taking an additional trip actually fell slightly, going from 14 percent to around 8 percent per year (Massey 2007). While IRCA had little effect on the rate of in-migration from Latin America, it did have a strong effect on the rate of out-migration from the U.S. The new enforcement regime tripled the death rate at the border and quadrupled smuggling costs (Massey, Durand, and Malone

2002), and in response to these new costs and risks undocumented migrants did the rational thing—they minimized border crossing.

Rather that deciding not to leave for the United States in the first place, undocumented migrants instead chose to stay longer. Once they had run the gauntlet at the border and made it successfully into the country they hunkered down to stay (Durand and Massey 2003). Among undocumented Mexicans, the probability of returning home within 12 months of entry declined from an average of close to 50 percent before IRCA to just 25 percent by 2000 (Massey 2005). The probability of their remaining in the United States more than 12 months without documents rose from 39 percent in 1986 to 80 percent ten years later (Rios-mena 2004).

The falling rate of out-migration and the steady rate of in-migration combined to increase the rate of net population growth and led to an unprecedented acceleration in the number of undocumented migrants living north of the border. Restrictive U.S. immigration and border policies were worse than ineffective; they were counterproductive. Instead of reducing the net annual inflow of Mexican migrants, they doubled it. U.S. policies transformed what had been a circular flow of male workers into a settled population of families, and by the year 2005, the total number of undocumented migrants living in the United States had reached 12 million.

These figures imply that one of every ten people born in Mexico now lives in the United States, and around 55 percent of Mexican immigrants are presently in illegal status. Immigrants have come to comprise a growing fraction of all Mexican Americans—roughly 40 percent as of 2005—and the large number of undocumented among them means that midway through the first decade of the twenty-first century, more than half of all Mexican-born persons and more than a fifth of all persons of Mexican origin lack any social, political, or economic rights in the United States.

At the same time, Latinos face a much more hostile and daunting economic environment because of IRCA's criminalization of hiring undocumented workers. This provision obviously did not stop migration by removing the "magnet" of jobs in the U.S., as its proponents had hoped. It did, however, transform the structure of the U.S. labor market in ways that were detrimental to the economic well-being not only of undocumented migrants but of legal immigrants and U.S. citizens as well, including African Americans (Massey, Durand, and Malone 2002).

Congress intended to induce employers to discriminate against Latinos on the basis of legal status, and in this sense the legislation was successful. Whereas before 1986, legal and illegal immigrants earned similar wages once human capital characteristics were controlled, afterward a significant gap opened up in the wages of documented and undocumented migrants (Donato, Durand, and Massey 1992b; Donato and Massey 1993). According to estimates by Phillips and Massey (1999), in the wake of IRCA illegal migrants came to earn 25 percent less than their legal counterparts after controlling for differences in background characteristics.

Besides this intended effect in promoting discrimination against undocumented migrants, IRCA had a spillover effect in promoting discrimination against Latinos in general (U.S. General Accounting Office 1990). Given that the vast majority of undocumented migrants are Latin American, an easy way for employers to reduce the risk of violating IRCA's sanctions is simply not to hire anyone who "looks Hispanic," and this is apparently what many bosses did after 1986 (Lowell, Teachman, and Jing 1995). For those migrants who did manage to get hired in the wake of IRCA, wages were much lower than before, suggesting that employers engaged in wage discrimination to compensate themselves for the perceived risk of hiring foreigners (Lowell and Jing 1994; Sorensen and Bean 1994; Fry, Lowell, and Haghighat 1995; Cobb-Clark, Shiells, and Lowell 1995).

A final consequence of IRCA was a radical transformation in the hiring process for all workers regardless of legal status. Whereas before IRCA most employers hired undocumented workers themselves, afterward they shifted to a practice of indirect hiring through subcontractors, an arrangement that historically has been associated with the most exploitive labor conditions, especially among immigrants (Zolberg 2006). Under a subcontracting arrangement, a U.S. citizen or resident alien contractually agrees with an employer, usually a corporation, to provide a specific number of workers for a certain period of time to undertake a defined task at a fixed rate of pay per worker. As the workers themselves are technically not employees of the firm but of the subcontractor, the employer escapes liability under the law. In return for providing this legal buffer, the subcontractor retains a portion of the workers' wages. Whether this deduction represents "income" for services rendered to employers or "profit" from the exploitation of workers is a semantic distinction of little importance to the workers themselves.

Such arrangements quickly became standard in industries with high turnover rates and significant numbers of immigrant workers, such as agriculture, construction, gardening, and custodial services (Taylor and Thilmany 1993; Taylor 1996; Martin 1996; Durand 1997; Taylor, Martin, and Fix 1997). As indirect hiring became the norm, it was imposed on all workers regardless of legal status. If a citizen or legal resident—black, white, Asian, or other—wished to get a job in agriculture or construction, he or she had to work through a subcontractor and forfeit a share of wages in return for the opportunity to work. In this way, a perverse consequence of IRCA's employer sanctions was to lower the wages and working conditions not only of undocumented migrants but also of legal immigrants and U.S. citizens who compete in the same markets, including African Americans (Durand and Massey 2003).

Under labor subcontracting arrangements, moreover, workers experience fewer returns to experience, education, and job tenure, yielding falling returns to human capital. By eradicating the routes to higher earnings that had prevailed before 1986, IRCA not only undermined the wages paid to undocumented migrants but had an even greater effect on the wages of legal immigrants and citizens. Whereas the real value of wages earned by undocumented migrants fell by 12 percent from 1986 to 1996, the real value of wages earned by documented migrants fell by 29 percent. Along with lower wages came greater informality in the terms of employment, with migrants experiencing longer hours and more payments in cash (Massey, Durand, and Malone 2002).

In sum, IRCA's employer sanctions radically restructured the market for unskilled labor in the United States, increasing discrimination on the basis of legal status, exacerbating discrimination on the basis of race and ethnicity, and pushing employers toward labor subcontracting as the principal hiring mechanism. Moreover, as IRCA's provisions were raising the penalties for being illegal, Hispanic, and unskilled in the U.S. economy, its militarization of the border backfired, acting to increase the relative number of people in marginalized categories (Massey and Bartley 2005). In other words, as the rules of the political economy were rewritten to become more exploitive, the number of people in exploitable categories expanded, with predictable results.

Racialization Redux

After 1986, analysts began to detect stronger and more negative influences of immigration on the economic standing of native-born citizens. Whereas studies based on the 1980 census (before employer sanctions) had shown positive or tiny negative effects of immigration on the wages and employment rates of domestic workers, those based on the 1990 and 2000 censuses (after employer sanctions) found larger and more negative effects, particularly on unskilled workers and minorities (Borjas, Freeman, and Katz 1992, 1996; Borjas 1993, 1994, 1997, 1999). The political economy of the United States became dramatically less favorable to working men and women, whether immigrant or native-born, black or white.

Rather than blaming the deterioration of wages and negative labor market effects on structural changes in the political economy, however, conservative economists such as George Borjas (1995) attributed the trend to a "declining quality of immigrants." Although the demonization of Latino immigrants as "invaders" and "terrorists" slackened somewhat during economic boom of the 1990s, these framings returned with a vengeance after September 11, 2001, both inside and outside academia. Within the academy, figures such as Harvard University political scientist Samuel P. Huntington (2004, 30) have used the protections of the ivory tower to offer a thinly veiled reprise of earlier racist assertions about the unassimilability of immigrants:

The persistent inflow of Hispanic immigrants threatens to divide the United States into two peoples, two cultures, and two languages. Unlike past immigrant groups, Mexicans and other Latinos have not assimilated into mainstream U.S. culture, forming instead their own political and linguistic enclaves—from Los Angeles to Miami—and rejecting the Anglo-Protestant values that built the American dream. The United States ignores this challenge at its peril.

Former Nixon speechwriter and conservative pundit Patrick Buchanan warned of an "Aztlan Plot" fomented by Mexican conspirators to recapture lands lost in 1848, to bring about a "reconquista" of the American southwest. Comparing Mexicans to the barbarians invading ancient Rome, he characterized "the Third World invasion and conquest of America" as a "state of emergency." In an interview with *Time*, he warned: "If we do not get control of our borders and stop this greatest invasion in history, I see the dissolution of the U.S. and the loss of the American southwest—culturally and linguistically, if not politically—to Mexico. It could become a part of Mexico in the way that Kosovo is now a part of Albania" (August 28, 2006, 6). Even more hyperbole was forthcoming from Chris Simcox of the Minutemen Civil Defense Corps, a vigilante group he founded to patrol the Mexico-U.S. border. On the organization's website, he rhetorically asks "Are terrorists exploiting our porous borders?" and then supplies this answer: "We know drug dealers, gang bangers and way too many criminal foreign nationals are creating havoc in our communities and threatening our public safety."

The legal foundations for the criminalization of undocumented migrants themselves, as well as those who hire undocumented workers, were laid by the 1996 Antiterrorism and Effective Death Penalty Act, which gave the federal government new police powers for the "expedited exclusion" of any alien who had ever crossed the border without documents, no matter what his or her current legal status, or who had ever committed a felony, no matter how long ago. These provisions, coming on the heels of a decade of draconian drug laws and three-strikes legislation, instantly rendered thousands of legal resident aliens deportable, many of whom had entered as infants and spent their entire lives in the United States.

The law delegated to the State Department absolute authority to designate any organization as "terrorist," thereby making all members of groups so designated immediately excludable and deportable. It narrowed the grounds for asylum and added alien smuggling to the list of crimes covered by the Racketeer Influenced Corrupt Organizations statute (RICO, which was passed in 1970 to combat organized crime), while severely limiting the possibilities for judicial review of deportations. According to Washington University law professor Stephen H. Legomsky (2000, 1616), this legislation constitutes "the most ferocious assault on the judicial review of immigration decisions" ever launched "by creating new removal courts that allow secret procedures to be used to remove suspected alien terrorists; by shifting the authority to make 'expedited removals' to immigration inspectors at ports of entry; and by setting unprecedented limits on judicial review of immigration decisions."

The events of September 11 occurred against a background of rising animus toward immigrants and a growing assault on their civil liberties and social rights. In response to the terrorist attacks, Congress on October 26, 2001, passed the USA PATRIOT Act, which granted the executive branch expansive new powers to deport, without any hearing or presentation of evidence, all aliens—legal and illegal—that the Attorney General had "reason to believe" might commit, further, or facilitate acts of terrorism. For the first time since the Alien and Sedition Act of 1798, Congress voted to permit the arrest, imprisonment, and deportation of noncitizens upon the orders of the Attorney General without judicial review.

The PATRIOT act not only gives the federal government sweeping powers of surveillance and incarceration with respect to immigrants but, as in past instances of political hysteria and fear-mongering, to U.S. citizens as well. As Zolberg (2006, 450) notes, "while the challenges posed by international migration are real and warrant a worldwide reconsideration of prevailing regimes, the resurgence of nativist responses constitutes a more immediate threat to liberal democracy than immigration itself." It is no coincidence that the only U.S. citizen held in indefinite detention under the act without charge and without a hearing was a dark-skinned, Afro-origin Latino named Jose Padilla.

All the work being done by academics, pundits, and politicians to frame Latin American immigrants as a threat and categorize them socially as undesirable has affected public opinion, turning it steadily against Latinos. According to polls conducted by the Pew Charitable Trusts, as late as 2000 only 38 percent of Americans agreed that "immigrants today are a burden on our country because they take our jobs, housing, and health care." Five years later, the proportion had risen to 44 percent; and as the drumbeat of anti-immigrant rhetoric reached a crescendo in 2006 it increased to 52 percent. In keeping with this shift, the proportion of Americans who rated immigration as a moderately big or very big national problem rose from 69 percent in 2002 to 74 percent in 2006 (Kohut and Suro 2006).

As of the year 2006, almost half of all Americans (48 percent) opined that "newcomers from other countries threaten traditional American values and customs" and 54 percent said that the United States needed to be "protected against foreign influence." In accordance with these views, 49 percent said they believed that "immigrants kept to themselves and do not try to fit in"; 56 percent said they "don't pay their fair share of taxes"; 58 percent believed that immigrants "do not learn English in a reasonable amount of time"; and 60 percent of those who had heard of the Minutemen approved of their activities. Amid the hysteria surrounding immigration and border control, Americans drastically overestimate the relative number of immigrants present in the country. Although the proportion of immigrants in the U.S. population stands at around 12 percent, 53 percent of poll respondents thought that it was 25 percent or greater (Kohut and Suro 2006).

Latinos and Blacks in the New Political Economy

Just as the criminal justice system has emerged as a new and powerful institution in promoting inequality between blacks and whites, the U.S. immigration system has assumed a new centrality in the exploitation and exclusion of Latinos. The implementation of employer sanctions increased discrimination against Hispanics in U.S. labor markets, lowered their wages, depressed returns to human capital, and closed off long-established pathways of upward mobility. At the same time, IRCA promoted a wholesale shift to subcontracting in the unskilled labor market. The militarization of the Mexico-U.S. border raised the rate of undocumented population growth and increased the number of people in exploitable, powerless categories. Finally, as private discrimination increased and larger shares of the population were being exploited economically, Congress increased the social penalties for being poor, foreign, and undocumented, cutting even legal immigrants off from public services for which they had heretofore qualified.

As a result of these deliberate policy changes, the political economy facing Latinos in the United States is now substantially harsher and more punitive than the situation that prevailed before 1986. Historically, Latinos occupied a middle position between blacks and whites in the American stratification system, but with the restructuring of the political economy of immigration in the late 1980s and early 1990s, their relative standing deteriorated and they unambiguously joined African

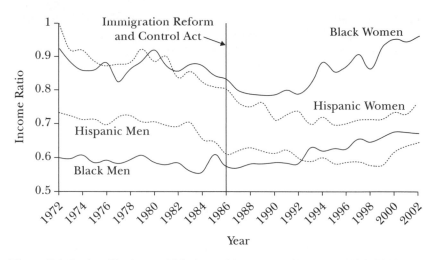

Figure 7.1. Ratio of Latino and black to white personal income, 1972–2002.
U.S. Bureau of the Census.

Americans at the bottom of the class hierarchy. Figure 7.1 illustrates this change by showing the ratio of minority to white income for blacks and Latinos from 1972 to 2002.

The bottom two lines show income ratios for Latino and black men. In the early 1970s, the average black male earned roughly 60 percent of what the average white male earned, while Latino males earned around 70 percent of what white males enjoyed. These relative income ratios prevailed through the early 1980s, but in the middle of that decade IRCA transformed the structure of the low-wage labor market and the bargaining position of Latino men deteriorated. From 1983 to 1986, the ratio of Latino to white income fell from .70 to around .60, where it hovered until 1991; then it dropped below .60 for the first time ever. At about the same time, black male incomes began rising relative to those of white males. In 1993 the black-white income ratio crossed over the Latino-white ratio, and from that point onward Latinos replaced blacks at the bottom of the male earnings hierarchy.

The top two lines, showing trends in the relative earnings of Latino and black women, reveal a switching of positions that occurred even earlier than among minority men. In 1972 Latino women earned the same average incomes as white women, while black women earned around 92 percent of what their white counterparts enjoyed. During the 1970s and 1980s, the earnings of women in both minority groups deteriorated relative to those of white women; but the decline was more rapid among Latino women. In 1981 the two lines crossed, and from then on Latinas replaced black women at the bottom of the female earnings hierarchy. Despite this early crossover, the Latino-white and black-white income ratios remained quite close to one another until IRCA was passed in 1986. After this date the deterioration in black female income slowed down, and then in the early 1990s reversed and began to move upward. In contrast, the deterioration in Latinas' earnings accelerated, and the two income ratios began pull apart at a rapid pace. From 1987 to 2002 the ratio of black female income to white female income rose from .80 to around .96, while the income ratio for Latinas fell from .80 to around .70 before coming back up to end the decade at around .77.

The shifting fortunes of Latinos and African Americans in U.S. labor market are clearly visible in American poverty statistics. Historically, poverty rates among Latinos were much lower than those among blacks, but over the course of the 1980s and 1990s the differential disappeared and the two groups ended the twentieth century at rough parity in terms of material deprivation. Figure 4.2 shows the ratio of Latino to black poverty from 1972 to 2002. Through the 1970s and early 1980s, Latino poverty fluctuated at around 70 percent to 80 percent of the black level, but during the late 1980s and early 1990s Latino poverty rates rose and came to range between 80 percent and 90 percent of black rates. With the increase in settlement by undocumented migrants and the shift to family migration following the military build-up on the border that began with Operation Blockade in El Paso, Latino rates of poverty came to equal or exceed those of blacks, and the ratio pushed above 1.0 for the first time since poverty statistics had been collected (Figure 7.2).

The deterioration in the labor market position of Latinos relative to blacks was accompanied by a parallel shift within housing markets, for the 2000 Housing Discrimination Study revealed a significant increase in discrimination against people of Latino origin. Whereas in 1989 Latinos were 19 percent less likely than blacks to experience adverse treatment in America's rental markets, in 2000 they were 8 percent more likely suffer discrimination. Although the incidence of discriminatory treatment fell for both groups in the sales market, the decline for Latinos was much smaller. As a result, whereas blacks in 1989 were twice as likely as Latinos to experience discrimination in home sales, by 2000 Latinos were 18 percent more likely to experience it (Turner et al. 2002). Consistent with these data, in their audit of rental housing in the San Francisco Bay area, Purnell, Idsardi, and Baugh (1999) documented extensive "linguistic profiling" that excluded speakers of Chicano English as well as black English from access to housing.

As discrimination against Latinos in housing markets increased, so did levels of Latino residential segregation. While the overall level of

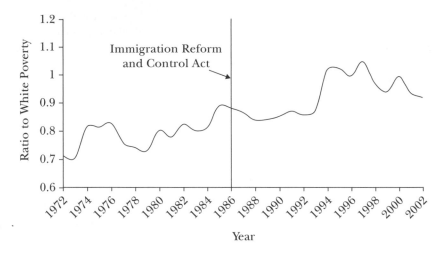

Figure 7.2. Ratio of Hispanic to black poverty rates, 1972–2002. U.S. Bureau of the Census.

black-white segregation fell by 10 points over the past decade and black neighborhood isolation dropped by 12 points, Latino-white segregation rose by six points and isolation increased by ten points (Charles 2003). Latinos did not satisfy the criteria for hypersegregation in any metropolitan areas during 1980 or 1990, but by 2000 both New York and Los Angeles had earned the dubious distinction of becoming hypersegregated for Latino residents (Wilkes and Iceland 2004).

In the social realm, researchers have documented a "chilling effect" of the 1996 immigration and welfare legislation on the use of public services by immigrants (Zimmerman and Fix 1998; Fix and Zimmerman 2004). Among undocumented migrants, the use of social services, which was always quite low, fell even further, so that after 1996 fewer than 5 percent reported receiving food stamps, welfare, or unemployment insurance while in the United States, and just 7 percent reported putting their children in public schools. More surprising was the decline in services consumed by legal immigrants. After 1996, permanent residents' utilization rates for welfare, unemployment insurance, and food stamps all fell sharply to 10 percent or less (Donato, Massey, and Wagner 2006), and according to estimates by Borjas (2004), every 10 percent cut in the fraction of the public on public assistance raised the relative number of food-insecure households by five percentage points.

In 1996 Congress sent a clear signal to legal as well as illegal immigrants that they were unwelcome in what remained of the American welfare state, and both sets of immigrants got the message loud and clear. In addition to restricting the eligibility of legal immigrants for means-tested federal benefits, Congress also raised the income threshold required to obtain an Affidavit of Support. This document is required of all persons seeking to sponsor the legal entry of a family member and requires a household to prove it has enough resources to support the immigrant should he or she become indigent. Congress sought to curtail family immigration, but rather than standing by and allowing the government to declare them ineligible to bring in relatives, immigrant households fought back by sending more family members into the workforce to bolster collective earnings so they could meet the higher income threshold. After 1996, older children in Latino families increasingly dropped out of school and went to work, depressing already low levels of education among Latino children and permanently undermining their economic prospects (Donato, Massey, and Wagner 2006).

Although Latinos have not been swept into the prison industrial complex to the same extent as African Americans, they nonetheless comprise a sizeable share of inmates that is disproportionate to their share of the U.S. population. Around 5 percent of Latino males aged twenty to forty were in prison or jail in 2000, compared with 12 percent of blacks and just 2 percent of whites (Western 2006). Moreover, in the spring of 2006 the U.S. House of Representatives passed legislation (HR4437) sponsored by Republican Representative James Sensenbrenner to make "unlawful presence" in the United States a felony. It defined unlawful presence so broadly that almost every immigration violation, no matter how minor, technical, or unintentional, became a federal crime subject to imprisonment and deportation. If this act were to be passed by the Senate and become law, it would render 12 million people instantly subject to incarceration and represent the largest expansion of the prison industrial complex ever, potentially tripling the size of America's prison population, already the largest on earth.

In *American Apartheid*, Massey and Denton offered a blueprint of how to build an underclass:

To begin, choose a minority group whose members are somehow identifiably different from the majority. Once the group has been selected, the next step in creating an underclass is to confine its members to a small number of continuous residential areas and then to impose on them stringent barriers to residential mobility. . . . Once a group's segregation in society has been ensured, the next step in building an underclass is to drive up its rate of poverty. . . . The interaction of poverty and segregation acts to concentrate a variety of deleterious social and economic characteristics. . . . Through prolonged exposure to life in a racially isolated and intensely poor neighborhood, poverty will quite likely be passed to children in the next generation. When this point is reached, a well-functioning and efficient structure for the construction and maintenance of an urban underclass will have been created. (1993, 182–85)

The evidence reviewed in this essay suggests that U.S. policies are moving Latinos steadily away from their middle position in the economic hierarchy and toward the formation of a new underclass. Segregation levels are rising, discrimination is increasing, poverty is deepening, educational levels are stagnating, and the social safety net has been deliberately poked full of holes to allow immigrants to fall through. Whether or not Latinos become a new urban underclass remains to be seen; but it is already clear that, after occupying a middle socioeconomic position between whites and blacks for generations, the economic fortunes of Latinos have now fallen to levels at or below those of African Americans.

In one crucial way, Latinos are much worse off than African Americans. Whatever discriminatory barriers African Americans still face, they at least have the legal right to live and work in the United States. In contrast, one fifth of all Mexican Americans now lack any legal claim on American society because they are present without authorization, and this fraction is rising rapidly. If the proportion of Latinos in undocumented status continues to rise, the resulting underclass will become even more intractable than the one that emerged in black inner cities during the 1980s. Not only will its members be exploited and excluded, they will be outside the law itself, deportable at a moment's notice and perhaps even at risk of incarceration for the felonious crime of living and working in the United States without permission.

It is difficult to see how much progress can be made in raising employment levels, wages, and working conditions for young black males as long as they must compete in labor markets where a large and growing fraction of their fellow workers are so vulnerable and exploitable. In this sense, immigration reform must be seen as part of a broader agenda of civil rights and economic opportunity in the United States. Regularizing the status of undocumented migrants already in the country will give them labor rights and make it possible to enforce labor legislation as well as occupational safety and health regulations. Creating a temporary worker program will reduce the rate of Latino population growth in the United States to minimize labor market competition; and bringing currently irregular flows of labor above ground will facilitate unionization and enable more systematic taxation to offset the inevitable costs of immigrants to natives. In sum, African Americans and Latinos have much more to gain by working together than by moving apart.

References

Alba, Richard D., and Victor Nee. 2003. *Remaking the American Mainstream: Assimilation and Contemporary Immigration.* Cambridge, Mass.: Harvard University Press.

Andreas, Peter. 2000. *Border Games: Policing the U.S.-Mexico Divide.* Ithaca, N.Y.: Cornell University Press.

Borjas, George J. 1993. The impact of immigrants on the employment opportunities of natives. In *The Changing Course of International Migration,* 217–30. Paris: Organization for Economic Cooperation and Development.

———. 1994. The economics of immigration. *Journal of Economic Literature* 32 (4): 1667–1717.

———. 1995. Assimilation and changes in cohort quality revisited: What happened to immigrant earnings in the 1980s? *Journal of Labor Economics* 13: 201–45.

———. 1997. The economic impact of Mexican immigration. In *Coming Together: Mexico-U.S. Relations,* ed. Barry P. Bosworth, Susan M. Collins, and Nora Claudia Lustig, 155–71. Washington, D.C.: Brookings Institution Press.

———. 1999. *Heaven's Door: Immigration Policy and the American Economy.* Princeton, N.J.: Princeton University Press.

———. 2004. Food insecurity and public assistance. *Journal of Public Economics* 88: 1421–43.

Borjas, George G., Richard B. Freeman, and Lawrence F. Katz. 1992. On the labor market effects of immigration and trade. In *Immigration and the Work Force: Economic Consequences for the United States and Source Areas,* ed. George J. Borjas and Richard B. Freeman, 213–44. Chicago: University of Chicago Press.

———. 1996. Searching for the effect of immigration on the labor market. *American Economic Review* 86: 246–51.

Charles, Camille Z. 2003. The dynamics of racial residential segregation. *Annual Review of Sociology* 29: 67–207.

Chavez, Leo R. 2001. *Covering Immigration: Population Images and the Politics of the Nation.* Berkeley: University of California Press.

Cobb-Clark, Deborah A., Clinton R. Shiells, and B. Lindsay Lowell. 1995. Immigration reform: The effects of employer sanctions and legalization on wages. *Journal of Labor Economics* 13: 472–98.

Doherty, Carroll. 2006. Attitudes toward immigration in black and white. Washington, D.C.: Pew Research Center for the People and the Press. http://pewresearch.org/obdeck/?ObDeckID=21, accessed January 8, 2007.

Donato, Katharine M., Jorge Durand, and Douglas S. Massey. 1992a. Stemming the tide? Assessing the deterrent effects of the Immigration Reform and Control Act. *Demography* 29: 139–57.

———. 1992b. Changing conditions in the U.S. labor market: Effects of the Immigration Reform and Control Act of 1986. *Population Research and Policy Review* 11: 93–115.

Donato, Katharine M., and Douglas S. Massey. 1993. Effect of the Immigration Reform and Control Act on the wages of Mexican migrants. *Social Science Quarterly* 74: 523–41.

Donato, Katharine M., Douglas S. Massey, and Brandon Wagner. 2006. The chilling effect: Public service usage by Mexican migrants to the United States. Paper presented at the Annual Meetings of the Population Association of America, Los Angeles.

Dow, Mark. 2004. *American Gulag: Inside U.S. Immigration Prisons.* Berkeley: University of California Press.

Dunn, Timothy J. 1996. *The Militarization of the U.S.-Mexico Border, 1978–1992: Low-Intensity Conflict Doctrine Comes Home.* Austin: Center for Mexican American Studies, University of Texas at Austin.

Durand, Jorge. 1997. Les nouveaux scénarios de l'immigration Mexicaine aux États-Unis. *Revue Tiers Monde* 150: 359–69.

Durand, Jorge, and Douglas S. Massey. 2003. The costs of contradiction: U.S. immigration policy 1986–1996. *Latino Studies* 1: 233-52.

Durand, Jorge, Douglas S. Massey, and Emilio A. Parrado. 1999. The new era of Mexican migration to the United States. *Journal of American History* 86: 518–36.

Fix, Michael, and Wendy Zimmermann. 2004. The legacy of welfare reform for U.S. immigrants. In *International Migration: Prospects and Polities in a Global Market*, ed. Douglas S. Massey and J. Edward Taylor, 337–53. Oxford: Oxford University Press.

Fry, Richard, B. Lindsay Lowell, and Elhum Haghighat. 1995. The impact of employer sanctions on metropolitan wage rates. *Industrial Relations* 34: 464–84.

Huntington, Samuel P. 2004. The Hispanic challenge. *Foreign Policy* 153 (March/April): 30-45.

Jacobson, Matthew Frye 1998. *Whiteness of a Different Color: European Immigrants and the Alchemy of Race*. Cambridge, Mass.: Harvard University Press.

Kamen, Al. 1990. Central America is no longer the central issue for Americans. *Austin American Statesman*, October 21.

Kohut, Andrew, and Roberto Suro. 2006. *No Consensus on Immigration Quandary or Proposed Fixes*. Washington, D.C.: Pew Research Center for the People and the Press and Pew Hispanic Center.

Legomsky, Stephen H. 2000. Fear and loathing in Congress and the courts: Immigration and judicial review. *Texas Law Review* 78: 1612–20.

Lowell, B. Lindsay, and Zhongren Jing. 1994. Unauthorized workers and immigration reform: What can we ascertain from employers? *International Migration Review* 28: 427–48.

Lowell, B. Lindsay, Jay Teachman, and Zhongren Jing. 1995. Unintended consequences of immigration reform: Discrimination and Hispanic employment. *Demography* 32: 617–28.

Martin, Philip L. 1996. *Promises to Keep: Collective Bargaining in California Agriculture*. Ames: Iowa State University Press.

Massey, Douglas S. 2007. *Categorically Unequal: The American Stratification System*. New York: Russell Sage.

———. 2005. Backfire at the Border: Why Enforcement Without Legalization Cannot Stop Illegal Immigration. Cato Institute Trade Policy Analyses 29. Washington, D.C.: Center for Trade Policy Studies, Cato Institute.

Massey, Douglas S., and Katherine Bartley. 2005. The changing legal status distribution of immigrants: A caution. *International Migration Review* 34: 469-84.

Massey, Douglas S., and Nancy A. Denton. 1993. *American Apartheid: Segregation and the making of the underclass*. Cambridge, Mass.: Harvard University Press.

Massey, Douglas S., Katharine M. Donato, and Zai Liang. 1990. Effects of the Immigration Reform and Control Act of 1986: Preliminary data from Mexico. In *Undocumented Migration to the United States: IRCA and the Experience of the 1980s*, ed. Frank D. Bean, Barry Edmonston, and Jeffrey S. Passel, 182–210. Washington, D.C.: Urban Institute.

Massey, Douglas S., Jorge Durand, and Nolane J. Malone. 2002. *Beyond Smoke and Mirrors: Mexican Immigration in an Era of Economic Integration*. New York: Russell Sage.

Nevins, Joseph. 2001. *Operation Gatekeeper: The Rise of the "Illegal Alien" and the Making of the U.S.-Mexico Boundary*. New York: Routledge.

Phillips, Julie A., and Douglas S. Massey. 1999. The new labor market: Immigrants and wages after IRCA. *Demography* 36: 233–46.

Purnell, Thomas, William Idsardi, and John Baugh. 1999. Perceptual and phonetic experiments on American English dialect identification. *Journal of Language and Social Psychology* 18: 10–30.

Roediger, David R. 2005. *Working Toward Whiteness: How America's Immigrants Became White: The Strange Journey from Ellis Island to the Suburbs.* New York: Basic Books.

Riosmena, Fernando. 2004. Return versus settlement among undocumented Mexican migrants, 1980 to 1996. In *Crossing the Border: Research from the Mexican Migration Project,* ed. Jorge Durand and Douglas S. Massey, 265–80. New York: Russell Sage.

Smith, James P., and Barry Edmonston. 1997. *The New Americans: Economic, Demographic, and Fiscal Effects of Immigration.* Washington, D.C.: National Academies Press.

Sorensen, Elaine, and Frank D. Bean. 1994. The Immigration Reform and Control Act and the wages of Mexican origin workers. Evidence from current population surveys. *Social Science Quarterly* 75: 1–17.

Taylor, J. Edward. 1996. IRCA's effects in California agriculture. In *Immigration Reform and U.S. Agriculture,* ed. Philip L. Martin, W. Huffman, R. Emerson, and J. Edward Taylor, 181–206. Oakland: California Division of Agriculture and Natural Resources.

Taylor, J. Edward, Philip L. Martin, and Michael Fix. 1997. *Poverty amid Prosperity: Immigration and the Changing face of Rural California.* Washington, D.C.: Urban Institute Press.

Taylor, J. Edward, and Dawn Thilmany. 1993. Worker turnover, farm labor contractors, and IRCA's impact on the California farm labor market. *American Journal of Agricultural Economics* 75: 350–60.

Turner, Margery A., Fred Freiberg, Eerin B. Godfrey, Carla Herbig, Diane K. Levy, and Robert E. Smith. 2002. *All Other Things Being Equal: A Paired Testing Study of Mortgage Lending Institutions.* Washington, D.C.: U.S. Department of Housing and Urban Development.

U.S. General Accounting Office. 1990. *Immigration Reform: Employer Sanctions and the Question of discrimination.* Washington, D.C.: U.S. Government Printing Office.

Western, Bruce. 2006. *Punishment and Inequality in America.* New York: Russell Sage.

Wilkes, Rima, and John Iceland. 2004. Hypersegregation in the twenty-first century: An update and analysis. *Demography* 41: 23–36.

Zimmermann, Wendy, and Michael Fix. 1998. *Declining Immigrant Applications for Medi-Cal and Welfare Benefits in Los Angeles County.* Washington, D.C.: Urban Institute.

Zolberg, Aristide R. 2006. *A Nation by Design: Immigration Policy in the Fashioning of America.* New York: Russell Sage.

Part III
Engaging Urban Youth in Social Institutions

Chapter 8

Youth Entrepreneurship Training in the Inner City: Overcoming Disadvantage, Engaging Youth in School

LUKE ANDERSON

The National Foundation for Teaching Entrepreneurship (NFTE) provides at-risk urban youth with entrepreneurship training as a means of engaging them in school and improving their life chances, self-esteem, and career aspirations. As program director of NFTE's Chicago office and after several years spent as a graduate student in sociology, I have been working directly with students, teachers, and administrators at 33 of Chicago's most troubled high schools for the past two years. In most urban public school systems throughout the U.S., high schools fail to provide an engaging curriculum, a supportive learning environment, or any serious incentive for students to stay in school for four years, creating unacceptably high dropout rates. The NFTE program fills this educational gap by providing students with a practical application for math, reading, and communication skills and, equally important, by supporting their aspirations beyond high school. NFTE helps to enrich the educational experience by supplying three basic incentives for students to stay engaged in the entrepreneurship program: giving students the freedom to pursue their interests or passions in an academic setting during the writing of a business plan; offering concrete financial rewards through the business plan and a student competition; and providing students with enhanced personal contact with positive role models through a wide range of experiences, including field trips, guest speakers, internships, and, most important, meaningful mentor relationships. These three elements of the program are essential for engaging students in school and can be adapted to many different core subjects and grade levels.

Fractured Learning Environments, Wasted Potential

As you approach Richard Wright High School,[1] the first thing you notice is the noisy group of students crowded around the front door, waiting to pass through the school's security checkpoint. Four or five guards in yellow jackets herd the students through three metal detector lanes, randomly opening bookbags and barking instructions. You smell whiffs of marijuana as you walk through the crowd of teenagers, who are laughing and chatting. Even though the school day officially begins at eight o'clock, students are still trickling in at nine. One teacher who has a first period class tells me he rarely has more than half his students in their seats when the bell rings.

Wright is located in Englewood, one of Chicago's most racially segregated and disadvantaged neighborhoods. Englewood began as an upper-middle-class suburb, initially housing German and Swedish immigrants and Anglo migrants. As the city grew, the neighborhood became predominantly working class, with a massive influx first of Irish factory workers in the mid-nineteenth century and then of African Americans during the Great Migration. Englewood became notorious as a site of race riots, starting with the infamous 1919 riot, which extended from the Loop into the South Side's "Black Belt," when mobs of Irish and other white working men attacked black people and some black men—particularly World War I veterans in uniform—fought back to defend themselves and their community. The area's shift from working-class white to poor black residents was accelerated by unscrupulous "block busting" real estate practices and systemic discrimination against African Americans. The departure of stable employment opportunities, a trend that began after World War II and intensified at the end of the century, left many of Englewood's residents destitute. Almost all of its current residents are African American; 43 percent of the population live below the poverty line. There are 2,473 vacant buildings and 215 empty lots in the neighborhood.

John Evans High School also serves the Englewood section of Chicago's South Side. The standardized test scores of its 1,300 students are regularly ranked among the lowest in the city. Over 400—more than one third of the entire student body—are listed as special education students by Chicago Public Schools (CPS). According to the teachers at Evans, these students are at such low reading and math levels for their age and grade that the school system has concluded they must have some sort of learning disability. However, the actual number of learning disabled students and the nature of their disabilities may never be ascertained, because overworked teachers have so little time to spend with the students and dropout rates are astronomical.

The environment at Evans, like most public high schools on the South Side, is simply not conducive to learning. Smells of mold, mildew, and rust permeate the decrepit building. The hallways echo with shouts and shrieks from both students and security personnel. Evans has perhaps the most visible police presence of any public high school in the city. Each time I have visited, a Chicago Police Department paddy wagon has been parked just outside the front door. One afternoon, as I left the school just before the final bell, I noticed cars parked in the middle of the intersection at either end of the street. Sitting on the hoods or leaning against the car doors were men whom I took to be plainclothes Chicago police detectives, their badges dangling on chains around their necks. I counted 14 officers waiting to greet the students as they left school for the day. When I asked one officer if this was routine, he simply looked away and smiled.

The School of Economics is an equally chaotic scene. It is one of the flagships of CPS's Small Schools Initiative, a program designed to break up massive, comprehensive schools into smaller institutions with more focused curricula. Small Schools is part of the city's larger school reform strategy, Renaissance 2010. The CPS website features a quotation from Mayor Richard M. Daley, who describes the goals of Renaissance 2010: "To turn around Chicago's most troubled elementary and high schools by creating 100 new schools in neighborhoods across the city over the next six years, providing new educational options to underserved communities and relieving school overcrowding in communities experiencing rapid growth." Despite these good intentions, Ren10, as it is known among CPS personnel, has been controversial and faces some opposition from the Chicago Teachers' Union, local school councils, and community leaders concerned with a policy they perceive as abandoning the most troubled and disadvantaged communities in the city.

What was once Metro High School has now been divided into a School of Economics, a School of the Liberal Arts, a School of Management, and a School of the Physical Sciences. Opened in 2002, the School of Economics serves a student body that is almost entirely African American. Despite significant progress in recent years, the environment is not much more conducive to learning than Evans and Wright. Some students sleep in class; others talk among themselves unchecked during the teacher's lesson. Fights are all too commonplace. One teacher there told me that he breaks up at least one fight each day. As is the case at most high schools in Chicago's low-income communities, students must cope with the daily threat of violence on school grounds. In an incident that received virtually no local media coverage, a student at the School of Economics was implicated in the weekend shooting of a youth from an adjacent neighborhood that has been

labeled "Terror Town" by the students because of its high levels of drug-
and gang-related violence. The following Monday, as the final bell rang,
a melee involving more than 40 young African American males broke
out on the school's front steps as Terror Town youths fought with the
students; teachers, administrators, and the rest of the student body
looked on, incapable of stopping the violence. Police and emergency
medical vehicles rushed to the scene of the brawl as a Chicago Police
Department helicopter hovered overhead. As I sat with a handful of
NFTE students in the school's library several days later, they spoke
about the fight as though describing a school basketball game, completely unfazed. When I naively asked if this sort of thing has happened
before, they laughed and related dozens of similar instances involving
vicious fights in school bathrooms, the cafeteria, and on the surrounding streets. When I pressed these students about how it makes them feel
to attend a school where this sort of violence is the norm, they laugh-
ingly conceded that while it may serve as a distraction and negatively
affect their performance in school; they have all been desensitized:
"We're used to it!"

CPS lists the graduation rate at the School of Economics at 68 percent,
actually higher than the citywide average of 54 percent. Between 1991
and 2004 only 39 percent of Chicago's African American male high
school students graduated by age nineteen (Allensworth 2005). Understandably, the noise and chaos in school, coupled with the violence,
stress, and visible effects of urban poverty outside school, leave many of
the students feeling disconnected, angry, and exhausted. Despite the
bravado the students display when they talk about the harsh environments in which they live, their lack of life or career aspirations and poor
performance in school indicate the true toll their reality takes on them.

Violence and an intimidating police presence are common throughout the city school system. After the 2005–2006 school year, Shaker High
School, just three miles from Chicago's affluent Gold Coast neighborhood, doubled its security force. Violent incidents spiked in the school
that year, garnering negative coverage in the local media. While teachers
and administrators at Shaker have dealt with their share of drug- and
gang-related school violence in the past, many teachers attribute this new
surge to the changing character of the school's population. Five years
ago, Shaker's students were predominantly working-class and low-income youth of Mexican and Puerto Rican descent. As Renaissance 2010
has taken shape, several large high schools on Chicago's West Side have
been shut down because of high dropout rates and low student performance. When two major high schools closed in the notoriously destitute
Austin and Englewood sections of the city, each enrolling 1,000–1,500
students, these youth were suddenly left without a neighborhood school.

These students are by and large African American, as well as poor. They are now forced to leave their neighborhoods to attend schools with different populations, social hierarchies, and, most importantly, drug-dealing gangs.

One incident that occurred in February 2007 typifies the tense atmosphere at Shaker. A fight broke out between a Mexican student and an African American student that escalated to a brawl involving dozens of students, police officers, and teachers; the school was locked down for two hours, with no one allowed to enter or leave the building. In the local media coverage, teachers and parents immediately fixated on the racial nature of the fight. It was observed that the Latino students were fighting the black students. What was the offense that started the fight? The Mexican student had stolen the African American student's hat the day before. It was clear to all of the teachers and students with whom I spoke that the simmering animosity between the different racial groups at the school had finally boiled over. One side-effect of Small Schools programs may be an increase in violence in schools that absorb student overflow. Transience among the student body is a common feature at many of CPS' underperforming schools. It is not uncommon for students to attend two or three different high schools during their four years—provided they stay in school that long.

Although vocational programs are intended to connect formal schooling with young people's career aspirations, the dropout rate at such schools as South Central Vocational High demonstrates that these schools also fail to educate low-income African American youth. Students are required to enroll in a three-year major after completing their freshman year. Each major prepares the student for work in a highly specialized field such as cosmetology, horticulture, culinary arts, automobile repair, or business administration. This massive school on the South Side, which enrolls over 2,000 students, is housed in an enormous converted army barracks and armory. Several senior girls told me that of the 800 students in their freshman class, only 200 remain as seniors. When I asked several girls how many of those 200 are going on to college next year, they laughed, looked at one another, and said, "Maybe 20."

What are the root causes of the alienation and discontent felt by so many young people in low-income, inner-city communities? Educators, sociologists, and policy analysts have offered a range of more or less useful explanations linked to possible remedies for the problem. Lack of engagement with school is a symptom of young people feeling abandoned and out of touch with mainstream society. In *The Truly Disadvantaged*, William Julius Wilson debunks arguments that define an "underclass" with a "culture of poverty" to explain the social and spiritual fracture of African American communities in the inner city. Instead, Wilson looks at the concentration effects of poverty when coupled with extreme social isolation. He defines social isolation as "the lack of contact or of sustained interaction with individuals and institutions that represent mainstream society." "Social isolation . . . not only implies that contact between groups of different class and/or racial backgrounds is either lacking or has become increasingly intermittent but that the nature of this contact enhances the effects of living in a highly concentrated poverty area" (Wilson 1987, 60–61). Like most sociologists, Wilson presumes that individual behavior is influenced by those with whom the individual has the most contact, so the concentration and isolation of poor people magnifies the effects of poverty. I share Wilson's view that members of disadvantaged communities such as those on the South Side of Chicago suffer from social isolation; it particularly afflicts students in Chicago's underperforming high schools. This concept suggests one important avenue for enabling youth to escape their isolation and alienation, which so often give rise to deviance and destructive behavior: quality exposure. To remove students from this limited and limiting environment through field trips, internships, guest speakers, and inventive, experiential lesson plans shows them the practical value of education. In the learning environments that continue to exist in Chicago's most disadvantaged neighborhoods, school offers few legitimate means of escaping poverty.

Increasing human capital, as conceived by economists such as Glenn C. Loury and Gary Becker, is also central to enhancing young people's engagement with school and improving their life chances. As Becker puts it: "Schooling, a computer training course, expenditures on medical care, and lectures on the virtues of punctuality and honesty also are capital. That is because they raise earnings, improve health, or add to a person's good habits over much of his lifetime" (Becker 1975). In the current educational context of "No Child Left Behind" and the ubiquitous and nearly exclusive use of standardized test scores to gauge student achievement, we could argue that this sort of investment in real human capital does not exist on any large scale. Providing real-world experiences and contacts with individuals from outside the students' environment does not take priority when principals must have students prepare for standardized tests so their failure does not affect the school's funding or probationary status. Nonetheless, increasing human and social capital may be a means of raising students' expectations of themselves and improving outcomes once they graduate from high school.

The Chicago public schools serve over 430,000 students in 511 elementary schools and 103 high schools. During the early 1990s, CPS was panned as one of the worst big-city school districts in the nation. So bleak was the state of Chicago's schools that Mayor Daley was given control of the entire system. In 2001, Daley hired Arne Duncan as CEO of

CPS, with the mandate to rejuvenate a school system that was failing more than half of the students enrolled. Duncan began to implement a series of reforms aimed at making the widely variable school curricula more uniform, increasing student literacy, and providing new experiential learning activities for students (Elmore, Grossman, and King 2006, 2). These reforms wrought significant improvements in student test scores between 2001 and 2005. Almost 50 percent of elementary students met or exceeded state standards on the Illinois Standards Achievement Test (ISAT), jumping 10 percentage points from the test scores in 2001. In Illinois all eleventh graders are required to take the Prairie State Achievement Exam (PSAE), which tests achievement in math, reading, and science. In 2005, 31 percent of CPS students met or exceeded state standards on the PSAE compared to 27 percent in 2001. However, these overall gains diminish or evaporate when we consider the wide variations in test scores between schools. The number of students meeting state standards ranged from 48 percent in schools located on Chicago's North Side to only 20 percent in some of the city's most troubled schools. Only 29 out of Chicago's 103 high schools had more than 30 percent of their students meeting state standards in 2005. Only 12 had more than half of their students earning the minimum ACT score required to attend a four-year university. Despite the school reformers' best intentions, the system continues to fail the majority of students of color from impoverished communities. According to a September 2005 article in the *Chicago Sun-Times*, only 54 percent of Chicago public high school students who started school in 1999 had graduated by 2003. The proportion for African Americans was reportedly well under 50 percent. These high dropout rates and low achievement scores have a devastating impact on students as they face severe obstacles to finding employment, earning a living wage, and participating in civic life.

Within this poor substitute for a learning environment, there are students who do want to achieve. Despite what the mainstream media tell us about the pervasive apathy and lack of motivation among African American teenagers, disadvantaged students can rise to take advantage of the opportunities that are offered to them. Through my time as program director of the NFTE office serving the students in these Chicago high schools, I have seen the potential of many young, underprivileged students when actively engaged with school.

Making School Relevant

The National Foundation for Teaching Entrepreneurship (NFTE) is an international nonprofit organization whose official mission is to teach entrepreneurship to young people from low-income communities in order to enhance their economic productivity by improving their academic, business, and life skills. NFTE's strategy for achieving this mission is to partner with schools, community-based organizations, and universities; create innovative, experiential curricula; train and support teachers and youth workers; and provide supportive alumni services. This strategy, while expressly intended to teach the basic concepts of entrepreneurship and the market economy, also serves to decrease social isolation while increasing human capital among NFTE students. A unique aspect of NFTE's curriculum is that every student who goes through the program writes a business plan generated from an idea of his or her choosing.

NFTE's approach grew out of the experiences of its founder, Steve Mariotti. After working as an executive for a major U.S. automaker and founding a successful import/export business in New York, Mariotti decided to become a high school teacher. In the mid-1980s, he worked in some of the most troubled and underperforming high schools in the South Bronx and Bedford-Stuyvesant section of Brooklyn. After a frustrating and demoralizing year of failed attempts to reach his students, Mariotti realized that his pupils only tuned in to his lectures when he spoke about his business experiences. He began giving weekly lectures on marketing and financial concepts and soon realized he was on to something. He organized a field trip to New York's wholesale district, gave each of his students $50 to spend on merchandise to be sold at the school, and NFTE was born. Officially receiving a non-profit 501(c)3 status in New York City in 1987, NFTE has reached over 150,000 young people and trained more than 4,100 Certified Entrepreneurship Teachers. Currently NFTE has active programs in 25 states and 13 countries. In May 2003, NFTE opened the Chicago office and successfully launched a partnership with the Chicago Public Schools. NFTE's curriculum has been adopted as the lead business curriculum within CPS, and during the 2006–2007 academic school year we are working with 1,800 students in 34 schools and 3 community-based organizations, bringing our cumulative total to more than 5,000 young people served by June 2007. Looking ahead, NFTE Chicago has developed an aggressive growth plan and aims to reach 13,200 youth by 2010.

Every few years NFTE publishes a new edition of its award-winning textbook on how to own and operate a small business. The textbook covers many basic financial and marketing concepts and offers how-to instructions on the daily operation of a small business, from keeping income statements to the rules of a good sales call. In the classroom, students learn about the market economy and are encouraged to come up with their own idea for a business that, realistically, they could operate. While the educational incentive is to learn business sense and to improve math and reading skills, creating a business plan is more of an exercise in visualizing future success based on the student's talents and interests. Students' ideas for their businesses range across all industries, including music production, pet care, fashion design, food service, photography, lawn care, and computer repair. Students often focus on niche industries, such as lizard breeding, sneaker customization, or teen athletic networking sites. The key to the business plan is that every student comes up with an idea based on his or her passion or interest, and fleshes out all the details during the course of the school year. Their plans are often the main class project and determine their grades. The business plan project is intended to create a sense of ownership over the student's future occupation, to turn a job into a career over which the student has control. Steve Mariotti often remarks that through creating a business plan students are able to understand the importance of ownership, the rationale being that in a free market the real power lies in whoever owns the means of production. The lack of ownership in an impoverished community, whether it is a home, business, or other viable asset, is one of the main barriers to significant wealth creation. Mariotti is fond of referring to this lack of business ownership as "the great civil rights issue of our era."

The NFTE course ends with an in-class competition during the last month of school. Students are required to dress in formal business attire and present their business plan in a 22-page Power Point template to their classmates or, in some places, the entire school. Typically, I judge these competitions along with local entrepreneurs, NFTE alumni, and businesspeople. The competition is an important component of the NFTE curriculum because it provides students with the essential experience of presenting their ideas coherently. The competitions often have small monetary rewards of $100 or $200; however, the money seems secondary to the pride students take in successfully communicating their vision for a business plan. The NFTE business plan template includes slides about Career and Educational Goals and a Philanthropy Plan that serve as a statement of purpose for many students. They are rewarded for critically analyzing their strengths and weaknesses and then devising a plan to capitalize on those strengths and fortify those weaknesses for the sake of profit and the good of the community.

Integral to the NFTE curriculum is a strong sense that each student is valuable and has a positive contribution to make. This orientation is reinforced through casting low-income communities as places that students should look to improve and give back to, rather than flee in order to achieve success. As sociologist Pedro Noguera (1996) found in his study of a public high school in northern California, many well-intentioned programs aimed at supporting disadvantaged black youth actually reinforce their marginalized status and cement an identity as the inferior, victimized "other." In order to combat this view, NFTE students take a field trip within their own community called an "opportunity walk." Teachers and NFTE staff walk with 20–30 students through the neighborhood surrounding the school, through the vacant lots and empty buildings, past liquor stores and fast food restaurants. The purpose is to force students to reexamine their community critically and ask themselves tough questions: for example, why are there so many places to buy junk food and liquor, yet no places to buy books? The students then imagine what store or business they might like to open. They are prompted to ask: what's missing from my community?

The NFTE curriculum has been embraced by CPS administrators and principals who have recognized the value and resources the program adds to the classroom experience. The district's vocational education department, Education-to-Careers (ETC), has named NFTE as the standard business curriculum in 16 of Chicago's most troubled high schools. First, NFTE identifies a school where at least 40 percent of the student body are low-income as classified by CPS; most of the schools where NFTE Chicago works serve almost entirely low-income students. Next NFTE identifies teachers who are able to integrate NFTE into their class and trains them at a four-day program implementation seminar called NFTE University. The flexible curriculum can be adapted to classes in business, economics, social studies, mathematics, and vocational subjects. Throughout the school, NFTE provides professional development to the teachers and a myriad of supports to the students.

Ideally, NFTE students would all start their own businesses, but the reality is that many do not. Lack of sufficient start-up capital and lack of time, given that they are full-time high school students, are among the barriers they face. But the program's aim is not to turn youth into entrepreneurs. The main goals are to get NFTE students engaged in school, educate them about basic business concepts, and raise their career and life aspirations. This last goal is critical, as many NFTE students enter the program without having a strong sense of what they might be capable of achieving in their careers. Several studies have been conducted to test the program's effectiveness in improving students' life skills and their educational and career goals. From 2001 to 2003, researchers from the Harvard Graduate School of Education, led by Michael Nakkula, Ed.D, administered a comprehensive survey to 312 NFTE and non-NFTE students at six Boston-area public high schools. Utilizing questionnaires completed at the start and end of the school year, the survey was designed to test the effects of the NFTE program on academic and psychosocial development. The researchers found significant differences in responses related to college and career aspirations and interest in school. Over the year, NFTE students' interest in college increased 32 percent while that of the non-NFTE comparison group declined by 17 percent. Occupational aspirations were measured by the level of education required to achieve the professional goals to which the students aspire. Before the course, NFTE students had career aspirations requiring less education than those in the comparison group. After the course, the NFTE students occupational aspirations increased by 44 percent, while the comparison group only increased by 10 percent (Nakkula 2004).

In 1998, the Koch Foundation sponsored research addressing the impact of the program on NFTE alumni aged eighteen to twenty-eight. A total of 765 young adults from Washington, D.C., and New York City were included in the study. Half had gone through a NFTE program; the other half had never participated in a NFTE course. Utilizing a randomized control design, researchers looked at a number of variables tracking subjects' occupations, career aspirations, and so on. Among NFTE alumni, researchers found significant jumps in the young adults' desire to start a business, become an economically productive member of society, and attend college (Koch 1998a, 1998b).

My experiences in the field have shown the substantial benefits of the NFTE curriculum. Three components are vital to its effectiveness: the possibility of financial rewards, pursuing a passion, and personal contact with mentors. First, the hook to getting these students excited about NFTE lies in the immediate financial gains they stand to make. At the end of each school year, NFTE holds a citywide business plan competition on the Kellogg School of Management's campus in downtown Chicago. Here the top students from each class compete for over $3,000 in venture capital funding. These immediate gains do motivate youth, but not nearly as much as the promise of the income they stand to earn from expanding their business or going to college. At South Central, I have seen students tearful at not winning the in-class business plan competition. Jennifer Jones, a senior at South Central, combined her natural charisma with her contacts in the local music scene to launch a talent agency and party-promoting business in the fall of 2006. Jennifer's company hosts three or four concerts per year. She recently won NFTE's 2007 Young Entrepreneur of the Year Award, earning a $1,000 grant and a free trip to New York City to be recognized at NFTE's Annual Awards Gala.

The potential monetary rewards that serve as an initial incentive for students to become involved in the competition are soon superseded by students' own interests in their projects. In April 2007, during CPS Spring Break, NFTE Chicago held an advanced camp for 22 of the most dedicated students from around the city. BizCamp, as it is known among the students, is an interactive week of seminars, workshops, guest speakers, and one-on-one coaching, capped by a business plan competition at the end of the week. A stipend of $200 was offered to each student for attending all five days. NFTE Chicago was allowed to use a state-of-the-art "smart" classroom at Kellogg's Chicago campus for the camp. As Noguera (1996) found, at-risk youth can make solid educational gains when provided with supportive teachers and mentors.

Like Noguera's experimental program, BizCamp was facilitated by a great instructor who emphasized new-age visualization techniques and positive energy and made sure to give each student a chance to participate fully and receive personal attention. In this supportive atmosphere, students arrived early and prepared to work. Students were treated to guest lectures by Ralph Faison, CEO of AndrewCorp, a major telecommunications company, Sharan Tash, a consultant specializing in networking and public relations, and Craig Huffman, an African American who cofounded Ascendance Partners, a large real estate firm specializing in the development of properties on the South Side. When it comes to guest speakers and mentors, NFTE tries to find as many people of color as possible; however, a more important criterion is to find someone who can engage directly with the students and make a business concept or personal history relevant. Students perfected their business plans through one-on-one coaching with mentors from Fifth Third, a large Midwestern bank. The camp created a cohesive group dynamic and atmosphere of mutual respect, as it gave participating students access to institutions with which they would normally have no contact. While the students enjoyed the camp thoroughly, the stipend was a tremendous incentive for them to take full advantage of the opportunity.

Second, the NFTE program gives students the opportunity to pursue a project in which they have a personal stake and feel a compelling interest. While we do offer venture funding as prizes for our business plan competitions, money is not the sole motivating factor. Students are engaged because they are working on something about which they are passionate. As program director, I am constantly advising students to create a business plan involving something that they enjoy doing or their business will not succeed.

One of NFTE Chicago's most successful students is Lawrence Yamoah, who is entering Howard University in the fall of 2007 to major in business administration. He graduated from John Williams College Prep, one of NFTE Chicago's higher achieving schools on the South Side. The population is almost entirely African American, but because of the school's policy of selective enrollment, only about 55 percent are low-income; at most NFTE Chicago schools, the overwhelming majority of students are poor as well as black. Lawrence is an artist and a hip hop devotee. Like most teenagers, he is very concerned with fashion and his own appearance. His business, In Touch Customz, a shoe customization service he runs out of his parents' basement, began when he was a junior in his NFTE Small Business Ownership class. Always a very quiet, thoughtful student, when Lawrence goes into his business plan presentation he exudes confidence, cracking jokes and engaging the audience. Lawrence leaped into the limelight last May when he won NFTE Chicago's City-Wide Competition. He won over $1,200 from the Chicago competition, appeared on the front page of the *Chicago Sun-Times*, was featured in a personal interest news story on the local ABC news affiliate, and was flown to New York to compete in NFTE's national competition, where he was a crowd favorite and placed third overall, earning an additional $2,500. He has now become a superstar at his school. His business involves an ingenious method of painting custom designs on sneakers that is guaranteed not to crack. He has a Website, and so far has generated over $6,000 in profit. I have gotten to know Lawrence and dozens like him very well over the past two years. The students continually remark that they enjoy the process of running their business as much as the net profits projected on their income statement and the return on investment they have calculated.

The third and equally important way NFTE engages kids in school is through increased personal attention. NFTE Chicago has a partnership with the Kellogg School of Management, and in 2005 it established a mentoring program in which Kellogg MBA students visit NFTE classrooms on a weekly basis and coach the students on their business plans. Aside from being a unique opportunity for mutual cultural exchange, these mentoring sessions engender self-confidence in NFTE students. It might seem difficult for a NFTE student to establish a meaningful relationship with an affluent, well-dressed, articulate member of the United States ruling class, yet mentor relationships develop remarkably quickly as the two communicate through the common language of economics and markets. The NFTE students, at first shy and withdrawn, open up when asked to explain some aspect of their business plan. The eight schools that regularly receive Kellogg mentor visits tend to produce the most competition winners. When these students see outsiders taking an interest in them and asking them what they want or what they are thinking, it raises their level of engagement with school. The key is that NFTE students have a higher level of control over the subject matter in the business curriculum. One of our best teachers is fond of saying to his students: "If you're ever bored in my class, it's your fault for not changing your business plan." Most students take on this sort of challenge when given the opportunity.

NFTE provides dozens of other opportunities for intensive, extracurricular mentoring relationships. During the lead-up to the citywide competition every year, competitors are required to attend a business plan coaching session at Goldman Sachs or Citigroup. Like the Kellogg program, these sessions give the students entrée into a world quite different from their own. Every detail of the experience, from working in a plush wood-paneled office on the 73rd floor of the Sears Tower to receiving expert assistance from financial advisors, helps students conceive of a wider range of future possibilities for themselves.

Another wildly popular program is the JobOne Internship program started by the Rotary Club of Chicago, NFTE, and Chicago Public Schools. Through this program, 100 students from low-income communities are offered paid eight-week internships at major banks, law firms, utility companies, museums, and universities. Each student accepted into the program must attend three Saturday morning job-readiness workshops and is assigned a Rotary Club member as a mentor. In the weeks before the start of the internship, the Rotarian takes the student to lunch and meets with the student in his or her office to prepare the student for the work world.

NFTE Chicago works to bring local entrepreneurs, executives, and business leaders into our classrooms on a regular basis. Through a 2006 partnership with the Chicagoland Entrepreneurial Center, a division of the Chamber of Commerce, NFTE has brought in dozens of local African American, Latino, or female entrepreneurs who operate small businesses in the Chicago community. In addition, neighborhood Rotary Clubs, small business associations, and small banks have acknowledged the importance of the program, providing guest speakers, competition judges, and classroom funding.

When mentoring and internships are coupled with the unique in-class curriculum, students perform better and see the practical applications of schooling. Recent research on the astronomical dropout rates in big-city school systems suggests that students are bored in school and see little reason to graduate; the long-term financial returns seem remote and uncertain. NFTE attempts to engage youth by facing the critical situation they confront in a direct way, by attempting to show that they can escape poverty by developing their academic skills. The NFTE curriculum and the program's extracurricular supports provide students with a rationale for pursuing their education. Through internships, guest speakers, and field trips, NFTE is able to increase students' contact with individuals and institutions that represent mainstream society. The program diminishes the students' social isolation while investing in their human capital. Entrepreneurship and business skills are the vehicle through which NFTE motivates students to move from passive place-holders to active participants in their education. The NFTE formula for effecting change in students' lives has been successful for the disadvantaged youth it serves and can be replicated in other places and settings.

References

Allensworth, Elaine. 2005. Graduation and dropout trends in Chicago: A look at cohorts of students from 1991 through 2004. *Consortium on Chicago School Research* (January).

Becker, Gary. 1975. *Human Capital: A Theoretical and Empirical Analysis, with Special Reference to Education.* 2nd ed. New York: National Bureau of Economic Research, distributed by Columbia University Press.

Elmore, Richard, Allen S. Grossman, and Caroline King. 2006. Managing the Chicago Public Schools. Public Education Leadership Project at Harvard University. June.

Koch Foundation. 1998a. Entrepreneurship for Young Adults: A National Evaluation of Entrepreneurship Training. New York. http://nfte.com/impact/kochresearch.asp

———. 1998b. Evaluation report: New York City and the National Foundation for Teaching Entrepreneurship program. New York. http://nfte.com/impact/kochresearch.asp

Nakkula, Michael. 2004. Initiating, Leading and Feeling in Control of One's Fate. Project IF: Inventing the Future. Harvard Graduate School of Education, June. http://nfte.com/impact/harvardresearch.asp

Noguera, Pedro. 1996. Responding to the crisis confronting California's black male youth: Providing support without further marginalization. *Journal of Negro Education* 65 (2) (Spring): 219–36.

Wilson, William Julius. 1987. *The Truly Disadvantaged: The Inner City, the Underclass, and Public Policy.* Chicago: University of Chicago Press.

Chapter 9

Black Male Students and Reflections on Learning and Teaching

L. JANELLE DANCE

In *Pedagogy of the Oppressed* (1999) and *Pedagogy of Hope* (2004), Paulo Freire distinguishes between the reading and teaching of the word and the reading and teaching of the world. Freire implores educators to respect the local realities in which students are enmeshed and to teach in a dialogic manner that facilitates critical reflection in both the educator (teacher-as-learner) and the "educand" (student-as-teacher). Before or in tandem with learning to decode written words (or studying science, social studies, or other subjects), students from marginalized backgrounds need to be empowered to read their worlds. Freire states, "The teaching of reading and writing of the word to a person missing the critical exercise of reading and rereading the world is scientifically, politically, and pedagogically crippled" (2004, 78–79). Literacy devoid of critical reflection is of little use to students. Teaching words and teaching students to name their worlds involve dialogue, and "dialogue cannot exist without humility" (1999, 71), Freire asks rhetorically:

How can [an educator] dialogue if [s/he] always projects ignorance onto others and never perceives [his/her] own? How can [an educator] dialogue, if [s/he] regards [him/herself] as a case apart from others—mere "its" in whom [s/he] cannot recognize the other "I"s? . . . Men and women who lack humility (or have lost it) cannot come to [students], cannot be their partners in [the] naming of the world.

By imploring educators to understand the reading of the world in which students find themselves, to be or become partners in the naming of students' worlds, Freire emphasizes respect for students' existential situation—not in the abstract, philosophical sense, but in the literal sense of learning about the local contexts in which students are enmeshed and the experiences, questions, and perspectives that they bring to learning. As Freire demonstrates, critical pedagogy aims to empower students not only to learn but also to emancipate themselves and to transform their world.

In this brief essay, I emphasize the importance of reading students' worlds alongside them, explore what it means to see ourselves in the young people we teach or mentor, explain the vital significance of both acknowledging and seeing beyond the intersecting labels of race, class or status, and gender that converge in the stigmatization of young, black males in the inner city, and outline what educators and schools can do to enable these students to defy expectations and succeed academically.

Reflection Back and Forth

The reading of the world is always a work in progress because the world is a dynamic place, even at the everyday level. A key ingredient of my success in recording and relaying the voices of marginalized students flows from the ability to humble myself, that is, to quiet my social scientific theoretical frames of reference and to listen attentively to students. The main ingredient, however, is my ability to look at students and see my own humanity reflected back. During the fall terms of 2004 and 2006, I had the opportunity to conduct research in Sweden in schools that have substantial ethnic minority and refugee populations from Middle Eastern countries. I realized that my previous work with African American and Latino students in the U.S. did not guarantee my success with different ethnic minority groups in a different society. I relied primarily on their willingness to engage with a newcomer and my genuine interest in the school lives of ethnic minority students—my deep respect for how they read, understand, and experience their day-to-day situations within and beyond the walls of the school. Respect for the complex humanity of youth should go without saying, but interviews with marginalized students reveal that many teachers and other representatives of mainstream institutions entirely fail to *see* them. Students regularly complain that teachers see "black" or "dangerous" or "failure" instead of recognizing them as individuals worthy of respect.

Mutual respect and partnering with students in reading the world involves reflection back and forth between educator and student. According to Sara Lawrence Lightfoot, mutual recognition is indispensable to effective teaching and real learning, yet it is often absent in relations between mainstream teachers and non-mainstream students. In Lightfoot's eloquent and poignant words:

In schools where teachers do not see their own destinies in the eyes of their [students] there's unlikely to be good teaching going on. In some sense, you have to see yourself reflected in the eyes of those you teach or at least your destiny reflected [in those you teach]. [By destiny I mean] your future after you're long gone. Part of what you're doing [as a teacher] in this [schooling] process is handing it over, is sharing what it is you know and how you perceive the world and your angle on it. What we might call the most pernicious discriminatory behavior on the part of teachers, which is often expressed quite passively, is, it seems to me, when teachers can't imagine themselves in their students at all. When there is no reflection back and forth. (Moyer 1987, quoted in Dance 2002, 83)

Deliberately distancing herself from the all-too-prevalent assumption that effective teaching requires that teacher and students mirror one another by sharing a common racial-ethnic identity, Lightfoot shifts the term "reflection" to a quality of mutual recognition that enables dialogue and promotes reflective inquiry on the world.

Lightfoot's statement leads to another rhetorical question that may be added to those Freire posed: How can an educator engage in dialogue if there is no reflection back and forth? The ability of a teacher to see her/himself in students is an important ingredient for productive student-teacher relationships. Why do so many students complain that their teachers looked at them and saw a "thug" or "gangster" instead? The intersectional paradigm can shed light upon what gets in the way of educators' abilities to see themselves reflected back in the eyes of the Black and Latino boys they teach.

The Intersectional Paradigm

An understanding of what such scholars as Kimberlé Crenshaw (1989) and Patricia Hill Collins (2000) call the intersectional paradigm is very helpful when working with racial-ethnic minority students from segregated, low-income communities. Some teachers and mentors arrive at this understanding intuitively, without ever enrolling in a sociology course. In my 2002 book *Tough Fronts: The Impact of Street Culture on Schooling*, I explore in depth how Ms. Bronzic, who teaches sixth grade in an inner-city elementary school, and the mentors of the Paul Robeson Institute (PRI), an enrichment program in Boston, interact with their black male students in a way that deconstructs and challenges deep-seated stereotypes and nightmares about the intersections of "blackness," "maleness," and "young poor people from the inner city." The PRI mentors and Ms. Bronzic do not pretend to be color-blind, gender-blind, or class-blind, but instead attend to the complex humanity of students who, due to intersecting systems of discrimination and oppression, have been socially stigmatized as thug-like things.

The intersectional paradigm is an analytical framework that seeks to explain the interrelationships of social systems of ethnicity and/or race, social class and/or status, gender, age and other social divisions (Crenshaw 1989; Collins 2000; Weber 2001). The concept was initially developed to capture the complex oppression and marginalization of Black women, who are negatively affected not by race *or* gender *or* class singly or even additively but, instead, by the intertwined social divisions of race *and* gender *and* class. The intersectional paradigm can be applied to other groups as well. When the interrelations of race, social class, religious affiliation, and gender refer to "white," "middle/upper-class," "Protestant," and "male," these intersecting dimensions typically confer esteem and privilege on the individuals who "wear" them. For example, the substance abuse history of President George W. Bush is viewed quite differently from the substance abuse history of Marion Barry, former mayor of Washington, D.C., who is "middle-class," "Protestant," and "male," but "*black.*" Likewise, the adulterous behavior of President William Jefferson Clinton did not prevent him from pursuing and winning two terms in the White House. But imagine Hillary Rodham Clinton, who is "white," "middle/upper-class," and "Protestant," but "*female*," daring to run for president if she, like her husband, had committed adultery multiple times. As "white," "middle/upper-class," "Protestant" "men," presidents Bush and Clinton wear social identities that defy stigmatization; they expect to be seen as complex human beings who made a few mistakes.

The students I studied for *Tough Fronts* are labeled "young," "Black" or "Latino," "male," "poor," "inner-city," and "at-risk." According to my interviews and observations, teachers and other authority figures view these students as problems waiting to happen. The students tell stories of being reduced to mistakes that they have not made and have no intention of making. And, once they make a single mistake, they become that mistake.

The Weighty Baggage of Stigmatization

Three stories from *Tough Fronts* reveal how young Black and Latino male students are defined not by their individual promise but by educators' stereotypes about young males of color from segregated, impoverished communities. Malik, an African American eighth grader, tells a story of being judged by his science teacher as a thug-like special education student incapable of successfully completing a science project until he does so without her help (but with the help of an outside tutor). Robbie, a Latino (Dominican) American tenth grader, shares stories of negative encounters with the police, not because he has engaged in criminal acts but because the police do not recognize Robbie's right to challenge unfair treatment by the authorities of the state. Malcolm, an African American ninth grader to whom I devote an entire chapter, shares his frustration about teachers who do not go beyond the official curriculum to teach more complex content, and then treat him like a troublemaker when he requests a more advanced, culturally relevant curriculum. My research and that of others (Ferguson 2000; Stanton-Salazar 2001; Carter 2005) suggests that if Malik, Robbie, and Malcolm were middle-class, suburban, white male students facing the same predicaments they would be viewed as individuals instead of stereotypes.

During the countless hours I spent hanging out with and interviewing students like Malik, Robbie, and Malcolm, I observed that stigmatization was like "baggage" that teachers and other representatives of the mainstream constantly offered to young Black (and Latino) males. Every effort these students made to escape the assumptions of academic failure that their racial-ethnic identities, class position, and gender carried was met with a negative response. Malik's teacher was constantly and metaphorically running beside him saying, *"Excuse me Malik, but you dropped this!"*—meaning, *"You're a poor, black and male special education student destined to be a thug!"* From Malcolm's perspective, his teachers were frequently and metaphorically running alongside him repeating, *"Sorry Malcolm, I believe you dropped something!"*—meaning, *"You're young, poor, black, and male. Don't ask for a more challenging curriculum . . . be satisfied with what you have!"* What makes Ms. Bronzic and the PRI mentors especially effective is that they figuratively run alongside students like Malik and Malcolm and say, *"Put that stigmatization baggage down! Or, don't pick that baggage up, that's not yours! That's not you!"* This deliberate defiance of imposed cultural scripts by educators enables students to learn, rather than pushing them into marginal positions where learning is impossible.

Unlearning Implicit Racism in Schools

What do this Jewish American female teacher and the African American male mentors at the Paul Robeson Institute have in common? They look at their students and see their own complex humanity reflected back. Although their social positions and, in the case of several mentors, their class backgrounds differ markedly from those of the youth they teach and mentor, they see their own destinies and legacies reflected in these young people. Bronzic and the PRI mentors are aware of the harsh realities of inner-city life, but they actively resist weighing down young Black and Latino males with stereotypical baggage and help them unload any baggage they may already be carrying. By this I do not mean that they merely avoid stereotyping young Black and Latino males. They actively avoid the implicit biases associated with the intersections of "young," "male," "poor," inner-city," "at-risk," and black or brown. No one, including Bronzic and the PRI mentors, is entirely free from implicit biases; rather, I suggest, they are aware enough of prevalent societal problems not to act on those negative assumptions, and to make deliberate efforts to counteract their pervasive effects on students.

We all make implicit associations, as we learn from results derived from the Implicit Association Tests administered online by Harvard and other cooperating universities (www.implicit.harvard.edu or www .projectimplicit.net). The challenge for educators is to teach in a manner that does not reify the implicit associations we possess and does not objectify our students. Bronzic focuses on the complex humanity of each child she teaches regardless of the tough postures and "ghetto" demeanors the child may present. She sees her job as nurturing and educating them, rather than imposing low expectations and burdensome stereotypes on them. In interviews, Malcolm articulated that he felt recognized as an individual when Bronzic would pull him aside and request him to redo assignments that did not represent his best work. The PRI students also conveyed how they felt seen, regardless whether mentors were admonishing so-called "bad" behavior or praising accomplishments. Following the lead of Bronzic and the PRI mentors, what can educators and school officials do to enable young Black and Latino male students to succeed despite the many obstacles they face?

First, educators must comprehend the full complexity of the situation in which these boys find themselves. Teachers and other school officials must understand that young, Black, and Latino males from segregated, impoverished inner-city communities are maligned through the combination of these socially devalued identities. A color-blind, gender-blind, class-blind approach not only ignores the real burdens these students carry but glosses over how they cope with mutually reinforcing stereotypes.

Although young males of color from low-income communities share similar existential situations, they have distinct, individual ways of responding to multiple oppressions, including going with the flow, resisting the flow, giving up, fighting back, protecting others, bullying others, being a part of positive social networks, getting enmeshed in negative social networks, acting tough, being tough, being afraid, and so on. They may deploy different strategies in different situations, or shift from one to another as their existential realities change over time. Teachers must work with individual students at the same time that they acknowledge the systems of oppression that structure and influence students' lives. At best, they can reinforce students' positive coping strategies and support their resilient responses to the obstacles they face.

Second, educators should create opportunities for all students from segregated communities to learn about dominant group cultural codes without demeaning the experiences the students bring to the learning process (Delpit 1995). For example, Bronzic views it as her responsibility to help her students acquire mainstream cultural capital, such as writing and reading in standard English about topics that arise from their multi-dimensional social positioning. She does so through various types of literacy assignments in which she dialogically teaches students to read their worlds and their words:

> I never know where [discussion about a book] is going to go because I have a certain framework but if [students] go off into certain tangents because they bring in issues that they're dealing with that have . . . meaning for them [that's allowed] . . . [W]e might go for four, five, six weeks on a book. I mean we go into it so deeply . . . and get into such heavy duty discussions that it's incredible. (Dance 2002, 82)

In-depth discussion of written texts enables students simultaneously to decode mainstream culture and articulate their own perspectives, recreating the naming process literacy entails and making it their own.

At the same time that educators enable students to grasp the tools of mainstream culture, they should support viable alternatives closer to home and provide opportunities for youth in segregated communities to join positive social networks. The mentors and teachers at PRI, who include graduate students, college professors, university administrators, businesspeople, and working-class laborers, link young black male students to valuable social networks. Males and females of color may especially benefit from groups and activities that address their gender-specific experiences and difficulties. Educators and schools should appreciate and utilize the power of positive rituals. The mentors at PRI begin every Saturday morning session with empowering words and poems read in unison by students and mentors while standing in a circle. During this "Circle of Love," students are asked to come to the center to receive constructive critique and praise.

Third, educators and mentors should learn how to read their students' world by spending time in the communities from which they come. Educators may attend neighborhood churches, community centers, recreation centers like the local YMCA or Boys and Girls Clubs, youth leagues and sports activities, and meetings of grassroots organizations. If educators do not have the time, social skills, or will to spend time in the communities from which their students come, then, at the very least, they should show respect for how students understand and interpret their worlds. This sort of "reading of the world" may be done through classroom activities; for helpful examples, see books such as Mike Rose's *Possible Lives: The Promise of Public Education in America* (1995).

When it comes to disciplining students, which is as serious a factor as academics in alienating young men of color from schools, school officials should pay attention to the "experts." Students themselves have insights into which disciplinary measures are effective and which more often backfire. Many adults in and around schools have excellent relationships with students and positive approaches to providing discipline. Often these experts work in the school and share the community origins of students. While conducting ethnographic research in an inner-city school in Philadelphia, I frequently observed that Ms. Johnson—whose job was to operate the elevator—was one of the most productive disciplinarians in the school. While the school police would chase, yell at, and "manhandle" students who would then yell back at them, Johnson would invoke the power of "I know your grandmamma raised you better"— that is, the power of community connection. In response, students would often compose themselves and say, "Sorry, Ms. Johnson!" Expertise about positive disciplinary measures can also be found among those who work in neighborhood organizations, youth centers, sports clubs, and other community-based programs and activities that attract young males outside of school.

We need to all support structural changes that will strengthen public education, including school reforms such as the Comer Model, the Talent Development Model, and other measures aimed at making school settings more personable, inviting, teachable, and educative. Structural changes are the most important for facilitating school success. But teachers and community activists can take many constructive actions without the approval of school boards, state legislatures, and federal mandates. The most important is to connect with young people themselves. Young Black and Latino male students report that effective educators act on an explicit association that has the power to keep negative stereotypes and implicit associations in check. Students defined as Black or Latino, young, male, poor, inner-city, and at-risk are first and foremost complex individuals. Effective educators act uon the explicit belief that, though devalued by the mainstream, Black and Latino males are invaluable students who cope with burdens in their own ways and have strengths, insights, and promise that defy the limits imposed on their lives. We must look at them and see our own humanity reflected back, engage in dialogue, and critically reflect on our shared world and our unique and varied ways of interpreting it. Educators and mentors must partner with students as they name their worlds.

References

Carter, Prudence. 2005. *Keepin' It Real: School Success Beyond Black and White.* Oxford: Oxford University Press.

Collins, Patricia Hill. 2000. *Black Feminist Thought: Knowledge, Consciousness and the Politics of Empowerment.* New York: Routledge.

Crenshaw, Kimberlé. 1989. Demarginalizing the intersection of race and sex: A Black feminist critique of antidiscrimination doctrine, feminist theory and antiracist politics. *University of Chicago Legal Forum*: 139–67. Reprinted in *The Politics of Law: A Progressive Critique*, ed. David Kairys, 195–217. 2nd ed. New York: Pantheon, 1990.

Dance, L. Janelle. 2002. *Tough Fronts: The Impact of Street Culture on Schooling*. New York: Routledge Falmer.

Delpit, Lisa. 1995. *Other People's Children: Cultural Conflict in the Classroom*. New York: New Press.

Ferguson, Ann Arnett. 2000. *Bad Boys: Public Schools in the Making of Black Masculinity*. Ann Arbor: University of Michigan Press.

Freire, Paulo. 2004. *Pedagogy of Hope: Reviving Pedagogy of the Oppressed*. Trans. Robert R. Barr. New York: Continuum.

———.1999. *Pedagogy of the Oppressed*. Trans. Myra Bergman Ramos. New York: Continuum.

Moyer, Bill. 1987. Interview with Sara Lawrence Lightfoot. *A World of Ideas*. Mystic Fire Direct Video.

Rose, Mike. 1995. *Possible Lives: The Promise of Public Education in America*. New York: Penguin.

Stanton-Salazar, Ricardo D. 2001. *Manufacturing Hope and Despair: The School and Kin Support Networks of U.S.-Mexican Youth*. New York: Teachers College Press.

Weber, Lynn. 2001. *Understanding Race, Class, Gender, and Sexuality: A Conceptual Framework*. Boston: McGraw-Hill.

Chapter 10

Fighting like a Ballplayer: Basketball as a Strategy Against Social Disorganization

SCOTT N. BROOKS

Many inner-city black neighborhoods in South Philadelphia are variations of the 'hood—places with high rates of poverty, violence, single-headed households, drug dealing, and premature death. Here and in similar urban American neighborhoods, people are indirectly monitored and supervised through physical boundaries, fraternal and compound policing,[1] and limited access to mainstream social services. These conditions are symptomatic of social disorganization. Children are raised under tenuous conditions where relationships and trust are strained early on and adult efforts must be combined. Parents and guardians seek to keep young males from the street, hoping that they will resist the allure of the corner—both a metaphor for street culture and a real place in the poorest communities—and avoid the inevitable violence, incarceration, or death that is associated with the street. In South Philadelphia, basketball is used to combat social disorganization and give young men some tools to counter the draw of the corner.

Elijah Anderson (1990) theorizes about the place of the black, poor, urban, young male in public. He describes what it means to be at this intersection: a young black man is stereotyped and has a negative history based upon the social position of his group; he is considered dangerous, criminal, and guilty. Black men's understanding of this presumption operates as part of their double consciousness; to be successful, they must understand that this stereotype operates and use it to inform them when dealing with others, black and non-black, in most public and formal institutional settings. This stereotype is a direct function of growing social disorganization: poor people who are increasingly impoverished and socially isolated offer displays of "ghetto-specific behavior" and get characterized as having a "culture of poverty." This viewpoint ignores the larger systemic and institutionalized framework of racism. Behavior is an adaptive response to the ongoing assault of macro- and microlevel processes, including cuts in federal, state, and city social spending, racialized policing, and historic and continuing segregation, that has adverse racial and class effects. The black poor get poorer and become more isolated from any possibility of geographic and economic mobility. Social organization at micro-levels can work to mitigate these effects, although with limited microlevel results.

In this context, basketball is a critically important activity. The sport is organized in many different ways that bring adults and youth together, and serious participation and integration into basketball activities build and bridge networks, providing additional resources and opportunities for young men. Young men are encouraged to maintain or regain positive senses of self through being given an opportunity to show that they can succeed at something positive and should not be presumed criminal, guilty, and inherently bad.

According to numerous articles, academic and journalistic, black men, particularly from the inner city, have an athleticized identity. This identity is not developed spontaneously through peer groups; it is passed down from older black men and propagated via media images and the racialization of such sports as basketball and football. Black youth are likely to learn about and develop an intense passion for sports at early ages and come to see athletic achievement as a significant measure of their masculinity and peer group status.[2] Athletic performance is a vehicle through which young black men may express their masculinity. Moreover, the importance of athletic achievement for perceptions of masculinity and status extends into adulthood, particularly for black men who earn high basketball status in their youth but work in blue-collar or low-level white-collar professions where their work rarely provides high occupational prestige or economic returns. For these men, basketball identity becomes their preferred "master status"; it represents the peak of their social career, at the same time that it highlights their skewed life course and low-status position in adulthood.

This chapter demonstrates the importance of basketball as an effective social organization of men, young men, and their families against social disorganization.[3] Basketball seen from this vantage point is not simply a "hoop dream"—young men's unrealistic hope and fixation on basketball and other athletic endeavors as a ticket out of the ghetto. Rather, basketball is an institution and way of life that enables young men to cope in the current context and reduces the social-psychological impact of being negatively stereotyped and marginalized. I learned about the significance of basketball in young men's lives while coaching young black men from impoverished communities in South Philadelphia through the Blade Rodgers League. Over a period of four years, I conducted formal and informal group and individual interviews and hung out with kids, tutoring them in school work, going on errands, and accompanying them to juvenile court. Participant observation on the basketball court and in players' neighborhoods and homes enabled me to understand the real difference their involvement in the sport and the social networks surrounding basketball made in their lives.[4]

Avoiding the Corner by Being a Ballplayer

Many adult black men who are involved with youth basketball leagues and play at local parks and gyms are actively engaged in the lives of young men. Their presence is significant, as studies of black families and poor black inner-city communities often highlight the "disappearance" or absence of black male role models—fathers, uncles, and other males—from the households in which young men live.[5] Notably, the adult black men who are the backbone of organized basketball activities in Philadelphia act as role models and advisors to younger black men, both inside and outside basketball.[6]

The Blade Rodgers League was created primarily to give kids, especially young black males, a place to go to escape the draw of the corner and street activity. The league emphasizes respecting and listening to adults because adults are valuable resources. Kids who participate are taught to respect elders, especially those involved with the league. League coordinators and the founder remove kids from games and expel them from the league altogether for poor behavior during games and league events. Often, players as well as coaches are pulled aside and spoken to regarding their behavior toward referees, league staff, or one another. League officials speak regularly of basketball's usefulness, but acknowledge that young men need help from others to be successful.

The most important aspect of this league is its network of adult men who coach, referee, and serve various administrative and coordinating roles. Without the network, the explicit and implicit missions of the league would fail. The network is made up of older men who have all worked with kids. Most have been a part of the league for over twenty years. The rest are younger men who enjoy working with kids as a way to give back. Many work in the juvenile criminal justice system. The league's coordinator, T.D., is a retired probation officer; Chuck, the co-coordinator and one of the founders, worked as a nonteaching assistant in a local public school and as a drug counselor and therapist; another staff member is a retired police officer; and others work in schools as security officers and non-teaching assistants. The network is tied together through basketball. It is a web of former "great" local ballplayers connected to the larger network of Philadelphia basketball, local college coaches, and professional coaches and players. These men are in a position not only to help some kids get a chance to play in college and even the professional ranks but also to teach young basketball hopefuls how to navigate the world beyond basketball and outside their communities.

I coached under Chuck, an "old head"—a term used by the kids in South Philly to describe older men, particularly those who mentor younger men. Chuck, now in his late sixties, has played and coached basketball for most of his life, and been a part of the Blade Rodgers League since its beginnings in 1968. He is called a youth advocate by some and praised by women and men, mothers and fathers, current and former players for his commitment to young people. Chuck loves basketball and claims that it saved his life, and he coaches young men to save as many as he can. Still, he is realistic about basketball and young men's possibilities. "Scott, for one of these kids to make it outta here, it's a miracle. Most of them end up on the corner." For adult men like Chuck and others who support young men who are not their own kin, the major reward is emotional, seeing someone succeed (generally measured by educational and occupational attainment) and having played a role in his success.

Basketball remains valuable and necessary in the eyes of Chuck and other men involved with youth basketball. It can have significant short-term and potential long-term benefits as an activity that kids want to do and that brings them to adults for help; kids regard it as worthwhile, rewarding, and effective in social and economic mobility. Being a basketball player is a positive identity and can possibly lead to a good life, free from drugs, incarceration, and violence. In many respects, being a basketball player or an athlete is deemed the opposite of being a thug and hanging on the corner, although some athletes do hang out on the street, run wild, and get into trouble. Players, coaches, and others believe that basketball players are largely distinguishable from other young men in their community because they devote themselves to trying to be the best basketball players they can be; this is how they gain status in their communities, and, hopefully, how they can achieve upward mobility.[7] In this way, basketball players have formed a group identity that is in direct opposition to other types of poor young black male peer groups. This positive valuation is justified by the activities associated with being an athlete. Playing ball seriously requires goal setting, discipline, and commitment and often leads to higher self-esteem and increasing social pressure to live up to idealized expectations. Thus basketball, as an institution, is a cultural force that socializes youth, reinforcing normative values and beliefs in democracy, fair play, and meritocracy.[8]

One evening after practice, I gave rides home to three high school players: Jermaine (fifteen years old), Ray (sixteen), and Darrell (fifteen). I asked them about some men, both older and younger, whom we saw standing on a corner. Our interaction illustrates what young men mean when they identify themselves with basketball players rather than with thugs (also called hustlers or drug dealers).

"Who are those guys on the corner?" I inquired.

"Drug dealers," Darrell responded without much thought.

"How do you know?" I questioned, wanting to know what he knew about these guys that clued him in to their being drug dealers as opposed to loafers, kids waiting for their parents to come home, or men who had just gotten off work.

"Everybody know," he said matter-of-factly.

"Do you *know* them?" I probed further.

"Yeah. I mean no. They know me, but I don't know them," he replied.

"I know them, Scott," Ray said. "Well, I don't *know* them, know them. But I know them. One of them used to go to our school."

Jermaine added, "Yeah, that Turk. But he don't go to school no more. He just hang out on the corner."

"How do *they* know *you*, then? They know you from school or the neighborhood . . . ?" I asked.

"Because we play ball," Darrell shot back.

"Just because you play ball they *know* you?" I asked with some disbelief.

"Yeah, 'cause they seen me play," Darrell said.

"They know us because we play ball and get girls, Scott," Jermaine added.

Darrell grew frustrated with my questioning and tried to summarize his point. "Basically, you either a thug or an athlete. And if you an athlete then you get respect, and girls like that. They [the thugs we saw] just wasting they lives."

In identifying different segments of the local population, Darrell, Jermaine, and Ray make it clear they are choosing to be part of a certain group. Each camp has its own characteristics and predicted behaviors. Thugs are young men who hang out on the corner and sell drugs, but ballplayers are respected and perceived as doing something positive, since playing well adds to their chances for upward mobility. A more immediate reward is that young women find athletes attractive.[9] Moreover, if a youth is perceived to have the potential to escape poverty through basketball, his social position is enhanced. Known basketball players are seen as "good" kids, and kids who hang out on the corner are not viewed as positively. For thugs, local "respect" is based on fear, not admiration, because they are considered "wastes" and negative influences or forces in the community.

One individual's experiences in high school illustrate how race, gender, and class scripted his interactions with civil authorities, yet his connection with basketball and the Blade Rodgers League staff were useful in his negotiating the juvenile justice system. Some adult men with whom he was connected indirectly through the league mentored and advised him, appealing to his basketball identity.

Paul's Story

I met Paul at basketball practice. He did not really stand out, although he always seemed to be in a good mood. He smiled and laughed often, especially when other kids were being scolded and picked on. His ability did not set him apart either; he was an average basketball player, but gave a lot of effort. He was finishing his tenth grade year, which meant that he would be moving up to the advanced high school level of the Rodgers League. This was a big jump, because the eleventh and twelfth graders in the Rodgers League were the best players in the city and neighboring areas. Paul established himself early in league play as a leader; he was vocal on the court and knew how plays were to be run. A problem was that he was emotional and explosive, sometimes having too many words for referees. Referees often warned Chuck and me to calm Paul down.

Paul's childhood was fairly typical for a kid growing up in South Philly. His father had never been around. His mother, Tasha, married twice, though neither marriage was to Paul's father, and had three sons, all of whom had different fathers. According to Tasha, she and Paul's father had intended to get married, but he deserted her when she told him of the pregnancy. In his absence, Paul's "stepfathers" had been father figures. Tasha's first husband, the father of her oldest son, played a large role in Paul's life. Paul said he was the father he never had, even though Paul was the product of a relationship Tasha had after their divorce. Tasha and her second husband, Paul's actual stepfather, separated when Paul was in middle school. Paul did not care much for him, and referred to him as "*his* dad," meaning his younger brother's dad.

Paul's brothers and his mother live in different places but remain close. Paul lives with Tasha and her boyfriend, "Mr. Larry," in a home that they rent a block south of Tasha's mother's home. Paul's older brother, Tommy, lives with the grandmother, and his younger brother, Andre, lives with his father. Andre comes "down" to stay with him and their mother on the weekends from Germantown, a neighborhood about ten miles north of South Philly. Paul sees Tommy throughout the week because of their proximity. They attend high school basketball and football games, go clothes shopping, and eat together regularly. Within this living arrangement, Paul has gotten used to a significant amount of freedom and self-management. Paul often cooks and shops for himself and abides by his own rules. In a real sense, Paul has already entered adulthood. No one acts as an authority disciplining him and making decisions for him. He interacts with his mother as though they are peers.

On one visit to Paul's home with Chuck, we took note of the interaction between Paul and his mother. After leaving, Chuck asked me, "You see how he talks to his mother? He don't have no respect for her. But when he wants some new sneaks or some grub [food] then it's all sweetness. But I don't blame the kids, I blame the parents. They let them get away with that shit. For a kid like Paul basketball may be his only hope. We might be the only adults that can speak to him, the only ones telling 'em right."

Chuck observed that Paul's condescension toward his mother during their interaction suggested that Paul felt equal or superior to his mother, perhaps smarter, while he remained her dependent. In Chuck's eyes this was out of order: a dependent child should act as a dependent and defer to a parent or guardian. More important, this stance highlighted Paul's sense of independence and manhood. He was much bigger than his mother, managed his own activities, and made his own decisions. But he was still a child who needed parental guidance; he needed to understand and respect authority as a means of growing up and becoming self-sufficient. Paul's situation is typical, but youthful independence often has grave implications in the context of urban poverty and social conditions in the community.

One day changed Paul's plans. Paul called me very late one Friday night. I asked him "what's up" and began to scold him about calling so late. He told me that he had been trying to get in touch with Chuck because his father, meaning his first stepfather, had been murdered a few days earlier and the funeral had been postponed to Saturday. I offered my condolences, told him I would let Chuck know about the change in the funeral date, and confirmed our next meeting for algebra tutoring.

The next morning I called Chuck to relay the message regarding the new time for the funeral. I told him about the late night call and he abruptly asked me if Paul was okay. I was a little confused. I explained that Paul had called to tell him and me about the new funeral time, but as I finished my thought, my voice trailed off; I couldn't believe that I had been so insensitive. Chuck jumped in, "I'm sorry to bring up the psychological stuff, Scott. But you know that's my thing." Chuck was right. It made no sense that Paul would call me to look for Chuck. He didn't really call to tell me about the funeral, he wanted to talk. I had missed the opportunity to be an emotional support for him.

I tried to reach Paul three times over the next two days, but either no one answered or Tasha or Mr. Larry told me that they would give him the message that I had called. Paul did not return my call. Tuesday afternoon came and I called, as I normally did, to make sure that we were still going to meet; he had stood me up once or twice, and I found that checking in reminded him and ensured that he would be home. This time Tasha answered the phone.

I called her by name, "Hey Tasha, it's Scott."

"Weren't you supposed to be meeting Paul today?"

"Yeah, that's why I'm calling."

"Well, you ain't gonna meet him today. It'll have to be tomorrow or Thursday or some other time."

She spoke curtly and in a very stern tone. I was taken aback. I was not sure what to take from her tone, but it did not sound good. I wondered if I had done something. I asked her why.

"You never guess where he at."

"Where?"

"In jail."

Tasha told me that Paul had gotten into a fight with a school police officer and been charged with assault. She claimed she knew the policeman, he was a friend of the family, and she was confident that the charges would be dropped.

"But I ain't worried. Paul's a good kid, he ain't never had no trouble with the law. He probably be released later tonight."

I told her I was sorry to hear about all the trouble, but she reassured me that everything would be alright. She asked me how late Paul could call me, so that he could return my call, and she thanked me for agreeing to tutor Paul in algebra.

Paul called me a couple of days later. He was his usual upbeat self and sounded in pretty good spirits. I asked when he had got home and he told me that he got home that night I spoke with his mom. I asked him about what had happened at school.

Paul told me that he was leaving the lunchroom and heard someone call his name when he was outside. He turned to see another young man approaching him and talking "smack" or insulting him. The young man, it seemed, was "showing out" to a bunch of girls; insulting Paul as a means to show that he was tough and unafraid of Paul despite his reputation for fighting. As the young man approached and continued to talk, he began taking off his coat. Paul did not wait for the young man to shed the coat; the movement to remove it triggered Paul's response. He saw this move as getting ready to fight, so he beat him to the punch. He hit him in the face, knocking him down, and then jumped on top of him, pounding him with his fists. After a number of blows, Paul got up and left the young man.

Paul began to walk toward the principal's office to face the inevitable when someone yelled, "Who was fighting?" Some girls pointed at Paul and yelled, "He was." Paul stood still as the school police officer ran toward him. The officer grabbed Paul's shirt with a punch. Paul was taken off guard and fought back until other officers came to help and Paul felt a barrage of hits and kicks to the face and body. Paul's girlfriend, Mia, tried to assist Paul and fought the officers. She got involved because of the excessive blows to his face, head, and body that the officer and back-up inflicted upon him. Paul felt that she had done the proper thing in "standing by her man." When the altercation was over, Paul and Mia were both charged with assault, Paul with 5 counts and Mia with 3. They both were given a court date for a month later and expelled from their school. The young man Paul fought, who had started the whole ordeal, had no charges brought against him because he did not fight the officers.

Paul was given two different court dates, a school disciplinary hearing regarding his educational future, and a civil case for assaulting a police officer. In the disciplinary hearing the judge would determine if he could return to Jackson Street High School or be reassigned. The judge ruled that Paul was not allowed to return to Street and was reassigned to Woodland, considered the worst and most dangerous school in the city. Upon hearing the ruling, Tasha said, she and Paul both broke down and cried. Both felt that Paul's actions were right and the officer was in the wrong. The policeman had hit him first and Paul responded by retaliating and protecting himself. The judge told Paul that on the street this reaction might have gotten him killed by regular police officers. He was probably right, but Tasha still felt that Paul had not been treated fairly.

Tasha believed this judge had made up his mind before they had even arrived. The judge claimed that Paul had a "history," a record of past troubles over his public school career. The judge recounted from some file that Paul had received four "pink notices" (detention slips) during the last three years and had been held back in the first grade. Tasha was amazed that the judge had used information about Paul's past to make a judgment about his present character. In her eyes, Paul was a "good" kid because he was not involved in drugs, had been an active athlete and steered clear of gangs, and had not been arrested before. But the judge's construction of Paul fit the common construction that Anderson (1990, 1999) calls the "black male in public." In this way, Paul was guilty as a function of his social position in relation to civil authorities. Paul's behavior was regarded as reflecting his antipathetic relationship to police and teachers, institutional authorities, and the wider white social system. He was inherently deviant and needed to be punished, controlled, and dominated by formal authorities because he was poor, young, black, and male.

The fate of many young men in Paul's neighborhood has been negatively determined by one event combined with their "past" and intersectional identity: being urban, poor, black, young, and male. This identity carries little or no social, economic, or political capital when confronted with formal civil authorities. No recourse or appeal can be made when a judge says a young man is of bad character and gives a judgment with possible adverse and life-changing consequences. Paul was expelled from the school that his mother, brother, and friends attended. He was reassigned to a school with a bad reputation where several probation officers had offices and worked full-time on site. This outcome was only half of Paul's problems; he still had to await his date in family court (where juvenile cases are heard) for assaulting the officer. Might he be incarcerated just months before he turned eighteen? Could they charge him as an adult?

At that critical juncture, Paul found out that his girlfriend, Mia, was pregnant. He was unsure not only about his education but also about his whole future. How would having a child affect his life? He had said before the pregnancy that he knew that Mia was "the one," his soulmate, and that he wanted to marry her after he went to college and got a good job. Becoming a parent would undoubtedly put a strain on these plans. Could he attend college and be a father? Would he marry her now? Could he still get the good job?

Paul's connections with the adult men in the basketball league meant that his story differs from that of other young black men in trouble with the formal authorities. Paul's association with the Blade Rodgers League had increased his social networks. He had me, Chuck, and others in his corner, to offer knowledge and support, and even to vouch for him to the officials wielding the power to shape his future.

I talked to Chuck about what had happened to Paul. He told me to have Paul come down to the league so we could come up with a game plan for how Paul might proceed in family court in front of a judge. Chuck believed we could help Paul because TD, the league coordinator and Chuck's longtime assistant coach, was a probation officer who worked at the courthouse. I went down to the league and met with Chuck and Paul before we spoke with TD. Chuck listened closely to Paul's story and instructed Paul to say as little as possible so that he could focus on what TD had to say. TD had often worked in this capacity, helping one of the league's guys, and had little tolerance for excuses.

We found TD after the day's games, and Chuck told TD that Paul needed his help. TD looked to Paul and asked, "What's up, man?" Paul explained that he had been in a fight and that he was in trouble for assaulting a school police officer. TD shook his head and started in: "What are you doing, man? You better than that. You a ballplayer. You not supposed to be getting into stuff like that." Paul tried to defend himself, and talked about the officer pushing him while handcuffing the other kid. Paul said that he told the officer not to touch him but the officer hit him in the face and then he fought back. Evidently, Paul did not understand what he had done wrong. When TD asked him why he fought back, Paul said that the officer wasn't supposed to put his hands on him. TD shook his head and told Paul that his attitude and disrespect for authority was the problem. Chuck tried to tell Paul not to say too much, "Just listen, man." TD asked if Paul had played for the school's team and Paul responded that he had not because he had broken his ankle.

Then TD asked Paul why he wasn't in school. Paul explained that the judge had told him to go to Woodland. TD asked him why that mattered: "If you trying to go to school, then you go to school. It don't matter where you at." Chuck stood up for Paul and tried to explain that Woodland was a bad school and gang territory. Paul said that he would just get into more trouble. TD replied that he needed to get rid of that "macho bullshit." He told Paul that as a basketball player he should have had social carte blanche in school.

TD was suggesting that there were benefits to being an athlete: if he had been on the ball team he might have been treated differently by the school and been able to avoid the fight. And at Woodland Paul might be able to avoid problems if he were involved with sports. Athletes generally are not brought into gang stuff, especially if they are promising athletes. Being part of a team implies that a youth has backup, the support of his teammates, who tend to be taller and bigger than others.

Wrapping up the conversation, Chuck told TD that Paul had a court date later that month. TD instructed Paul how to dress for court and speak with the public defender and judge. Last, TD reminded Paul that his attitude had gotten him into trouble. TD had an office in the same building as the courtroom and told Paul to visit his office before seeing the judge. Chuck told Paul to go to TD's office the next day between 10 and 11:30 A.M. to try to get TD to work on the judge before the date. After the meeting Chuck scolded Paul for trying to defend his behavior to TD, who, as a probation officer, understood the system and could possibly help him.

All this happened within the context of the league. I was the point person between Paul and the league's network, and in regular contact with Paul and Chuck. Then Paul, Chuck, and I arranged to meet at the league. Chuck listened to Paul's story and scolded him for being out of control. Still, he told Paul that we had a plan and explained what came next—talking to TD, what to expect from this meeting, and how Paul was to behave. TD then heard Paul's situation and questioned and reprimanded him before offering a solution and speculating on the outcome. Paul had resources because as a basketball player he had developed relationships with men who were in positions to help him, inform him of critical information: how to behave (yes sir, yes ma'am), how to dress for court, and what outcomes to expect. At the same time, Paul received feedback and admonishments from each of us. All this guidance lessened Paul and Tasha's worries.

The time finally came for Paul to go before the family court judge. Paul and Tasha had been down to court for his original trial date in December, but the proceeding was postponed until January. I was able to make the second "notice to appear." I entered the building, went to the security desk, checked in my cell phone, and signed a guest list, after checking the docket and finding which courtroom Paul was scheduled to be in. I went through the metal detector and followed the signs to courtrooms A and B. I entered an adjoining room where those being tried waited with friends and family.

There was a buzz of activity and talk as people waited their turn. The kids were quieter than their parents. They seemed nervous and unsure of their fate, having nothing to distract them from what was looming. One black woman, the mother of a child, said to an older black woman, who seemed to be the grandmother, "This is worse than waiting in the hospital." Many folks seemed to know each other. Paul recognized and spoke to a young woman who attended his school about her reason for being in court. She said that she was there for truancy because she had missed too much school. This young woman seemed almost cavalier; she smiled and laughed easily as though her impending case was of little consequence. Was she putting on a front?

Most of the action was the lawyers making deals. They were wheeling and dealing, moving between a courtroom, which was closed and seemed secretive, and the huge waiting room. Three lawyers, two women and a man, interacted and moved between the waiting room and courtroom. The women were public defenders serving the entirety of the room. Periodically they would go to the front of the room, identified by the direction in which half the chairs faced, and call names to meet their next client.

Each case was put into the queue and handled in pieces. The lone male district attorney (DA) fielded the multitude of cases on the docket. The system worked as an assembly line. First came the public defender's introduction to the client; followed by a brief negotiation with the DA. The public defender returned to the client to discuss the options and specifics of disposition and sentencing, and then checking with the client before making the final deal with the DA regarding how he or she wished to plead. The court proceeding before the judge seemed a mere formality; the cases were generally decided before the kids even saw the judge.

The young woman whom Paul had spoken with entered the courtroom and exited only ten minutes later. Her mother stood crying, her head down. When Paul went up to her to ask what happened, she said she was ordered to go to a group home. A young, pregnant white woman entered the courtroom before being brought out in cuffs. Her mother was distraught; the young woman was downcast, with tears staining her face. The mother's emotion filled the air and left a hush in the room. Prior to sentencing she had seemed so confident, meddling with her younger brothers and sisters and speaking loudly and boldly in her conversation. This was serious now. The room became thick with tension and fear. Waiting kids could no longer believe that this was play; something real was happening in the courtroom.

Tasha, Paul, Mia, and Mia's mother were clearly nervous, and their nervousness grew with each horrifying scene of a young person being sentenced. But Paul had me there, to speak with the public defender and clarify questions and answers, and more important, he had someone helping him on the inside. Paul had already gone to TD's office to remind him that the day had come. TD came into the courtroom periodically to check with the public defender and reassure all of us. After TD's third and final trip, he returned and told us that Paul was going to get six months' probation. He asked how old Paul was (just a month from his eighteenth birthday) and then optimistically said that he'd be fine because this offense would be on his juvenile record, which would not matter when he turned eighteen.

Inside the courtroom, the proceedings went quickly. The DA gave the brief story: Paul got into a fight in school and then resisted arrest, fighting the school officers and injuring the officer, who was present. The judge then looked toward Mia, and the DA added that Mia assaulted the officer, kicking him, while Paul was being restrained. The DA also informed the judge that an agreement had been made. The judge stopped reading the paperwork to address Paul and Mia.

Judge O'Malley was the fifty-something son of a retired Philadelphia judge, called an "a-hole" by one probation officer who said "he ain't nothing like his father. His father was real cool. He act like he got something to prove." O'Malley sat tall on the bench, as though a god, but leaned over and looked down at the "criminals" to give effect.

"This is why our schools are in the shape that they're in," Judge O'Malley said firmly. "It's because of students like you." He went on: "Young lady, it looks like you've been nothing but trouble." He perused some paperwork and continued: "Fights, disrespecting your teachers, and disobedience. How would you feel if someone kicked your father in the head?"[10] The judge shook his head disapprovingly and then told Paul and Mia that they were to take a drug test by giving a urine sample upstairs immediately. "Are you clean? I am not going to get these tests back and have them say that you're dirty, am I? Tell me now. Because if they come back positive for drugs, I'll hold you in contempt of court for lying and then you will be tried as an adult. You hear me, son?"

The judge's statements and questions reflected his tough love approach to sentencing young persons, and a general pessimism held toward young black women and men. He claimed that kids, and Paul and Mia as representatives, were the root of Philadelphia's educational woes. Of course, the judge was simply trying to make a point: kids have a role in the plight of public schooling. But this point is particularly meaningful when considering Paul's two court appearances. In the first hearing, Paul was said to have a troubled past that ran back ten years to first grade; in his second appearance, he was considered emblematic of what is wrong with the whole educational system. Paul was questioned about smoking weed and threatened with being tried as an adult if he had a positive urine test. An altercation with another youth at school had led to something much more serious with long-term implications. This escalation of an ordinary conflict into an event with major educational and legal consequences highlights the layered aspersion that comes with being black and male.

After the urine tests proved negative, Paul and Mia were given six months probation and 25 hours of community service. Paul, Tasha, and I were directed to the probation office to get the necessary paperwork for processing, including a community service record sheet. A black man in his mid-thirties named Randy greeted us and spoke to Paul with familiarity. "Paul. Man, what you doing in here?" Paul sheepishly responded that he had gotten into a fight. Tasha looked at the man quizzically, trying to place him.

"Aw, don't worry, Ma. This happens to many young bulls. Paul used to play ball for me. Yeah, and he used to come over and ride my [motorcycle] bikes. I'll have to tell Tony [another coach] I saw you." Randy tried to comfort Tasha. "Ma, he a good kid, he'll be all right. But I wouldn't have pleaded guilty. If it were my son, I'll tell you what I would have done. I would have pleaded innocent because probation and community service, that's the worst they could have given you. I would have held out for community service only. But it's all right. I got a guy who works at the school and he'll take care of him."

The dealings between the public defender and DA are efficient. Clients are given very few options for how they are to plead and estimates of their sentence connected with their options. Appealing for different representation, going to trial, or taking some other action that slows efficiency is not offered. Each defendant is assumed to be guilty; the cases are simply negotiations of what punishment will be given. Paul did not have the resources to retain his own attorney, nor did he, Tasha, or I understand the rules of the game. TD played into the game. In his eyes, Paul had clearly done wrong by assaulting an officer and needed to be taught a lesson that would stay with him only if he accepted responsibility and completed his community service while staying clean from criminal activity. New knowledge of alternatives came up after Paul serendipitously met with his former basketball coach, Randy, from the league. Seeing Randy and talking about past times lightened Paul's mood and even brought a smile and some laughs. Randy added to Paul's experience by giving him a shortcut to completing his service hours.

Then Randy looked at all of us. "Where you gonna do your community service?"

"I don't know," Paul said.

"You wanna put down Blade Rodgers?" Randy asked.

Paul said, "Yes."

"You could work in the league right away, do whatever they need you to do—sweep, keep score, know what I mean, and you could have it all finished before he [the probation officer] even contacts you. And I'll put you with my man [a probation officer Randy knew]. He already full, but I'll talk to him. He'll take care of you."

Meeting Randy was a fortunate but fortuitous event; there was no other probation officer in the office when we arrived. Randy affirmed Paul's goodness and spoke of his trouble as common. Treating a young black man getting in trouble as a normal situation is not a positive thing, but Randy's words lifted Paul's head, rather than shaming him. Ultimately, the presence of Chuck, TD, Randy, and me countered Paul's interactions with the judges and court system. Rather than having a history that he could not overcome and living under a cloud of suspicion, Paul was reminded of his basketball identity and supported with words, given encouragement and advice, and accompanied and spoken for.

The End of Dreams

The whole ordeal represented an end of dreams for Paul and his mother. He had hoped to attend college and get a well-paying job, but this was contingent on playing sports. How else would Paul get to college? His grades were not good, but being a promising athlete might make teachers think of him differently, as an athlete, and if he were considered a high-caliber athlete he would be given information regarding college that he would most likely not otherwise get. Being expelled and sent to another school and having to give up high school sports ended Paul's dream of upward mobility via athletics. Tasha wanted Paul to do something to make her proud, and she felt that the local corner and street life were too alluring. She implored Paul to do something, to try harder in school if he wanted to go to college, or to join the military.

"I would rather see my son die serving his country, than die on the street corner," Tasha declared.

After completing his GED in night school, Paul enlisted and remains active in military service. Paul visited Chuck and me at practice to let us know how he was doing. He felt connected to us because of our assistance, but also because he maintained a sense of himself as an athlete. This identity gave him an alternative perspective to interpret his experiences and consider options for his future. He felt accountable for his actions: fighting in school and resisting an officer, we had told him, was stupid and therefore his punishment was deserved. He made unusual decisions, relative to other young men in his community, by continuing school and joining the military in line with his positive identity. He did not have to see his life as over or unredeemable; he had committed himself to steering clear of the corner and street.

Basketball is important, not simply as a form of recreation or means to fame and riches, but as an institution where kids can gain a positive social identity as a basketball player and develop contacts with networks of "decent" men. The league was created as a response to community decline, the growing dearth of male role models, and limited opportunities for youth to learn and play basketball. With its explicit mission to help kids, the league is an organization of "decent" men who help young, poor, black men by being able to provide guidance, offer support, counter the pessimism surrounding young black male identity, and create shortcuts for navigating otherwise tricky and adversarial systems. While this assistance does not guarantee positive outcomes, Paul's case clearly demonstrates how resources have been organized and men have gathered to improve the lives of young men in the midst of the social disorganization found in poor urban and black communities.

However, basketball does not offer a cure for poverty and social marginality. As Harry Edwards (1969) has reminded us time and again, basketball leaves little room for luck, injury, or errors, and it develops few, if any, skills that can be transferred into other occupations. Rather, the organization of basketball demonstrates the importance of a perceived route toward upward mobility and self-esteem. Young black men see black men succeeding at various levels of basketball, in college and in the professional ranks; what it takes to succeed seems clear, and black men are supported in this endeavor. In what other occupational areas can this be said? To solve the structural problems of black education and employment, we need local and federal policies that not only link jobs to growing industries, as has been done in some welfare policy, but also create transparent processes, organizations, direct links to other more practical activities and careers, and support networks to build confidence and self-worth for young urban poor black men and women.

References

Adler, Patricia, and Peter Adler. 1991. *Backboards and Blackboards: College Athletes and Role Engulfment.* New York: Columbia University Press.

Anderson, Elijah. 1999. *The Code of the Street: Decency, Violence, and the Moral Life of the Inner City.* New York: W.W. Norton.

———. 1990. *Streetwise: Race, Class, and Change in an Urban Community.* Chicago: University of Chicago Press.

———. 1976. *A Place on the Corner.* Chicago: University of Chicago Press.

Blumer, Herbert. 1958. Race prejudice as a sense of group position. *Pacific Sociological Review* 1 (Spring): 3–6.

Brooks, Scott N. 2004. Putting the blessings on him: Vouching and basketball status work. In *Being Here and Being There: Fieldwork Encounters and Ethnographic Discoveries,* ed. Elijah Anderson, Scott N. Brooks, Raymond Gunn, and Nikki Jones. *Annals of the American Academy of Political and Social Science* 595 (September): 80–90.

Duncier, Mitchell, with photographs by Ovie Carter. 1992. *Slim's Table: Race, Respectability, and Masculinity.* Chicago: University of Chicago Press.

Edwards, Harry S. 1969. *The Revolt of the Black Athlete.* New York: Free Press.

Furstenberg, Frank. 1995. Fathering in the inner city. In *Fatherhood: Contemporary Theory, Research, and Social Policy,* ed. William Marsiglio, 119–47. Thousand Oaks, Calif.: Sage.

Furstenberg, Frank, and Kathleen M. Harris. 1993. When and why fathers matter. In *Young Unwed Fathers: Changing Roles and Emerging Policies,* ed. Robert I. Lerman and Theodora J. Ooms, 117–38. Philadelphia: Temple University Press.

Goffman, Erving. 1963. *Stigma: Notes on the Management of Spoiled Identity.* Englewood Cliffs, N.J.: Prentice-Hall.

Harris, Othello. 1997. The role of sport in the black community. *Sociological Focus* 30: 311–20.

Hartmann, Douglass. 2003. Theorizing sport as social intervention. *Quest* 55: 118–40.

———. 2001. Notes on Midnight Basketball and the cultural politics of recreation, race and at-risk urban youth. *Journal of Sport & Social Issues* 24 (November): 339–71.

Hoberman, John. 1997. *Darwin's Athletes: How Sport Has Damaged Black America and Preserved the Myth of Race.* New York: Houghton Mifflin.

Jones, Nikki. 2004. "It's not where you live, it's how you live": How young women negotiate conflict and violence in the inner city. In *Being Here and Being There: Fieldwork Encounters and Ethnographic Discoveries,* ed. Elijah Anderson, Scott N. Brooks, Raymond Gunn, and Nikki Jones. *Annals of the American Academy of Political and Social Science* 595 (September): 49–62.

Liebow, Elliott. 1967. *Tally's Corner: A Study of Negro Streetcorner Men.* Boston: Little, Brown.

Messner, Michael S. 1988. Masculinities and athletic careers. *Gender & Society* 3: 71–88.

Sailes, Gary A. 1998. *African Americans in Sport: Contemporary Themes.* Piscataway, N.J.: Transaction Publishers.

———. 1996. An examination of basketball performance orientations among African American males. *Journal of African American Men* 1 (4): 37–46.

———. 1987. A socio-economic explanation of black sports participation patterns. *Western Journal of Black Studies* 11: 164–67.

Spradley, James P. 1980. *Participant Observation*. New York: Holt, Rinehart, Winston.

Whyte, William Foote. 1981. *Street Corner Society: The Social Structure of an Italian Slum*. 3rd ed. Chicago: University of Chicago Press.

Wilson, James Q. 1968. *Varieties of Police Behavior: The Management of Law and Order in Eight Communities*. Cambridge, Mass.: Harvard University Press.

Wilson, William Julius. 1987. *The Truly Disadvantaged: The Inner City, the Underclass, and Public Policy*. Chicago: University of Chicago Press.

Young, Alford. 2004. *The Minds of Marginalized Black Men: Making Sense of Mobility, Opportunity, and Future Life Chances*. Princeton, N.J.: Princeton University Press.

Chapter 11

"Tell us how it feels to be a problem": Hip Hop Longings and Poor Young Black Men

IMANI PERRY

> . . . *fantasy*
> *parodies desire*
> *replacing longing . . .*
> —*Audre Lorde, "Addiction"*

In "Of Our Spiritual Strivings," the autobiographical essay that opens *The Souls of Black Folk*, W. E. B. Du Bois reflected on his response to provocative (and insulting) white peers: "To the real question, How does it feel to be a problem? I answer seldom a word" (1903, 1). In the United States today, perhaps no one is made to feel like a problem more acutely than the poor young Black man who, despite his great social vulnerability, is so often presumed to be a predator or threat.[1] These youths, proclaimed to be "in crisis" by commentators ranging from academics to *New York Times* headlines, respond to the question, "How does it feel to be a problem?" in the lyrics of our popular music. The answer offered there often seems more problematic than problem-solving; indeed, it seldom even identifies the nature and sources of the problem.

The problematic character of this answer is due in part to the fact that today hip hop is dominated by corporations. Choices about what kinds of songs and artists are marketed and what music is most popular are no longer rooted in urban Black communities but rather flow from executive decisions and the voyeuristic interests of a national and international audience. As rapper Nas argues, "Heinous crimes help record sales more than creative lines."[2] However, within the lyrics of hip hop we can find significant commentary on the lives and consciousness of poor young Black men.

Hip hop remains a useful context for social observation. Although its audience has dramatically broadened, hip hop continues to be the music of choice for America's young Black men. The consistent themes found throughout the history of hip hop are not merely a reflection of corporate choices but rather originate in the Black male experience that is represented in the music. While young Black men are often the fantastic and fantasized "subjects" of entertainment—in athletics, in sensationalized news media (Gilliam and Iyengar 2000), and in reality television—the exhortations of hip hop provide one of the few arenas in which we hear their voices, in either the literal or the role-playing "everyman" voice of the rapper. The voices of hip hop are still over-whelmingly young, Black, and male. The authors remain so as well, even as their words are vetted and evaluated by a wide range of people in the music industry before they hit the clubs, airwaves, and iPods. Moreover, because of the great value placed on the image of authenticity in the art form, some degree of loyalty to urban experience has been sustained even though the music is sensationalized and often resorts to stereo-types to improve sales.

British cultural theorist Stuart Hall and his colleagues in the emerg-ing field of cultural studies argued that the meaning of a mass media product exists somewhere between the producer and the audience (Hall et al. 1978). Today cultural products are often produced with ambiguous meanings, and different audiences latch on to different meanings within the music. In 1971, Hall observed presciently: "The mass media play a crucial role in defining the problems and issues of public concern. They are the main channels of public discourse in our segregated society. They transmit stereotypes of one group to other groups. They attach feelings and emotions to problems. They set the terms in which problems are defined as 'central' or 'marginal'."[3] The mass media that propagates hip hop constitutes both mass culture—produced by an industry and channeling stereotypes of Black culture as pathological—and Black popular culture—offering insights into Black experience and appealing to the Black music aesthetic. This music speaks in multiple registers.

Nonetheless, any straightforward interpretation of mainstream hip hop might reasonably yet incorrectly lead one to understand young Black men as the sole or dominant authors and creators of the condi-tions they depict—including urban decay, poverty, and the flood of guns in poor neighborhoods—rather than simply authors of the narra-tives they tell. The narrative dimension of hip hop tells the story of nav-igating these conditions, which forms one part of its appeal for Black young men. As The Game boasts, "The hood love me, hoodrats gotta hug me."

While pundits offer important critiques of the messages in hip hop, this essay does not intend to analyze the various messages hip hop communicates to different audiences.[4] Instead, it extricates some sense of the desires, longings, and absences that exist in the lives of young Black men through an analysis of the content of the music. This analysis does not stand in as a substitute for ethnographic or survey research among this population; rather, it complements more direct observational studies.

The intersections between the social sciences and cultural studies merit greater interdisciplinary inquiry. Cultural studies scholars examine cultural products—film, literature, television, and new media—in order to assess ideas, values, and trends in society, while social scientists use quantitative data and/or qualitative analyses of particular locations to do similar work. In a collection of articles on young, poor, Black men authored mostly by social scientists, this essay complements other contributors' observations and arguments with a cultural studies analysis.[5]

As the conversation about the crisis facing young, poor, Black men has grown, hip hop is often used as an example of the antisocial behavior and attitudes that are responsible for the conditions they face (Martino et al. 2006; Wingood et al. 2003; American Academy of Pediatrics 1996). The explanatory narrative suggests that their pathological view—not poverty, not imprisonment, not lack of educational or professional access—explains what is going on in their lives. Critical assessments of this interpretation of the music are found both in the humanities and the social sciences. Blake Lloyd (2000) offers an alternative perspective on the role of music videos in adolescent development. He argues that the videos transmit implicit social knowledge and inform young people about ways of responding to problematic social encounters and methods of social negotiation. This observation is supported by Elijah Anderson's seminal work, *Code of the Street*, which describes how young children from "decent" families must learn to navigate the demands of the street and become "street smart." Indeed, the rapper who personifies the "stick up kid" may be educating the non-stick up kid as much as he is playing the role of the thief. The theater of hardness in hip hop provides instruction about the self-protective strategies that young Black urban men adopt, which are a response to, rather than a cause of, the critical situation they face. This music provides troubling answers to the kind of fundamental questions Jay Z asks in "Justify my Thug" about what you do "When you play the game of life and the win ain't in the bag / When your options is none and the pen is all you have"—the word "pen" a double entendre for the penitentiary and the writing instrument.[6]

Given a rather flip neglect of widely available social scientific data that demonstrates the damaging effects of inequality, along with a set of class, generational, and racial biases that are implicit in the "blame it on hip hop" perspective, it is easy to see how the drive for "money power respect" at all costs that is articulated in hip hop becomes an explanatory narrative for the state of young, poor, Black men. The "culture of pathology" arguments that have taken hold in American popular culture as descriptors of Black life dovetail with an implicit cultural policy that keeps its hands off destructive or vulgar expression at the same time it argues that entertainment has greater social power than economics or education and abdicates aggressive social policy in favor of private resolutions to public problems. Nonetheless, when we hear lyrics that seem to celebrate violence, the exploitation of women, and illegal activity, it appropriately raises some alarm bells. We ask, have these values become representative of hip hop's voice?

I am not certain how to answer that question, and I am hesitant to offer any absolute answer about a rapidly changing and diffuse art form. Instead, I suggest that we change our frame of reference for looking at hip hop in relation to social questions. Because the music is so often a corporate creation, we cannot reductively assume that it is a clear expression of Black youths' values or priorities. Rather than seeking a direct correlation between these songs and the people who are its subjects, we should explore what is being sought by the listener and what resonates for artist and audience. What is the yearning, longing, or aspiration of the artist? What does the music meditate upon? What problems are the artists seeking to answer? How are they attempting to connect with listeners?

When we consider these questions, we are impressed by the deep sense of longing in the music. The lyrics express yearning for what the subject does not have, or for what seems fragile and fleeting in life but is nonetheless cherished. The words from Audre Lorde's poem that begin this essay suggest that behind the excessive fantasy of the world of hip hop and the desire-fueled lyrical escapades it recounts are more profound longings. These longings, I argue, express the needs and interests of young, poor, Black men.

With this perspective, we find that hip hop expresses a longing for things that have been destabilized or unattainable in the Black community during the post-civil rights era. This yearning is buried underneath a desire for late-capitalist versions of the American Dream—for better or worse. This longing is not merely evidence of deprivation, but also may operate to give us instruction on how to respond to the needs of the population depicted in the music.

We should not be so simplistic as to think of this as music of deprivation or absence; it is also music of creation. For many, hip hop constitutes an arena of creativity; prospective and professional emcees and producers are constantly developing new forms of this music. Creativity as habit is at the heart of a classically African American jazz posture; virtuosity in improvisation develops out of repetition as well as a ritual of allowing space for spontaneity. This is a deep affirmation of humanity and human potential when the music is experienced as such, and harnessing that force in hip hop is as important as thwarting the expression of antisocial forces in poor communities that are expressed in the music. The task is extremely challenging because of both the market forces that shape the music and the dire state of many poor urban communities. In communities with few professional opportunities, this creative energy is meant to generate an alternative existence. The refrain to the Nas song "Hold Down the Block" goes, "I gotta lay down the block, when the block is hot. I gotta use my imagination, to change the situation."[7] This aspiration is similar to other mythic exits from the 'hood, such as athletics. The narratives in hip hop lyrics are American Dream stories about rhyming one's way to success. This use of creative power is about becoming a self-made person as opposed to a person whose life is entirely shaped by social determinants. Unfortunately, the selves that we see created in hip hop today are so often meager approximations of full personhood, identified by consumption rather than humanity and responsive to a market that is driven by long-standing stereotypes of Black people as violent, hypersexual, and generally criminal. Nonetheless, the idea of self-creation is a powerful one and should lead us to understand that hope persists for the men called "a problem," a hope that merits response and revision.

A Story of Guns, Girls, and Gangsters

The embarrassingly formulaic hip hop video is an adolescent male fantasy: fawned over by half-naked women, the young man wears accoutrements of ready cash and is backed up by his artillery. This kind of masculine fantasy is deeply American. Byron Hurt, maker of the acclaimed documentary film "Hip Hop: Beyond Beats and Rhymes," explained: "I think the way you see manhood portrayed in hip hop is deeply entrenched in American culture, not just hip hop culture. Like if you watch cowboy movies, gangster movies, action movies—you can see the same elements of manhood and masculinity in those areas that you will see in hip hop. What distinguishes hip hop from the rest of the culture is that hip hop is so blatant. Also, with hip hop you have a lot of young men who come from poverty, and other situations, that make this quest for hyper-masculinity seem much more essential" (Cantwell 2006).

Wealth, women, and the use of weapons in the violent assertion of power are central to the construction of American masculinity from

Horatio Alger stories and Western movies through the "War on Terror" and Donald Trump's reality television fare "The Apprentice." But, as Hurt's commentary about the effect of poverty on the quest for hyper-masculinity suggests, the masculine fantasy expressed in hip hop should not be treated merely as a multicultural version of the dominant fantasy. In considering the relationship between art and society, we must ask how artistic representations relate to conditions within these communities. Taking the sexist fantasy representations of women in particular, we find that the question merits a two-fold response. One is a response to the ideas it articulates: that it is appropriate to objectify women, and that women are valuable for what sexual or menial services they can provide men. The other is a response to the emotions it expresses: beyond lust, the man desires an idealized sexual relationship with women. The first dynamic that should prompt a critical assessment of this fantasy is that rates of employment and household headship are higher for black women than for black men, particularly in poor communities (Holzer, Offner, and Sorensen 2005). Neighborhoods of concentrated poverty are not locations of conventional patriarchal domination. The fantasy may reflects a longing for a kind of masculinity that is both appropriate to criticize for its implicit or explicit advocacy of male dominance and appropriate to empathize with because Black men have a vulnerable position within families, especially as women's partners in heterosexual relationships.

The sexist fantasy about women in hip hop is not only about physical domination but, perhaps even more centrally, about economic dominance. In the prevailing images propagated by the lyrics, women are "bought" with luxury items. This aspiration directly contradicts the material realities for poor Black men in urban America. As Ghostface Killah says, "When marinating in the slums, you gotta practice survival/ Now everybody wants to be the next American idol/ But these are more than just songs pressed up your vinyl/ Being rich is a poor man's dream, and we all wanna shine/ But we all can't green, know'a' I mean?"[8] Even small-time hustlers, who have more "cash" than the average poor working man, do not live like men in hip hop videos—for that matter, neither do hip hop artists themselves. Although poverty among black children overall has decreased in recent years, extreme poverty (defined by a family income no more than half of the established poverty level for a family of three, set at $7,064 in 2003) has sharply increased since welfare reform.[9] According to the National Center for Children in Poverty, Washington D.C. has the highest rate of child poverty in the U.S. (30 percent), and nearly one in five children (19.2 percent) in this largely African American city live in extreme poverty. In Illinois, whose black population is concentrated in Chicago, 44 percent of black children live in poverty (Fass and Cauthen 2005). These families are significantly more vulnerable to robbery and assault.[10] Black boys growing up in poor families are often watching their mothers struggle to provide for them. Only 35 percent of black children live with two parents; the majority live with their mothers.[11] In 1965, Dr. Martin Luther King, Jr. said: "the Negro male precedes his wife in unemployment. As a consequence he lives in a matriarchal society within the larger culture which is patriarchal."[12] While King's (and others') descriptions of the Black community as "matriarchal" have been appropriately interrogated for both their veracity and the implicit negative value judgment of cultures that are matrifocal or approaching gender equity, his observation does serve to support the claim that patriarchy is more fantasy than reality for poor Black men.[13] Two decades ago, William Julius Wilson (1987) persuasively argued that jobs were the answer for this problem. The need for employment opportunities is undeniable, and certainly the fixation upon money in hip hop reflects the prevalence of economic anxiety. The fantasies about wielding financial power over women in hip hop, I contend, manifest a longing for patriarchal security—economic, physical, and domestic—as well as men's deep anxieties about their potential as mates in the absence of economic security.

We should have a similar critical assessment of the image of violent power in hip hop. While access to guns is rampant in urban America, the reality is that a poor black young man is more likely to be the victim of crime and violence than to be a violent bully. According to the FBI's Uniform Crime Reports, in 2005, 27 blacks, 20 whites, and 14 persons of other races sustained a violent crime per 1000 persons within that racial group. Black men ages fifteen to twenty-four are victims of homicide at a rate of 85 per 100,000, while the rate in the general population is only 6 per 100,000. In 2005, 49 percent of murder victims were black, and the majority of that black victim population was male. More black men are hospitalized for assault injuries annually than women of all races combined.

In Byron Hurt's documentary, James Peterson discusses how rapper 50 Cent acquired a mystique in the eyes of Black men because he had survived multiple gunshot wounds. According to the account Peterson provided, this acclaim was not a romanticization of violence, but a sense of awe at his survival against extraordinary odds. The point of these examples is that the fantasy must be understood as imagination, but the longings driving that fantasy for young Black men should enlighten us and motivate progressive social policy. Trumpeted in various iterations in virtually every sector of American popular culture, these lyrical fantasies may encourage unsuccessful and potentially destructive mimicry of the kind of masculinity that eludes men who live in poverty. I do not mean to sound reductive, as though music dictates behavior; rather, I suggest that there is a dynamic relationship between our economic, political, racial, gender, and social position, how we process that existence, and how we see it processed by the interpretive texts that surround us. The violent and misogynistic fantasies in hip hop are easily condemned, but the greater challenge is to reveal the more humane underlying longings found in the music.

A deep longing for economic autonomy and other forms of security and self-actualization are apparent in the entrepreneurial ventures that are part of the world of hip hop: clothing companies, independent record labels, sneaker designs. This entrepreneurial fantasy in the world of hip hop, which occasionally translates into reality, manifests a longing for economic success outside of a job market that provides limited opportunity for meaningful work or for any work at all. The ideal, as unrealistic as it may be except for a few, is to create one's own opportunity.

My Boys, My Crew, My Block

Hip hop expresses a deep celebration of affiliation. Rappers often wax poetic about their friends, crew, community, city, or region. This celebration has been widely critiqued when it slides into accounts of violent conflict to assert the honor of one's group. The regional conflict that led to the deaths of Biggie Smalls and Tupac Shakur is the most dramatic display of the dangers of affiliation in hip hop history.

On the other hand, the strong identification with male friends, in conjunction with misogynistic lyrics, has been described as a homoerotic thread in hip hop. While homoerotic images do occur in this music, I find the assumption that male friendship is homoerotic implicitly homophobic, as though men's love for other men raises anxieties about its nature and heterosexual love is more appropriate for celebration than same-sex emotional intimacy. Moreover, there are out gay rappers (exclusively in the underground of the music) who are more justly identified as the source of a gay presence in hip hop precisely because they are challenging the oppressiveness of the closet and asserting identity and community.

Although these critical inquiries are important, we should consider the longing that is expressed in the enshrinement of friendship and membership in various kinds of groups. These relationships are important in part because of the prevalent concern with finding safe spaces. Among friends or with the crew, men can feel secure that violence will not occur; here the conflicts of romantic relationships that arise because of poverty and the imbalance in Black male and female economic realities do not exist. The love that surrounds friendship and membership provides a way of sustaining tenderness in contexts that may be quite brutal. Perhaps it expresses a deeper longing for a life which does not require such hyper-vigilance. The enshrinement of a particular kind of relationship implicitly entails a wish that the world could be so trustworthy.

The discourse about affiliation that is so prevalent in hip hop also signals a desire to create organization in poor urban communities. Whether or not disorganization actually exists, the physical environment may create internal and external perceptions, as the blighted state of Black neighborhoods is seen as evidence of social disorder (Sampson and Raudenbush 2004). Even for highly organized communities, this persistent perception creates anxiety. As well, while one dimension of life may be highly organized, others might be troublingly disorganized. For example, children who live in well organized homes often must attend urban schools that are chaotic. I do not mean to fetishize organization: Jim Crow and slavery were organized systems. But healthful organization can create valuable emotional securities, and we should consider the longing for membership suggested by the affiliation discourse in hip hop as a guide in our responses to this community.

Membership Rather Than Institutionalization: A Social Policy Response

One of the most powerful predictors of black males entering the prison system is failing to graduate from high school (Pettit and Western 2002; Holzer, Offner, and Sorenson 2005; Eckholm 2006). If school can be a place for membership, then it has a much greater chance of working for poor Black males who clearly value belonging and a sphere of emotional connection. Currently the school is a space where youth yearn for affiliation, but seldom find it a responsive environment. The success of films like *Drumline* and *Stomp the Yard* among Black audiences indicates a romantic yearning for the kind of membership that was ubiquitous before desegregation but is absent from the lives of many African Americans today. Strong affiliations used to be forged in all-black elementary and high schools (J. Anderson 1995, 1999). It is essential that we support locations for healthy membership development in school as well as out of school. To do so, we need to be involved in the creation of healthy social institutions for these young men to participate in. Such institutions have historically been most successful when they have emerged organically from communities. Nonetheless, social policy can and should have a hand in this goal. To the extent there can be a social policy effort to enhance, create, or sustain such institutions, what follows are a few modest recommendations.

First, effective social policy must respond to cultural realities. In the contemporary U.S., social policy is quite disconnected from cultural studies or serious cultural analysis. For example, the necessity of positive institutional membership has, generally speaking, not been part of any explicit policy initiative. Policy experts have appropriately highlighted the role of education, job training, and reentry strategies for offenders as responses to the challenges faced by young poor Black men (Edelman, Holzer, and Offner 2006). But surely facilitating a sense of membership through institution- or community-building is a critical component to success in any of these initiatives, particularly for someone who might find alternative spheres of belonging through illegal or antisocial activities. We must understand what institutional cultures must do in order to be successful. Institutions that are vehicles for access must provide a sense of belonging, safety, and affiliation.[14] This goal can only be achieved by intentional practices that accept the knowledge of the cultural community as legitimate sources for developing that cultural sophistication.

Social policy with respect to African Americans is often spoken about in terms of either a humanitarian responsibility to alleviate suffering or a "mutual self-interest" model concerned with the health of the entire society. In contrast, I advocate a democratic conception of social policy which seeks to maximize the experience of all members of our society as rights-bearing individuals. To do so with respect to young poor Black men requires not only protection of their safety but also vehicles for civic engagement and participation. This is another critical arena for affiliation.

Before the civil rights movement, African Americans were subject to comprehensive forms of social neglect and humiliation. Under these adverse conditions, the sustaining force of institutional membership in schools, churches, clubs, and civic organizations allowed a healthy community to develop and facilitated the formation of social movements to counter those destructive forces. Places for being fully human and loved despite our negative characterization in the larger society are essential. The absence of those institutions in the lives of poor young Black men today is a crucial deficit (Moss et al. 1993, 27). The support of institutions that are operated and developed by members of African American communities based in historic and culturally rooted models should be an important policy goal.

Living Critical Masculinity: A Cultural Response

We are challenged to consider what to do about a society that proclaims that to be a man one is required to have both a certain kind of economic success that is not available to everyone and a certain degree of power over others that is inaccessible and highly problematic. Counternarratives about masculinity such as those provided by Byron Hurt in his film *Hip Hop: Beyond Beats and Rhymes* are vitally important. Critical masculinity must become not simply an academic enterprise but an educational activity. Revising images of masculinity is just as important as gaining access to the economic vehicles that would allow Black men to attain conventional standards of masculinity.

Our current reality is unacceptable on both counts. The proportion of African American households that are headed by women more than doubled between 1970 and 1990 (Hamer 2006, 102). The displacement of black men as family heads, resident fathers, and spousal partners occurred simultaneously with the rapid rise in rates of black male imprisonment and the deconstruction of civil rights gains made in the 1960s and early 1970s. High rates of incarceration among poor black men affect not only their presence and their ability to provide economically but also their emotional and psychological well-being.

The value of fathers, sons, and boyfriends should not be seen as residing solely in their earning potential as long as their income and employment are limited by economic factors beyond the control of individuals. Research shows that men who cannot provide economically have less interaction with their children than those who can (Crowell and Leeper 1994, 14). That connection arises from our image of masculinity and fatherhood. The problem is exacerbated by the fact that we tend to define the role of non-custodial fathers almost exclusively in economic terms as providers of child support (Hamer 2006, 53). Black children who have non-custodial fathers are frequently referred to as "fatherless" in both the media and in social scientific research. The image of men as nurturers, as companions, and as participants in household management is obscured and even denied by such constructions. One potentially illustrative piece of data is that black men are reportedly less likely to serve as caregivers for elderly or infirm relatives than are white men, white women, or black women (U.S. DHHS 1995). If this duty were not regarded as contrary to images of Black masculinity, caregiving would be an important social role for a population that is disproportionately jobless in a community with high rates of infirmity. This issue is not an exclusively or even primarily one for poor and Black people to tackle. In middle-class households working women still carry a disproportionate burden of household duties. Americans' gender ideas are far less progressive than we often assume. Poor men are made to feel humiliated for failing to meet these gender ideas and then lambasted for taking on hyper-masculine postures. I do not mean to suggest that since poor Black men do not have jobs, we should just shuttle them into domestic responsibilities. Rather, a critical masculinity approach would entail both advocacy for public policy that could transform their economic and educational access and a refusal to devalue these men as men because they are denied that access. This refusal will occur only if we acknowledge the human value of males in far broader terms than mogul fantasies and masculine domination.

References

American Academy of Pediatrics, Committee on Communications, Policy Statement RE9144. 1996. Impact of music lyrics and music videos on children and youth. *Pediatrics* 98 (6): 1219–21.

Anderson, James D. 1995. Literacy and education in the African American experience. In *Literacy Among African American Youth*, ed. Vivian L. Gadsden and Daniel A. Wagner, 19–37. Cresskill, N.J.: Hampton Press.

———. 1988. *The Education of Blacks in the South, 1860–1935*. Chapel Hill: University of North Carolina Press.

Cantwell, John. 2006. Byron Hurt: On manhood in Hip Hop. *Vibe Magazine Online Exclusive*, posted June 28.

Correll, Joshua, G. L. Urland, and T. A. Ito. 2006. Event-related potentials and the decision to shoot: The role of threat perception and cognitive control. *Journal of Experimental Social Psychology* 42: 120–28.

Crowell, Nancy A., and Ethel M. Leeper, eds. 1994. 1994. *America's Fathers and Public Policy: Report of a Workshop*. Board on Children and Families, Commission on Behavioral and Social Sciences and Education, National Research Council, Institute of Medicine. Washington, D.C.: National Academy Press.

Du Bois, W. E. B. 1903. *The Souls of Black Folk.* Chicago: A. C. McClung.

Eckholm, Erik. 2006. Plight deepens for Black men, studies warn. *New York Times*, March 20.

Edelman, Peter, Harry J. Holzer, and Paul Offner. 2006. *Reconnecting Disadvantaged Young Men.* Washington, D.C.: Urban Institute Press.

Fass, Sarah, and Nancy K Cauthen. 2005. Who are America's poor children? Fact Sheet, National Center for Children in Poverty, September.

Ford, Thomas E. 1997. Effects of stereotypical television portrayals of African Americans on person perception. *Social Psychology Quarterly* 60 (3): 266–78.

Gilliam, Franklin D., Jr., and Shanto Iyengar. 2000. Prime suspects: The influence of local television news on the viewing public. *American Journal of Political Science* 44 (3): 560–73.

Hall, Stuart, Charles Critcher, Tony Jefferson, John Clarke, and Brian Robert. 1978. *Policing the Crisis: Mugging, the State, and Law and Order.* London: Palgrave Macmillan.

Hamer, Jennifer F. 2006. *What It Means to be Daddy: Fatherhood for Black Men Living Away from Their Children.* New York: Columbia University Press.

Holzer, Harry J., Paul Offner, and Elaine Sorensen. 2005. Declining employment among young black less-educated men: The role of incarceration and child support. *Journal of Policy Analysis and Management* 24 (2): 329–33.

King, Martin Luther, Jr. 1986. *A Testament of Hope: The Essential Writings and Speeches of Martin Luther King. Jr.*. Ed. James F. Washington. San Francisco: HarperCollins.

Lloyd, Blake Te'Neil. 2000. Media influence on identity formation and social competence: Does music video impact adolescent development? Ph.D. dissertation, University of Pennsylvania.

Martino, Steven C., Rebecca L. Collins, Marc N. Elliott, Amy Strachman, David E. Kanouse, and Sandra H. Berry. 2006. Exposure to degrading versus nondegrading music lyrics and sexual behavior among youth. *Pediatrics* 118 (2) (August): e430–e441.

Moss, E. Yvonne with Tobe Johnson, Diane Pinderhughes, Michael B. Preston, Susan Welch, and John Zipp. 1993. Black political participation: The search for power. In *African Americans: Essential Perspectives,* ed. Wornie L. Reed, 81–118. Westport, Conn.: Praeger Greenwood.

Payne, B. Keith. 2001. Prejudice and perception: The role of automatic and controlled processes in misperceiving a weapon. *Journal of Personality and Social Psychology* 81: 181–92.

Perry, Theresa. 1993. Toward a Theory of African American School Achievement. Center on Families, Communities, and Children's Learning, Report 16. Baltimore. March.

Perry, Theresa, Claude Steele, and Asa G. Hilliard. 2003. *Young, Gifted, and Black: Promoting High Achievement Among African American Students.* Boston: Beacon Press.

Pettit, Becky, and Bruce Western. 2002. Inequality in Lifetime Risks of Imprisonment. Washington, D.C.: National Science Foundation. July.

Sampson, Robert J., and Steven W. Raudenbush. 2004. Seeing disorder: Neighborhood stigma and the social construction of "broken windows." *Social Psychology Quarterly* 67 (4) 319–42.

U.S. Department of Health and Human Services (DHHS). 1995. Informal Caregiving: Compassion in Action. Booklet prepared under the direction of Jeanette Takamura and Bob Williams summarizing data from the 1982, 1989, and 1994 National Long-Term Care Surveys, 9. Accessed 27 April 2007 at http://aspe.hhs.gov/daltcp/reports/Carebro2.pdf

Wilson, William Julius. 1987. *The Truly Disadvantaged: The Inner City, the Underclass, and Public Policy.* Chicago: University of Chicago Press.

Wingood, Gina M., Ralph J. DiClemente, Jay M Bernhardt, et al. 2003. A prospective study of exposure to rap music videos and African American female adolescents' health. *American Journal of Public Health* 93: 437–39.

Wolff, Janet. 1988. Cultural studies and the sociology of culture. *Invisible Culture: An Electronic Journal for Visual Studies* 1 (Winter), http://www.rochester.edu/in_visible_culture/issue1.wolff/wollf.html, accessed April 27, 2007.

Part IV
Social Policy Matters

Chapter 12

Social Issues Lurking in the Over-Representation of Young African American Men in the Expanding DNA Databases

TROY DUSTER

In early May 2007, the governor of New York announced a plan to expand the state's criminal forensic database by requiring DNA samples from "those found guilty of any misdemeanor, including minor drug offenses" (McGeehan 2007). While several commentators were invited to reflect on some of the social consequences of this proposal, not a single word in the report or in the governor's plan mentioned the 800-pound gorilla in this database: race. Even the most cursory review of incarceration rates by sex, race, and age reveals an astonishing level of overrepresentation of young black males in the nation's prisons and jails. A striking but not atypical case is Washington State, where in 1998 blacks were only 3 percent of the general population, but 23 percent of the prison population (Palmer 1999).

To put this situation in recent historical perspective, in 1970 there were approximately 133,000 blacks in prison in the United States. Just three decades later, that figure had increased a stunning sevenfold, and by the year 2000, one million blacks were behind bars. In this essay, I explain the dramatic social and political implications of the racialized character of what may appear at first glance to be a race-neutral expansion of DNA databases.

Geometric Expansion of the National DNA Forensic Database

When criminal justice officials began collecting and storing DNA evidence in the early 1980s, the cases were always about sex crimes. Three factors converged to make this practice acceptable to politicians and the public: sex offenders are those most likely to leave body tissue and fluids at the crime scene; they rank among the most likely repeat offenders; and their crimes are often particularly reprehensible because they violate other persons, in acts ranging from rape to molestation and abuse of the young and most vulnerable. The rationale for having a DNA database of sex offenders was clear. By the mid-1980s, most states had begun to collect and store forensic data for those convicted of sexual crimes. In the ensuing two decades, these databases have expanded to include not only sex offenders and people convicted of violent crimes but also those convicted of felonious assault, arson, and a host of other crimes against property.

Today, all fifty states store DNA samples of sex offenders, and most do the same for convicted murderers (Simoncelli 2006, 1). But the original rationale seems inapplicable to the types of cases now included in the forensic database, such as burglary, car theft, and mere misdemeanors. In an even more dramatic departure from the original purpose, the federal government and six states now *collect and store DNA from anyone even arrested* (Simoncelli 2006). Why is the policy of storing the DNA of anyone who is arrested such a potentially explosive issue? The answer lies in the social patterns of arrest, independent of whether there are adequate grounds for specific arrests.

Comparing data on marijuana use with data on arrests for marijuana possession among youth who belong to different racial-ethnic groups reveals a significant bias: whites, who are more likely to use marijuana, are less likely to be arrested for possessing it. Figure 12.1 shows patterns of marijuana use by race and ethnicity. Among all those under thirty-five, who are most likely to be arrested, whites' rates of marijuana use actually exceed those of Blacks and Latinos.

Figure 12.2 shows a remarkably different arrest pattern for marijuana possession. In fifteen major metropolitan areas across the U.S., blacks are arrested, routinely and systematically, at about twice their proportions in the local population. Atlanta, Georgia, tops the list; 90 percent of all those arrested for marijuana possession are black, while only about 45 percent of the population is black. The story is very similar in every jurisdiction: only about a quarter of New York City's residents are black, but well over half those arrested for marijuana possession in New York are black.

How do we explain the fact that blacks are twice as likely as whites to be arrested for marijuana possession, yet are less likely to possess marijuana than whites? The answer lies in U.S. government policy, which dates back to a 1987 decision by law enforcement officials to train law enforcement personnel to "stop and search" suspects based on a particular social profile.

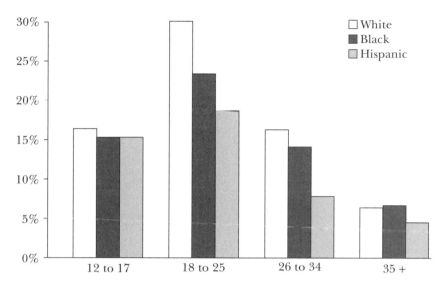

Figure 12.1. Age of last year of marijuana use, by ethnic group. SAMHSA
Office of Applied Studies, National Household Survey on Drug Abuse, 1997.
http://www.oas.samhsa.gov/?NHSDA/1997Main/?nhsda1997mfWeb-27.htm#,
Table3.5.

Operation Pipeline as the Major Funnel to the DNA Tunnel

In 1986, the federal Drug Enforcement Administration initiated Operation Pipeline, a program designed in Washington, D.C., that trained
27,000 law enforcement officers in 48 participating states over the ensuing
decade. The project was designed to alert police and other law enforcement officials to "likely profiles" of those who should be stopped and
searched for possible drug violations. High on the list are young, male
African Americans and Latinos driving in cars that signal that something
might be amiss. For example, a nineteen-year-old African American driving a new Lexus would be an "obvious" alert, based on the assumption that
the family could not afford such a car so the driver must be "into drugs."

In a study of the I-95 highway corridor just outside Baltimore, police
records indicated that Latinos and blacks were eight times more likely
to be stopped by police than were whites (Duster 2004). A young white
male in his early twenties driving a Lexus would not be considered "suspicious" since the police are likely to assume that he is driving the family
car. In this real-life example, we can see that if we control these statistics
for class, we still find a racial difference; see Figures 12.3 and 12.4.

Of course, many appreciate that DNA evidence can be and has been
used to exonerate the innocent. But, while there have been only a few

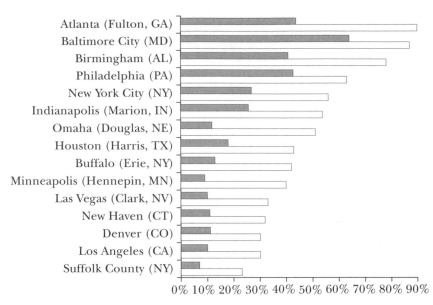

Figure 12.2. Racial arrest pattern for marijuana possession, fifteen metropolitan areas.

hundred exonerations of the wrongfully convicted, thousands languish behind bars because of prosecutors' claims of a match of DNA evidence. Despite public perceptions to the contrary, fueled by television drama series, movies, popular novels, mystery stories, and other fictions, *jury trials are the exception.* Fewer than 10 percent of those serving time in prison have been convicted by a jury. The overwhelming majority of convictions are secured by a plea bargain, a deal done out of public sight between the prosecutor and the defendant's legal representative—typically the Public Defender in the case of young black males. This is where the racial bias in the collection of DNA evidence has the greatest potential to produce a high level of unexamined social and racial injustice.

In September 1999, Louisiana passed the first state law permitting DNA samples to be taken from all those arrested for a felony (Tracy and Morgan 2000). Four other states quickly followed. Today, thirty-eight states include some misdemeanants' samples in the DNA databank. Twenty-nine states require that tissue samples be retained in their DNA databanks after profiling is complete (Kimmelman 2000, 211); only Wisconsin requires the destruction of tissue samples at that point. While thirty-nine states

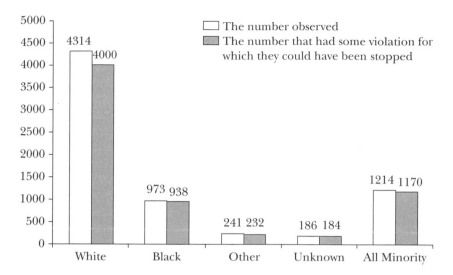

Figure 12.3. Drivers stopped, by race, I-95 North Corridor, January 1995 to September 1996. Maryland State Police files, http//www/aclu.profiling/report/index/html Gray: number observed; black: number with some violation for which they could have been stopped.

permit expungement of samples if charges are dropped, destroying the sample and permanently removing the DNA from the database, almost all those states place the burden on the individual to initiate expungement. Civil privacy protection, which in the default mode would place the burden on the state, has been reversed.

What started as a tool to deal with sex offenders has now "crept" into a way to "capture" those arrested on far less serious charges. Citizens should worry about what policy analysts have come to call "mission creep," which occurs when a policy intended for one specific purpose "creeps" or expands into many other uses—for example, when a military mission is extended to accomplish political goals. The best example is the history of the Social Security number. When the idea was first introduced in the mid-1930s, skeptical members of Congress warned that it could become the equivalent of a national identification card. Advocates assured the Congress that the Social Security card would only be used to track and allocate employment-related benefits. With clear hindsight, we can see how "mission creep" has affected the Social Security Number during the ensuing seven decades. A similar trend is already visible regarding DNA samples.

On January 5, 2006, President George W. Bush signed into law HR 3402, the Department of Justice's reauthorization of the Violence

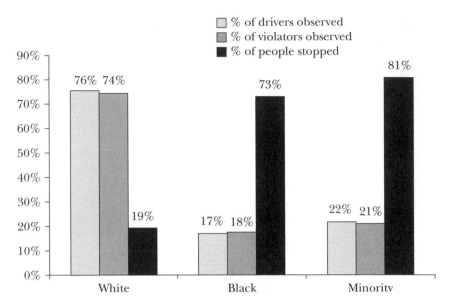

Figure 12.4. Percentage of drivers stopped, by race, I-95 North Corridor, January 1995 to September 1996. Maryland State Police files http//www/aclu .profiling/report/index/html. Light gray: number of drivers observed; dark gray, number of violators observed; black, number of drivers stopped.

Against Women Act of 2005. This legislation for the first time permits state and federal law enforcement officials to enter DNA profiles of those arrested for federal crimes into the federal Combined DNA Index System (CODIS) database. Previously, only convicted felons could be included. Those DNA profiles will remain in the database unless and until those who are exonerated or never charged with the crime request that their DNA be expunged. The default will be to store these profiles, and getting them expunged requires vigilance and vigorous proactive behavior on the part of those arrested. Given their youth, low economic status, and lack of access to legal counsel, the overwhelming majority will not even know of their right to have this information expunged.

This expansion is certainly a boon for those in the business of providing DNA testing services. Just after President Bush signed the bill authorizing collection of DNA samples on arrestees, the chief executive officer of Orchid Cellmak, one of the leading providers of DNA testing, issued a statement applauding this development:

This is landmark legislation that we believe has the potential to greatly expand the utility of DNA testing to help prevent as well as solve crime . . . . It has been shown that many perpetrators of minor offenses graduate to more violent crimes, and we believe that this new legislation is a critical step in further harnessing the power of DNA to apprehend criminals much sooner and far more effectively than is possible today. (Orchid Cellmak press release, January 6, 2006, 1)

Twenty states authorize the use of databanks for research on forensic techniques. Based on the statutory language in several of those states, this research could easily mean assaying genes or loci that contain other types of information, even though current usage is restricted to analyzing portions of the DNA which are useful only as identifying markers. Since most states retain the full DNA (and every cell contains all the DNA information), it is a small step to using these DNA banks for other purposes. The original purpose has been pushed to the background, and the "creep" accelerates.

Biased Policies and Practices of Genetic Profiling

While the U.S. has been pushing ahead rapidly, the United Kingdom has been in the vanguard of these developments.[1] In April 2004, a law was passed in the UK permitting police to retain samples from anyone arrested for any reason, including those who are not charged with a crime. Anyone can have their DNA taken and stored. The database already contains 2.8 million DNA "fingerprints" taken from identified suspects; plus another 230,000 from unidentified samples collected from crime scenes.[2] Samples are being added at the rate of between 10,000 and 20,000 per month.[3] The aim is to have on file the DNA of a quarter of the adult population—a figure that exceeds ten million, making it by far the largest DNA database in the world. It was recently disclosed that nearly four in ten black males in the UK are in the forensic database, compared with fewer than one in ten white males (Randerson 2006). Civil liberties groups and representatives of the black community worry that this disparity is not only a sign of racial biases in the criminal justice system but will actually exacerbate them. Dominic Bascombe of *The Voice*, the black newspaper based in London, expressed his concern that these data reflect police attitudes more than they do the behavior of those apprehended: "It is simply presuming if you are black you are going to be guilty—if not now but in the future." He called this "genetic surveillance" of blacks: "We certainly don't think it reflects criminality" (quoted in Randerson 2006). The reporter concluded: "Anyone in the database—and family members—can more easily be linked to a crime scene if their DNA is found there. This may be because they are a criminal, or because they visited the scene prior to the crime" (Randerson 2006).

When representative spokespersons from the biological sciences say that "there is no such thing as race" they mean, correctly, that there are no discrete categories that have sharp boundaries, that there is nothing mutually exclusive about our current or past categories of "race," and that there is more genetic variation within "racial" categories than between them. All this is true. However, when Scotland Yard or the police force of Birmingham, England, or New York City want to narrow the list of suspects in a crime, they are not primarily concerned with tight taxonomic systems of classification with no overlaps. That is the stuff of theoretical physics and logic in philosophy, not the practical stuff of trying to solve crimes or the practical application of molecular genetics to health delivery via genetic screening—and all the messy overlapping categories that will inevitably be involved with such enterprises. For example, some African Americans have cystic fibrosis even though the likelihood is far greater among Americans of North European descent, and in a parallel if not symmetrical way some white Americans have sickle cell anemia even though the likelihood is far greater among Americans of West African descent. But in the world of cost-effective decision making, genetic screening and testing for these disorders are routinely based on common-sense versions of the phenotype. The same is true for the quite practical matter of naming suspects.

In 2000, the New York Police Department, with the urging and support of Mayor Guiliani, was chafing to use a portable DNA lab kit (Mathis 2000). New York Police Chief Howard Safir said that a DNA sample should be taken from "anyone who is arrested for anything" (Tracy and Morgan 2000, 665). This lab kit, which was developed by the Whitehead Institute for Biomedical Research, emerged at the convergence of molecular genetics with concerns about the identification of criminal suspects. During the next decade, it is more likely that we will be using these technologies for purposes of forensics and law than to develop medical therapies. California passed a ballot proposition in 2004 that permits the collection and storage of DNA data not only on all felons but on some categories of arrestees and misdemeanants by 2008.

New York State has since 1994 collected fingerprints from persons receiving public assistance in order to prevent duplicate claims, but does not generally share those data with law enforcement. In New York, arrest records must be sealed, and employers cannot ask if a job applicant has ever been arrested, but only if he or she has been convicted. When a mere arrest triggers DNA sampling and storage, and when those samples are not expunged, the forensic record becomes analogous to stored radioactive waste, in that it keeps emitting its effect (Kimmelman 2000).

Population-Wide DNA Databases

Many scholars and public policy analysts now acknowledge the substantial and well-documented racial-ethnic biases in police procedures, prosecutorial discretion, jury selection, and sentencing practices. Racial profiling is but the tip of an iceberg (Mauer 1999). Racial disparities penetrate the whole criminal justice system, from biased policies of stopping and searching drivers all the way up to racial disparities in seeking the death penalty for a given crime.

If the DNA database is primarily composed of those who have been touched by the criminal justice system, and that system is pervaded by practices that routinely select disproportionately from one group, there will be an obvious skew or bias toward this group. Some have argued that the best way to handle the racial bias in the DNA database is to include everyone. But this proposal does not address the far more fundamental problem of the bias that generates the configuration and content of the criminal (or suspect) database. If the lens of the criminal justice system is focused almost entirely on one part of the population—young men of color in the inner city—for a certain kind of activity—drug dealing and street crime—and ignores a parallel kind of crime—cocaine sales at the fraternity a few miles away—then even if the fraternity members' DNA is in the data bank, they will not be subject to the same level of matching, or of subsequent allele frequency profiling research to "help explain" their behavior. *That behavior itself will not have been recorded.* That is, if the police are not stopping to arrest the fraternity members, it does not matter whether their DNA is in a national database or not, because they are not *criminalized* by the selective aim of the artillery of the criminal justice system.

In the aftermath of the 1965 Watts rebellion, bookended by the dramatic news of burning cities with rioting and looting that continued for several days in Detroit and Newark, two sharply contrasting images of the police emerged in the public consciousness. These opposing views were distilled in two bumper stickers: "The Police Serve and Protect the Community" and "The Police are a Brutal Occupying Alien Force." Which viewpoint predominated depended upon the community's social location. This phenomenological separation of the races, predicted in 1968 by the Kerner Report, explains the remarkably divergent responses to the O. J. Simpson verdict. Cameras trained on audiences of white viewers showed shock, dismay, and anger. But cameras trained on African Americans just after the verdict was announced showed people shouting affirmation, laughing, and hugging.

Just as the Tuskegee experiment has had far greater resonance and traction in cultural memory among African Americans than among whites, so the Rampart police scandal, uncovered in Los Angeles in 1999, is the subject of far more barber-shop theorizing along Martin Luther King Jr. Drive and Cesar Chavez Street than in affluent suburbs and country clubs. Beginning in late 1999, nine months of testimony revealed that officers in the Rampart division of the Los Angeles Police Department were planting drugs and guns on defendants, mainly African Americans and Latinos, and then testifying in court, under oath, that they had found these items on the suspects, in order to secure convictions (Cannon 2000, 32). These machinations came to light only because a police officer working in a special unit of Rampart (Community Resources Against Street Hoodlums, or CRASH) began testifying against his fellow officers while he was awaiting retrial on charges of stealing impounded cocaine. The officer, Rafael Perez, testified that he and other police officers had planted guns on suspects, fabricated drug evidence, and lied in arrest reports. As a result, more than 120 criminal defendants had their convictions vacated and dismissed, and more than $42 million has been paid in civil settlements (Glover and Lait 2003).

During the last fifteen years, serious police corruption has come to light in Dallas, New Orleans, Philadelphia, and Chicago. In Dallas, the police framed 39 Latinos and had them deported by planting what they testified to be cocaine on them. The substance turned out to be powdered wallboard gypsum.[4] In the infamous Tulia, Texas, drug bust, a corrupt police officer jailed and then helped convict nearly three dozen people by planting drugs and testifying against them. These convictions were later overturned when the governor pardoned 35 persons, and the police officer was indicted for perjury (Gold 2003, A11). The scandal came to national attention only after Bob Herbert kept up a steady stream of revelations in his column in the *New York Times*. This racially biased pattern has a substantial bearing upon the degree to which citizens do or do not trust supposedly neutral DNA technology when wielded by law enforcement.

A few more examples fill in the contours of a national pattern, a mosaic of dotted lines that can be connected to provide a plausible account of suspicion. In the early 1990s, Philadelphia's 39th police district was rocked by scandal. Five officers pleaded guilty to setting up suspects, bribing witnesses, and planting evidence, resulting in the vacating of more than 50 convictions and an investigation of another several thousand arrests. "What's most disturbing about the Philly corruption," said Lynn Washington, legal scholar and editor of the Philadelphia *New Observer*, "is that the DA knew what the cops were up to, but tolerated their use of planted evidence because it boosted conviction rates" (quoted in Parenti 1996, 4). New York's police were rocked by a similar scandal, when 16 officers of the Bronx 48th precinct were arrested and indicted "on charges ranging from falsifying evidence to stealing weapons and money from illegally raided apartments (Parenti 1996, 2).

This pattern of racial bias and police corruption sets the context for the discussion about DNA, genetic technologies, and crime fighting as it relates to the African American and Latino community. On the basis of their divergent experiences with law enforcement, some groups are likely to see DNA evidence as definitive, while others maintain strong skepticism, thinking that DNA technology might not be used fairly in a criminal justice system that is tainted. African Americans and Latinos in the poorest neighborhoods in our major cities are far more likely to approach DNA evidence with a general mistrust. Indeed, these divergent perspectives on just how definitive DNA testing is arise directly from groups' divergent experiences with the law enforcement system. On the one hand, when analysis of the DNA left at the crime scene does not match that of the person who has been convicted, an innocent person may be exonerated. On the other hand, when there is a match between the DNA found at a crime scene and that in a databank (known as a "cold hit"), a person who was not previously a suspect may be arrested and convicted.

If DNA is the only evidence against the accused, and citizens are aware of the fact that in many cities police have been caught framing people of color, some will worry about the possibility that evidence will be abused by rogue police officers who are committed to obtaining a conviction. If the police can plant cocaine and guns on those whom they later testify against and obtain a conviction, they can surely "plant DNA." The legitimacy of the criminal justice system rests primarily on the citizenry's belief that the laws are applied fairly. Two matters affecting that legitimacy come to the fore regarding DNA evidence. First, who, or what part of the society, would believe that the police would do such a thing as plant DNA evidence? Second, even if they did, can DNA evidence ever stand alone without other circumstantial evidence?

Police Departments' Organizational Imperative

Powerful organizational motives push police departments to demonstrate effectiveness in "solving crimes." It is a considerable embarrassment for a police department to have a long list of crimes on their books for which no arrest has been made. No police chief with this problem wishes to face a city council concerned about crime. Backlogs of unsolved cases count more than almost anything else when it comes to reporting to the public about what the police are doing (Skolnick 2002; Skolnick and Fyfe 1993). Working under these organizational imperatives, police departments clean up the books by a procedure known as "cleared by arrest." To understand how arrest rates are influenced by "clearing," it is vital to ground this procedure empirically by close observation.

Here is the pattern. Someone, "P," is arrested and charged with committing a crime, for example, burglary. There are a number of other unsolved burglaries in this police precinct. The arresting officers see a pattern to these burglaries and decide that the suspect is likely to have committed a number of those on their list. Thus, it sometimes happens that when P is arrested for just one of those burglaries, the police can clear 15 or 20 crimes with that single arrest. The defendant can show up in the statistics as a "repeat offender," even though there may never be any follow-up research to verify or corroborate that the "rap sheet" accurately represents the burglaries now attributed to P.

This pattern can be corroborated empirically only by "riding around in police cars" and observing police work close-up (Jackall 2005). Yet, if social theorists take the FBI Uniform Crime Reports as a reflection of the crime rate, with no observations as to how those rates were constructed, they will make the predictable "policy error" of assuming that a very small number of persons commit a large number of crimes. The resulting error in theorizing would be to look for the "kind of person" who repeatedly engages in this behavior—as if criminal acts, rather than the police procedure of "clearing by arrest," generated the long rap sheet.

The racial composition of the U.S. prison population has shifted dramatically over the past thirty years. The convergence of this social trend with the burgeoning redefinition of race as something that can be determined by DNA patterns will generate challenges to equal justice at many levels, from the attempted reinscription of race as a biological or genetic category to the attempted explanation of a host of complex social behaviors. Those challenges can only be met by doing what the social researchers of a previous generation did with police work: going to sites at which those data are generated and scrutinizing the procedures through which they are produced for racial biases and other violations of civil rights.

Unreasonable Searches and DNA Dragnets

To understand the historical and political context of the right of citizens "to be secure in the persons, houses, papers, and effects, against unreasonable searches and seizures" as specified in the Fourth Amendment to the U.S. Constitution, we must go back to the period when the British ruled the American colonies. In this period, an officer of the Crown, armed with only the most general warrant for collecting taxes, could break down the door of a person's home, enter, search for taxable goods, and seize whatever items appeared not to have been taxed by going through customs (Chapin 2004, 1847). Colonial officials' exercise of these powers was one of the key issues that triggered the American Revolution, so protection against unreasonable search and seizure was enshrined in the Bill of Rights.

The Fourth Amendment does not specify what constitutes a " reasonable search," but most courts have interpreted this language substantively as requiring the government to conduct only searches that are "warranted" and, procedurally, to obtain a search warrant in advance. However, a search is sometimes permissible without a warrant. In issuing a warrant, the state must balance the "government's special needs" against the individual's right to personal privacy. "Special needs" encompass the safety of passengers on public conveyances, so the courts have ruled that it is permissible to test airline pilots, bus drivers, and train and subway operators for alcohol and drugs. The police have been allowed to search citizens on other grounds, such as "suspicious behavior," without obtaining a warrant.

Police are usually prohibited from carrying out a general dragnet of those who exhibit no suspicious behavior—*unless that suspicious behavior is being in a population group that is thought to contain the likely suspect.* In such circumstances, privacy rights have been limited; for example, the U.S. Supreme Court has ruled that ex-convicts have fewer protections of the expectation of privacy (see the discussion of *Griffin v. Wisconsin* in Chapin 2004, 1843). The federal DNA Act of 2000 provided funds for states to expedite the admission of DNA evidence of crimes without suspects. The lower courts have been challenged on this, but the law has so far withstood the challenge, and the Supreme Court has yet to rule on the issue (Chapin 2004, 1854). In late December 2005, the President of the United States acknowledged that he had authorized warrantless electronic eavesdropping on U.S. citizens in the wake of the September 11, 2001, terrorist attacks (Sanger 2005, 1). Which socially designated groups would be singled out for such invasions of their privacy is obvious: people whose appearance can be interpreted as placing them in a suspect group, such as immigrants from the Middle East, North Africa, and South Asia, and people who seem to be Muslim. Similarly, Latino and African American males in the inner city or as "bodies out of place" in predominantly white settings are targeted. Just being part of a group, or being perceived as belonging to a group, becomes "suspicious behavior." DNA dragnets are the empirical extension of this biased limitation of rights.

DNA dragnets originated in England and are most advanced in Europe and Great Britain. The first DNA dragnet was conducted in Leicestershire, England, in 1987. Two teenage girls were raped and murdered in the same area, and police requested "voluntary" blood samples from more than 4,500 males in the vicinity. When a man was overheard boasting that he had asked a friend to submit a DNA sample in his place, he was immediately a prime suspect, and he turned out to be the killer (Wambaugh 1989). Germany is the site of the largest DNA dragnet ever conducted. In 1998, the police collected samples from more than 16,000 people, and finally they matched the DNA of a local mechanic to that found on the body of an eleven-year-old girl who had been raped and murdered (Hansen 2004, 42).

While the United States has only had about a dozen DNA dragnets, what is most notable about them is their racialized character. San Diego was among the first jurisdictions to conduct the practice when, in the early 1990s, a serial killer murdered six persons in their homes. The suspect was African American, and more than 750 African Americans were tested. The man who was eventually apprehended and convicted was identified only after being arrested for an unrelated crime. In 1994, Ann Arbor, Michigan, police obtained nearly 200 samples from African Americans in the hunt for yet another serial rapist and murderer. In that case, too, the perpetrator was apprehended in the course of committing another crime. He was among approximately 400 men who had refused to be tested, and his conviction seemed to validate the police chief's conclusion that merely refusing DNA testing was grounds for suspicion. Men who had been subjected to the DNA dragnet, including one who had been fired from his job after a detective informed his coworkers that he was being interrogated, brought a class action suit and won damages. In 2004, Charlottesville, Virginia, a racialized DNA dragnet generated such intense criticism from civil liberties groups that the police suspended the operation.[5]

Despite serious grounds for concern about the pervasive violation of citizens' civil rights, the expansion of national DNA databases is inevitable. The House of Representatives passed a bill (H.R. 3214, "Advancing Justice Through DNA Technology Act of 2003") that would expand the original CODIS to include persons merely indicted. In 2004, California voters passed a proposition (No. 69) that permits collection and storing of DNA for those *merely arrested* for a select number of crimes by 2008, joining four other states collecting DNA on arrestees. The Violence Against Women Act of 2005 contains a provision that DNA samples can be obtained from those merely "detained" under federal authority.

As the number of profiles in the databases increases, researchers will propose to provide DNA profiles of specific offender populations. Twenty states authorize the use of databanks for research on forensic techniques (Kimmelman 2000). Simoncelli (2006) analyzes the civil liberties implications of the U.S. Senate's approval of the reauthorization of the Violence Against Women Act (S. 1197, October 2005). Senator Kyl's amendment to this reauthorization bill included a provision that persons merely *arrested* or *detained* by federal authorities would have their DNA taken, profiled, and stored. A similar amendment was attached to the H.R. 3132, the Children's Safety Act of 2005, approved by the U.S. House of Representatives that September. The DNA Fingerprint Act of 2005 goes even farther, allowing states to upload DNA profiles from anyone whose DNA samples are collected under applicable legal authorities. Moreover, it eliminates the current protections that prevent the collection and storing of DNA profiles from arrestees who have not been charged in an indictment and permits the retention of DNA samples that are voluntarily submitted solely for elimination purposes.

All of these developments point to an ever-expanding national forensic DNA database. When this is coupled with an increasing commitment to use the DNA to estimate racial identity in order to reduce the number of suspects that are needed in a mass screening program (Lowe et al. 2001), we can see the ingredients for what Wacquant (2005) called a "deadly symbiosis." Sixty-two percent of all prisoners incarcerated in the United States are either African American or Latino (Gross et al. 2004), while these groups account for only about a quarter of the nation's population.

Three forces are converging to produce a dangerous challenge to the idea that the new DNA technologies can deployed as neutral advances to achieve greater social justice: the highly selective aim of the artillery of the War on Drugs on young African American and Latino males; political pressure on police departments in major urban areas to demonstrate their effectiveness in crime fighting; and police scandals in many of those cities that have shown a remarkable pattern: abusive treatment of the members of the poorest communities of African Americans and Latinos, including the planting of evidence. Thomas Jefferson is credited with the phrase: "Eternal vigilance is the price of freedom." As the nation seems increasingly mesmerized by popular media renderings of DNA technology as a device for exoneration and more effective crime scene investigation, those watching the astronomical incarceration rate of young African American males should pay special heed to Jefferson's exhortation.

References

Cannon, Lou. 2000. One bad cop. *New York Times Magazine*, October 1, 2.

Chapin, Aaron B. 2005. Arresting DNA: Privacy expectations of free citizens versus post-convicted persons and the unconstitutionality of DNA dragnets. *Minnesota Law Review* 89 (6) (June): 1842–74.

Duster, Troy. 2006a. Comparative perspectives and competing explanations: Taking on the newly configured reductionist challenge to sociology. *American Sociological Review* 71 (February): 1–15.

Duster, Troy. 2006b. Explaining differential trust of DNA forensic technology: Grounded assessment or inexplicable paranoia? *Journal of Law, Medicine and Ethics* 34 (2) (Summer): 293–300, http://www.gene-watch.org/DNADatabases/DusterBrief.html, accessed June 25, 2007.

———. 2006c. The molecular reinscription of race: Unanticipated issues in biotechnology and forensic science. *Patterns of Prejudice* 40 (4/5) (November): 827–41.

———. 2004. Selective arrests, an ever-expanding DNA forensic database, and the specter of an early twenty-first-century equivalent of phrenology. In *DNA and the Criminal Justice System: The Technology of Justice*, ed. David Lazer, 315–34. Cambridge, Mass.: MIT Press.

Franklin, Raymond. 1991. *Shadows of Race and Class*. Minneapolis: University of Minnesota Press.

Glover, Scott, and Matt Lait. 2003. Lack of funds stalls Rampart probe: The LAPD seeks private donations so that an independent panel can begin investigating the department's handling of the scandal. *Los Angeles Times*, November 6, B1.

Gold, Scott. 2003. 35 are pardoned in Texas drug case. *Los Angeles Times*, August 23, A11.

Gross, Samuel R., Kristen Jacoby, Daniel J. Matheson, Nicolas Montgomery, and Sujata Patil. 2005. Exonerations in the United States, 1989 through 2003. Manuscript, University of Michigan Law School, 2004. www-mickunas.cs.uiuc.edu, accessed December 17, 2005.

Hansen, Mark. 2004. DNA dragnet. *American Bar Association Journal* (May): 38–43.

Jackall, Robert. 2005. *Street Stories: The World of Private Detectives*. Cambridge, Mass.: Harvard University Press.

Kimmelman, Jonathan. 2000. Risking ethical insolvency: A survey of trends in criminal DNA databanking. *Journal of Law, Medicine and Ethics* 28: 209–21.

Lowe, Alex L., Andrew Urquhart, Lindsey A. Foreman, and Ian W. Evett. 2001. Inferring ethnic origin by means of an STR profile. *Forensic Science International* 119: 17–22.

Mathis, Ayana. 2000. New York police ponder portable DNA labs. *Village Voice*, June 6, 26.

Mauer, Marc. 1999. *Race to Incarcerate*. New York: New Press.

McGeehan, Patrick. 2007. New York plan for DNA data in most crimes. *New York Times*, May 14.

Palmer, Louise D. 1999. Number of blacks in prison nears one million. *Boston Globe*, February 28.

Parenti, Christian. 1996. Police crime. http://zmag.org/ZMag/articles/mar96parenti.htm, accessed June 24, 2007.

Risch, Neil, Esteban Burchard, Elad Ziv, and Hua Tang. 2002. Categorization of humans in biomedical research: Genes, race and disease. *Genomebiology* (July 1): 1–12, http://genomebiology.com/2002/3/7/comments/2007, accessed November 19, 2005.

Randerson, James. 2006. DNA of 37% of black men held by police. *Guardian*, January 5, 1.

Roberts, Dorothy. 1997. *Killing the Black Body: Race, Reproduction, and the Meaning of Liberty*. New York: Pantheon.

Sanger, David E. 2005. In address, Bush says he ordered domestic spying. *New York Times*, December 18, A1.

Simoncelli, Tania. 2006. Dangerous excursions: The case against expanding forensic DNA databases to innocent persons. *Journal of Law, Medicine and Ethics* 34 (2): 390–97.

Skolnick, Jerome H. 2002. Corruption and the blue code of silence. *Police Practice and Research* 3 (1).

Skolnick, Jerome H., and James J. Fyfe. 1993. *Above the Law: Police and the Excessive Use of Force*. New York: Free Press.

Taylor, Anne L. et al., for the African-American Heart Failure Trial Investigators. 2004. Combination of isosorbide dinitrate and hydralazine in Blacks with heart failure. *New England Journal of Medicine* 351 (20) (November 11): 2049–57.

Touchette, Nancy. 2003. Genome test nets suspected serial killer. *Genome News Network*, June 13.

Tracy, Paul, and Vincent Morgan. 2000. Big Brother and his science kit: DNA databases for 21st century crime control. *Journal of Criminal Law and Criminology* 90 (2): 635–90.

Wacquant, LoÔc, 2000. Deadly symbiosis: When ghetto and prison meet and mesh. *Punishment and Society* 3 (1): 95–134.

Wambaugh, Joseph. 1989. *The Blooding: The Dramatic True Story of the First Murder Case Solved by Genetic Fingerprinting*. New York: Morrow.

Wendler, D., R. Kingston, J. Madans, G. Van Wye, H. Christ-Schmidt, L. A. Pratt, O. W. Brawley, C. P. Gross, and E. Emanuel. 2006. Are race and ethnic minorities less willing to participate in health research? *PLOS Medicine* 3 (2) (February): 1–10. www.plosmedicine.org, accessed December 20, 2005.

"You can take me outta the 'hood, but you can't take the 'hood outta me": Youth Incarceration and Reentry

JAMIE J. FADER

Each year, over 100,000 young offenders are incarcerated in facilities designed to reform them and end their criminal careers (Sickmund, Sladky, and Kang 2004). These institutions employ a wide variety of strategies to "rehabilitate" their young targets, but all are based on the common assumption that children and youth are especially malleable and can be transformed through resocialization. Despite widespread belief among policymakers that any treatment is better than none, substantial empirical evidence suggests that many, or even most, forms of intervention have little measurable effect. Worse yet, they may have unintended negative consequences, particularly for the disadvantaged (McCord 2003; Petrosino, Turpin-Petrosino, and Finckenauer 2000; Sampson and Laub 1997).

The experiences of young people in the juvenile justice system vary widely. Even among those who are placed in a single facility under similar conditions, outcomes are disparate: some are rearrested soon after release; some continue to offend but are not brought to the attention of authorities; some appear to have made a complete turnaround as a result of their time away from home; and some seem simply to have outgrown offending. Many staff people say that they are unable to predict who will succeed and who will fail after returning home based on their behavior inside the institution. Poverty, lack of opportunities, and other community-level or societal factors seem as important in shaping outcomes as individuals' responses to treatment programs. Among young black men who occupy a marginal position in mainstream social institutions such as schools and workplaces, formerly incarcerated youth may desist from criminal behavior—ceasing criminal activities or substantially reducing their frequency and severity—but continue to struggle on a daily basis with maintaining a safe place to live, finding stable employment, and pursuing an education and job training. When using a broad definition of reintegration, distinguishing between "success" and "failure" becomes increasingly problematic.

Recently, research on youths returning from juvenile facilities has identified structural barriers to successful reintegration and offered suggestions for providing developmentally appropriate transitional services to adolescents (Altschuler and Brash 2004; Snyder 2004). The small but growing literature on the topic of reentry for incarcerated youth tends to treat community reintegration as independent from youths' institutional experience, however. Furthermore, just as community reentry studies have neglected programmatic experiences, program evaluations have generally failed to consider the cultural context in which young people must put these interventions to work.

Applying both an institutional and a cultural lens to the study of reentry allows for a critical examination of the underlying assumptions behind efforts to rehabilitate young offenders. This perspective invokes a debate that exists both in the scholarly literature and in the practice of juvenile corrections about the nature and source of change. Specifically, is a cognitive transformation a necessary or sufficient condition for desistance to occur, as Giordano, Cernkovich, and Rudolph (2002) suggest? Or, as Laub and Sampson (2001, 2003) argue, does desistance, which they define as the process that leads a person to cease offending, occur "by default"? If change is more than skin deep, how must urban youth meet the performative requirements set by facilities which demand behavioral evidence of a cognitive transformation? By attending to the contextual dynamics of reentry, looking backward at the institutional experience and forward to the cultural exigencies of the street, we can begin to meet Maruna's call to explore *how* and *why* desistance occurs—or fails to occur (2001, 27).

Scholarly analyses of desistance have presented somewhat paradoxical findings regarding the role of incarceration in "going straight." Aggregate analyses suggest that incarceration is linked to unstable employment, higher rates of re-offending, and increasing social inequality, particularly among black males (Laub and Sampson 2003; Sampson and Laub 1997; Western, Kling, and Weiman 2001; Holzer, Raphael, and Stoll 2004). Research that examines the effects of incarceration at the individual level has more mixed results. For some individuals, incarceration provides a "time out" to think about their behavior and their plans for the future (Anderson 2001; Edin, Nelson, and Paranal 2004). Some young men even identify incarceration, particularly in conjunction with experiences such as being in the military or fatherhood, as a turning point in their criminal careers (Laub and Sampson 2003). For others, the institutional experience appears to make no visible difference in their lives or, worse, puts them "off time" in terms of their psychosocial development, schooling, or employment (Steinberg, Chung, and Little 2004; Sullivan 2004).

Given the billions of dollars spent incarcerating youthful offenders each year and the possibility that confinement may actually reduce rather than enhance their life chances, it is critically important to scrutinize and explain the conflicting findings about the role of incarceration and the power of structural and cultural forces in determining future offending. I argue that these discrepant findings are in part a function of a monolithic view of these institutions. The literature is largely silent on a number of dimensions that comprise the institutional experience. In addition to the intervention modality employed there, the relationships that young people forge with both staff and other clients; time spent away from home and loved ones; opportunities for social mobility, such as completion of a high school diploma or GED; living in a "safe community"; lack of control over one's physical person; and even fun and play are important aspects of life inside juvenile facilities. Moreover, I argue that cultural orientations, specifically the "street code," shape the ways young people respond to and interact with the various elements of the institutional experience.

This essay examines these questions through a longitudinal study of young men who were incarcerated at a juvenile facility that extends from their institutionalization through their reentry into the community. Using ethnographic observations and in-depth interviews with a prospective sample of fifteen young black and Hispanic men incarcerated at "Santana Foundation," I document their experiences both inside and outside institutional walls.[1] I begin by exploring the program's daily rituals and requirements, in the course of carrying out an intervention designed to confront "criminal thinking errors." Next, I examine how urban culture shapes the way my informants perceive this intervention and how they rationalize the conflicting demands of the facility and their knowledge of the street code. Finally, by following them for up to two years after their return to Philadelphia, I can say something about whether and how they ultimately put their experience of incarceration to use in the community context.

I posit that the intervention employed by Santana and other similar "therapeutic" institutions confronts the "code of the street" (Anderson 1999), attempting to eliminate thoughts and behaviors that stem from street culture. Unable directly to address the structural and cultural causes of criminality, the facility instead targets "street" behavior, interpreting it as a reflection of individual propensities for delinquency. By equating street behavior with street culture and street culture with criminality, the institution fails to recognize the fundamental role that street culture plays in constructing masculinity and in providing an important source of respect (Anderson 1999).

Although the intervention employed by Santana Foundation is couched in individual-level explanations of criminal offending, I contend that young men embedded in the street code view it as a cultural assault, often in explicitly racialized terms. In rejecting this perceived racial and cultural stigma, they also resist the more positive aspects of the intervention. Over time, they learn to suppress "street" behavior with the goal of earning release, while at the same time maintaining that their identity is firmly grounded in street culture. Facing unchanged structural circumstances upon their return to the community, they are unable to translate the concrete advantages conferred by the facility, such as a high school diploma, into meaningful opportunities for improving their life chances. Moreover, because of the limited understanding of culture within Santana and other institutions, these young men are not provided with alternative cultural repertoires to help them navigate social institutions that are essential for successful community reintegration.

"Santana Foundation"

Santana Foundation is just over five hours' drive from Philadelphia, nestled deep within a national forest. It is a privately run institution that belongs to a larger for-profit company that is traded on the stock market. The facility itself is "staff secure": in theory, security is provided by intensive staff supervision. No fences surround the property, and the dorms where the program's clients sleep have no locks or window bars. Nevertheless, escape is nearly impossible, given the facility's location six miles from the nearest road. To avoid stigmatizing the program's residents, counselors and staff refer to them as "students," and indeed, the facility contains a well-funded school on site where the majority of young people spend a large part of their weekdays.

Judges and probation officers consider Santana a high-quality program for treating drug and alcohol abuse, including drug use and selling, and the findings of a Philadelphia-based independent evaluation bear out this opinion.[2] Juveniles often remain for a considerable period at Philadelphia's detention facility waiting for a bed to open up at this highly valued facility. Sending a youth to Santana is recognized as a fairly intrusive intervention, particularly given its distance from Philadelphia. Decision makers in the juvenile justice system believe that young people will not be coddled at Santana, as they might be at other facilities. For that reason, many consider it the last stop before young offenders move into the less therapeutically oriented state system which, in turn, is considered by most to be the last stop before the adult system.

Santana stands apart from most other juvenile facilities in some important ways, but it generally conforms to the model employed by a wide range of total institutions for the last two centuries. Perhaps the most important difference is that, in comparison with youth sent to other facilities that have contracts with the Philadelphia juvenile justice system, youth sent to Santana are more likely to complete the program successfully and less likely to be charged with a new offense during their time in the institution and during the six months following release. The facility distinguishes itself by its carefully constructed program design. Santana's theory of change, which is explicitly stated in its staff training manual, is based in criminal personality theory, an empirically derived (though problematic) explanation for delinquent and other antisocial behavior. The program's theoretical framework, short- and long-term objectives, and activities are tightly linked.[3] Among probation officers and administrators in the city's Department of Human Services, the facility generates fewer informal accounts of physical and sexual abuse than most other institutions utilized by Philadelphia's Family Court. In these ways, the young men sent to Santana are given one of the best possible institutional alternatives for delinquent youth. Yet few of my informants experienced substantial success upon their return to the community. The vast majority resumed regular marijuana use, continued to employ drug selling as a sporadic means of earning income, and have spotty work histories. Several have ongoing housing problems. We can only assume that the graduates of less well-run facilities might experience even greater difficulties when returning home.

In many ways, Santana looks like many other institutions. Historians have argued persuasively that today's reform schools retain many of the features of their predecessors since the birth of the reformatory in the nineteenth century (Miller 1998; Platt 1977; Schlossman 2005; Schneider 1992) Schneider argues that the history of reform schools is characterized by the repetition of three key themes: the organizational structure of reformatories; the failure of the Progressive movement (the attempt to address problems of industrialization and urbanization through governmental initiatives, characterized by many historians as paternalistic and moralistic in nature); and the identification of deviant— that is, successful—cases to legitimate their continued operation.[4] First, he points to several features of the organizational structure of institutions that are virtually identical to reformatories of the 1880s: their "sentimental pastoralism," the notion that the countryside has curative properties; the identification of lower-class youths' behavior as most problematic and worthy of intervention; and the methods that inmates use to "get by," such as lying. The conflict between "snitching" and solidarity, he contends, is integral to the workings of these facilities, and the targeting of the "street code" as problematic is only the most recent version of this issue. Next, he cites seventy years of social science literature demonstrating the persistent failure of institutions to promote change in their young targets. Finally, Schneider argues that proponents of these institutions always offer some "slim reed" of hope by sharing success stories in the face of overwhelming evidence that their efforts are ineffective, or even downright harmful. Reform schools have retained these features over a remarkable span of time, despite the profound social changes that have affected young people (see also Schneider 1992).

Goffman's (1961) study of asylums demonstrates that "total institutions" such as prisons, boarding schools, military camps, and mental hospitals share an astonishing degree of similarity. His work documents the processes of identity stripping and other mortification rituals, the manner in which staff creates and maintains social distance, and the strategies that inmates and mental patients use to maintain a coherent sense of self and narrative inside and outside the walls of institutions. These themes are echoed in my own observations inside Santana and in the personal accounts of my informants.

Goffman's research, like Schneider's, reveals cause for concern about the effects of institutionalization.

Total institutions frequently claim to be concerned with rehabilitation, that is, with resetting the inmate's self-regulatory mechanisms so that after he leaves he will maintain the standards of the establishment of his own accord . . . . In fact, this claim of change is seldom realized, and, even when permanent alteration occurs, the changes are often not of the kind intended by the staff. (Goffman 1961, 71)

Thus, while Santana is unique is several meaningful ways, young people's experience inside the facility is in many other ways similar to those in other institutions.

"Criminal Thinking Errors"

The guiding theory behind Santana's intervention is criminal personality theory, which is based on empirical evidence that offenders tend to share a similar set of cognitive characteristics distinguishing them from law-abiding members of society. During their time at Santana, youths must memorize 22 criminal thinking errors (sometimes known at other facilities as "cognitive distortions") and practice standard correctives for each. These errors include failing to endure adversity, succumbing easily to suggestion, adopting a victim stance rather than seeing oneself as a self-determining agent, taking unwarranted pride in antisocial behavior, expressing anger, and imaging oneself as unique. To be released from the program, young people must demonstrate a willingness to accept criticism (known inside the institution as "feedback") and a desire to make a change in their lives. These changes, while ostensibly occurring internally—that is, cognitively—must be demonstrated behaviorally.

Santana's program design is based largely on the work of Yochelson and Samenow (1976), forensic psychologists who developed the notion of "criminal thinking errors" after fifteen years of work with offenders in Maryland. Frustrated with the ineffectiveness of traditional therapeutic efforts, they concluded that criminals were distinct from law-abiding individuals because they had well-defined thought patterns that led them to make criminal decisions. The criminal can be identified by his need for excitement; his drive for power and status; his tendency to see himself as a victim and blame others for his station in life; and his exploitation of others for personal gain. He is a habitual liar and manipulator; has "abundant energy"; sees himself as worthless but argues that he is a "good person"; and is haunted by irrational fears, particularly of allowing others to see personal weakness. One moment sentimental, the next violent, the criminal mind moves quickly back and forth between contradictory emotional states, an error Yochelson and Samenow term "fragmentation."

Despite the fact that criminal thinking patterns were present in most of their sample as early as age four and were manifested in a number of antisocial behaviors, Yochelson and Samenow assert that altering criminal thinking patterns is possible. For change to occur, the personality must be broken down and built back up. A total rejection of the old self and acceptance of the new identity is necessary for meaningful change to be sustained. A successful "conversion" requires "a total destruction of a criminal's personality, including much of what he considered the 'good' parts. Converting involve[s] a 'surrender' to a responsible agent of change." This transformative process, they believe, is most likely to occur during periods of confinement, "when his options are considerably reduced and he is more likely to reflect on his past" (Yochelson and Samenow 1976, 36). In the terms used by contemporary research on desistance, young people must undergo a "cognitive transformation" whereby they begin to see themselves as wholly different from before (Giordano, Cernkovich, and Rudolph 2002).

Although Yochelson and Samenow maintain that their theory is race- and class-neutral (and, indeed, they developed it at a time when color-blindness appeared to be the most appropriate way to deal with issues of race), contemporary scholars can hardly ignore the significance of racial and class disparities as they relate to issues of crime and incarceration.

Even if we set aside for the moment the implications of a state-sanctioned effort to inculcate a disproportionately minority population of confined men with the belief that their bleak prospects in the labor market are a function of their personal shortcomings, some important questions remain. How do young black men experience "criminal thinking errors" or "cognitive distortions" interventions while incarcerated, especially as delivered by counselors and other staff who are nearly all white? What are the other meaningful aspects of the incarceration experience? How do the ways in which young black men make sense of these two vastly different worlds—the pastoral, structured setting of a juvenile facility and the gritty, violent realities of the poorest communities in Philadelphia—affect the choices they make and opportunities they find upon their return? I turn to a discussion of how the effort to eliminate "thinking errors" is implemented at Santana Foundation.

Implementation of Cognitive Behavioral Therapy

Cognitive Behavioral Therapy (CBT) at Santana Foundation consists of getting clients to recognize thinking errors as they occur in their daily thought patterns and teaching a series of correctives that are intended to deter criminal and antisocial behavior. Young people are given daily "feedback" on their behavior around their dorms, in school, and during mealtimes. This feedback is the basis of the client's "status" or level in the program; as he moves up through the highly structured level system, he is accorded an increasing number of privileges. Rarely do young people advance through these levels without backsliding. Failing to abide by the program's rules results in a drop in status and a loss of privileges. Serious misconduct is deemed a "Major Norm Violation," and in MNV status all privileges are suspended. To earn home passes and to be successfully discharged, clients must maintain a status 3—that is, be a positive role model for others—for four to six consecutive weeks.

In addition to CBT, Santana's program model includes a twelve-step component. At the beginning of each day, a morning meeting is held inside the dorms where the counselors announce the day's theme and which of the twelve steps and traditions will be highlighted. No distinction is made between drug users and drug sellers, or between grades of drug use. This blurring of distinctions is significant, given the near ubiquity of marijuana use among inner-city youth, particularly boys; users are lumped together with dealers, and marijuana is not distinguished from cocaine, prescription drugs such as Oxycodone, or hallucinogens. Group counseling sessions are employed both to practice thinking errors correctives and to disseminate information about the dangers of drug use. Young people are responsible for completing "thinking errors reports" in which they describe their regular thinking patterns and plans for change.

Days and weeks at Santana are highly structured. Clients have limited time for activities such as showering and shaving and must ask permission to move about the dorm (even to the bathroom) and the campus. Civility is strictly enforced. When traveling between buildings, the first in line must hold the door open for the other 31 people behind him, saying "you're welcome" to each of their required "thank you"s. Thanks are also required whenever young men get "feedback" from staff, such as directives to retie their shoelaces correctly or tuck in their shirt. When a client's behavior deviates too far from program rules, any staff person who witnesses it may intervene. Though the employee training manual forbids screaming in a client's face, all my informants characterize interventions in this manner. Because of this lack of control over their physical person and the inability to stick up for themselves during confrontations, many former residents say that doing adult time in jails or prisons is actually easier than incarceration in a therapeutic setting such as Santana.

Santana Foundation is a fascinating place to study the ways in which young offenders make sense of and address expectations for thinking and behavior that lies far outside their repertoire of experience. The facility's distance from Philadelphia is not simply a symbolic break from the norms and routines of daily street life. Freedom quite literally hinges on their ability to interact with and adapt to the culture at Santana, including its isolated, rural setting; its nearly all-white staff; and its demands to abandon the trappings of the street as a demonstration of a commitment to conventional values. Baggy pants and "street" labels such as RocaWear or State Property are forbidden, along with any clothing that suggests that a youth is too "image conscious." Handshakes and fist-thumping are seen as indications of gang membership. Prolonged eye contact with other clients while passing in hallways and on sidewalks is discouraged to avoid the potential for confrontations. Team sports, particularly basketball, are carefully monitored for their potential for posturing, verbal put-downs, and aggression masked as play. Listening to or writing rap or hip hop music is not allowed except on special occasions. "Strutting" is continually pointed out as young men move about the campus. In short, to regain their freedom, young inner-city men at Santana must learn how to eliminate or conceal the behavioral repertoire associated with street culture.

The people responsible for implementing "thinking errors" interventions are culturally very different from their clients. Aside from the program director and one staff person, all counselors, teachers, and staff (at least during my subjects' period of incarceration) are white. Most reside in the small, rural communities surrounding the facility and are avid hunters and outdoorsmen; they regard Philadelphia and other urban areas with suspicion and disdain. Based on my discussions with staff at other facilities in rural locations, I believe this attitude arises in part from a general distaste for urban life and in part from a feeling of frustration that their hard work is so easily lost when their clients return to the city. Nonetheless, some counselors and staff members overcome their vast differences to establish warm and caring relationships with the young men in the program. Their concern about the difficulty associated with returning to Philadelphia is often expressed in their desire to help clients move to smaller communities to work or attend school. One counselor offered two of my informants a job and free place to live if they were willing to move to western Pennsylvania; they both declined.

Tensions Between the Institutional and Street Codes

Anderson's ethnographic work in inner-city communities of Philadelphia has led him to conclude that they are socially organized around a tension between orientations that community members term "decent" and "street." Both orientations are available to young people, regardless of their upbringing, and as children grow older, they engage in the "social shuffle," testing and trying on new roles and statuses and attempting to identify their own personal orientation. The street is an important institution of socialization for inner-city youth, especially as their parents' influence over them begins to weaken.

The "code of the street," according to Anderson, "amounts to a set of informal rules governing interpersonal public behavior, particularly violence. The rules prescribe both proper comportment and the proper way to respond if challenged. They regulate the use of violence and so supply a rationale allowing those who are inclined to aggression to precipitate violent encounters in an approved way" (1999, 33). Anderson points out that knowledge of the code of the street is required of every community member, particularly young black males, in order to navigate public spaces safely. The use of defensive posturing is performative, deflecting the potential for victimization that is an ever-present reality of the street. Those who are socialized into the street code adopt a set of behaviors that may as easily reflect knowledge of the interactive demands of public space as they demonstrate a commitment to an oppositional culture. Youths' selective and tactical use of street behaviors makes determining who has "changed" as a result of "thinking errors" intervention particularly difficult.

Anderson argues that a campaign for respect is at the heart of the street code. "In the inner-city environment respect on the street may be viewed as a form of social capital that is very valuable, especially when various other forms of capital have been denied or are unavailable. Not only is it protective; it often forms the core of the person's self-esteem, particularly when alternative avenues of self-expression are closed or sensed to be" (1999, 66). As adolescents begin their transition into young adulthood, manhood, self-esteem, and respect become inextricably intertwined. In the social context of limited job opportunities, failing schools, the stigma of deprivation, and an ever present threat of violence, the street orientation provides a sense of identity, belonging, and pride. With that comes a sense of loyalty, even among those whom the street life appears to have failed, who are incarcerated as a result of their activities on the corner. A commitment to the street is hard to shake. This complex situation is the starting point from which juvenile facilities such as Santana must operate to promote pro-social changes in young offenders.

Young men view their time at Santana as a departure from the real world. They refer to life outside as "the real world" or more commonly, "out there, in the world." Inside the carefully constructed buffer world of Santana, young men are forced to step outside their comfort zone to engage in behaviors that they perceive as risky or dangerous in an urban setting. "Loner behavior" is eschewed inside the facility, and young men are expected to interact with other young men from a variety of settings, though in a very controlled manner. Many say that they don't normally "conversate" with people they don't know. In some instances, forced interaction facilitates the development of friendships with young men from other cities and from other racial-ethnic backgrounds.

In other instances, abandoning loner behavior brings about an altogether new danger: discipline resulting from others' behavior. Interacting with others raises the possibility that a young man might become aware of rule infractions. Failing to "hold others accountable" brings severe consequences, including a drop in status and possible loss of home pass or other privileges. "Holding others accountable" by reporting them to staff is seen by the clients themselves as "snitching," one of the most serious rule violations in the code of the street. Warren, an eighteen-year-old from South Philly, discussed his technique for managing the tension between the street code that prohibits snitching and the program's demands that he hold his peers accountable for misbehavior.

If they're doing something that's going to get me caught up, of course, I'm going to come to them like a man, I'm not going to go to staff and say, look, he's doing this, he's doing that, I'm like look, you're doing this, and you're doing that, and you need to chill, and if they don't fix it, you say, I'm not going to get myself jammed up, I brought it to them first and that's when I've got to say, look, he's doing this and I told him . . . . Somebody else that's going to get brownie points they go right to staff and say, he's doing this, and he's doing that, no, that's not even my style. They tell you how to hold people accountable and you've got to hold yourself accountable, I looked at it as snitching, so I didn't do it, but then you've got to get to a point where somebody is doing something around you that's going to let you stay here longer and when you think about it, them or my family, you've got to pick, and you're going to pick your family, so, that's how I looked at it.

I learned first-hand the consequences of snitching very early in my study. Five weeks after returning home to Philadelphia, Sharif, an eighteen-year-old from North Philadelphia, was fatally shot less than 24 hours after he signed a subpoena to testify in a murder trial. Though he maintained that he could not shed any light on the case, his status as a probationer had likely made him vulnerable to pressure to cooperate with the authorities. Another informant, Hassan, who is also eighteen and from North Philadelphia, opted to take his chances on the run instead of snitching after he was the victim of a shooting following his release. His probation officer and reintegration worker believe that the police trumped up charges of gun possession when he refused to cooperate by naming his assailant. Facing what he predicted would be swift retaliation or a probation violation and possible arrest, he chose to flee. According to official records, he is still at large.

Honesty, called an "open channel of communication," is another requirement that places young, inner-city men in what they perceive to be a double bind. In the context of the street, a display of emotions other than anger suggests weakness that can make young men vulnerable to violence or aggression. Inside the "safe community" of Santana, however, counselors expect to see evidence of emotional growth in the form of honesty during individual and group sessions. To advance through the level system, clients must admit their mistakes and identify their own failings. In addition to making them feel vulnerable, which from the staff's perspective is a desired outcome, my informants report that the requirement of total honesty put them in a no-win situation. "If I tell them that I'm angry about being locked up, then I've [avoided one thinking error, closed channel of communication, but] made another thinking error, anger. I tell them I'm angry, that goes in my file and comes back up again during the status meeting," one young man tells me. Clients express confusion about which behavior is most desired by staff.

As with any intervention that incorporates the AA model, relapse and failure are an expected part of recovery. During the initial interview, each client is read a series of statements intended to inform him that he fits the profile of someone with a criminal personality. The last of these is "We are aware that you may go through a period of 'monasticism' where you will try to avoid all criminal thinking and actions. You will eventually grow tired of this and start looking for excitement again. Violation equals excitement. You will seek it out because that is the way you are." Because relapse is expected, those who sail through the program without hitting any setbacks are suspected of "faking it to make it." Gabe, an unusually mature eighteen-year-old from Southwest Philly, tells me that his stay at the facility was longer than average because his behavior was *too* good. "I got intervened with on the third day for not saying 'thank you' after I asked the staff if I could go to the bathroom. That was the last time I got intervened with, because I didn't see any reason to act a fool like the other bols there." "Fake it to make it" is a common mode of adaptation to the performative requirements at Santana and other facilities. According to Gabe, his counselors thought he had learned the rules a little too quickly for his behavior to be a genuine reflection of cognitive transformation (although interviews with staff may have produced other reasons for the delay in his release).

Criminal personality theory posits that "criminals" need to control others and respond swiftly and negatively to verbal putdowns by others. For this reason, counselors often test young men's mettle by verbally baiting them. A common way to do this is to tell them that they are destined for failure after discharge from the program. Some young men are astute enough to recognize staff's motivation for saying this; indeed, dire predictions of failure are grounded in the recidivism statistics for this and similar programs. But other clients see it as a "cheap shot," as bullying someone who is in no position to fight back without significant consequences. James, an eighteen-year-old from Southwest Philly, thought that one staff person took it too far when he made a similar prediction about his baby daughter. Furious, he recounts a situation in which his counselor announced, for the group to hear, that his continued lack of progress was why his daughter was going to end up at Santana's facility for delinquent girls. While he was prepared to deal with direct insults within the milieu of cognitive behavioral therapy, challenging his claim to good fatherhood replicated a "street" exchange too closely for him to hold his tongue. After he responded in anger during an intervention, a situation in which residents are not allowed to speak or move without permission, his status was dropped.

As the theme of "fake it to make it" emerged early in the pre-release interviews, I asked young men to explain what it meant to them and how they could tell when another client was faking it. Sincere, an eighteen-year-old from Kensington, explains:

Like, I don't know, but I know people have, like, tell people what they want to hear. I could tell you what you want to hear, like, if you're my counselor and you want to hear something like, "I'm really feeling bad about stuff I used to do," stuff like that. I'm basically telling somebody what they want to hear to get [the] benefits of going on a home pass.

Keandre, an eighteen-year-old from North Philly, was so astoundingly good at faking it that he was able to achieve a successful discharge after only six months, which was unusual for an older youth and for anyone from Philadelphia. Unlike Gabe, who was held longer for what staff believed to be a performance, Keandre used his twin babies at home as leverage to earn a quick discharge. Moreover, his charming personality made him easy to like and a believable moral character within the walls of the institution. Within weeks of his release, however, he was rearrested for drug selling and presently has an open bench warrant after failing to appear at his hearing.

Many young men report being confused by the labyrinth of seemingly conflicting expectations at the facility. Leo, an eighteen-year-old from North Philadelphia, illustrated his confusion with an analogy: "Sometimes I feel like I've been dropped into a video game and there are all these doors, and I don't know how to get out. If I open one door, I get to the end of the game. If I open another, I'm back to the beginning again and I have to start all over." Sincere reports his frustration at having to prove to staff that he has changed as a result of the program:

I see myself as a completely changed person, Miss. . . . Staff here, they don't know me out in the world, so they can't really say, so they just go by what they see me doing here and stuff like that. They want to see the change that I've made inside, they want to see it outside before anything ever happens. Before we can even talk about me going [home], they want to see an outside change . . . . I believe they see the change to the inside, but it seems like the change starts outside, you've got to show me the outside change. My beliefs and stuff like that changed a lot.

In sum, young men frequently experience incarceration at Santana as a double bind in which they must choose between fidelity to the street code, which they view as "reality," and meeting the behavioral expectations of the facility, which they must do in order to obtain release. For some, rationalizing these contradictions involves a tightrope walk: temporarily suspending behavior that is associated with the code of the street while at the same time maintaining that their sense of identity is still firmly rooted in the street. For other young men, this tension results in confusion about what is required and how to demonstrate cognitive change on the "outside," behaviorally. Others seemingly "fake it to make it," pretending to have a newfound commitment to the "decent" orientation. What seems clear is that they do not learn how to "code switch" between the decent and street behavior. This pattern is one important reason why they find such limited success after their return.

Returning to Philadelphia

Two years after recruiting the sample, most of my informants have been home at least eighteen months; the last to be released has been home for over a year. Of the fifteen, eight have been rearrested on new charges (Isaiah, Malik, Keandre, Tony, Warren, Jose, Hassan, and Eddie). Three have been arrested on three separate occasions (Eddie, Luis, and Hassan), and another has been arrested twice (Keandre). The vast majority of new charges are for drug selling or possession. As a result of these charges, Luis and Malik were reincarcerated at juvenile facilities. Luis, my only informant with a serious substance abuse problem, is currently being held at an adult facility on charges of theft and receiving stolen property. Malik completed a year at a state-run juvenile facility and is currently on the run after failing to complete probation. Four (Isaiah, Tony, Warren, and Eddie) have spent time in adult jails while their cases were processed. Two are fugitives (Malik and Hassan), and one was the victim of a homicide (Sharif). At least ten returned to drug selling after their return, though some did so for only a short time.

Of the eight who are not incarcerated or fugitives and whose employment status is known, only one is employed. Sincere, now twenty, works approximately eight days per month doing day labor in construction and demolition. During his first year home, his commitment to finding a job waxed and waned. While on probation, he was required to fill out job applications, but he never turned them in. In order to complete probation, Sincere had his brother-in-law write him a letter saying he worked for him. After his son was born and he and his baby's mother started living together as a family, over a year after he left Santana, he settled into a semiregular work schedule.

The work experiences of all but one of the other men in the study can only be characterized as sporadic. Most encountered difficulty while seeking employment. Many low-paying employers do not respond to applications dropped off by job seekers and prefer to hire through referrals or after in-person meetings. James had difficulty passing a series of screening tests on attitudes and values because he refused to lie about his past drug use. Many of my informants became discouraged after weeks of searching for work. The jobs they did get were typically low-paid positions as dishwashers, fast food cooks, or members of a night-time cleaning crew. Isaiah worked as a security guard until he was fired for tardiness and absenteeism. Their time since returning home from

Santana has been characterized by long periods of unemployment and jobs that were typically terminated after an argument with a supervisor. Importantly, there are whole sectors of the labor market, as well as sections of the city, that my informants view as "white" spaces. While many make an effort to overcome this feeling, most express extreme discomfort in settings where they are the racial minority; their lack of cultural capital in this world is one reason why they choose work that is "behind the scenes."

James, now twenty, has been employed for nearly the whole time he has been home, although he recently quit his job as a cook at IHOP because he was not getting enough hours. James's experience is different from those of his counterparts in the study for several reasons beyond the scope of this essay. Most important, he sees himself as a new person as a result of his period of incarceration. Although he cannot now name more than five of the thinking errors he learned to identify at Santana, and he still reports getting a strange taste in his mouth and a pain in his chest every time he thinks about the facility, he credits the time away from home with this change. Being away from his baby daughter, now three, was enough to help him reorganize his priorities. He says, "I wouldn't change anything [about the experience], 'cause that made me the person I am today." James has more stable social supports than most of my other informants. Nevertheless, his post-release time has been anything but easy.

Twelve of the fifteen young men in my sample completed their high school diplomas or GEDs before leaving Santana; in fact, several chose to remain at the facility for a couple of months past their release date in order to finish. Of the three who did not complete a degree while incarcerated (Luis, Keandre, and Akeem), none went back to public school or completed a GED. All my informants, regardless of their reentry experiences, agree on the value of the educational component at Santana. In Philadelphia, most were attending school only sporadically if at all, and few had experienced any sort of academic success. A few, such as Isaiah, eighteen, told me that his time at Santana allowed him to believe in his own intelligence. Most said that the experience of the school had to do with the commitment of the teachers. Warren, eighteen, explained:

You get more attention here. The teachers up there, it ain't even a word to describe them. They're like great . . . . When I first came here, I think my Pre-GED was like in Social Studies was like 3 something, now when I took the real GED it was 470. He got me ready for the real test, but it's like, these teachers up here care, like, you can tell all these teachers up here care. So far, all these teachers, I don't know about none of the other ones, but the ones I encountered, they all care.

For Sincere, the teachers' approach and the school environment made a real difference:

Here, it's like, you've got to pass. Seriously, you've got to pass. There is no failing here. If you fail a test, you take it and retake it again until you pass it. That's a good thing, the teachers here are on you, but at home, it's like, right here, this is considered a private school. There are no girls here to distract people, because that was a big distraction for me. Nobody with drugs around saying here, you want to hit this or, here, we're about to go smoke, do you want to smoke, or something like that, so that's a good thing.

Four young men began advanced education and training upon their return to the community. One attended a four-year university (Eddie), one went to a community college (Isaiah), and two enrolled in for-profit technical schools (Tony and James). All have dropped out. It is discouraging to report, but critical to understand, why none of the academic successes these young men experienced inside the facility were maintained or built upon when they returned home. None of the four completed more than a couple of months before the pressures of balancing school and work or fatherhood (or, in Eddie's case, a return to offending) ended their academic careers. While their experience at Santana provided most with a high school diploma, they returned to economically depressed sections of the city and resumed a hand-to-mouth existence that is simply incompatible with investment in the future.

Family and fatherhood have emerged as important themes. At least six of my informants have conceived children since their return; seven were already fathers while incarcerated. Four established households with their baby's moms upon their return (Sincere, Isaiah, Gabe, and Warren), although Warren moved out when his girlfriend's pregnancy revealed they were unable to coexist. Isaiah's partner, Dominique, recently got a restraining order after several appalling incidents of domestic abuse. The stress of providing for three children drove them to near-constant conflict that turned violent whenever Isaiah drank. Now five months pregnant, Dominique is working to get Isaiah some anger management counseling, hoping he will someday be able to return to their family.

With the exception of Luis, who has no contact with his child, the young fathers in my study strive to be actively involved with their children and provide more than compulsory financial assistance. Their commitment to parenthood contradicts the journalistic portrayal of inner-city black men as absentee fathers and sexual predators. Most ultimately fail as stable partners and providers because of their marginal position in the labor market (see also Liebow 1967). Drug selling constantly looms in the background as a viable option for regaining their lost sense of self-esteem and respect after failing to establish themselves in either the family or the workplace.

This study of formerly incarcerated young men of color paints a fairly grim picture of reentry experiences, even though my informants came from one of the highest-quality facilities available to Philadelphia's juvenile court. If we use a wider definition of desistance and reintegration than simple avoidance of recidivism, it seems clear that these young men are ill prepared for a life of meaningful participation in mainstream social institutions. Even among those who were not rearrested, most have engaged in some sort of "hustle" to make ends meet: typically drug selling, but also hawking sexual services to the women in communities where the disproportionate impact of incarceration has resulted in a noticeable lack of available men. As they approach adulthood, they are armed with a high school diploma, experience as a drug seller, a spotty work history, and little else. While only a carefully designed and executed randomized experiment could determine what their lives would have been like if they were not incarcerated, it is clear that the same conditions that existed in the 'hood when they were locked up— widespread poverty, violence, discrimination, lack of access to jobs that pay a living wage—are still waiting for them when they return.

As Goffman (1961) points out, institutions are in the business of change, but they cannot afford to acknowledge the structural and cultural determinants of action. By focusing only on individual-level explanations for delinquent offending and strategies to promote personal transformation, they fail on two grounds. First, they dismiss or ignore the structural circumstances that shape individual choices (Schneider 1992). These are the fundamental barriers that young men from poor urban neighborhoods confront upon reentry to the community, yet inside the facility they are dismissed as mere excuses for antisocial behavior, as employing a "victim stance" and "failing to endure adversity." Because their time inside the institution does nothing to change their material conditions, these young men are unable to build on even the most tangible of advantages, such as a high school diploma.

Second, these institutions' view of "street culture" is problematic. They fail to acknowledge the performative demands of the urban milieu, where "acting street" is an adaptation to a specific situation in which violence is an ever present threat. As Anderson's (1999) work reveals, physical comportment such as strutting, scowling, making eye contact, clothing, and language are strategically manipulated by the ghetto poor to reduce the chances of victimization while navigating urban terrain. Moreover, because institutions posit a conceptual link between culture and values, viewing any adherence to street culture as evidence of a criminal lifestyle, they miss an opportunity to provide young people with alternative cultural repertoires.

Instead of learning how to "code switch" between "street" and "decent" behavior, inmates learn how to "switch off" street behavior inside the confines of the institution, temporarily suspending or hiding conduct associated with street culture. Without new strategies for action in their cultural "toolkit" (Hannerz 1969; Swidler 1986), these young men leave the facility without added capacity for negotiating milieus where the "code of the street" does not dominate, such as in interactions with potential employers or educators. Santana and similar facilities take these young men out of the 'hood, but taking the 'hood out of them seems both unrealistic and unwise. As long as they lack access to mainstream institutions and support for investing in their own futures, their only option is to remain firmly embedded in street culture.

References

Altschuler, David M., and Rachel Brash. 2004. Adolescent and teenage offenders confronting the challenges and opportunities of reentry. *Youth Violence and Juvenile Justice* 2 (1): 72–87.

Anderson, Elijah. 2001. Going straight: The story of a young, inner-city convict. *Punishment & Society* 3 (1): 135–52.

———. 1999. *Code of the Street: Decency, Violence, and the Moral Life of the Inner City.* New York: W.W. Norton.

Edin, Kathryn, Timothy J. Nelson, and Rechelle Paranal. 2004. Fatherhood and incarceration as potential turning points in the criminal careers of unskilled men. In *Imprisoning America: The Social Effects of Mass Incarceration,* ed. Mary Pattillo, David Weiman, and Bruce Western, 21–45. New York: Russell Sage.

Giordano, Peggy C., Stephen A. Cernkovich, and Jennifer L. Rudolph. 2002. Gender, crime, and desistance: Toward a theory of cognitive transformation. *American Journal of Sociology* 107: 990–1064.

Goffman, Erving. 1961. *Asylums: Essays on the Social Situation of Mental Patients and Other Inmates.* New York: Doubleday Anchor.

Hannerz, Ulf. 1969. *Soulside: Inquiries into Ghetto Culture and Community.* Chicago: University of Chicago Press.

Holzer, Harry J., Steven Raphael, and Michael A. Stoll. 2004. Will employers hire former offenders? Employer preferences, background checks, and their determinants. In *Imprisoning America: The Social Effects of Mass Incarceration,* ed. Mary Pattillo, David Weiman, and Bruce Western, 205–46. New York: Russell Sage.

Jones, Peter R., Philip W. Harris, and Jamie J. Fader. 1999. "Evaluating Services to Delinquent Youth in Philadelphia: The *ProDES* Information System." *PAPPC Journal* (Pennsylvania Association for Probation, Parole, and Correction) 59 (1): 10–13.

Laub, John H., and Robert J. Sampson. 2003. *Shared Beginnings, Divergent Lives: Delinquent Boys to Age 70.* Cambridge Mass.: Harvard University Press.

———. 2001. Understanding desistance from crime. *Crime and Justice: A Review of Research* 28: 1–69.

Liebow, Elliot. 1967. *Tally's Corner: A Study of Negro Streetcorner Men.* Boston: Little, Brown.

Maruna, Shadd. 2001. *Making Good: How Ex-Convicts Reform and Rebuild Their Lives.* Washington, D.C.: American Psychological Association.

McCord, Joan. 2003. Cures that harm: Unanticipated outcomes of crime prevention programs. *Annals of the American Academy of Political and Social Science* 587 (1): 16–30.

Miller, Jerome G. 1998. *Last One over the Wall: The Massachusetts Experiment in Closing Reform Schools.* Columbus: Ohio State University Press.

Petrosino, Anthony, Carolyn Turpin-Petrosino, and James O. Finckenauer. 2000. Well-meaning programs can have harmful effects! Lessons from experiments of programs such as Scared Straight. *Crime and Delinquency* 46 (3): 354–79.

Platt, Anthony M. 1977. *The Child Savers: The Invention of Delinquency.* 2nd ed., enlarged. Chicago: University of Chicago Press.

Sampson, Robert J., and John H. Laub. 1997. A life-course theory of cumulative disadvantage and the stability of delinquency. In *Developmental Theories of Crime and Delinquency*, ed. Terence P. Thornberry, 133–61. Advances in Criminological Theory 7. New Brunswick, N.J.: Transaction Publishers.

———. 1993. *Crime in the Making: Pathways and Turning Points Through Life.* Cambridge, Mass.: Harvard University Press.

Schlossman, Steven. 2005. *Transforming Juvenile Justice: Reform Ideals and Institutional Realities, 1825–1920.* De Kalb: Northern Illinois University Press.

Schneider, Eric C. 1992. *In the Web of Class: Delinquents and Reformers in Boston, 1810s–1930s.* New York: New York University Press.

Sickmund, Melissa, T. J. Sladky, and Wei Kang. 2004. Census of juveniles in residential placement databook. http://www.ojjdp.ncjrs.org/ojstatbb/cjrp/, accessed January 17, 2005.

Snyder, Howard N. 2004. An empirical portrait of the youth reentry population. *Youth Violence and Juvenile Justice* 2 (1): 39–55.

Steinberg, Laurence, He Len Chung, and Michelle Little. 2004. Reentry of young offenders from the justice system: A developmental perspective. *Youth Violence and Juvenile Justice* 2 (1): 21–38.

Sullivan, Mercer L. 2004. Youth perspectives on the experience of reentry. *Youth Violence and Juvenile Justice* 2 (1): 56–71.

Swidler, Ann. 1986. Culture in action: Symbols and strategies. *American Sociological Review* 51: 273–86.

Western, Bruce, Jeffrey R. Kling, and David F. Weiman. 2001. The labor market consequences of incarceration. *Crime & Delinquency* 47 (3): 410–27.

Yochelson, Samuel, and Stanton E. Samenow. 1976. *The Criminal Personality.* Vol. 1, *A Profile for Change.* New York: J. Aronson.

Chapter 14
Suicide Patterns Among Black Males

SEAN JOE

> *Regretting my very existence because doomed to a life of bondage, and so goaded and so wretched as to be even tempted at times to take my own life.*
>
> —*Frederick Douglass*

Several high-profile suicides and suicide attempts by young black males have recently aroused public concern about self-harming behaviors among African Americans. Interest in the suicidal behavior of young black males has been fueled by incidents such as the highly publicized suicide of eighteen-year-old James Dungy, eldest son of Indianapolis Colts head coach Tony Dungy, and the reported suicide attempt of Terrell Owens, one of professional football's most talented, misunderstood, and taunted stars. Public dismissal of the possibility that Owens might have attempted suicide arises in part from the notion that people who are rich and famous could not possibly consider suicide, but also from the common assumption that African Americans are less prone to suicidal behavior than members of other racial-ethnic groups. If men like Dungy and Owens, who seem to have so much to live for; can fall into suicidal despair, then what about other young black men, whose prospects are much more limited? Suicide is a form of self-destructive behavior that differs from the more prevalent risk-taking behaviors (e.g., getting killed through drug use and street violence) that young black men living in areas of concentrated poverty may seem prone to; in those cases, the individual accepts the possibility that physical harm could result from his actions, but does not intend or expect to die (Joe 2003). Widespread disbelief that black Americans would engage in suicidal behavior continues despite recent epidemiological research documenting a rise in suicide and nonfatal suicidal acts among young black males (CDC 1998; Joe and Marcus 2003). For too long, data have been lacking on the prevalence of suicidal behavior among African Americans and plausible causal explanations.

This essay presents the most recent research on the prevalence of suicide and nonfatal suicidal behavior among young black males and provides a framework for understanding population-level changes in their pattern of self-destructive behavior over time. The traumatic legacy of African Americans' historical experiences with racism and discrimination in the new developmental context of urban decay is connected to their affective coping strategies—the ways they manage emotional stress—and their attributional orientations—whom or what they blame for their distressing predicament. Considering gender differences in black suicidal behavior suggests varied responses to racism-induced stressors and divergent attributional tendencies, illuminating the salience of hypermasculinity. Finally, the essay explores how these attributional styles lead to pathological emotional and behavioral responses to negative life events and eventually contribute to the recent increase in blacks' risk of committing suicidal acts.

Patterns of Black Suicidal Behavior

Suicide is the eleventh leading cause of death among all Americans, and rates vary across specific demographic subgroups; for example, suicide is the eighth leading cause of death among Native Americans, Asian/Pacific Islanders, and males (CDC 2007; Miniño, Heron, and Smith 2006). Across age, race, and gender, national suicide rates are highest among the elderly, particularly white males eighty-five and older, who have a suicide rate of 51.6 per 100,000 (CDC 2007). In 2004, the risk of dying from suicide was more than twice as high among whites as among blacks, with suicide rates of 12.3 and 5.5 per 100,000 respectively (Hoyert et al. 2006). Men are four times more likely to die of suicide than women (Goldsmith et al. 2002). In 2004, the ratio of male to female suicide rates for blacks was 5:1, considerably wider than the approximate 4:1 ratio among whites (Hoyert et al. 2006). Figure 14.1 illustrates that across the life span black males are at substantially higher risk for suicide than black females. In 2004, males accounted for 82 percent of all black Americans who died by suicide. Among black females, rates of suicide across the life span have remained the lowest in the nation; they have not experienced a rise in self-destructive behavior as have males.

Silent Epidemic: Rise in Young Male Suicidal Behavior

In recent years, suicide has emerged as a crucial health issue for African Americans, particularly among young males (CDC 1998; Goldsmith et al.

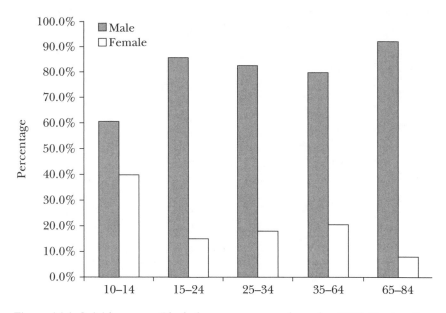

Figure 14.1. Suicide among Blacks by age groups and gender, 2004. Centers for Disease Control, Web-based Injury Statistics Query and Reporting System, 2004, ICD-10 X60-X84, Y87.0, *U03.

2002; U.S. PHS 2000). Although suicide has been viewed as a problem that affects more whites, the prevalence of suicide among blacks has risen significantly since the mid-1980s (Griffith and Bell 1989), with increases in both the rate of suicide completion (Garlow, Purselle, and Heninger 2005) and that of nonfatal suicidal behavior, especially among younger black males (Joe and Marcus 2003). Several studies have shown that black males are more likely to commit suicide before age thirty-five than are white males (Garlow, Purselle, and Heninger 2005; Joe 2006; Willis et al. 2003). A precipitous increase in the rate of suicidal behavior among younger black males has reduced racial disparities in suicidal behaviors, irrespective of the recent overall decline in the national suicide rates. The difference in suicide rates between whites and blacks aged fifteen to twenty-four narrowed from a ratio of 1.7 in 1980 to 1.4 in 2003 (CDC 2006a).

Suicide is now the third leading cause of death for black males aged fifteen to twenty-four (Hoyert et al. 2006). Among this group of adolescents and young adults, the data show marked increases in suicide over a fifteen-year period ending in 1994; the suicide rate rose from 14.0 per 100,000 in 1979 to 20.4 per 100,000 in 1994 (see Figure 14.2). A

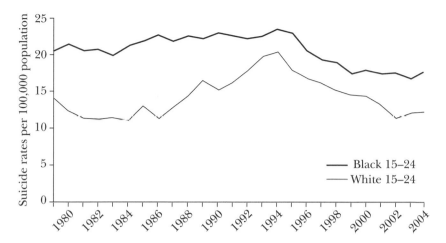

Figure 14.2. Suicide rates for black and white men aged fifteen to twenty-four, 1979–2004. Centers for Disease Control, National Center for Health Statistics, compressed mortality files, 1979–1980; Centers for Disease Control, Web-based Injury Statistics Query and Reporting System, 1981–2004.

detailed breakdown by age reveals that black males aged ten to fourteen and fifteen to nineteen experienced the steepest rise in suicide rates during that period. Suicide rates among the latter age group more than doubled, from 6.7 per 100,000 in 1979 to 16.5 per 100,000 in 1994. (Rates also rose among black males aged ten to fourteen, from 0.3 to 2.1 per 100,000, although this finding must be treated with caution because of the small numbers involved.) Since 1995 the rate of suicide in the United States has declined steadily for all racial and age groups. Amid this overall decrease in suicide rates, the increase in young black male suicide has altered the racial disparities in suicide. As Figure 14.3 shows, the racial disparities in suicide between black and white males aged fifteen to twenty-four declined 21 percent from 1.83 in 1981 to 1.45 in 2004. Previously, suicide risk was considered an exception to the more general pattern of health disparities that are unfavorable to blacks, but recent trends give us reasonable cause for concern.

Some analysts point to the very recent decline in suicide to suggest that the rate of suicide among blacks will return to historically lower patterns. However, data from the Centers for Disease Control Youth Risk Behavioral Survey (YRBS), which are the only data on nonfatal suicidal behavior among young Americans based on a representative national sample collected regularly over time, suggests an alternative prediction. As seen in Figure 14.4, while the rate of suicide has declined, the rate of

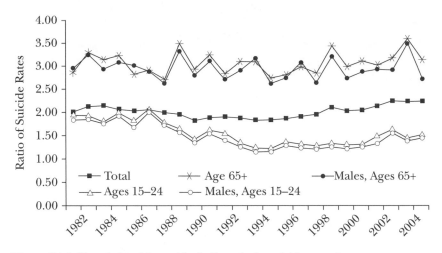

Figure 14.3. Trends in white to black disparity in suicide rates by age group, 1981–2004. Centers for Disease Control, Web-based Injury Statistics Query and Reporting System.

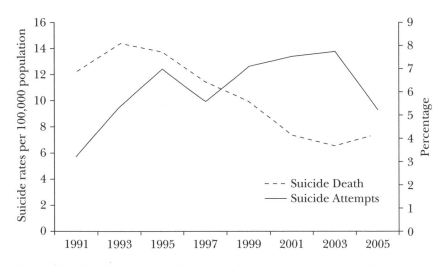

Figure 14.4. Suicide deaths and attempts among late adolescent black males, 1991–2006. Centers for Disease Control, National Center for Health Statistics, compressed mortality files, 1991–2002; attempt data from Centers for Disease Control, Youth Risk Behavioral Surveillance System (YRBSS), 1991–2003.

attempted suicide for black males has risen. If younger cohorts of black males continue to carry their increased suicide risk into later life, then the recent decline in black male suicide rates will be reversed. Joe and Marcus (2003) examined the YRBS data and found that ever since the CDC began collecting these data in 1991, black males have reported more attempted suicide than white males of similar age. In fact, according to the most recent CDC report, the prevalence of attempted suicide for white (7.3 percent) and black (7.6 percent) high school students was roughly the same (CDC 2006b).

Despite increasing recognition of the public health and social significance of these changes in suicidal behavior among black Americans, more comprehensive data on the prevalence and risk profiles of young black males are lacking. This sort of information would enable us to ascertain whether the current programs for the prevention and treatment of antecedents to suicide are effective in reducing risk among this population. Equally or more troubling is the fact that plausible causal explanations for black suicidal behavior cannot be tested against adequate evidence, so reasoned speculation continues to dominate current discussions about whether a call to action is warranted. The epidemiological evidence is unequivocal in its support of the call to action outlined in the landmark 1999 report of the U.S. Surgeon General, Dr. David Satcher, which emphasized the importance of a national scientific blueprint for a suicide prevention strategy that addresses the unexpected increase in self-inflicted death among black males (U.S. PHS 2000). The next section presents a framework for understanding the rise in suicide among young black males and explores some of the most useful causal explanations.

Explanations for the Rise in Black Male Suicidal Behavior

When we look back upon the systematic cruelty and immense suffering that previous generations of African Americans endured over centuries of enslavement and oppression, we are amazed that so few of them succumbed to despair. As we look at contemporary black youth, who are growing up in a society that asserts a belief in equal opportunity without respect to race, we worry that so many of them feel hopeless. How can we explain the increasing prevalence of suicidal behavior among the young, especially the suicide rates of young men? At a time when the healthy development of young black men is under attack from interpersonal violence, incarceration, and HIV/AIDS, it is deeply disconcerting to know that some turn to suicide, their young spirits brutally and severely bruised by their life experiences. Black youth are more vulnerable to suicide than adults. In order to examine the plausible reasons for the rise in suicide among young black males, we must view the phenomenon in a temporal perspective. The increase in suicide rates has occurred among successive cohorts of young black males, marking it as a cohort effect. In analyzing cohort effects, we assess to the extent to which developmental factors or previous life events result from the impact of societal events, or a combination of external events, upon a group of young persons in a particular age group and explore the ways in which the situations in which they matured continue to influence their behavior throughout the life span (e.g., black males who were adolescents during the onset of the crack cocaine epidemic). Joe et al. (2004) found that black people under thirty-two years of age (born after 1975) are nine times more likely to attempt suicide than those age seventy or older (born before 1935).

Suicide occurs in the context of a wide range of complex and interrelated underlying etiological factors, so the increased rate of suicide among successive black birth cohorts (Joe et al. 2006; Joe and Kaplan 2001), particularly for males, must be placed in a broader context of psychosocial development. The growing body of research on black suicidal behavior has confirmed that many of the known suicide risk factors for whites are also important risk factors for blacks, including mental disorders such as depression (Horwath, Johnson, and Hornig 1993; Kaslow and Kingree 2002; Willis et al. 2003) and substance abuse (Castle et al. 2004; Garlow 2002; Marzuk et al. 1992). This body of research has produced equivocal findings, in part because of the lack of clear operationalization of terms (McKeown et al. 1998) and the lack of attention to contextual factors such as gender, race, and socioeconomic status that may influence suicidality. Although this line of research is relatively important for understanding those black persons who are most at risk for suicide, it is generally based on individual-level analyses and must be distinguished from research on the cumulative effects of population-level factors that have resulted in the tragic trends in suicide among black males evident in the last fifteen years.

Importance of Population-Level Explanations

In order to explain this unprecedented increase in suicidal behavior, it is important to distinguish between research on individual suicide risk and investigations of historical societal factors that might have caused large-scale changes in patterns of suicidal beliefs and behavior (Joe 2006). Although these two investigative tracks are linked, we cannot interpret the results from individual risk studies as explanations for societal-level changes. Failure to make this distinction in the analysis of patterns of suicide among black men could, at the very least, lead to the inappropriate and ineffective use of resources for suicide prevention or, at worst, cause counterproductive, even iatrogenic outcomes.

Societal-level examination of suicide patterns dates back to Durkheim (1897), and social-scientific research on suicide among African Americans began with the work of Prudhomme (1938). Both focused on suicide as a social pathology and emphasized the importance of social structure in determining population suicide rates. In order to identify factors associated with changes in the perpetuating and precipitating risk factors for suicide in an ethnic minority group, population-level studies often employ a historical perspective, which illuminates group-level changes over time in patterns of suicide (Joe 2006). Implicit in this perspective is a plausible assumption that the factors related to suicidal behavior are similar across all ethnic groups. This framework implies that all groups' exposure to and psychosocial interpretation of similar historical changes might eventually result in comparable levels of suicide vulnerability.

The growing similarities between young black and white males provide some evidence that the factors related to suicidal behavior might well be similar across ethnic groups (Joe, Clarke, et al. in press). Individual-level risk studies are informative in this regard. Recent studies have shown that many of the known risk factors for the general population are also related to suicidal behavior among blacks (Castle et al. 2004; Garlow 2002; Joe, Clarke, et al. in press; Joe, Marcus, and Kaplan 2007; Kaslow and Kingree 2002; Kung, Liu, and Juon 1998; Willis et al. 2003). Despite the growing similarities, well-established racial disparities in suicide in the United States continue to suggest that this hypothesis is not yet tenable. Moreover, groups' reactions to broad, societal-level changes vary by ethnic, gender, class, and other characteristics. Research on population-level changes in suicide patterns among Americans of African descent should encompass the process of acculturation, including adoption of a new language, historical experiences of trauma, and the effects of colonization, and would require cross-sectional or longitudinal data (Joe 2006). In historical perspective, although African Americans have experienced more of the common stressors that are suicide risk factors, their suicide rates have been well below those of whites.

This population-level explanation of trends in the suicidal behavior of black men is guided by Charles Prudhomme's insightful acculturation framework. Prudhomme (1938) noted that what determined black Americans' attitudes toward suicide and suicidal behavior were not "racial" factors, such as variations in skin color or physical features, but the degree to which they absorbed the culture of whites and shared similar experiences regarding social advancement. He hypothesized that as black Americans became more assimilated or acculturated by the white majority, their suicide rates would invariably increase. In sum, the more that black Americans shared in the American Dream, the more suscepti-ble they would become to the cultural beliefs and experiences associ-ated with suicidal behavior among whites.

In a modern presentation of this acculturation process, civil rights scholar Lani Guinier explains, "the problem with the American Dream is that it offers no explanation for failure other than that you deserve your lot in life, and that if you fail there must be something wrong with you. Many people are perfectly willing to believe that success is individ-ual but don't want to think about failure as individual, and no one wants to believe that they deserve to fail" (Parrish 2006). As younger cohorts of black Americans become more assimilated, they become more sus-ceptible to depression and the other pathogenic factors that also make whites at increased risk for suicide. Prudhomme provided a clear idea regarding when and for whom population-level changes in the black ex-perience might cumulate in ways that increase their vulnerability to sui-cidal forces.

Cohort effects as described by Prudhomme become manifest over the long term. A typical example is a change of social norms, which are usually determined early in life but continue to act on human behavior throughout the life span (Stevenson et al. 2005). A developmental per-spective is especially important in understanding the implications of normative changes for the trend of suicide incidence. Cohort effects can have relatively long-lasting impacts on the suicide pattern as the co-hort ages, affecting overall trends in suicide for the entire population. The next section explores a number of possible explanations for the cohort effects observed for black people, particularly for men: a new macro-level developmental context; changes in attributional coping styles; race-induced gender role strain; and attitudes toward suicidal be-havior. Although these plausible explanations are moderately sup-ported by evidence, they remain speculative and should be confirmed in future research examining their direct effects on young black males' risk for suicide.

New Developmental Context

First, recent changes in the pattern of suicide among younger African Americans may reflect their experience of growing up in more extreme and concentrated poverty at a time when the protection formerly pro-vided by parents, the church, and other community institutions has been considerably weakened. The rise in suicide rates among black men, which began in 1983, coincided with the peak of deindustrialization, which disproportionately burdened black families and communities

(Massey and Denton 1993; Wilson 1996). Changes in the macrostruc-
ture of American cities during the 1970s and 1980s induced the formation of neighborhoods of concentrated poverty: black male joblessness
markedly increased (Wilson 1987, 1996), families were disrupted, residential and commercial real estate decayed, and social organization was
eroded (Almgren 2005). The young and the old tend to be most susceptible to environmental changes. Growing up in poverty increases the
possibility of being exposed to air pollution, lead paint, and other con-
taminants that may affect mental as well as physical health (Bernard and
McGeehin 2003; President's Task Force 2000; Krieger, Williams, and
Moss 1997). During this same period, the onset of the crack cocaine
trade resulted in the proliferation of semiautomatic firearms in these
neighborhoods (Wilson 1996; Zimring 2004). Previous research has
demonstrated that the increase in suicide among blacks was due primarily to increases in firearm-related suicide of young males (Joe and Kaplan 2002). Firearms are the most common method used by black males
to commit suicide.

Substantial research supports the relationship between concentrated
social and economic deprivation and suicide risks among blacks. Burr
and colleagues (1999) provide data showing that the suicide risk for
black males ages fifteen to twenty-four was highest in areas where occupational and income inequities between African Americans and whites
were greatest. A more recent study examining Wilson's (1996) hypotheses found a direct relationship between concentrated economic disadvantage resulting from deindustrialization and increased suicide risk for
young black males across U.S. cities (Kubrin, Wadsworth, and DiPietro
2006).

The rise in suicide among black males provides significant evidence
of the most important societal consequence of growing up amid extreme deprivation and isolation. The new developmental context leaves
many youth without access to traditional symbols and sources of hope
(Gibbs 1988) and bereft of the coping strategies that helped earlier
generations face the challenges of adverse life circumstances. Equally
ominous, the social-structural landscape, marked by unprecedented underemployment and ineffective social institutions, has led to profound
hopelessness, despair, demoralization, loneliness, and depression, as
well as changes in the coping styles of many young African Americans
(Spencer, Dupree, and Hartman 1997; Wilson 1996).

Rising rates of suicide may also reflect reactions to the social up-
heavals taking place in the United States in the post-civil rights movement era, including the growing power of ultraconservative movements
in politics and public policy. These societal changes created an environment of high personal expectations and goal striving among young

African Americans, while weakening or even eliminating major social services and much-needed developmental programs. Forced to cope with chronic underpreparation for gainful occupations, unemployment and underemployment, and fewer avenues for success, young black males realize that society has no place for them and feel isolated and alienated (Bell and Clark 1998). Many contend with the difficult transition to young adulthood after emerging from dilapidated and disadvantaged institutions, such as public schools. Regrettably, investigations into generational differences in coping styles that might have resulted from major social changes and increased suicide risk among African American males are marginal in the field of suicidology.

Growing Pattern of Self-Blame

Another important line of investigation is to discern whether a generational change to a more maladaptive coping style is one mechanism through which the cohort and period effects resulting from social changes are associated with the increase in suicide among younger black males. Coping styles are the cognitive and behavioral efforts employed to manage the adverse demands resulting from interactions between a person and his environment that are appraised as stressful, as well as the emotions they generate (Lazarus and Folkman 1984, 19). According to attributional style theory (Abramson, Metalsky, and Alloy 1989), a maladaptive style is manifested when positive events are explained in specific, yet unstable external explanations and negative events with stable internal, yet global attributions. For instance, a black youth sees his academic success as a result of "acting white" in conformity with the school's demands and sees the difficulties into which he is drawn by his peers as confirmation that, as a young black man, he is destined to failure, violent conflict, and an early death.

Several researchers have used attributional orientation to explain higher risk for poor mental health and death among African Americans (Jackson et al. 1996; LaVeist, Sellers, and Neighbors 2001). Maladaptive attributional styles have also been associated with depressive symptoms among black adolescents who have attempted suicide (Summerville et al. 1994) and with a perceived risk for suicide among adolescents (Greening and Stoppelbein 2002). The strength of the association between attributional style and internalizing symptoms of psychological distress that are known risk factors for suicide, such as depression (Gladstone and Kaslow 1996; Johnson et al. 2002) and anxiety (Luten, Ralph, and Mineka 1997), suggests that attributional style is a cognitive variable that may serve as a pathway between black youths' new developmental context and their higher suicide risk.

The generational change in attributional style and other coping strategies among African Americans represents an unexpected outcome of the movement for civil and social rights, which has been crucial in raising the personal expectations, achievement opportunities, and aspirations of black youth. The successes of this movement may have inculcated a greater belief among black youth that their opportunities are limited only by their skills and motivation—a common feature of the dominant American ethos. In turn, many black males may become frustrated, angry, and depressed when those expectations do not materialize, because, although normative achievement expectations may well have changed, many of the institutional and structural barriers associated with the legacy of racism continue to thwart black youths' development, individual effort, and achievement (Powell and Arriola 2003; Prelow et al. 2004; Spencer et al. 1997). Today, younger African Americans may be more likely than previous generations to believe that their life course depends solely on their actions. In the face of adverse circumstances, this orientation may increase their susceptibility to depression and other risk factors for suicide (Joe 2003). Although the role of attributional orientation in blacks' suicide risk requires empirical verification, it is a promising and potentially fruitful line of inquiry.

Several important hypotheses are worthy of empirical examination. In the past, did an external attributional orientation, which blames the system for the difficulties people experience, buffer this group from internalizing limited individual success or negative outcomes, given their exposure to such chronic psychosocial stressors as discrimination, marginalization, and concentrated disadvantage dictated by a racist society? Has this mindset been replaced more recently with a more internal orientation, which leads to self-blaming, particularly among youth? A system-blaming attributional style, particularly in the context of high-effort coping (Bennett et al. 2004), may well have helped previous generations of African Americans to manage their potentially deleterious chronic exposure to psychosocial stressors (L. P. Anderson 1991; Paradies 2006). This orientation may have deflected or attenuated the negative consequences of encountering discrimination by ascribing personal setbacks to the external realities of racially unequal social structures that are endemic to life in America. This assertion is not to suggest that many of the psychological and sociocultural parameters associated with decreased suicide risk in earlier cohorts of blacks, including attributional style, entailed no risk for other adverse outcomes. For instance, high-effort coping, which is often regarded as a source of African Americans' psychological resiliency, has been linked to poor health outcomes (Bennett et al. 2004).

Racism and Masculinity

African Americans must negotiate a racialized social terrain in their
everyday lives, because racism remains a pervasive feature of contemporary society (Clark et al. 1999). Surprisingly, no research has examined
what role racism and discrimination may have played in the increase in
black male suicidal behavior, but race-based stress has been clearly associated with risk for poor health and psychopathology among African
Americans (Sellers and Shelton 2003; Sellers, Caldwell et al. 2003).
Today, the racism that young black males encounter may not be as observable as the more blatant forms of racial discrimination were in previous generations, but it is just as noxious. One major arena in which
young black males suffer as a result of racial discrimination is their inability to fulfill conventional gender expectations by being wage earners
and fathers in households they share with their wives and children.
Today, young black males living in concentrated poverty come to believe
that society is constructed to relegate them to a position of economic
and social marginality, which may lead many to despondency.

Racial discrimination has always played a role in defining black masculinity and limiting the black man's role as a provider (Ferber 2007).
Black job applicants commonly encounter discrimination, which places
them at a decided disadvantage in the labor market. Any experience of
discrimination, whether objectively verifiable or subjectively perceived,
can injure even the best prepared young black male, and is even more
damaging to those who are poorly prepared for the world of work.
Until very recently, young black males who did not graduate from high
school could not turn to the military, because before the long wars in
Afghanistan and Iraq the U.S. military was less likely to accept high
school dropouts, closing an alternative route from aimlessness that had
sustained earlier generations of young black males (Edelman, Holzer,
and Offner 2006). The dire situation of young black males goes well beyond the fact that growing numbers are jobless (Mincy, Lewis, and Han
2006) or in prison; even more are becoming entirely disconnected from
mainstream society. More than one in six young black males experiences long-term idleness without any major childrearing responsibilities
(Edelman, Holzer, and Offner 2006).

Researchers must examine the psychological consequences of young
black males' experiences of joblessness and personal failure and assess
their causal attributions, which can determine the risk for psychological
distress. Young men of the post-civil rights generation are caught in a
difficult situation: because many are less likely to run up against the
overt racial discrimination that existed in the past and are in a somewhat better position to do well than previous birth cohorts, they are

more likely to be chastised for personal failure. Criticism certainly comes from the dominant society, but admonition also comes from the family or the black community, because previous generations were able to do great things when they had less freedom and more limited access to gainful employment. Many African Americans are more likely to attribute negative life events to internal causes, even in the context of extreme disadvantage and challenging developmental experiences, and this attribution increases their risk of psychological distress and suicide.

Many young black males have a strong sense of personal agency and exhibit little psychological distress, despite being confronted by many challenges; only a few tend toward suicidal thinking and behavior. The resiliency exhibited by many young black men is probably related to a strong sense of self-efficacy and racial identity, buttressing their self-esteem while under duress. African Americans with higher generalized self-efficacy are less likely to experience psychological distress regardless of the level of discrimination they experience (Lightsey and Barnes 2007). Previous studies have found that high public or private regard for one's own ethnic group mitigates the deleterious effects of racism on psychological well-being (Sellers and Shelton 2003; Sellers et al. 2003). African Americans may be able to retain a positive sense of self-efficacy despite the discrimination they experience because they can appropriately identify the negative outcome as related to being disadvantaged and attribute it to external factors. The key components of the psychological armor that once protected blacks from suicide are probably the ability to make the appropriate attribution when confronting discrimination or disadvantage, a strong sense of self-efficacy, and a positive racial identity.

Yet African Americans' history of resiliency does not prevent racism from having devastating effects today. Among those with a weak racial identity and low self-efficacy, attributions to discrimination are associated with low levels of social self-esteem, perceived social control, and perceived control over the ability to perform an action (Lightsey and Barnes 2007). Males exhibiting these characteristics are less likely to make an external causal attribution, regardless of how much disadvantage they face, because they do not want to be seen as complainers. Men are expected not to complain when challenged; they must "man up" and get through it. Moreover, research shows that a social cost accompanies attributions to discrimination (Kaiser, Dyrenforth, and Hagiwara 2006), such as extreme social isolation or verbal harassment (e.g., being labeled a less competent, "Affirmative Action" hire at work). Therefore, the consequences of attributions to discrimination encourage the minimization of discrimination, even when there is evidence to suggest it has occurred. The negative outcomes many African Americans experience are not easily attributed to overt discrimination; like members of other ethnic minority groups, blacks often experience attributional ambiguity (Crocker and Major 1989). Since external attributional strategies have been shown to protect or enhance beliefs about self (Crocker and Major 2003), shifting blame for an ambiguous negative outcome to an external or specific factor can shield self-esteem and psychological health (Lightsey and Barnes 2007).

In sum, the social constructions of black masculinity shape men's interpretations of interpersonal interactions, including their perceptions of racism, self-efficacy, self-esteem, and help-seeking attitudes and behaviors. Racism reinforces black men's negative self-images, causing them to doubt their abilities, the quality of their work, and even their successes, and leading some to depression and psychological distress. The subjective concept of masculinity conditioned by racism intensifies the stigma of mental illness and discourages men from seeking professional help, increasing their risk for severely debilitating psychiatric illness and suicide. As black journalist John Head describes his experiences with depression and suicidality, the roots of black men's depression lie in the complex relationships between their masculinity and racism. Racism not only brings on depression but also exacerbates its effects. Racism intensifies the sense of hopelessness when depression hits. Head puts it succinctly: "to face racism is to struggle to maintain hope," and depression forces an individual to abandon hope (2004, 59). Racism's coercive power is manifest not only in instrumental concerns but also in black men's psychology and levels of self-doubt. Psychiatric illness such as depression exacerbates those feelings and causes the person to feel shame for his resulting behaviors. This sense of shame is heightened by the belief that personal failure confirms the worst stereotypes of black men, increasing his risk for suicide and other self-destructive behaviors.

These social, ecological, and psychological changes may explain the rising rates of suicidal behavior among young black males, but the consistently lower rates of attempted and completed suicide among young black females must also be explained. Among the many possible explanations for the visible gender differences in suicide risk, the more plausible analyses maintain that women are more likely to seek and receive emotional support (Gibbs 1988), have different achievement expectations and experiences with role strain, have less access to firearms, and have stronger religious affiliations than men (Gibbs and Hines 1989). Females' lower rates may also be attributed to greater perceived gender discrimination and less perceived racism. Sellers and Shelton (2003) found that black males report more experiences of racial discrimination than do black females. Although women are making more social gains than men, many experience or perceive gender discrimination and are less likely to attribute their experiences primarily to personal efficacy. There is some evidence to suggest that women cope with the negative consequences of perceived discrimination by increasing their identification with women as a group (Schmitt et al. 2002). Research is needed to consider whether females' attribution orientation is more consistent with the perspective that protected many African Americans from suicidal forces in the past.

Suicide Acceptability and the Stigma of Mental Illness

The final component of this explanatory framework focuses on how African Americans' social norms have changed, influenced by structural changes and their greater acculturation into mainstream American society. Culture—a product of people living together and creating a conglomeration of ideas, habits, thoughts, traditions, norms, and values that manifests as a pattern of thought and action in the group—powerfully shapes and constrains the behavior of group members in ways that the structural aspects of society may not (Bille-Brahe 2000). In this context, the primary question is whether the normative religious belief that African Americans once held about suicide, which may have served as a protective factor (Neeleman, Wessely, and Lewis 1998; Prudhomme 1938), continues to be held by younger generations. The religious taboo on suicide may have declined along with participation in organized religion.

The mainstream culture's view of suicide as relatively acceptable may have influenced young African Americans to regard it as normal and increased their likelihood of committing suicide in times of personal crisis. While the stigma of suicide was never unique to black culture, it was extremely powerful. Traditionally, African Americans have been less accepting of suicide than European Americans, an opinion researchers attribute to their religious beliefs (Neeleman, Wessely, and Lewis 1998). Early's (1992) unique study of religion and suicide found that black people condemn suicide on the basis of both religious beliefs and a secular attitude that defines it as a "white thing." Although blacks continue to report a less accepting attitude toward suicide our recent study confirms that younger blacks are more likely than older blacks to be accepting of suicide (Joe, Romer, and Jamieson 2005), attenuating the protective effects of this factor.

This explanation assumes that acceptance of suicide plays an important role in regulating people's consideration of suicide as a solution to life problems (Goldsmith et al. 2002). We conducted a study based on a nationally representative sample of 3,301 youth ages fourteen to twenty-two and found that adolescents and young adults who strongly believe that it is acceptable to end one's life are more than fourteen times more likely to make a plan to kill themselves than those who strongly reject suicide (Joe, Romer, and Jamieson 2007). This connection between regarding suicide as acceptable and making a suicidal plan was found among black youth as well as those in other racial-ethnic groups, and it was not simply the result of prior symptoms of hopelessness or differences in sensation-seeking. The effect of attitudes toward suicide was particularly striking among young persons who had experienced hopelessness during the previous year; nearly half of those with the most accepting attitudes had planned their suicide, while only less than 10 percent of those who expressed strong disapproval of suicide had done so. Youth endorsing such attitudes and reporting previous experiences of hopelessness and sensation-seeking should be considered at higher risk for suicidality.

It may be possible to use attitudes toward the acceptability of suicide as a predictive tool for identifying adolescents and young adults who are likely to make a suicide plan when they become depressed. Several studies show that individuals who approve of suicide tend to score higher on suicide risk scales; and when comparing suicidal to non-suicidal adolescents and young adults, suicidal youth tend to be more accepting of their own suicidal behavior and that of others (De Wilde et al. 1993). Changing individual attitudes toward suicide should be considered as a possible approach to suicide prevention (Pokorny 1992).

The pervasive social stigma associated with mental illness in African American communities is a significant barrier to efforts to reduce the risk of suicide (Poussaint and Alexander 2000). Cultural interpretations and views of mental illness shape how individuals act upon psychological or emotional distress, and individuals from racial-ethnic minority groups are less inclined to use formal mental health services as a first option. Some segments of the population, including the poor and racial-ethnic minorities, rely more heavily on psychiatric emergency services because of their social and economic circumstances (Chow, Jaffee, and Snowden 2003; Hu et al. 1991; Neighbors 1986). Current evidence confirms that blacks are less likely to receive mental health services than whites and are overrepresented among those who receive mental health care in emergency services and psychiatric hospitals, partly because they delay seeking treatment (U.S. PHS 2001).

The reluctance of young African Americans, particularly males, to use mental health services is a major public health problem, which arises both from the relative absence of health insurance among the poor and unemployed and from the cultural stigma attached to seeking help (U.S. PHS 2001, U.S. DHHS 2003). Suicidal black adolescents and young adults underutilize mental health services (Garland et al. 2005; Joe et al. 2006). Any delay in treatment often requires more intensive care because of the greater severity of impairment in functioning that results (Wilson and Klein 2000; Lindsey et al., in press). Although the stigma of psychiatric illness is not unique to African Americans, it has particularly severe consequences in this community. Suicidal black persons with psychiatric disorders who do not seek treatment promptly are at risk of an untimely death.

Conclusion

The most recent information on suicidal behavior among African Americans and current research on gender differences in both risk and protective factors refute the conventional belief that suicide is rare in this population. The epidemiological data on trends in suicidality among black men, particularly among youth, is cause for serious concern. A population-level framework for understanding the rise in suicidal behavior among young black males includes the changing contexts in which successive generations grow up and the coping strategies they adopt. Today, young men are moving toward adulthood in a developmental context that differs significantly from previous generations, making them more likely to cope with racism, segregation, discrimination, and low socioeconomic status, including extreme poverty and increasingly limited economic opportunities, in a maladaptive manner. These young men are more likely to internalize negative life events, leading to an increased risk for psychiatric disorders and other suicide risk factors.

Like many other men in American society, but to a more extreme degree, black men are caught in the gender straightjacket of hyper-masculinity, which discourages help-seeking and undervalues emotional concerns, while exaggerating the importance of work and material indicators of success in a context in which economic success may be almost unattainable. The values and norms that define masculinity among African Americans contribute to black males' risk of suicide and their use of firearms as the primary method to complete suicide. Examining specific expectations rather than treating masculinity as a global gender category might well yield more significant insights into the problem. Additional research is needed to enhance our understanding of whether the components identified in this essay are potentially modifiable protective factors that can be targeted in any prevention program or treatment service. The paucity of research on suicide among African Americans leaves many mental health professionals and policy makers concerned about the plight of young black men inadequately prepared to respond to their needs. If younger cohorts of black males carry their increased suicide risk into later life, then the recent declines in suicide rates among African Americans will be reversed. The higher suicide mortality among young black males and their growing use of firearms should be addressed in future research and considered by clinicians when screening, intervening, and treating them. Since black males have the greatest likelihood to use a firearm to complete suicide (Joe, Marcus, and Kaplan 2007), priority should be given to identifying black men who are depressed and suicidal and developing strategies for limiting their access to firearms.

Greater awareness of the risk of suicide among black men is vital, especially among those who work with them in schools and other social institutions. If they remain unaware of the patterns of suicide among black youth, their practice may be based on the erroneous but commonly held belief that African Americans do not commit suicide (Early 1992), leading to misinterpretation of their self-destructive behaviors. Mental health professionals and others working with young black males should become aware of this problem and of the social factors that are making it more serious today. All Americans can support the National Strategy for Suicide Prevention, the mental health parity legislation that requires insurance companies to cover mental health treatment in the same way they do treatment for physical health, and support national efforts to limit access to firearms. To save the lives of more young black men, we must also invest in key protective factors, including social and emotional supports and the reduction of stigma related to mental illness and help-seeking (Greening and Stoppelbein 2002; Marion and Range 2003; Poussaint and Alexander 2000). Recognizing suicidal behavior among people in our families and communities is the first step toward treatment and prevention.

References

Abramson, Lyn Y., Gerald I. Metalsky, and Lauren B. Alloy. 1989. Hopelessness depression: A theory-based subtype of depression. *Psychological Review* 96: 358–72.

Almgren, Gunnar. 2005. The ecological context of interpersonal violence: From culture to collective efficacy. *Journal of Interpersonal Violence* 20 (2): 218–24.

Anderson, Louis P. 1991. Acculturative stress: A theory of relevance to Black Americans. *Clinical Psychology Review* 11: 685–702.

Anderson, Robert N., and Betty L. Smith. 2003. Deaths: Leading causes for 2001. *National Vital Statistics Reports* (National Center for Health Statistics) 52 (9): 1–86.

Bell, Carl C., and David C. Clark, 1998. Adolescent suicide. *Pediatric Clinics of North America* 45 (2): 365–80.

Bennett, Gary G., Marcellus M. Merritt, John J. Sollers III, Christopher L. Edwards, Keith E. Whitfield, and Dwayne T. Brandon. 2004. Stress, coping, and health outcomes among African Americans: A review of the John Henryism hypothesis. *Psychology and Health* 19 (3): 369–83.

Bernard, Susan M., and Michael A. McGeehin. 2003. Prevalence of blood lead levels (5 (g/dL among U.S. children 1 to 5 years of age and socioeconomic and demographic factors associated with blood lead levels 5 to 10 (g/dL. Third National Health and Nutrition Examination Survey, 1988–1994. *Pediatrics* 112 (6): 1308–13.

Bille-Brahe, Unni. 2000. Sociology and suicidal behaviour. In *The International Handbook of Suicide and Attempted Suicide*, ed. Keith Hawton and Kees van Heeringen, 193–207. Chichester: Wiley.

Burr, Jeffrey A., John T. Hartman, and Donald W. Matteson. 1999. Black suicide in U.S. metropolitan areas: An examination of the racial inequality and social integration-regulation hypotheses. *Social Forces* 77: 1049–81.

Castle, Kathryn, Paul R. Duberstein, Sean Meldrum, Kenneth R. Conner, and Yeates Conwell. 2004. Risk factors for suicide in blacks and whites: An analysis of data from the 1993 National Mortality Followback Survey. *American Journal of Psychiatry* 161: 452–58.

Centers for Disease Control and Prevention (CDC). 2007. Web-Based Injury Statistics Query and Reporting System (WISQARS). www.cdd.gov/ncipc/wisqars, retrieved May 22, 2007.

———. 2006a. Web-based Injury Statistics Query and Reporting System (WISQARS). www.cdd.gov/ncipc/wisqars, retrieved September 29, 2006.

———. 2006b. Youth Risk Behavior Surveillance—United States, 2005 (No. 55, SS-5). Atlanta.

———. 1998. Suicide among African American youths—United States, 1980–1995. *Morbidity and Mortality Weekly Report* 47: 193–96.

Chow, Julian C.-C., Kim D. Jaffee, and Lonnie R. Snowden. 2003. Racial/ethnic disparities in the use of mental health services in poverty areas. *American Journal of Public Health* 93 (5): 792–97.

Clark, Rodney, Norman B. Anderson, Vanessa R. Clark, and David R. Williams. 1999. Racism as a stressor for African Americans: A biopsychosocial model. *American Psychologist* 54 (10): 805–16.

Crocker, Jennifer, and Brenda M. Major. 2003. The self-protective properties of stigma: Evolution of a modern classic. *Psychological Inquiry* 14 (3–4): 232–37.

———. 1989. Social stigma and self-esteem: The self-protective properties of stigma. *Psychological Review* 96 (4): 608–30.

De Wilde, Eric Jan, I. Keinhorst, Rene F. Diekstra, and W. Wolters. 1993. The specificity of psychological characteristics of adolescent suicide attempters. *Journal of the American Academy of Child and Adolescent Psychiatry* 32 (1): 51–59.

Durkheim, . . . mile. 1897. *Suicide: A Study in Sociology*. Trans. John A. Spaulding and George Simpson. New York: Free Press, 1961.

Early, Kevin E. 1992. *Religion and Suicide in the African-American Community*. Westport, Conn.: Greenwood Press.

Edelman, Peter B., Harry J. Holzer, and Paul Offner. 2006. *Reconnecting Disadvantaged Young Men*. Washington, D.C.: Urban Institute Press.

Ferber, Abby L. 2007. The construction of black masculinity: White supremacy now and then. *Journal of Sport & Social Issues* 31 (1): 11–24.

Garland, Ann F., Anna S. Lau, Meh Yeh, Kristen M. McCabe, Richard L. Hough, and John A. Landsverk. 2005. Racial and ethnic differences in utilization of mental health services among high-risk youths. *American Journal of Psychiatry* 162 (7): 1336–43.

Garlow, Steven J. 2002. Age, gender, and ethnicity differences in patterns of co-
    caine and ethanol use preceding suicide. *American Journal of Psychiatry* 159 (4):
    615–19.
Garlow, Steven J., David Purselle, and Michael Heninger. 2005. Ethnic differ-
    ences in patterns of suicide across the life cycle. *American Journal of Psychiatry*
    162: 319–23.
Gibbs, Jewelle Taylor. 1988. Conceptual, methodological, and structural issues
    in black youth suicide: Implications of assessment and early intervention. *Sui-
    cide and Life-Threatening Behavior* 18: 73–89.
Gibbs, Jewelle Taylor, and Alice M. Hines. 1989. Factors related to sex differ-
    ences in suicidal behavior among black youth: Implications for intervention
    and research. *Journal of Adolescent Research* 4: 152–72.
Gladstone, Tracy R. G., and Nadine J. Kaslow. 1996. Depression and attributions
    in children and adolescents: A meta-analytic review. *Journal of Abnormal Child
    Psychology* 23: 597–606.
Goldsmith, Sara K., Terry C. Pellmar, Arthur M. Kleinman, and William E. Bun-
    ney, eds. 2002. *Reducing Suicide: A National Imperative.* Washington, D.C.: Insti-
    tute of Medicine, National Academies Press.
Greening, Leilani, and Laura Stoppelbein. 2002. Religiosity, attributional style,
    and social support as psychosocial buffers for African American and white
    adolescents' perceived risk for suicide. *Suicide and Life-Threatening Behavior* 32
    (4): 404–17.
Griffith, E. E. H., and Carl C. Bell. 1989. Recent trends in suicide and homicide
    among blacks. *Journal of the American Medical Association* 262: 2265–69.
Head, John. 2004. *Standing in the Shadows: Understanding and Overcoming Depres-
    sion in Black Men.* New York: Broadway Books.
Horwath, Ewald, Jim Johnson, and Christopher D. Hornig. 1993. Epidemiology
    of panic disorder in African Americans. *American Journal of Psychiatry* 150:
    465–69.
Hoyert, Donna L., Melonie P. Heron, Sherry L. Murphy, and Hsiang-Ching
    Kung. 2006. *Deaths: Final data for 2003. National Vital Statistics Reports* 54 (13)
    (April 19). Hyattsville, Md.: National Center for Health Statistics.
Hu, Teh-Wei, Lonnie R. Snowden, Jeanette M. Jerrell, and Tuan D. Nguyen.
    1991. Ethnic populations in public mental health: Services choice and level of
    use. *American Journal of Public Health* 81 (11): 1429–34.
Jackson, James S., Tony N. Brown, David R. Williams, Myriam Torres, Sherrill L.
    Sellers, and Kendrick Brown. 1996. Racism and the physical and mental
    health status of African Americans: A thirteen-year national panel study. *Eth-
    nicity and Disease* 11 (1–2): 132–37.
Joe, Sean. 2006. Explaining changes in the patterns of black suicide in the
    United States from 1981–2002: An age, cohort, and period analysis. *Journal of
    Black Psychology* 32 (3): 262–84.
———. 2003. Implications of focusing on black youth self-destructive behaviors
    instead of suicide when designing preventative interventions. In *Reducing
    Adolescent Risk: Toward an Integrated Approach,* ed. Daniel Romer, 325–32.
    Thousand Oaks, Calif.: Sage.
Joe, Sean, Raymond E. Baser, Gregory Breeden, Harold W. Neighbors, and
    James S. Jackson. 2006. Prevalence of and risk factors of lifetime suicide at-
    tempts among blacks in the United States. *Journal of the American Medical Asso-
    ciation* 296 (17): 2112–23.

Joe, Sean, Jenell Clarke, Asha Z. Ivey, David Kerr, and Cheryl A. King. In press. Impact of familial factors and psychopathology on suicidality among African American adolescents. *Journal of Human Behavior in the Social Environment* 15 (2/3).

Joe, Sean, and Mark S. Kaplan. 2002. Firearm-related suicide among young African American males. *Psychiatric Services* 53 (3): 332–34.

———. 2001. Suicide among African American men. *Suicide and Life-Threatening Behavior* 31 (supplement): 106–21.

Joe, Sean, and Steven C. Marcus. 2003. Trends by race and gender in suicide attempts among U.S. adolescents, 1991–2001. *Psychiatric Services* 54 (4): 454.

Joe, Sean, Steven C. Marcus, and Mark S. Kaplan. 2007. Racial differences in the correlates of firearm suicides in the United States. *American Journal of Orthopsychiatry* 77 (1): 124–30.

Joe, Sean, Daniel Romer, and Patrick E. Jamieson. 2007. Suicide acceptability is related to suicidal behavior among U.S. adolescents. *Suicide and Life Threatening Behavior* 37 (2): 165–78.

———. 2005. Race and gender differences in U.S. trends in suicide acceptability. Paper presented at the American Association of Suicidology annual meeting, Bloomfield, Colorado.

Johnson, Renee M., Jonathan B. Kotch, Diane J. Catellier, Jane R. Winsor, Vincent Dufort, Wanda Hunter, and Lisa Amaya-Jackson. 2002. Adverse behavioral and emotional outcomes from child abuse and witnessed violence. *Child Maltreatment* 7: 179–86.

Kaiser, Cheryl R., Portia S. Dyrenforth, and Nao Hagiwara. 2006. Why are attributions to discrimination interpersonally costly? A test of system- and group-justifying motivations. *Personal and Social Psychology Bulletin* 32 (11): 1523–36.

Kaslow, Nadine J., and J. B. Kingree. 2002. Risk factors for suicide attempts among African American women experiencing recent intimate partner violence. *Violence and Victims* 17 (3): 283–95.

Krieger, Nancy, David R. Williams, and Nancy E. Moss. 1997. Measuring social class in U.S. public health research: Concepts, methodologies, and guidelines. *Annual Review of Public Health* 18: 341–78.

Kubrin, Charis E., Tim Wadsworth, and Stephanie DiPietro. 2006. Deindustrialization, disadvantage and suicide among young black males. *Social Forces* 84 (3): 1559–79.

Kung, H.-C., X. Liu, and H.-S. Juon. 1998. Risk factors for suicide in Caucasians and in African Americans: A matched case-control study. *Social Psychiatry and Psychiatric Epidemiology* 33: 155–61.

LaVeist, Thomas A., Robert Sellers, and Harold W. Neighbors. 2001. Perceived racism and self and system blame attribution: Consequences for longevity. *Ethnicity and Disease* 11: 711–21.

Lazarus, Richard S., and Susan Folkman. 1984. *Stress, Appraisal, and Coping*. New York: Springer.

Lightsey, Owen Richard, Jr., and Peter W. Barnes. 2007. Discrimination, attributional tendencies, generalized self-efficacy, and assertiveness as predictors of psychological distress among African Americans. *Journal of Black Psychology* 33 (1): 27–50.

Lindsey, Michael A., Wynne S. Korr, Marina Broitman, et al. in press. Help-seeking behaviors and depression among African American adolescent boys. *Social Work*.

Luten, A. G., J. A. Ralph, and Susan Mineka. 1997. Pessimistic attributional style: Is it specific to depression versus anxiety versus negative affect? *Behaviour Research and Therapy* 35: 703–19.

Marion, Michelle S., and Lillian M. Range. 2003. African American college women's suicide buffers. *Suicide and Life-Threatening Behavior* 33 (1): 33–43.

Marzuk, Peter M., Kenneth Tardiff, Andrew C. Leon, Marina Stajic, E. B. Morgan, and J. J. Mann. 1992. Prevalence of cocaine use among residents of New York City who committed suicide during a one-year period. *American Journal of Psychiatry* 149: 371–75.

Massey, Douglas S., and Nancy A. Denton. 1993. *American Apartheid: Segregation and the making of the underclass.* Cambridge, Mass.: Harvard University Press.

McKeown, Robert E., Carol Z. Garrison, Steven P. Cuffe, Jennifer L. Waller, Kirby L. Jackson, and Cheryl L. Addy. 1998. Incidence and predictors of suicidal behaviors in a longitudinal sample of young adolescents. *Journal of the American Academy of Child and Adolescent Psychiatry* 37 (6): 612–19.

Mincy, Ronald B., Charles W. Lewis, Jr., and Wen-Jui Han. 2006. Left behind: Less-educated young black men in the economic boom of the 1990s. In *Black Males Left Behind,* ed. Ronald B. Mincy, 1–10. Washington, D.C.: Urban Institute Press.

Miniño, Arialdi M., Melonie P. Heron, and Betty L. Smith. 2006. Deaths: Preliminary Data for 2004. *National Vital Statistics Reports* 54 (19).

Neeleman, Jan, Simon Wessely, and Glyn Lewis. 1998. Suicide acceptability in African- and White Americans: The role of religion. *Journal of Nervous and Mental Disease* 186 (1): 12–16.

Neighbors, Harold W. 1986. Ambulatory medical care among adult Black Americans: The hospital emergency rooms. *Journal of the National Medical Association* 78 (4): 275–82.

Paradies, Yin. 2006. A systematic review of empirical research on self-reported racism and health. *International Journal of Epidemiology* (April 3), 1–14.

Parrish, Rebecca. 2006. The meritocracy myth: A Dollars & Sense interview with Lani Guinier. *Dollars & Sense: The Magazine of Economic Justice.* January–February.

Pokorny, Alex. 1992. Prediction of suicide in psychiatric patients: Report of a prospective study. In *Assessment and Prediction of Suicide,* ed. Ronald W. Maris, Alan L. Berman, John T. Maltsberger, and Robert I. Yufit, 105–29. New York: Guilford Press.

Poussaint, Alvin F., and Amy Alexander. 2000. *Lay My Burden Down: Unraveling Suicide and the Mental Health Crisis Among African Americans.* Boston: Beacon Press.

Powell, Cecil L., and Kimberly Ruth Jacob Arriola. 2003. Relationship between psychosocial factors and academic achievement among African American students. *Journal of Educational Research* 96: 175–81.

Prelow, Hazel M., Sharon Danoff-Burg, Rebecca R. Swenson, and Dana Pulgiano. 2004. The impact of ecological risk and perceived discrimination on the psychological adjustment of African American and European American youth. *Journal of Community Psychology* 32: 375–89.

President's Task Force on Environmental Health Risks and Safety Risks to Children. 2000. Eliminating Childhood Lead Poisoning: A Federal Strategy Targeting Lead Paint Hazards. February. http://www.hud.gov/offices/lead/reports/fedstrategy2000.pdf, retrieved May 2, 2007.

Prudhomme, Charles. 1938. The problem of suicide in the American Negro. *Psychoanalytic Review* 25: 187–204, 372–91.

Schmitt, Michael T., Nyla R. Branscombe, Diane Kobrynowicz, and Susan Owen. 2002. Perceiving discrimination against one's gender group has different implications for well-being in women and men. *Personality and Social Psychology Bulletin* 28 (2): 197–210.

Sellers, Robert M., Cleopatra H. Caldwell, Karen H. Schmeelk-Cone, and Marc A. Zimmerman. 2003. Racial identity, racial discrimination, perceived stress, and psychological distress among African American young adults. *Journal of Health and Social Behavior* 43: 302–17.

Sellers, Robert M., and Nicole J. Shelton. 2003. The role of racial identity in perceived racial discrimination. *Journal of Personality and Social Psychology* 84 (5): 1079–92.

Spencer, Margaret Beale, Davido Dupree, and Tracey Hartmann. 1997. A phenomenological variant of ecological systems theory (PVEST): A self-organization perspective in context. *Development and Psychopathology* 9: 817–33.

Stevenson, Howard C., J. Derek McNeil, Teresa Herrero-Taylor, and Gwendolyn Y. Davis. 2005. Influence of perceived neighborhood diversity and racism experience on the racial socialization of black youth. *Journal of Black Psychology* 31 (3): 273–89.

Summerville, Mary B., Nadine J. Kaslow, Maureen F. Abbate, and Shade Cronan. 1994. Psychopathology, family functioning, cognitive style in urban adolescents with suicide attempts. *Journal of Abnormal Child Psychology* 22: 221–35.

U.S. Department of Health and Human Services (U.S. DHHS). 2003. *New Freedom Commission on Mental Health, Achieving the Promise: Transforming Mental Health Care in America. Final Report* (DHHS Pub. No. SMA-03-3832). Rockville, Md.: U.S. Department of Health and Human Services.

U.S. Public Health Service (U.S. PHS). 2001. *Mental Health: Culture, Race, and Ethnicity—A Supplement to Mental Health: A Report of the Surgeon General.* Rockville, Md.: U.S. Department of Health and Human Services.

———. 2000. *The Surgeon General's Call to Action to Prevent Suicide, 1999.* Washington, D.C.: U.S. Public Health Service.

Willis, Leigh A., David W. Coombs, Patricia Drentea, and William C. Cockerham. 2003. Uncovering the mystery: Factors of African American suicide. *Suicide and Life-Threatening Behavior* 33 (4): 412–29.

Wilson, Karen M., and Jonathan D. Klein. 2000. Adolescents who use the emergency department as their usual source of care. *Archives of Pediatric Adolescent Medicine* 154: 361–65.

Wilson, William Julius. 1996. *When Work Disappears: The New World of the Urban Poor.* New York: Knopf.

———. 1987. *The Truly Disadvantaged.* Chicago: University of Chicago Press.

Zimring, Franklin E. 2004. The discrete character of high-lethality youth violence. *Annals of the New York Academy of Sciences* 1036: 290–99.

Chapter 15

Why Are Handguns So Accessible on Urban Streets?

DAVID KAIRYS

Why are handguns so accessible on urban streets? Why is it easier for young black men to obtain a handgun than an up-to-date school textbook or a regular job?

This question has two components: How does the gun market work to make a product designed to kill so easily available? And why do we allow it to function this way? The answers differ significantly from conventional wisdom. The common image of an underground, illegal market is largely fictional. Most of what goes on is the predictable result of simple distribution and marketing choices, and is surprisingly legal.

The statistics on handguns are familiar. There are about 60 handgun deaths each day in the United States, with a yearly total of about 24,000. About three times that many people are injured but not killed each day. This level of non-war-related handgun deaths is among the highest in the world, and many times greater than in other countries of comparable development and wealth. Handguns have been the biggest and most consistent threat to urban safety and public health in the United States for the last several decades. Research has shown that bringing a gun into your home increases the probability that someone in the home will be the victim of a gun homicide by three times and increases the probability of a suicide in your home by five times. If there is a teenager in the household, the suicide risk is multiplied by ten.

The toll of these grim statistics falls hardest on poor and black communities, particularly black young men. Black males aged twenty to twenty-four have the highest homicide rate of all groups, and homicide—about 90 percent of which is by guns—is the leading cause of death for black youth. The introduction of easily available handguns into communities that are deprived and struggling has created a daily disaster, fed false stereotypes (only a small proportion of black young men shoot people), provided a rationalization for the failure to deal with poverty or discrimination, and sapped efforts to reform and regain hope.[1]

Yet most Americans seem oddly immune to concern about the gun problem, unable to take it seriously. The dominant public attitude toward handgun homicide is "regrettably normal." Every day on television, news anchors, reporters, pundits, and politicians express sadness about the latest deaths, but there is a pervasive acceptance, a strange sense that this extraordinary level of death and killing is a normal or inevitable aspect of life in urban America.

How Does the Handgun Market Work?

I was introduced to the gun issue in 1996 when I served on a Philadelphia task force on youth, crime, and guns established by Recreation Commissioner Michael DiBerardinis. We had access to data and to people knowledgeable about the various aspects of the problem. What I learned and figured out belied what I thought I knew about guns, and led to my conceiving the city handgun lawsuits brought by over 40 cities and one state (Kairys 2003a,b, 2000a,b, 1998).[2]

I had assumed that there was an underground, illegal market and that the handguns criminals and youth used in crimes were largely stolen. This is wrong. The market makes new handguns so easily available—often for less than a hundred dollars new, right out of the box—that it makes no sense to steal one. New guns have no traceable history and are so cheap that they can be thrown away after each use.

Some facets of the handgun marketing system that contribute to easy availability are well known: gun shows, mail order and online sales, and straw purchases, in which someone who does not have a criminal record buys a gun for someone who does. What is not commonly understood is that, within the law, anyone who does not have a record can go to a licensed gun store in most states, legally buy as many handguns as he or she wants, and walk out the door with them. The only limit would be the one on the credit card; buyers can purchase as many weapons as they want and can pay for.

A dealer who sells a lot of guns to one person is supposed to comply with some reporting requirements; in certain circumstances, a dealer is required to send a notice of multiple purchases to the federal Bureau of Alcohol, Tobacco, and Firearms (ATF). But this requirement has little significance because the purchase is not illegal. The purchaser legally owns those guns and has no legal duty to report or explain what he does with them.[3]

Nor are there meaningful limits on resale of handguns. Under federal law and the law of most states, a gun owner can sell guns to someone else without any record check. The Brady Act requires that a purchaser pass a record check (aimed mostly but not solely at criminal records) when buying from a licensed dealer. The dealer checks the purchaser's record by an instantaneous computer link or by phone. Purchases from a non-dealer, which are common at gun shows and on the streets, are not subject to a record check, because the Brady Act only applies to licensed dealers.

The bottom line is this. Under federal law and the laws of most states, any person so inclined can buy huge quantities of cheap, easily concealed handguns and sell them to others indiscriminately, often without violating any law and usually without having to worry much about getting arrested, prosecuted, or convicted. Nor are the identities of owners of handguns, or the persons to whom they transfer ownership, registered or maintained by government, unless state law so provides—and most do not. Convicted felons are not allowed to buy or possess handguns, but the marketing system up to that point is largely legal. The person who sells a handgun to a person with a felony conviction has no meaningful or enforceable responsibility. Though the handgun debate is commonly cast in terms of "illegal guns," the central problem resides in what continues to be legal.

The level of multiple sales by licensed dealers is extremely high. The Philadelphia task force did a statewide study in 1997 that covered a 15-month period. Most of the guns purchased from licensed dealers were bought by someone who bought at least one other gun during that same period; 30 percent were purchased by someone who bought three or more, and 17 percent by someone who bought five or more.[4] The 17 percent who bought five or more guns are the best customers of this industry, and industries tend to design and market what their best customers want.

The high volume of multiple sales is why the proposal to impose a limit of one gun per person per month represents a reform. Why would someone want twelve handguns in one year, and twelve more the next? What are they doing with these guns? The one-a-month proposal establishes a limit, but it still legitimates purchasing a lot of handguns.[5]

We know that the handgun industry produces more guns than could be sold to law-abiding people—and that handgun manufacturers are well aware of that fact. They channel large quantities of handguns to particular places where gun laws are weak, knowing that people from places where gun laws are strict will go there to buy. Over the past decade, Philadelphia and Pennsylvania, where I live, have become a major source of guns for the northeastern and mid-Atlantic states. New Jersey and New York have strict laws, but there are almost no limits on purchases in Pennsylvania. As you travel south down the I-95 corridor on the East Coast, guns are generally easier to buy. People from the Northeast who want to purchase large quantities of guns can drive to Pennsylvania or continue further south and bring handguns back to sell on the street.[6]

In the 1980s and 1990s, a gun industry market assessment, which was revealed in litigation, showed that the legal market for 9 millimeter handguns was saturated, but manufacturers produced more of them anyway. Manufacturers do not produce more of something than they think they are going to sell. The 9 millimeter has been the gun of choice for murder in the United States (Kairys 2003b).

Manufacturers sometimes advertise features of guns that appeal to criminals. Some advertisements are amazingly blatant. I was shocked to see a brochure for a handgun that listed as one of its features "excellent resistance to fingerprints." This feature would not matter to someone wanting a handgun for self-defense (Kairys 1998, 21).

We know that the crime-gun distribution system—from manufacturer to distributor to dealer to purchaser to criminal—is efficient. According to the ATF, the time between the dealer sale to a purchaser and the handgun's subsequent use in a crime is particularly short. Most of the guns used in crime were first bought within two years of the crime.

Criminals and youth gain access to guns through a small number of dealers. Only one percent of the dealers sell 57 percent of the guns involved in crime. The manufacturers could easily monitor the distributors and dealers who sell their products. They have data from the ATF that reveal which dealers down their distribution chain are selling a lot of guns that wind up being used in crime. But manufacturers refuse to use these data, or even to follow the usual practices of tracking inventory and sales that are routine in business.[7]

The 2007 Virginia Tech shootings have drawn attention to the inadequacies of the database used for Brady Act record checks. This gap needs attention, but the more important, and often ignored, truth is that it is easy for mentally deranged people contemplating mass murder to get handguns. The Virginia Tech shooter sidestepped Virginia's one-a-month law by waiting a month before going back to the dealer for his second semi-automatic. He could have bought them both without any record check at the frequent gun shows in Virginia or from easily located non-dealers.

One aspect of the market puzzled me from the beginning of the task force's work on youth, crime, and handguns. The handguns that wind up being used in crimes are not a large proportion of the total number of handguns sold; the best estimate is in the range of 10 to 15 percent. Why would manufacturers continue to conduct their businesses as they do for an additional profit of only 10 to 15 percent when they could stop supplying criminals and youth or at least seriously reduce the supply? People sometimes do awful things to make money and often find strange ways to justify themselves. But the gun trade has such a clear connection to murder and mayhem. Gun manufacturers are already the object of public criticism and would like to avoid governmental regulation. Why not take some measures to reduce the supply of new handguns to criminals and youth?

I wound up concluding that a lot more than the visible 10 to 15 percent is at stake when we consider how the market functions and is structured. In the eyes of the public health community, gun deaths and injuries constitute an epidemic. But this epidemic is spread, not by bacteria or viruses, but by fear. Fear is the engine of demand for this industry's products. Oddly, the instrument of the harm and epidemic is commonly viewed as the solution: if you are afraid of gun violence, you buy a gun. We understand that it is best to keep away from other agents that cause epidemics. But here, the very same thing that is causing the harm is viewed as the solution. These handguns bought for self-protection pose a greater danger of death and injury to the family at home than they do to any potential intruder.

Anything that increases fear is great for gun sales. The worst things that could happen for the country are the best things for the handgun industry. The Oklahoma City bombing, Columbine, 9/11, and the Washington Beltway Snipers all led to huge spikes in handgun sales to frightened folks looking for what they believe is protection from harm.

In between the big scares and spikes in handgun sales, the usual level of fear that generates the bulk of handgun sales is provided by crime, particularly crimes with guns and all manner of shootings. The gun industry needs the daily local news accounts of shootings and murders—fed by easy access to handguns for criminals and youth—in order to maintain its high level of new handgun sales, over a million each year.[8]

Why Do We Allow It?

Why is this market in handguns allowed to thrive when the consequences are clear day after day, gloomy statistic after gloomy statistic?

The gun lobby, which includes the National Rifle Association (NRA), the gun industry, and other gun-focused groups, is well funded and very influential, especially with politicians.

After Robert Kennedy was killed with a small handgun in 1968, Congress was moved to ban the small, inexpensive handguns called "Saturday night specials." The political will to do something meaningful about gun control materialized in response to that traumatic event. At the last minute before the bill's passage, however, the gun lobby got an amendment that exempted Saturday night specials manufactured in the United States. So what did this accomplish? Made-in-America mayhem rather than foreign-made mayhem. The amendment undercut the purpose of the legislation, enabling the flow of new, cheap handguns to continue unchecked. Foreign handgun makers set up manufacturing plants in the United States in order to qualify for the exemption. Gun companies such as Beretta became our new corporate neighbors.[9]

In 1976, at the behest of the gun lobby, Congress limited the jurisdiction of the Consumer Product Safety Commission (CPSC), the federal agency where citizens can complain about a consumer product without hiring a lawyer, to exempt anything to do with guns or ammunition from the agency's authority.[10] If you have a tennis racket that is causing tennis elbow because of a design defect, you can file a complaint with the CPSC. However, if defective ammunition is blowing up in the hands of hunters, you cannot.

In the early 1990s, Congress reacted to the leading public health studies showing the danger of handguns in the home by barring the Centers for Disease Control (CDC), which had funded the studies, from conducting or funding any research on public health "to advocate or promote gun control." The next year, Congress removed from the CDC budget the exact amount of the grant that had funded the studies.[11]

Recently, Congress has let the ban on assault weapons expire, restricted ATF from providing important data and information on guns used in crime to the public, scholars, or law enforcement, and granted a broad immunity to the gun industry in response to the city handgun lawsuits.[12]

A lobby this strong operates on many levels. The gun lobby is politically active and visible; across the country, office-seekers must either gain its endorsement or worry about its opposition to their candidacies. It distributes a lot of campaign funds. The gun lobby also gains strength from the hinted or implicit threat of violence to anyone who opposes the unregulated flow of guns, when, for example, Charlton Heston, as head of the NRA, often held a rifle in the air and said menacingly, "From my cold dead hands." At a recent gun rights rally at the state capitol in Pennsylvania, a large banner said a state legislator who had introduced legislation that would require registration of guns should be "hung from the tree of liberty."[13]

There is a well-funded, well-connected, powerful, and sometimes intimidating gun lobby. But there are a lot of well-funded, well-connected, powerful, and sometimes intimidating lobbies that do not succeed to this extent. Lead paint and PCBs were banned despite rich, powerful lobbies representing those industries. Guns touch a deep nerve in American society.

The cultural and political dimensions of public opposition to gun control are often ignored by those who believe that there are too many handguns and want to do something about the problem. The wide-spread identification of guns with our highest ideals—freedom, liberty and, for some, patriotism—affects the politics of guns and of proposals for government regulation.[14]

Some Americans think and feel on a gut level that guns and the constitutional provision on guns in the Second Amendment are central to everything that they hold dear about America, and that any attempt to put limits on them is a terrible threat. Their thinking is similar to that of many more Americans about the protection of freedom of speech in the First Amendment. So I can disagree with what you say but defend your right to say it, even if what you say is deplorable or disgusting to me. Similarly, one can deplore what some do with guns, but defend the un-regulated right to them—sometimes accompanied by tortured denials of any connection between the two. There are, of course, differences; for one, usually no one dies from disgusting speech. But the logic is similar and embodies a very American conception of rights.

The most extreme form of this cultural and political identification of guns with freedom, the NRA version, leads to opposition to restrictions on Teflon-coated bullets called "cop-killers" because they can pierce bulletproof vests. Any government regulation of guns or ammunition, even that advocated by law enforcement officials, is seen as a threat to fundamental American ideals.

Less extreme versions of the identification of guns with freedom have more widespread and significant effects on American society and politics. Sometimes even the wildest arguments against regulation strike a chord with a broad segment of Americans, who think the NRA goes too far but still see guns as linked with freedom. They may accept that something should be done about the slaughter but feel deeply uneasy with gun restrictions. Those who support government regulation must understand this perspective in order to advocate effectively.

The moderate version of this cultural and political identification contributes to the gun lobby's success with the strategy of supporting and proposing meaningless laws and then arguing that all that is needed is enforcement of existing laws. Pennsylvania provides an instructive example. A Pennsylvania law provides that resales should be processed through a dealer, who would have to do a Brady Act record check. But the law is so narrowly worded and qualified that it cannot be enforced. There are not any reported cases on the law, and according to a law enforcement official familiar with gun prosecutions, no one has been charged with a violation. On the other hand, the Pennsylvania legislature prohibited the City of Philadelphia from taking any actions regarding guns in spite of having home rule. It overturned Philadelphia's ban on assault weapons. It forbade the police from requiring an explanation and good reason from people who request a permit to carry a concealed handgun. Because of this law, if somebody requests a concealed carry permit and does not have a record, the police have to give them the permit. There has been a huge increase in the number of people carrying handguns legally on Philadelphia streets and in their cars. There are no studies on the impact on handgun death rates as yet, but in recent years an argument between neighbors over shoveling snow erupted into a shootout after both men pulled out guns that they carried regularly and legally, and fights at bars seem more frequently to end with someone shot with a legally carried handgun.[15]

In Pennsylvania and many other states, the gun industry and the NRA effectively appeal to the widespread, moderate version of the cultural and political identification with guns by arguing that there are many gun laws on the books and we should enforce them rather than adding more—all the while knowing that these laws leave handguns all but unregulated. Many Americans who share the identification of handguns with freedom are also sincerely concerned about the catastrophic results of the current situation. But the industry has regularly and successfully tapped into that identification, as well as pervasive negative attitudes toward cities and urban dwellers that often have a racial dimension, to maintain a high level of new handgun sales.

What Can Be Done?

Solutions for most of the problems addressed in this book are hard to come by. Usually they require enormous funding that could only come from the federal government. There should be a Marshall Plan for the cities, but there is not the political will, and it is a challenge to come up with other meaningful measures that could improve the situation. Most meaningful measures to regulate handguns are also national in scope, although many do not require major funding. But many proposals that sound effective are not, so we should be leery of easy fixes and false promises, particularly with a problem that causes so much destruction and grief.

We should register handguns and license handgun owners. Several states have already adopted some version of this policy, and studies show that when registration and licensing are combined it is significantly harder for criminals and youth to obtain guns (Webster, Vernick, and Helpern 2001). All sales, transfers, and thefts of handguns should be mandatorily reported, maintained in government records, and subject to the Brady Act record check. We license and register our marriages, our cars, our cats and dogs; these rules do not seem to bother anybody. Why wouldn't we license and register a device that is designed to kill and that does such harm?

We should take sample shots from every handgun and keep them in a data bank, which would enable police to trace weapons from bullets recovered at crime scenes. Police could find out what gun fired them and track it down the distribution chain.

We should adopt strong, clear and specific "straw purchase" laws that make all of the parties to a straw purchase criminally and civilly responsible.

We should limit the purchasing of handguns. We could acknowledge the right to self-defense and the role of rifles in hunting and target shooting, but limit multiple purchases of handguns, perhaps by requiring a good reason for additional purchases. Why would anyone legitimately need many handguns, let alone one a month?

Finally, the large urban areas of the nation, where unregulated handgun markets have taken such a terrible toll, should have the power to regulate handguns within their borders.[16]

Measures like these could be effective, particularly at reducing the flood of new handguns to urban streets. But we must recognize that there are a lot of handguns out there now: best estimates are in the range of 65 million (Cook and Ludwig 1996). We are an armed nation, and there is no quick or easy solution.

We may have to come to grips with the cultural and political identification of guns with our nation's highest ideals and with the deadly legacy of that identification. Large cities facing declining job opportunities, losses in population and tax revenues, and rising levels of deprivation are being forced to accommodate virtually unregulated handgun markets. The cultural and political identification with guns and the unregulated handgun markets have continuing broad support almost exclusively in rural areas and have been imposed on urban and black communities. Laws that allow easy availability of handguns urgently require public attention and may well draw considerable opposition even in rural areas if debated openly and honestly. But denial and political expediency have reigned too long. The loss of life, the economic and social costs, and the undermining of safety and the quality of life in urban America are unacceptable.

References

Bureau of Alcohol, Tobacco, and Firearms (ATF), U.S. Department of the Treasury. 2000. *Commerce in Firearms in the U.S.* http://permanent.access.gpo.gov/lps4006/020400report.pdf

Center for Gun Policy and Research, School of Public Health, Johns Hopkins University. 2004. Firearm Injury and Death in the United States. Updated periodically to include latest research. http://www.jhsph.edu/gunpolicy/US_factsheet_2004.pdf.

Centers for Disease Control and Prevention (CDC). 2003. Web-Based Injury Statistics Query and Reporting System (WISQARS). http://www.cdc.gov/ncipc/wisqars/default.htm.

Cook, Philip J., and John Ludwig. 1996. *Guns in America: Results of a Comprehensive National Survey on Firearm Ownership and Use.* Washington, D.C.: Police Foundation.

Federal Bureau of Investigation (FBI). 2003. *Crime in the United States 2002: Uniform Crime Reports.* Washington, D.C.: U.S. Department of Justice.

Kairys, David 2005a. Legislative usurpation: The early practice and constitutional repudiation of legislative intervention in adjudication. *University of Missouri-K.C. Law Review* 73: 945–50.

———. 2005b. Fire sale: How the gun industry bought itself immunity from the rule of law. *Slate,* November 7.

———. 2003a. A Philadelphia story. *Legal Affairs* (May–June): 63. http://www.legalaffairs.org/issues/May-June-2003/story_kairys_mayjun03.msp

———. 2003b. The cities take the initiative: Public nuisance lawsuits against handgun manufacturers. In *Guns, Crime, and Punishment in America,* ed. Bernard E. Harcourt, 363–83. New York: New York University Press. http://ssrn.com/abstract=730843.

———. 2000a. The origin and development of the governmental handgun cases. *Connecticut Law Review* 32: 1163–74.

———. 2000b. The government handgun cases and the elements and underlying policies of public nuisance law. *Connecticut Law Review* 32: 1175–87.

———. 1998. Legal claims of cities against the manufacturers of handguns. *Temple Law Review* 71 (1): 1–21.

Kellermann, Arthur L., and James A. Mercy. 1992. Men, women, and murder: Gender-specific differences in rates of fatal violence and victimization. *Journal of Trauma* 33: 1–5.

Kellermann, Arthur L., Frederick P. Rivara, Norman B. Rushforth, Joyce G. Banton, Donald T. Reay, Jerry T. Francisco, Ana B. Locci, Janice Prodzinski, Bela B. Hackman, and Grant Somes. 1993. Gun ownership as a risk factor for homicide in the home. *New England Journal of Medicine* 329: 1084–91.

Kellermann, Arthur L., Frederick P. Rivara, Grant Somes, Donald T. Reay, Jerry Francisco, Joyce G. Banton, Jancice Prodzinski, Corinne Fligner, and Bela B. Hackman,. 1992. Suicide in the home in relation to gun ownership. *New England Journal of Medicine* 327: 467–72.

Krug, Etienne G., Kenneth E. Powell, and Linda L. Dahlberg 1998. Firearm-related deaths in the United States and 35 other high- and upper-middle-income countries. *International Journal of Epidemiology* 27: 214–21.

Lott, John R., Jr. 1998. *More Guns, Less Crime: Understanding Crime and Gun Control Laws.* Chicago: University of Chicago Press.

Webster, Daniel W., Jon S. Vernick, and L. M. Helpern. 2001. Relationship between licensing, registration and other gun sales laws and the source state of crime guns. *Injury Prevention* 7: 184–89.

Weil, Douglas S., and Rebecca C. Knox. 1996. Effects of limiting handgun purchases on interstate transfer of firearms. *Journal of the American Medical Association* 275: 1759–61.

Wintemute, Garen J. 1994. *Ring of Fire: The Handgun Makers of Southern California.* Sacramento, Calif.: Violence Prevention Research Program.

Chapter 16
What Do We Do Now? Toward a Brighter Future for African American Men

PETER EDELMAN

After reading to this point, you may well be wondering what anyone can say with any confidence about solutions to the problems confronting young black men in inner cities. These problems add up to a crisis that will not give way easily. It has developed over a long period of time, and will not disappear with the wave of a wand.

Nonetheless, much can be done—provided there is a will to act. The answers involve many actors and many actions. They include public policy and civic action in the larger community and help and support in black youths' immediate families and neighborhoods. All are vital. And there is one realm of responsibility without which success is impossible. No one will succeed unless he himself tries. But this is not either/or; it is both/and. As things are, try as they might, some youth face such overwhelming barriers that they cannot beat the odds. The entire community, in all its meanings, must be at the table.

Nor will change be easy. It requires a determined, collaborative effort that entails the participation of Americans both white and black, from outside the inner city as well as within it. Nothing less will maximize the chances of success in addressing the urban poverty and racial inequality that are embedded in our society.

There is a long list of steps that bear on the excruciating problems set forth in this volume. Most are hard to accomplish, because of societal and therefore political attitudes about race and poverty, because institutions are resistant to change even when money is available, and because the attitudes and expectations of the young men whose lives are at stake are hardened by history, current events in their lives, and messages they receive within their immediate communities and from mass culture.

But we can act, and we must.

Our discussion occurs at the intersection of race and poverty—a dangerous place indeed, as the foregoing chapters indicate so vividly.

The Debate

A vigorous debate rages between people who point to structural and societal issues as the major causes of the problem and the major focus of action going forward, and those who emphasize issues of personal responsibility as the cause and central point of necessary change. Books, speeches, and op-ed pieces teem with sharp accusations and retorts.

A more three-dimensional, more thoughtful, and, may I say, more anguished discussion can be found within the African American community about why so many young people are going astray. I can claim only limited and sporadic glimpses of this deeper conversation, and it is entirely understandable that it is less visible to the outside world. But it is important, and I hope it will be productive.

I find the public, more one-dimensional version of the debate an unhelpful caricature. The short answer is that both sides are right. Racism is a continuing fact. The results of the legacy of racism are a continuing, damaging reality. Structural problems, dysfunctional institutions, and flawed policies in the economy and the society as a whole are a major factor. But patterns of personal irresponsibility and negative influences close to home are facts, too, whatever their cause. So public policies and civic action are a crucial part of the answer. And assumption of personal responsibility is inescapable as well.

The History

To comprehend the current situation, it is important to understand its origins, especially beginning with the 1960s. History absolves no one from being responsible for him or herself, which of course includes responsibility for loved ones, neighbors, coworkers, and others who constitute the various communities to which we belong. The legacy of the past cannot excuse current behavior, but it is nonetheless vital to understand how it shapes the present.

The history as I see it has been amply set forth by William Julius Wilson and others (Wilson 1996, Sugrue 1996). The discussion really begins with slavery, Jim Crow, and the consequences of systemic exploitation and white supremacy, but starting in the 1960s the consequences of deindustrialization and globalization in the larger society combined with the concentration of African American poverty in inner cities to form a lethal mix. The intersection of race and poverty became a far more dangerous place.

Good jobs disappeared for millions of Americans of all races. The economy stagnated for half or more of American workers, and wages for the bottom half remain basically stagnant today (Mishel, Bernstein, and

Allegretto 2006). The financial difficulties families faced were ameliorated only by sending another worker—typically the wife in a two-parent household—into the job market. Low-wage work became a fact of life for something like half the labor force, and family income low enough to make daily subsistence a never-ending struggle became a pattern for nearly a third of American families (Wilson 1996).

African American poverty intensified within this broader economic context. Two stories have played out side by side in the African American community over the past half-century. A far stronger African American middle class developed, even as the tragedies described in this volume became a pattern in the inner cities. The gulf between two societies growing inexorably apart, which the Kerner Commission famously discussed in the 1960s as a gulf between whites and blacks, has become a class division among African Americans as well (Report of the National Advisory Commission on Civil Disorders 1968).

The economy has had a cold for half of America's workers for a third of a century, but it has had those symptoms for an even larger proportion of African American workers, and it has had pneumonia for a disproportionate section of the African American community, especially in the inner city.

Why? White workers always fare better than black workers, on average. They typically have higher wages and lower unemployment rates (Edelman, Holzer, and Offner 2006). But the story in the inner city is much more complicated.

As recounted elsewhere in this volume, in the past the segregated communities of the inner city were more three-dimensional in class and income terms. The mantra, at least in retrospect, is that "Mrs. Johnson" always knew what young people were doing and called their mama to report when someone went astray. And "Mr. Johnson" was far more likely to be present, have a stable job, and help young men navigate their way to work and a family of their own.

With the urban rebellions of the 1960s and the enactment of the Fair Housing Act of 1968, much of the African American middle class left the inner city for suburbs with better schools and public services. They left behind a heavily low-income populace far less able to move, which began to manifest a markedly higher incidence of problems reflecting social disintegration.

Other trends exacerbated the deterioration. During segregation, big-city schools had teachers with Ph.D.s who could not get jobs in white-dominated institutions. Other professionals and community workers were people whose initial career decisions were made within highly constricted frameworks, or with no opportunity to work in agencies and organizations outside the black community. Desegregation, antidiscrimination laws, and changing social attitudes opened up new career possibilities and new venues within which to practice and develop expertise. This development was good, of course, but it had one harmful side effect: to reduce the number of African Americans serving low-income African Americans in the helping professions.

Beyond the obvious point that the other side of the coin of the burgeoning African American middle class was a continuing gap that was especially acute at the low-income end of the continuum, the concentration of inner-city poverty spawned the destructive behaviors that some now characterize as cultural, with the negative implication that the culture is somehow genetic or at least environmentally inevitable.

The story is partly about the destruction of hope, too. I remember coming to New York State to be youth corrections commissioner in 1975 and being shocked to find a considerable number of black male fourteen- and fifteen-year-olds committing muggings in which they not only stole an elderly woman's purse but felt the need to push her to the sidewalk as well, too often fracturing her hip or inflicting other gratuitous injuries. What was this about? My theory was that these young people were channeling their anger in a different direction from their counterparts of a decade earlier. In the imagery offered by Geoffrey Canada, this was still the era of the fist and stick rather than the knife and gun, but it nonetheless involved apolitical violence against other people in a way that had not been characteristic of the 1960s (Canada 1995).

In the heyday of the 1960s, young people had hope. When the historic civil rights legislation of the period did not produce an immediate expansion in economic opportunity and improved incomes and resources for inner-city people, they erupted in violence. The riots were self-destructive, to be sure. But this unrest was also a revolution of rising expectations, an inarticulate, dramatic political statement of a demand for action to match the rhetoric of civil rights.

By 1975 when I came back to New York, only seven years after I had left that state's politics with the death of Robert Kennedy (for whom I had worked from 1964 to 1968), things were very different. Hope had been quashed. Richard Nixon was President. The inner cities of the nation were largely isolated and ignored. In New York City the teachers' union had successfully derailed the plan for community control of the schools, scoring a direct hit on the aspirations of the black community. As ostensibly friendly as the administration of Mayor John Lindsay had been to the African American and Hispanic communities, the sense that things could change was gone. Abe Beame, whose diminutive physical stature matched his accountant's personality, was now the mayor of a fiscally bankrupt city. There were more black faces in government and business, but to the young African American men in the inner city, the sense of possibility had been replaced by a sense of futility. The anger was still there, but its modus operandi no longer had any positive implications. It was now random violence against elderly women on the street.

What to Do

The strategies I suggest here are not limited to a direct focus on young black men, although attention to them in particular is vital. Their issues are inextricably connected to broader issues of both race and poverty, the health of the whole African American community, especially at the low-income end, and the health of American society generally. Much of what follows relates to those encompassing concerns, with the view that these framework measures are critical to the prospects of young African American men.

I don't know who knows how to end racism in the United States. I certainly don't. We have made great progress during the last half century, but a racial lens will reveal continuing issues throughout our society, and this book illuminates that the bottom end of the black community has lost ground.

We can confront racism when it takes the form of legally actionable discrimination, and we can analyze, confront, and take steps to remedy the structural racism of institutions and systems that do not operate according to a specific plan to discriminate, but do so as effectively as if they did have such a plan. If we do those things vigorously, we will undoubtedly have a reverberative effect on racism itself.

One task that must be taken on within the African American community especially is direct action to change attitudes on the street that disrespect and discourage the kind of achievement which we routinely value in the larger society. Some of the peer culture of nonachievement may yield to leadership, especially from faith leaders, which speaks out forcefully to condemn the self-fulfilling destructiveness of paying heed to those who say it isn't cool even to try. That leadership needs to confront as well the messages of mass culture that glorify violence, attack women, and suggest that being a thug is a great career. And renewed leadership from all corners is needed to reduce the flood of guns which makes it so much more likely that an altercation which used to end in a black eye now ends in a mortuary.

But messages are not enough. Messages cannot make up for schools that do not teach and a world in which all roads seem to lead to prison. In the remainder of this essay I set out some thoughts about how to change some of the frameworks and contexts in which the cancer of devaluing achievement metastasizes, changes that I believe would help toward reversing the malignant growth of negative norms.

The actions I suggest include (1) policies that are neutral as to race but will have disproportionate effects on different racial groups because the problems to be addressed appear disproportionately among people of color; (2) policies that are race-conscious, focusing on racial discrimination and on structural or institutional racism, the ways in which major societal institutions operate with an especially negative impact on people of color; and (3) policies that relate to place, directed at the problems that multiply when too many low-income people live in the same place, which in the United States is a phenomenon disproportionately associated with low-income people of color.

Race-Neutral Policies

Why start with race-neutral policies? Because poverty rates among African Americans (and Latinos and Native Americans) are about two and a half times higher than among whites, and African Americans who have jobs are disproportionately represented in the ranks of low-wage workers. Non-Hispanic whites' median family income was $50,784 in 2005, while that of African Americans was $30,858 (DeNavas-Walt, Proctor, and Lee 2006).

These racially unequal economic facts would be altered substantially by a number of race-neutral policies. Much of what I set out in this section is contained in the report of a poverty task force sponsored by the Center for American Progress (CAP) and released in April 2007, which I had the honor of cochairing.

These policies would affect all low-income Americans regardless of race. By raising wages and incomes in low-income neighborhoods and among low-income people wherever they live, their quality of life would be improved, the stresses of survival would be reduced, and their children would grow up with a better view of the returns that come from work.

INCOME FROM WORK AND INCOME TRIGGERED BY WORK

Raising the minimum wage, lowering legal barriers to union organizing, and improving the Earned Income Tax Credit (EITC) would all have a disproportionate effect on workers of color, because people of color are disproportionately represented in the ranks of low-wage workers, and because labor-market economics tells us that higher wages and increased wage supplements should have the effect of drawing more people into the labor force and, many including myself would say, encouraging more people to marry.

The minimum wage was raised in the spring of 2007 to reach $7.25 an hour over a two-year period. The CAP poverty task force recommended raising it further until it reaches 50 percent of the average wage, which would be $8.40 as of 2007, and then indexing it to inflation (CAP 2007).

For most of the 1950s and 1960s the minimum wage was at 50 percent of the average wage. There is good reason to restore that level. Sound research shows that setting the minimum at that level would destroy few jobs and have little effect on small businesses. Similarly, further success with living wage campaigns would be a great help to workers of color. These campaigns have produced wages of around $10 an hour for employees of companies in more than a hundred jurisdictions that contract with state and local governments to perform various services.

What is extremely unfortunate is that raising the minimum wage to a level of half the average wage will not get families of four or more people out of poverty. And the official federal poverty line, about $20,000 a year for a family of four in 2007, is a grossly insufficient measure of capacity to make ends meet. To put it simply, the American labor market is broken. A quarter of all jobs pay less than $20,000 a year, and half pay less than $30,000 (CAP 2007).

Recognizing this gap, in the mid-1970s Congress created the Earned Income Tax Credit to supplement the incomes of low-wage workers. The EITC adds more than $4,000 to the income of a minimum-wage worker with two children, and more than $2,500 to the income of such a worker with one child. It is a powerful antipoverty tool, currently reaching 22.5 million people at a cost of $40.6 billion. In 2007 twenty states, the District of Columbia, and a few local governments had their own EITCs, geared to state or local income taxes (CAP 2007). More states and local governments should take similar steps.

The EITC should be improved in a number of ways, all of which would have disproportionate benefits for the most disadvantaged members of nonwhite racial and ethnic groups. A category should be added for families with three children. Marriage penalties currently built into the EITC structure should be ameliorated. And the rate at which the EITC is reduced as income rises should be changed, because the current schedule eliminates income supplementation before a family's income is high enough to pay the bills.

One EITC reform with especially important implications for the young African American men who are the subject of this book is to increase substantially the very modest income supplement now available to low-wage workers who are childless or are noncustodial parents. It is capped for 2007 at $428 for the year and is not available to workers

younger than 25 (CAP 2007). Tripling the maximum payment and reducing the minimum age for eligibility to 18, as our CAP poverty task
force recommended, could help draw unmarried young men into the
job market and, when their wage is supplemented, help those who are
fathers to meet child support obligations and bring them closer to their
children.

"SOCIAL INCOME" MEASURES

Americans generally agree that in regard to health coverage and public
health policy, child care and preschool programs, housing assistance,
and the cost of higher education, we have a societal responsibility to assist lower-income people who cannot purchase (or pay the full market
price for) these items on their own. Public financing to help with each
of these essential goods is justified because each contributes to the quality of life of vulnerable people, but all effectively add to income as well.
Because people of color, having lower incomes, will benefit disproportionately from means-tested government assistance in these areas, or
from increased government support for services to lower-income people, all of these are matters of special importance to young, black men
in impoverished communities.

At the same time, all these matters present challenges that go far beyond money, for the country as a whole and for low-income people generally. Health care should be made universally available by national
policy. Financing alone is not enough, however. Are first-class hospitals
and physicians, rather than mediocre and uncoordinated services, available to lower-income people? Are prevention services targeted particularly to this population, which is disproportionately prone to a myriad of
health problems, many of which arise from or are exacerbated by
poverty? Do we have a system of child care, early childhood development, and pre-kindergarten in the community that is more than a
patchwork, available everywhere and of especially high quality for those
children who need an extra investment in order to be ready for school
by age 5? Is there an investment in increasing the supply of affordable
housing, beyond helping people to pay the astronomical rents produced by the current terrible shortage of such housing? Are community
colleges and other appropriate postsecondary programs not only physically accessible but also welcoming and responsive to the needs of students who may be underprepared and need some catching up?

All these are race-neutral policies that will have salutary, racially disproportionate effects.

Notice, too, the implications of these recommendations for the matter of who bears the responsibility to act. There will not be a first-class

universal health care system, a system of services for children under 5 to provide care while parents work and prepare children for kindergarten, a planned system to increase the supply of affordable housing, or an accessible and responsive system of higher education in any community unless local leaders and citizens, both those with professional expertise and those who are concerned as a civic responsibility, take the steps necessary to create these systems. The federal government can and should provide funding to help and set some national standards to assure certain key elements of content and quality, but unless there is local leadership, little good will come of the national investment.

GOING FROM K–12 TO P–16

The basic educational reform we need as a nation is, again, race-neutral, although certainly not income-neutral. Our sense of educational responsibility for all children and young people has to begin before kindergarten and continue past high school graduation. We may charge a fee for pre-kindergarten and college to those who can afford to pay a portion of the cost, although I was excited to read of Massachusetts Governor Deval Patrick's proposal to make community college free to all (*Boston Globe*, June 1, 2007). K–12 education is now free to all, but education from early childhood through postsecondary training should constitute a coherent system that concentrates especially on those children and young people who need extra attention. If we cannot make our schools work to educate all of our children, we would have to concede that we had failed to make good on the promise of equal opportunity that is a tenet of our democracy, a fundamental failure indeed.

Disconnected Youth

We are failing now. In every major city, high school graduation rates are appallingly low.

The massive dropout problem is in reality a racial issue. The urban school systems with these appalling dropout statistics have student bodies who are heavily African American and Latino. The proportion of young men who are disconnected—that is, who are both out of school and out of work—is much higher among African Americans and Latinos than among whites. Only half the African American men between eighteen and twenty-four who have no more than a high school diploma and are neither in school nor in jail have a job (Edelman, Holzer, and Offner 2006). What Wilson calls joblessness constitutes an immense problem with devastating effects for black families and communities. I raise it in the discussion of nonracial policies because the population in need of attention is by no means composed entirely of people of color, and the steps we need to take are not defined by race or ethnicity.

This is a challenge to every community, and especially every big city. Federal money is critical to meeting the challenge, but it is the community itself that must take responsibility for all its young people. We need clear pathways to economically stable adulthood and full inclusion in society for every young person.

The challenge can be divided into two big pieces: preventing disconnection, and achieving reconnection for those already disconnected.

Preventing disconnection is a responsibility of the schools and of a myriad of participants during the off-school hours. Beyond preparing for college every child who has the capacity to benefit from it, whether it is a community college or a four-year institution, the schools need to be connected much more closely than they are now to employers. Many employers hire high school graduates. In many cities, health care, computers, construction, and travel and entertainment are all sectors that work in partnership with high schools in career academies and other career and technical education programs.

Students in low-income neighborhoods need to see a reason to stay in school. Exhortations to stay in school are useless when nothing about the school engages them and some policies actively push them away. Elijah Anderson talks about "decent" and "street" orientations. You can't beat something with nothing. Young people who have seen wasted and thwarted lives as a daily diet need a very clear vision that there is something tangible in their immediate environment which offers a positive route forward.

But what goes on in the school may not do the whole job. What goes on in off-school hours is crucial. Young people need more caring adults in their lives, to supplement the support of a loving but hard-pressed parent and all too often to make up for what is missing at home. Coaches, pastors, youth workers, and mentors and tutors of all kinds need to be there in significant numbers. And such people will be only randomly successful if they have to operate as individuals, hit or miss. Communities—through Ys, Boys and Girls Clubs, scouts, sports leagues, churches, synagogues, and mosques, and after-school programs of all kinds (some using school buildings)—need to organize systemic frameworks for the off-school hours.

What occurs in the schools and what happens in the off-school hours form the substance of the strategy to counter the culture of nonachievement, the content that must accompany the message from the leaders that trying to make the most out of life is not acting "white."

These steps would reduce disconnection, but there also has to be a strategy to reconnect those who get disconnected—currently, a large number of young men of color. Youth get arrested or grow up in foster care, or both, and for too many a process of disconnection starts very early. Young women have babies and put aside their hopes for something else, if they even had such hopes. Whether or not incarceration or parenthood induces disconnection, thousands upon thousands of young people, disproportionately of color, drop out of school and lose their way.

So we must also commit ourselves to reconnection: for ex-offenders, for youth who have aged out of foster care, for young parents who have left school and are not working, and for the larger number who have just gotten lost along the way (Edelman, Holzer, and Offner 2006). What is reconnection? It is YouthBuild, in 200 sites across the country, teaching construction skills and building human strength. It is Job Corps, still going strong after more than four decades. It is the Service and Conservation Corps, which has reached hundreds of thousands of young people around the nation. It is community colleges, which in some places have an open door to youth without a high school diploma and bring them along to a two-year college degree and sometimes more. And it is hundreds of local organizations that are not part of any national system except perhaps for public funding they receive. It used to be the military for some, and should be again, but, for reasons which in 2007 trouble many people, that is not an attractive option for reconnection at present.

I could add other race-neutral policies. The social safety net in America has frayed badly, including a system of unemployment insurance that has deteriorated to the point where it helps only 35 percent of those who have lost a job (CAP 2007). We need to adopt policies that encourage saving and asset-building so lower-income people are not always just a paycheck away from poverty. But I hope I have made my point. This book walks through the door of race into the room where race and poverty dwell in a deadly embrace. Beginning to detoxify the situation means paying attention to poverty policy as well as to policies designed to redress racial inequality. Reducing poverty by race-neutral means is in fact not race-neutral in its impact. What I have described thus far will improve the quality of life in communities of color and will therefore, though often indirectly, attack the issues that are the topic of this volume.

Race-Conscious Policies

But some of what is terribly wrong is about race. Racial discrimination, which constitutes racism even though it is not always a matter of simple prejudice, persists. We passed historic laws, to be sure. And they have made a difference in employment, housing, public accommodations, and elsewhere. Nonetheless, every day, in many places across the United States, some employer, some real estate developer, or some hotel or restaurant is engaging in illegal discrimination based on race.

Someone could sue. Sometimes they do. Individuals can't enforce the laws by themselves, though. The government has to be involved, and it should do far more than it does. Beginning in 2001, particularly, the federal government greatly reduced its efforts when, if anything, it should have increased them.

So the good laws we have need to be enforced.

We have learned, though, that racism is not always embodied in deliberate, racially malignant policy. Sometimes it is embedded in the behavior of institutions and agencies even though no group of people sits down to make a plan. This is structural racism, institutional racism, or functional racism, and it is quite real.

Why are African Americans stopped by the police so disproportionately? Why, at every step of the way, through arrest, the filing of charges, the pursuit of prosecutions, sentencing, and incarceration, do African Americans become an ever-increasing proportion of the population in the system? To some extent this is connected to the disproportionate poverty of African Americans, as is the over-representation of African American children and youth in foster care and in juvenile jails.

But poverty is clearly far from the totality of what is at work. Race is doing its work as well, even when a significant proportion of the police, prosecutors, judges, probation officers, and the rest of the people running the system are African American. The system itself has a bias, reflecting perhaps a stew of attitudes about class and race.

We can make the same observation about our urban public school systems. Why do the teachers with the greatest seniority generally prefer not to work in inner-city schools? If those schools are the most poorly maintained and the most likely to lack up-to-date books and sufficient supplies, why is that? If there is an apparent assumption among many principals and teachers that their pupils are not capable of or interested in learning, why is that? If an African American child in an inner-city school misbehaves in some minor way, why is he or she far more likely to be suspended from school than a white child in a school in a better part of town?

Poverty is a part of this picture. But it seems inescapable that race is in the mix as well. As with the justice system, many of the teachers and principals involved are African American. Again, race and class bias are a hybrid poison.

We can be confident that the race-neutral steps set forth earlier will reduce poverty and will have a disparately positive effect on the poverty of people of color, although our capacity to bring those steps to fruition is another matter.

But what to do about structural racism? Not so clear. The first step is to call it out. Many have done so, of course, but we need voices both inside and outside the African American community to speak the truth. From there on, however, the going is tougher.

As for the justice system, perhaps a thorough scrubbing of all written policies would reveal places for constructive change. Maybe we need a different or additional set of criteria for hiring. Certainly we need different messages in both preservice and inservice training. Different policing policies to make the police into a community-building and supportive force instead of an occupying army. Far more in the way of diversion of non-violent first offenders and other minor offenders to community supervision, restitution, and activity—but real diversion, not just an admonition to go home and not do it again. Prisons that teach literacy and job skills to prepare offenders for a better future. The list is long.

The same goes for the schools, although with different details. Funding formulas that get more money to the schools which have a predominant population of low-income children. Principal and teacher assignment policies that walk a similar extra mile with the system's human resources. Math and science, art and music, culturally relevant materials. Parent involvement. Respectful disciplinary policies. Smaller schools. Extended school days and longer school years. And so on.

We should not give up the battle for racial diversity. All people should be able to choose to live and socialize and worship with people who have a different skin color or appearance or with people who look like themselves, so long as they do not violate any law, but children need the chance to understand the diversity of our society in a firsthand way. At the very least, going to school with children of the same race who come from circumstances of greater prosperity will help to alter the learning atmosphere and the educational outcomes for all the children (Century Foundation 2002). In 2007 the possibility for either racial or economic integration is in large part a matter of where people live.

We cannot address the justice and education systems in isolation. If families are stronger and parents have a better understanding of positive nurturing practices, if communities are stronger and supply multiple sets of shoulders on which children can stand as they grow up, if churches, synagogues, and mosques play an active role, the justice system and the foster care system will have less business and they along with the schools will possibly have a more positive view of how to carry out their own responsibilities.

Place-Based Policies

Many though not all the powerful stories and observations in the forego-ing essays concern young men who grow up in neighborhoods where poverty is endemic. By the numbers, the low-income population of those neighborhoods, insofar as they are predominantly African American, is perhaps a quarter of the African American poor (Jargowsky 1997). The problems chronicled by the various authors inevitably spill over from the inner city to other cohorts of African American young men.

Nonetheless, to recall again Elijah Anderson's evocative image of the "decent" and the "street," that struggle is at its apex in the inner city, so it is imperative that a discussion about African American young men ad-dress the question of place.

There are three possibilities, not at all mutually exclusive: enable peo-ple to move out of the inner city to lower-poverty neighborhoods; entice higher-income people to move into inner cities without forcing current residents out; and improve the circumstances of the people now living in the inner city. What should be done—indeed, what is being done in many cities—with the high-rise public housing projects that are now and have for some time been places where nearly everyone is poor is a ques-tion within the larger question of the future of inner-city residents.

All three possibilities are complementary and should be pursued in tandem.

First, through a greatly increased pool of housing vouchers (adminis-tered with teeth and supportive services to help people move anywhere that works financially), a new investment in the supply of affordable housing built throughout the region, and an aggressive job training and placement policy, people should be empowered to move out of the inner city and make new lives elsewhere.

Second, a wave of return to the central city is already under way in every city that is economically healthy, but in most places it is not occur-ring with much or any care or concern about its impact on the current population of those places. What is happening is gentrification, when what we should be talking about is equitable development. If inner-city neighborhoods can be safe, nurturing places with good schools and amenities, economic integration can occur.

That brings us to the third point: the urgent need for increasing the income and life possibilities of families who want to stay where they are. Among other things, this approach means making a far greater effort to help people find jobs in the regional economy and to provide the physi-cal mobility through mass transit or help with purchasing a car so peo-ple can get to those jobs. Of course, it also involves public safety, good public education, and working community institutions of all kinds.

None of this is simple, but if there is no policy about place, there will be far less progress toward addressing the crisis that stimulated this excellent set of essays.

Who Must Act and How Do We Get Them to Act?

It should be evident now, without need for reiteration, that the actors who need to be involved in the matters I have discussed are multiple—government at all levels and private actors of all kinds. Nearly all can be either advocates and leaders for change or, as the case may be, targets for advocates who press them to be part of the solution.

The mix of advocates and targets will differ from place to place. The mayor and other elected officials will be leaders or a problem. Local foundations will be leaders or will need to be pushed. Business and labor leaders, university presidents, the clergy, major figures both within and outside the African American community, will be leaders or will have to be pressed to act. The same goes for people and institutions at the state or national level.

I am often asked, if there were only one thing I would be able to do to address all these problems, what would it be? The question used to irritate me. There is no one thing, I would say somewhat heatedly. Then I figured out the answer: ORGANIZE.

There has to be a mix of bottom-up and top-down activities. Top-down programs, even if they come from self-starting efforts, will fail if they fall on apathetic or incompetent shoulders at the bottom. Bottom-up efforts are important to push for action and to do things that communities can do for themselves. Organizing is imperative.

The advocacy part requires involvement in the electoral process, to push for the election of people who care about these issues and affect the attitudes and commitments of those who otherwise would be uninterested or worse. Similarly, advocacy with those already in office to make them better than they would otherwise be is a necessary part of the process. Too many people who do good things in their communities to help others do not see the essential need to participate in the political process. This has to change.

Everyone who reads this book has a role to play. If they don't, we will continue for generations to suffer the tragedies and waste of lives that are portrayed so vividly in this volume.

References

Bernstein, Jared, and Dean Baker. 2003. *The Benefits of Full Employment: When Markets Work for People.* Washington, D.C.: Economic Policy Institute.

Canada, Geoffrey. 1995. *Fist, Stick, Knife, Gun: A Personal History of Violence in America*. Boston: Beacon Press.

Center for American Progress (CAP), Task Force on Poverty. 2007. *From Poverty to Prosperity: A National Strategy to Cut Poverty in Half.* Washington, D.C.: Center for American Progress.

Century Foundation, Task Force on the Common School. 2002. *Divided We Fall: Coming Together Through Public School Choice.* New York: Century Foundation Press.

Danziger, Sheldon, and Peter Gottschalk. 1995. *America Unequal.* Cambridge, Mass.: Harvard University Press.

DeNavas-Walt, Carmen, Bernadette D. Proctor, and Cheryl Hill Lee. 2006. *Income, Poverty, and Health Insurance Coverage in the United States: 2005.* Washington, D.C.: U.S. Department of Commerce.

Edelman, Peter. 2005. Where race meets class: The 21st century civil rights agenda. *Georgetown Journal on Poverty Law and Policy* 12: 1–12.

———. Welfare and the politics of race: Same tune, new lyrics? *Georgetown Journal on Poverty Law and Policy* 11: 389–403.

Edelman, Peter, Harry J. Holzer, and Paul Offner. 2006. *Reconnecting Disadvantaged Young Men.* Washington, D.C.: Urban Institute Press.

Holt, Steve. 2006. The Earned Income Tax Credit at Age 30: What We Know. Research Brief. Washington, D.C.: Brookings Institution.

Jargowsky, Paul A. 1997. *Poverty and Place: Ghettos, Barrios, and the American City.* New York: Russell Sage.

Lardner, James, and David A. Smith, eds. 2005. *Inequality Matters: The Growing Economic Divide in America and Its Poisonous Consequences.* New York: New Press.

Mishel, Lawrence, Jared Bernstein, and Sylvia Allegretto. 2006. *The State of Working America.* Ithaca, N.Y.: Cornell University Press.

Report of the National Advisory Commission on Civil Disorders. 1968. Washington, D.C.: U.S. Government Printing Office.

Sugrue, Thomas, J. 1996. *The Origins of the Urban Crisis: Race and Inequality in Postwar Detroit.* Princeton, N.J.: Princeton University Press.

Wilson, William Julius. 1996. *When Work Disappears: The World of the New Urban Poor.* New York: Knopf.

Notes

Chapter 1. Against the Wall: Poor, Young, Black, and Male

Copyright © 2008 Elijah Anderson.

Chapter 2. David's Story: From Promise to Despair

1. For a discussion of parents' involvement in youth sports see Coakley 2006; Chafetz and Kortarba 1995. See Cooper 2000 for an intriguing discussion of the ways fathers employed in the Silicon Valley knowledge industry at once reconceptualize and reinscribe traditional notions of fatherhood.

2. The advent of information technology has made domination by physical size and strength a thing of the past. Clad in sweater and shirt, a new hero is emerging, whose physical stature may not be imposing but whose technical knowledge and financial savvy carry a big punch. Think Bill Gates and Jeff Bezos, founders of Microsoft and Amazon respectively. Nevertheless, boys from marginalized groups, with little access to the resources to become an expert in the knowledge industry, are more likely to subscribe to outdated notions of masculinity that rely heavily on physical strength and size than do boys from the dominant group.

3. For Philadelphia's code of conduct, see http://www.phila.k12.pa.us/offices/otae/discipline/coconduct0607.pdf.

Chapter 4. The Economic Plight of Inner-City Black Males

This essay draws on field research that my colleagues, graduate students, and I conducted in Chicago's inner-city neighborhoods from the mid-1980s to the mid-1990s. These research projects include the Urban Poverty and Family Life Study (UPFLS), conducted in 1987 and 1988, which included a random sample of nearly 2,500 poor and non-poor African American, Latino, and white residents in Chicago's poor inner-city neighborhoods. As part of this broad project, the UPFLS included data from the Social Opportunity Survey, a subsample of 175 UPFLS participants who answered open-ended questions concerning their perception of the opportunity structure and life chances; a 1988 survey of 179 employers—in most cases, the information came from the highest-ranking official at each firm sampled—that were selected to reflect the distribution of employment across industry and firm size in the Chicago metropolitan area; and comprehensive ethnographic research, including participant observation research and life history interviews, conducted during the period 1986 to 1988 by ten research assistants in a representative sample of inner-city neighborhoods. The remaining projects include a 1993 survey of a representative sample of 500 respondents from two neighborhoods with high rates of joblessness and six focus group discussions involving residents and former residents of these neighborhoods.

1. The figures in this paragraph were calculated from data provided by the economist David Ellwood of Harvard University, based on data from the U.S. Department of Labor.

2. More recent studies report findings consistent with those in our research. See Holzer 1995; Waldinger and Lichter 2002.

3. See also Majors and Billson 1992; Anderson 1990.

4. Also see Young 2004.

Chapter 5. Blacklisted: Hiring Discrimination in an Era of Mass Incarceration

1. To some degree, these disparities reflect differences in the level of recorded criminal activity between groups. Particularly for violent crimes such as homicide, blacks are represented in roughly equal proportions among those arrested and those imprisoned. In contrast, in the case of drug crimes, which have been a major source of prison growth since 1980, the evidence suggests that whites outnumber blacks in both consumption and distribution, but blacks are disproportionately charged with and convicted of possession and dealing. See Sampson and Lauritsen 1997; Blumstein 1982, 1993; Tonry 1995.

2. Loïc Wacquant 2000 addresses the interdependent and reciprocal nature of racial disproportionality in punishment. In what he calls a "deadly symbiosis" between prison and ghetto, Wacquant finds a reinforcement of repression and social marginality driven by these twin institutions. In this formulation, the management and containment of poor black men becomes the dominant objective, with both prison and ghetto isolating this problematic population from the distant mainstream. As increasing numbers of blacks churn from poor neighborhoods to prison and back again, the functional equivalence of these institutions—in the eyes of residents, employers, and the general public—is powerfully reinforced.

3. Over 71 million criminal history records were maintained in state criminal history repositories by the end of 2003 (Bureau of Justice Statistics 2006a). As of 2005, 38 states provide public access to their criminal record repositories, and 28 make some or all of this information available online (Legal Action Center 2004).

4. In answering a question about their willingness to hire an applicant with a criminal record, roughly a quarter of employers responded, "it depends." This finding suggests that, at least for some employers, the type of crime, or the circumstances of the conviction, could be significant beyond the simple fact of conviction.

5. The literature on labeling provides a parallel approach to analyzing the effects of such formal negative markers as juvenile delinquent, mentally ill, homosexual, drug user, etc.; see Becker 1963; Goffman 1963; Garfinkel 1956.

6. As psychologist John Dovidio explains, because most Americans today "consciously endorse egalitarian values, they will not discriminate directly and openly in ways that can be attributed to racism; however, because of their negative

feelings they will discriminate, often unintentionally, when their behavior can be justified on the basis of some factor other than race" (2001, 835).

7. The criminal record in all cases was a drug felony, possession with intent to distribute (cocaine), and 18 months of prison time. Testers presented the information to employers by checking the box "yes" in answer to the standard application question, "Have you ever been convicted of a crime?" As additional cues, testers also reported work experience in the correctional facility, and listed their parole officer as a reference. For a more detailed discussion, see Pager 2003.

8. Employment services such as Jobnet have become a much more common method of finding employment in recent years, particularly for difficult-to-employ populations such as welfare recipients and ex-offenders. A survey conducted by Harry Holzer, Steven Raphael, and Michael Stoll (2006) found that nearly half of Milwaukee employers (46 percent) use Jobnet to advertise job vacancies in their companies.

9. Comparisons of outcomes by race are thus based on between-pair comparisons. Between-pair comparisons provide less efficient estimators, but they are nevertheless unbiased, provided that there are no systematic differences between the sample of jobs assigned to each pair or between the observed characteristics of the black and white pair apart from race. For a more extensive discussion, see Pager 2003, 2007, chap. 5.

10. A more in-depth discussion of methodological concerns, including limits to generalizability, representativeness of testers, sample restrictions, and experimenter effects, is presented in Pager 2007, app. 4A.

11. While not significant in the full sample, this interaction becomes significant when analyzed specifically for suburban employers, and among employers with whom the testers had extended personal contact; see Pager 2007a, chap. 7.

12. The sound bite that has emerged from this study is somewhat misleading. The research has been cited among politicians and the media as demonstrating that "whites with a felony conviction have a better chance at getting a job than do blacks with clean criminal histories." This isn't quite right. The difference between a callback rate of 17 percent (for white felons) and 14 percent (for black non-offenders) is small and not statistically significant. An accurate way to summarize these findings, then, is to conclude: A while felon has about the same chance of getting a callback as a black man with no criminal background.

13. There are several ways of calculating the level of racial segregation in a metropolitan area. The most common method is the dissimilarity index, which calculates the relative distribution of two racial groups (e.g., blacks and whites) across neighborhoods in a city. For U.S. city rankings according to this index, see http://www.censusscope.org/segregation.html.

14. The study by Bendick, Jackson, and Reinoso (1994) included an assessment of the full hiring process, from application to job offer. That the racial disparities reported here (at the first stage of the employment process) closely mirror those from more comprehensive studies provides further reassurance that this design is capturing a majority of the discrimination that takes place in the hiring process.

15. The lower callback rates overall in the Bertrand and Mullainathan study (2003) may reduce the observed contrasts between resume pairs. If for example, 5 percent of employers tend to call back *all* applicants as a matter of policy, the resulting contrast would be based on a very small number of employers who conduct any type of screening at the resume submission stage.

16. A recent study by the National Institute of Justice found that while black and white drivers were stopped by the police at roughly equal rates, once

stopped blacks were substantially more likely to have their cars and/or bodies searched. Contrary to arguments that the use of race is warranted by higher rates of illegal activity among blacks, searches of blacks produced significantly lower yield (evidence of contraband) compared to searches of whites (3.5 versus 14.5 percent). See Bureau of Justice Statistics 2003, tables 9, 11.

17. Such predicaments have been discussed elsewhere in many contexts. Some middle-class blacks indicate that they sometimes dress up even to go grocery shopping or to the mall, as a necessary precaution for dealing with street-wary whites. See Lacy 2004; Feagin and Sikes 1994. Having the luxury of wearing sweatpants to the grocery store is not something most whites think of as among the privileges they enjoy as a function of their skin color. The testers in this study dressed in "business casual," typically a button-down shirt and slacks.

18. The level of suspicion greeting black job applicants has been further documented in the work of Susan Gooden (1999). Comparing the treatment of black and white welfare recipients, Gooden found that black job applicants were required to complete a pre-application twice as often, and were significantly more likely to be subjected to drug tests and criminal background checks than were their white counterparts. Interviews with black applicants in Gooden's study were shorter and less thorough. In short, blacks faced additional hurdles in the application process, while simultaneously receiving fewer opportunities to demonstrate their qualifications.

19. Farmer and Terrell (2001) begin with the assumption that the higher rates of criminal activity among African Americans provide useful information in evaluating the criminal propensities of an unknown African American individual. Their estimates suggest that such inferences alone (without other mediating information) produce a rate of error whereby, at its logical extreme, an innocent African American would be almost five times more likely to be wrongfully convicted of a violent crime than an innocent white individual and, in the case of murder, eight times more likely.

20. A similar overrepresentation of African American involvement in crime has been shown in Sheley and Ashkins 1981 and Klite, Bardwell, and Salzman 1997.

21. Limiting attention only to serious crimes (felonies) yields identical results. Romer, Jamieson, and deCouteau (1998) find a similar over-representation of blacks as violent perpetrators and whites as victims relative to crime statistics in Philadelphia; Oliver (1994) does not find this over-representation in her analysis of "reality-based" police shows such as *Cops*.

22. This survey item comes from the 1991 National Race and Politics Survey, http://sda.berkeley.edu:7502/archive.htm. Of all those arrested for violent crimes in 1990, 45 percent were black; FBI, Uniform Crime Reports 1990.

23. When the race of the perpetrator was not identified, 44 percent of respondents falsely recalled seeing a black perpetrator; 19 percent falsely recalled seeing a white perpetrator. In conditions in which the race of the suspect was identified, subjects were better able to recall the suspect's race when he was presented as black (70 percent) than when he was presented as white (64 percent). Gilliam and Iyengar 2000.

24. The pervasive images of black offenders may have implications for perceptions of the "crime problem" as well. In a study I conducted with Lincoln Quillian, for example, we examined residents' perceptions of the crime problem in their own neighborhoods. We then compared these perceptions to actual

neighborhood crime rates, as measured by police statistics and victimization reports. After taking into account a whole host of individual and neighborhood-level factors that could influence perceptions of crime, including official crime rates, we found racial composition to be one of the strongest determinants. As the percentage of young black men in a neighborhood increased, so too did residents' perceptions of crime, above and beyond any real increases in crime. The strong attributions of criminality to young black men result in race being readily invoked as a visible proxy for danger. While there may indeed be a statistical basis for associating young black men with crime (there is a correlation between racial composition and neighborhood crime rates), this evidence suggest that residents significantly overestimate that correlation, assuming far more of an association between race and crime than actually exists. See Quillian and Pager 2001.

25. Duncan (1976) finds that mildly aggressive behavior is perceived as more threatening when the actor is African American as when the actor is white. Likewise, Sagar and Schofield (1980) presented subjects with verbal accounts of ambiguous interactions, and found that actors depicted as African American were viewed as more threatening than otherwise identical white actors. They find that this effect holds for both black and white subjects, suggesting that the underlying mechanism is likely a more generalized cultural stereotype rather than personal prejudice or racial animosity.

26. The effects of media representations are unlikely to be independent of the broader influence of racial stereotypes. Images of groups are easier to assimilate and remember when they are consistent with stereotypes of that group. See Bodenhausen and Lichtenstein 1987; Fiske 1998.

27. It is important to note that these dynamics can emerge even in the absence of conscious negative feelings or ill-will. Both race and criminal background are sensitive topics, which can lead to strained or uneasy interactions even among the most well-meaning individuals. Unfortunately, mere discomfort in interactions can produce some of the same consequences as intentional discrimination. For example, an experimental study in which subjects were asked to interview job applicants in a simulated hiring situation found that interviews with black applicants contained a greater number of pauses and speech errors, and were terminated more quickly. Job candidates (of any race) subjected to interviews characterized by these nonverbal disruptions were in turn evaluated as less qualified by external observers (Word, Zanna, and Cooper 1974). Anxiety or discomfort in interracial interactions and/or with ex-offenders can thus produce outcomes that look very similar to outright discrimination. See Crocker, Major, and Steele 1998.

28. Shawn Bushway (2004) and Henry Holzer, Steven Raphael, and Michael Stoll (2006) have argued that employers who have access to official criminal background information can replace generalized attributions and assumptions with objective information about actual criminal status, thereby reducing discrimination against blacks without criminal backgrounds. The audit data provide only limited support for this hypothesis: employers who conduct official background checks (identified by survey self-reports) are roughly 3 percent more likely to hire black non-offenders than are employers who do not do checks. Furthermore, only 15 percent of employers reported conducting background checks at the initial stages of selection. A great deal of informal screening thus takes place before more objective background checks are administered.

Chapter 6, The Effects of Immigration on the Economic Position of Young Black Males

1. The question and response options read: "Illegal immigrants should be: Required to go home; Allowed to stay"; "Legal immigration into the U.S. should be: Kept at present level, Increased, Decreased"; "Self or Family member lost job to immigrant"; "Immigrants take jobs away from U.S. citizens."

Chapter 8. Youth Entrepreneurship Training in the Inner City: Overcoming Disadvantage, Engaging Youth in School

1. All names of schools, teachers, and students have been changed to protect their privacy.

Chapter 10. Fighting like a Ballplayer: Basketball as a Strategy Against Social Disorganization

1. Fraternal and compound policing refer to a style of policing whereby police officers are typically assigned to areas whose residents share their racial-ethnic background—folks watching their own folks. This style of policing has predictable effects, increasing tensions within groups and limiting mobility for nonwhite police officers. This practice implicitly suggests that the best policing is done through cultural homogeneity rather than through training and objectivity, or "professional" policing. For more details, see J. Wilson 1968.

2. Many scholars discuss athletic identity and consider how race, gender, and class play significant roles in young black men becoming athletes and using athletic achievement as a status marker; see, for example, Sailes 1998; Messner 1988. Elsewhere (Brooks 2004), I consider the ways in which athletic identity endures into black male adulthood as a sign of inequality, since athletic achievement typically occurs between the ages of fifteen and thirty and represents the social status peak of poor black men. This pattern is in direct contrast with the social status and financial peaks in the life course of middle-class whites, which occur about ten years later and are accompanied with much higher economic gains.

3. At the same time, I recognize the obvious trope of the "endangered black male," which illustrates the continuing obsession with the black man as central to black politics, leadership, and family stability, while deemphasizing black women and implicitly suggesting that they are less important than men.

4. Spradley 1980 was an extremely useful guide to recording, coding, and analyzing information gathered through participant observation.

5. Previous research has measured the effects on children, particularly boys, of growing up without close adult male role models; young males from such backgrounds are more likely to be arrested for petty and serious crimes, join gangs and be drawn into the drug trade at young ages, and ultimately to be absent in the lives of their own children. While it is unclear whether men who are not kin can take the place of biological fathers, it is clear that father figures are important and can play a significant role in the outcomes of children in poverty, particularly if the father figure lives in the same household. See Furstenberg 1995; Furstenberg and Harris 1993. However, many researchers provide evidence and interpretations that contradict the idea that black adult men are

absent or irresponsible, lacking the desire to work and support their families. See especially Liebow 1967; Anderson 1976; Duneier 1992; Young 2004.

6. While studies on Midnight Basketball programs yield mixed results on basketball as an effective intervention in inner-city and violence-filled communities, many recreation programs lack the mentoring and rigorous involvement of positive male figures found in the league studied here. See Hartmann 2001, 2003.

7. For a discussion of role engulfment among college basketball players, see Adler and Adler 1991.

8. A critique of this positive view of basketball might be that young men are being taught to assimilate and conform to mainstream standards. But this is complicated. Young men look for opportunities to play, build a reputation, and be promoted. However, "black" sports are popular activities simply because black men are disproportionately represented and considered dominant. Therefore, involvement in basketball reinforces young black men's sense of black masculinity and difference from other men (particularly white men), while forcing them to conformity to mainstream white standards in some way.

9. Some say the fixation poor black males have on sports is a waste of human potential. See Edwards 1969; Sailes 1996; Harris 1997; Hoberman 1997 for discussions of the dangerous effects of high athletic achievement on the black urban poor. Blumer (1958) theorizes how groups define themselves favorably when comparing themselves to one or more additional groups. In *Stigma* (1963), Goffman suggests that individuals with stigma sometimes create their own groups, using different criteria, and raise the status of their stigma over the standards of the "normals." Whyte (1981) illustrates how this was done empirically. The "corner boys" ranked one another based on bowling ability, ease and ability to get along with young women, and fighting skills. A person's standing among the "college boys" was linked to performance in academic or intellectual endeavors in high school or college. Participation in highbrow cultural activities or potential for escaping their poor neighborhood was also taken into consideration.

10. Young black women have the fastest growing rate of incarceration, a phenomenon that is undertheorized. Nikki Jones's work (2004) fills some of the void, illuminating how social environment and culture lead to young women having similar rationales for fighting. In this case, Mia protected Paul's back, in line with male gang behavior.

Chapter 11. "Tell us how it feels to be a problem": Hip Hop Longings and Poor Young Black Men

Audre Lorde, "The Politics of Addiction," *Callaloo* 14, 1 (1991): 44–45, lines 15–17, copyright © 1990 Audre Lorde.

1. For example, on race and shooter bias, see Payne 2001, Correll, Urland, and Ito 2006.

2. Nas, "Can't Forget About You," *Hip Hop Is Dead.*

3. Stuart Hall quoted in "Revealed: How U.K. Media Fueled Prejudice," *Chronicle World–Changing Black Britain,* http://www.thechronicle.demon.co.uk/tomsite/8_6_1rev.htm, accessed April 27, 2007.

4. While we often hear commentary on what impact this imagery has on Black youth, it is equally important to consider what impact images in hip hop have on perceptions of African Americans generally. For research showing that stereotypic media representations shape perceptions of the group in general, see Ford 1997.

5. The critical importance of this move is articulated in Wolff 1988.

6. Jay Z, "Justify My Thug." *The Black Album*, 2003.

7. Nas, "Hold Down the Block," *Hip Hop Is Dead*, 2006.

8. Ghostface Killah, "Grew Up Hard," *More Fish*, 2006.

9. Children's Defense Fund press release, April 30, 2003.

10. U.S. Department of Justice Bureau of Justice Statistics, "Victim Characteristics," http://www.ojp.usdoj.gov/bjs/cvict_v.htm#race, accessed April 27, 2007.

11. "America's Families and Living Arrangements: 2005," Child Trends calculations of U.S. Census Bureau, Current Population Survey, 2005 Annual Social and Economic Supplement, table C-2.

12. "Next Stop: The North," in King 1986, 189.

13. Another oft-cited statistic is that currently 69 percent of black children are born "out of wedlock." I hesitate to use the data on single-parent households because the single parent is often identified by the simple fact of being unmarried and the category does not acknowledge cohabiting biological or informally adoptive parents. Moreover, assessments of whether children live with two parents leave out families in which children live with more than one child-rearing adult, such as aunts, uncles, or grandparents. Despite these reservations, the Black man seems to appear as a fungible member of the family when he cannot fulfill conventional masculine breadwinning and caretaking roles.

14. For discussion of what educational institutions must provide to ensure African American students' success, see Perry, Steele, and Hilliard 2003; Perry 1993.

Chapter 12. Social Issues Lurking in the Over-Representation of Young African American Men in the Expanding DNA Databases

Portions of the section on Operation Pipeline and on the police organizational imperative, and the section on population-wide databases, are based on Duster 2006c.

1. In early April 2005, the Portuguese government announced that it intended to collect DNA on all the nation's inhabitants; see http://www.newropeans-magazine.org/index.php?option=com_content&task=view&id=2059&Itemid=121, accessed June 6, 2007.

2. See http://www.bjhc.co.uk/news/1/2005/n502020.htm, accessed June 6, 2007.

3. The bombings in London in July 2005 were followed by intensified surveillance.

4. See http://www.november.org/razorwire/rzold/27/page03.html, accessed December 16, 2005.

5. See http://www.noblenational.org/news/publish/article_1019.shtml, accessed June 8, 2004.

Chapter 13. "You can take me outta the 'hood, but you can't take the 'hood outta me": Youth Incarceration and Reentry

The author wishes to acknowledge the following readers who made very helpful comments on previous versions of this paper: Faye Allard, Elijah Anderson,

Patrick Carr, Eric C. Schneider, and the members of the University of Pennsylvania Urban Studies Colloquium.

1. In order to protect the identities of informants, the name of the facility has been changed and all informants chose pseudonyms for themselves.

2. ProDES (Program Development and Evaluation System), Crime and Justice Research Center, Philadelphia. See Jones, Harris, and Fader 1999.

3. During my time as a program evaluator, I had the opportunity to review the program design, as well as those of other institutions that have contracts with the Philadelphia juvenile justice system. Our research team had ongoing communication about facilities with probation officers, judges, and administrators in the Department of Human Services.

4. Eric Schneider, personal communication, October 17, 2006; see also Schneider 1992.

Chapter 14. Suicide Patterns Among Black Males

Epigraph, Frederick Douglass, *My Bondage and My Freedom*, opening of chapter 14.

Chapter 15. Why Are Handguns So Accessible on Urban Streets?

I appreciate assistance with public health research from Jon Vernick, Co-director of the Center for Gun Policy and Research, Johns Hopkins University School of Public Health. Copyright © 2007 David Kairys.

1. The data for overall firearms deaths, about 80 per day or 30,000 per year, are known more accurately than those for handguns, estimated here at about three-quarters of the total; see National Center for Injury Control (WISQARS) 2003; FBI 2003. On homicide and suicide, see Kellermann, Rivara, Rushforth et al. 1993; Kellerman, Rivara, Somes et al. 1992. On other countries, see Krug et al. 1998. For the data for young black men, see WISQARS. Some have argued that more guns make us safer, most prominently Lott 1998, but the argument has been based on flawed research and exaggerated, or even distorted, interpretations of data. On the flaws in the research, see Center for Gun Policy and Research 2004, 7, nn. 52–58.

2. The public nuisance legal theory of the city handgun lawsuits has become the leading legal theory in a range of other cases against corporations accused of endangering public health or safety, for example, the manufacturers of lead paint. See "Public Nuisance Suits Keep Companies on the Defensive, Gun Suits Start an Unnerving Trend in Corporate America," *Corporate Legal Times*, August 2004.

3. Law enforcement is left with the difficult and arduous task of keeping track of multiple purchasers and seeking evidence related to their use or disposition of handguns. Federal law does not specifically prohibit straw purchases, but makes it a crime to make certain misrepresentations on forms filed with the government. The lack of effective legal tools or a clear legal foundation can make prosecution difficult even where the evidence is quite clear. See Kairys 2000b, 1183–84, and n. 35.

4. See Kairys 1998, 8–9, n. 22. "Multiple" purchase is used here in a general way, as buying more than one irrespective of timing or place, rather than in the more limited ways it is often defined in law and used in the literature on guns.

5. It is not yet clear whether the limit of one gun a month reduces deaths and injuries, but its adoption by the Virginia legislature made Virginia less often a source state for guns used in crimes. See Weil and Knox 1996.

6. The federal limits on purchases of handguns by out-of-state residents are easily overcome with straw purchasers and easily available drivers' licenses in some states.

7. See ATF 2000; Kairys 2003b, 364–69; Kairys 2000a, 1166–67; Kairys 1998, 6–9, nn. 15–16. Handguns often go through more than one dealer before they are sold to a non-dealer.

8. ATF reports that over a million new handguns were manufactured per year in recent years, not including handguns manufactured for export or military use. Figures through 2004 are available at the ATF website, http://www.atf .treas.gov/firearms/stats/index.htm

9. Pub. L. 90–618, 90th Cong., 82 Stat. 1213, Oct. 22, 1968. On the growth of the "Saturday night special" industry after the 1968 act, see Wintemute 1994.

10. Pub. L. 94–284, 94th Cong., 90 Stat. 503, May 11, 1976.

11. Pub. L.104–208, 110 Stat. 3009, Sept. 30, 1996. The same limit has been placed in successive CDC appropriations. On the removal of the amount that funded the Kellerman studies from the next year's CDC appropriation, see http://en.wikipedia.org/wiki/Arthur_Kellermann.

12. Protection of Lawful Commerce in Arms Act, Pub. L. 109–92, 119 Stat. 2095, October 25, 2005. The Tiahrt Amendment attached to appropriations bills since 2003 limits ATF release of information; see, e.g., Public Law 109–108, 119 Stat. 2290, H.R. 2862, November 22, 2005. On the industry immunity, see Kairys 2005a,b.

13. "Gun-control lawmaker threatened," *Philadelphia Inquirer*, April 27, 2007.

14. There is a gender dimension to this cultural and political phenomenon: guns are often identified with masculinity. Women are less likely to own a gun and are more likely to be shot with a gun than to shoot someone; see Kellerman et al. 1992. The gun industry saw women as an untapped market in the 1990s and directed advertising at them; see Kairys 1998, 11–12.

15. 18 Pa.C.S.A. § 6111(c) provides that a person who is not a licensed dealer selling a firearm to another person who is not a licensed dealer must sell on the premises of a licensed dealer and the dealer should do a record check. However, it applies only to the seller, requires a sale "knowingly and intentionally" in violation of the statute (an unusually strict requirement), and has exceptions and exemptions. Id. at §§ 6111(d)–(i). See "Man shot, killed in snow dispute," *Philadelphia Inquirer*, January 27, 2000 ("Police said both [neighbors] had permits to carry handguns"); "Man faces trial over shooting," *Philadelphia Inquirer*, February 3, 2000; "Man shot to death outside Phila. nightclub," *Philadelphia Inquirer*, January 22, 2002.

16. Other reforms have considerable merit, such as a waiting period, which can reduce the large numbers of suicides with guns and provide time for more serious checking on buyers.

Contributors

Elijah Anderson is William K. Lanman, Jr., Professor of Sociology at Yale University and formerly Charles and William Day Distinguished Professor of the Social Sciences at the University of Pennsylvania. He received a B.A. from Indiana University, an M.A. from the University of Chicago, and a Ph.D. from Northwestern University, where he was a Ford Foundation Fellow. He has served as Visiting Professor at Swarthmore College, Princeton University, and the Ecole des Hautes Etudes en Sciences Sociales in Paris. He also served on the National Research Council Panel on the Understanding and Control of Violent Behavior. He is the author of *A Place on the Corner: A Study of Black Street Corner Men*; *Streetwise: Race, Class, and Change in an Urban Community* (which received the Robert E. Park Award); and *Code of the Street: Decency, Violence, and the Moral Life of the Inner City*, as well as numerous articles and reviews on the black experience. Director of the Philadelphia Ethnography Project, he has served as editor of several professional journals, an officer of the American Academy of Political and Social Science and the American Sociological Association, and as a consultant to numerous government agencies.

Luke Anderson, a native Philadelphian, received a B.A. in English Literature from the University of Pennsylvania. While at Penn, he worked as a union representative for the United Food and Commercial Workers Local 1776, organizing supermarket workers and hospital employees. He spent two years in the graduate program in sociology at Northwestern University, specializing in ethnographic methods and the sociology of culture. He resides in Chicago, working in public high schools on the city's South and West Sides.

Scott Brooks teaches sociology at the University of California, Riverside, and is currently working on a book titled *Black Men Can't Shoot*, which describes the social work required for a young man to become an elite basketball player.

L. Janelle Dance, Associate Professor of Sociology, University of Maryland-College Park, is moving in spring 2008 to the University of Nebraska-Lincoln. She has conducted ethnographic research with ethnic minority students in the U.S. and Sweden. During the 2006–2007 academic year, she worked on a Swedish research team in a cross-national study funded by the National Science Foundation titled "The Children of Immigrants in Schools." In addition to ethnographic work with students, she often engages in dialogic interactions with K–12 public school teachers in workshops and seminars.

Waverly Duck is a Postdoctoral Fellow at Yale University. He earned his Ph.D. in Sociology from Wayne State University and a Master of Science in Community Medicine from Wayne State School of Medicine. He has taught at the Community College of Philadelphia and been Visiting Scholar at the University of Pennsylvania. His areas of interest are gender, social psychology, gerontology, and medical sociology. Duck has conducted research projects on a variety of topics including gender and health, welfare reform, and mental illnesses of children in foster care.

Troy Duster is Professor of Sociology and Director of the Institute for the History of the Production of Knowledge at New York University, as well as Chancellor's Professor at the University of California-Berkeley. Over his career, he has done research and writing on the sociology of knowledge and science, deviance and control, and race and ethnicity. He coauthored *Whitewashing Race: The Myth of a Color Blind Society* (2003), and was president of the American Sociological Association in 2004–2005. Duster has served on advisory committees for the National Academy of Sciences and the National Institutes of Health. He chaired the Ethical, Legal, and Social Issues Committee of the Human Genome Project.

Peter Edelman is Professor of Law at Georgetown University Law Center. He served as a legislative assistant to Senator Robert F. Kennedy, Assistant Secretary of the U.S. Department of Health and Human Services under President Bill Clinton, and Director of the New York State Division for Youth under Governor Hugh Carey. His most recent books are *Searching for America's Heart: RFK and the Renewal of Hope* and *Reconnecting Disadvantaged Young Men*, coauthored with Harry J. Holzer and Paul Offner. Edelman co-chaired a Task Force on Poverty for the Center for

American Progress in 2006–2007 and chairs the District of Columbia Access to Justice Commission.

Jamie J. Fader is a doctoral candidate in sociology at the University of Pennsylvania. Her research interests include social inequality, urban sociology, the consequences of incarceration, and transitions to adulthood. She was one of the organizers for the April 2006 conference, "Poor, Young, Black and Male: A Case for National Action?" Her dissertation, "Inside and Out: Community Re-Entry, Continuity and Change Among Incarcerated Urban Youth," uses ethnographic methods to document the experiences and outcomes of a longitudinal sample of fifteen young black and Hispanic men aged seventeen to nineteen who returned to Philadelphia from a facility designed to correct "criminal thinking errors."

Raymond Gunn, currently a Visiting Fellow in the Sociology and Anthropology Department at the College of Wooster, is completing a joint Ph.D. in sociology and education from the University of Pennsylvania. His research explores the points of intersection between race, class, gender, and academic achievement. His dissertation is an ethnographic account of the ways styles of self-presentation adopted by urban African American male high school students affect their postsecondary opportunities.

Gerald D. Jaynes is Professor of Economics and African American Studies at Yale University. Currently Director of Graduate Studies for African American Studies, he was chaired the program from 1990 to 1996. He was study director of the National Research Council's Committee on the Status of Black Americans and coedited *A Common Destiny: Blacks and American Society*. His books include *Branches Without Roots: Genesis of the Black Working Class in the American South* and *Race and Immigration: New Dilemmas for American Democracy*. He has authored many articles on race relations and has testified to Congress on race and immigration.

Sean Joe holds a joint appointment as Assistant Professor in the School of Social Work and the Department of Psychiatry at the University of Michigan Medical Center and is associated with the Program for Research on Black Americans at the Institute for Social Research. His current interests center on developing father-focused, family-based interventions to prevent urban African American adolescent males from engaging in multifarious self-destructive behaviors. He co-chairs the Emerging Scholars Interdisciplinary Network Research Study Group on African American Suicide and serves on the board of directors of the Suicide Prevention

Action Network, the scientific advisory board of the National Organization of People of Color Against Suicide, and the editorial board of *Advancing Suicide Prevention*, a policy magazine.

David Kairys is James E. Beasley Professor of Law at Temple University. The many articles, chapters, and book he has authored, co-authored, and edited included *The Politics of Law* and *With Liberty and Justice for Some*. Working full-time as a civil rights lawyer (1968–1990), he won the major race discrimination case against the FBI, won challenges to unrepresentative juries around the country, stopped police sweeps of minority neighborhoods in Philadelphia, and represented Dr. Benjamin Spock in a free speech case before the Supreme Court. In 1996 he conceived the city lawsuits against handgun manufacturers, and his public-nuisance theory has become the major basis for a range of challenges to corporate practices that endanger public health or safety. He is working on a memoir, *Philadelphia Freedom, Memoir of a Civil Rights Lawyer* (forthcoming 2008).

Douglas S. Massey is Henry G. Bryant Professor of Sociology and Public Affairs at Princeton University and Adjunct Professor of Sociology at the University of Pennsylvania. His recent research examines the racialized class structure that relegates both Latinos and African Americans to marginal positions, focusing especially on the residential segregation of African Americans and Latinos of African ancestry, which interacts with shifts in the income distribution to produce a rising concentration of urban poverty that, in turn, intensifies social disorder and violence. He is the author of *Categorically Unequal: The American Stratification System*.

Devah Pager is Associate Professor of Sociology and Faculty Associate of the Office of Population Research at Princeton University. Her research focuses on institutions affecting racial stratification, including education, labor markets, and the criminal justice system. Pager's current research involves a series of field experiments studying discrimination against young black men and ex-offenders in the low-wage labor market. Recent publications include *Marked: Race, Crime, and Finding Work in an Era of Mass Incarceration* and, with L. Quillian, "Walking the Talk: What Employers Say Versus What They Do." He holds Master's degrees from Stanford University and the University of Cape Town and a Ph.D. from the University of Wisconsin-Madison.

William Julius Wilson is Lewis P. and Linda L. Geyser University Professor at Harvard University. A MacArthur Fellow, he has been elected to the National Academy of Sciences, the American Academy of Arts and

Sciences, the National Academy of Education, the American Philosophical Society, the Institute of Medicine, and the British Academy. Past President of the American Sociological Association, he is a recipient of the National Medal of Science in 1998, and the Talcott Parsons Prize in the Social Sciences of the American Academy of Arts and Sciences in 2003. He has testified before U.S. congressional committees and advised policymakers on urban poverty and race relations.

Index

Acknowledgments

The papers collected in this volume were initially developed for a conference, "Poor, Young, Black, and Male: A Case for National Action?" held at the University of Pennsylvania in Philadelphia on April 20 and 21, 2006.

I first thank Waverly Duck, Jamie Fader, and Raymond Gunn, who formed the conference's organizing committee with me, as well as Carrie Stavrakos, Jelani Newton, Christine Szczepanowski, Onyx Finney, Randy Collins, and Kathy Hall, who provided organizational assistance.

Many thanks are due to the fine roster of speakers: Paul Allison, Robert Alsbrooks, Bernard Anderson, Luke Anderson, Scott Brooks, Keith Brown, Rebecca Bushnell, Camille Z. Charles, Randall Collins, Ellis Cose, L. Janelle "Tomni" Dance, Ronald Daniels, John DiIulio, Waverly Duck, Mitchell Duneier, Troy Duster, Michael Eric Dyson, Peter Edelman, Jamie Fader, Vivian Gadsden, Alice Goffman, Raymond Gunn, Amy Gutmann, Hakim Hasan, Bob Herbert, Harry Holzer, Gerald Jaynes, Sean Joe, Sylvester Johnson, David Kairys, Lawrence Katz, Douglas Massey, Joanie Mazelis, Ronald Mincy, Acel Moore, Aldon Morris, Devah Pager, Walter Palmer, Imani Perry, William Raspberry, Lawrence Sherman, Kenneth Shropshire, Stephen A. Smith, Margaret Spencer, Vaughn Taylor, Cornel West, Douglas Wiebe, and William Julius Wilson.

In addition, I thank Grey Osterud, whose fine editorial skills were essential for turning these conference presentations into a book.

Finally, I am deeply grateful to the conference sponsors at the University of Pennsylvania: the School of Arts and Sciences, Penn Institute for Urban Research, Center for Africana Studies, National Center on Fathers and Families, Graduate School of Education, Wharton Sports Business Initiative, and School of Social Policy and Practice. I particularly appreciate the support of the university's president, Amy Gutmann; its provost, Ronald Daniels; Rebecca Bushnell, dean of the School of Arts and Sciences; and Paul Allison, chairman of the Sociology Department.